Reinventing Free Labor

PADRONES AND IMMIGRANT WORKERS IN THE
NORTH AMERICAN WEST, 1880–1930

One of the most infamous villains in North America during the Progressive Era was the padrone, an immigrant boss who allegedly enslaved his compatriots and kept them uncivilized, unmanly, and unfree. In this first-ever history of the padrone, Gunther Peck analyzes the figure's deep cultural resonance by examining the lives of three padrones and the workers they imported to North America. He argues that the padrones were not primitive men but rather thoroughly modern entrepreneurs who used corporations, the labor contract, and the right to quit to create far-flung coercive networks. Drawing on Greek, Spanish, and Italian language sources, Peck analyzes how immigrant workers emancipated themselves using the tools of padrone power to their advantage. By excavating the geography of transnational labor mobility and padrone power, Peck fundamentally challenges the varieties of exceptionalism that still pervade U.S. western, labor, legal, and immigration history. Free labor remained an unstable fiction in North America between 1880 and 1930, one whose meaning was continuously redefined by border bureaucrats, padrones, and workers on the boundaries between regions, nations, and cultures.

Gunther Peck is an assistant professor in the History Department at the University of Texas at Austin. His pathbreaking scholarship in North American labor, immigration, and western history has already appeared in the *Journal of American History*, *Western Historical Quarterly*, *Journal of Social History*, and *International Labor and Working-Class History*. He won the Porter Prize from the Yale Graduate School for the best dissertation in 1995.

*To
Faulkner Fox*

Reinventing Free Labor

PADRONES AND IMMIGRANT WORKERS IN

THE NORTH AMERICAN WEST, 1880–1930

Gunther Peck
University of Texas at Austin

CAMBRIDGE
UNIVERSITY PRESS

CAMBRIDGE UNIVERSITY PRESS
Cambridge, New York, Melbourne, Madrid, Cape Town, Singapore, São Paulo

Cambridge University Press
The Edinburgh Building, Cambridge CB2 8RU, UK

Published in the United States of America by Cambridge University Press, New York

www.cambridge.org
Information on this title: www.cambridge.org/9780521641609

First published 2000

A catalogue record for this publication is available from the British Library

Library of Congress Cataloguing in Publication data

Peck, Gunther.
    Reinventing free labor : padrones and immigrant workers in the
North American West, 1880–1930 / Gunther Peck.
        p.   cm.
    Includes bibliographical references.
    ISBN 0-521-64160-8. – ISBN 0-521-77819-0 (pbk.)
    1. Padrone system – North America – History.   2. North America –
Emigration and immigration – History.   3. Right to labor – North
America – History.   4. Alien labor, Greek – North America – History.
5. Alien labor, Italian – North America – History.   6. Alien labor,
Mexican – North America – History.   7. Greek Americans – Employment –
West (U.S.) – History.   8. Miners – West (U.S.) – History.   9. Italian
Americans – Employment – History.   10. Mexican Americans – Employment –
History.   11. Railroad construction workers – North America –
History.   I. Title.   II. Title: Padrones and immigrant workers in
the North American West, 1880–1930.
HD4875.N7P43   2000
331.6′2′0978–dc21   99-26123
                                                                  CIP

ISBN 978-0-521-64160-9 hardback
ISBN 978-0-521-77819-0 paperback

Transferred to digital printing 2007

Contents

Illustrations and Tables

Maps

Figures

Plates

Tables

Map Tables

Acknowledgments

Research into the many meanings of mobility to transient men and their elusive padrones has taken me along both established paths and roads less traveled in the historical archives of North America. I have benefited from the expertise and patience of dedicated archivists and staff at each of the following research centers: the American West Center and the Greek Archives of the Marriott Library at the University of Utah; the Bancroft Library at the University of California at Berkeley; the Canadian National Archives in Montreal and Ottawa; the Center for American History at the University of Texas at Austin; the El Paso Public Library; the Hoover Library at Stanford University; the New York Public Library; the Pocatello Public Library; the archives of Idaho State University; Perkins Memorial Library at Duke University; the State Historical Society of Wisconsin; the Beinecke, Sterling Memorial, and Seeley Mudd Libraries at Yale University; the archives of the University of Texas at El Paso; the Utah State Historical Society; the Utah State Archives; and finally the U.S. National Archives in Washington and its branch office in Philadelphia. Special thanks go to James Danky of the Wisconsin State Historical Society for encouraging my initial queries into immigrant mobilizations nearly a decade ago. And in my many research trips to the North American West, both Helen Papanikolas and her son, Zeese, have been remarkably generous with their time and insights into the experience of working-class immigrants in the West. Special thanks also go to John Peter Sarbanes for introducing me to Greek culture, and to Lena Nikolaou for friendship and help on initial translations. Efcharisto para para poli!

The research and writing of this book have been made possible by the generosity of a variety of fellowships, grants, and awards. I gratefully acknowledge the financial support from the Summer Research Institute at the University of Texas at Austin, the Dora Bonham Fund from the Department of History at the University of Texas, the Department of History at Yale University, the Giles M. Whiting Foundation, the Helen Z. Papanikolas Charitable Trust for Greek-American Studies, the Charles Redd Center for Western Studies, the Jacob Javits Fellowship of the United States Department of Education, the Eugene V. Debs Foundation, the Western History Association, and the Eggleston and Porter Dissertation Prizes from Yale University.

Had I known where my first forays into the meanings of free labor and transience were ultimately headed ten years ago as a graduate student at the University
of Wisconsin or how long it would take to bring them to fruition, I might have
chosen a more sedentary topic for research. Fortunately, I discovered an idealistic
community of teachers and peers in Madison who nurtured a passion for getting it
right and finding political meaning in unlikely places. Thanks to professors Alan
Bogue and David Zonderman for their enthusiastic support, and to Susan Traverso,
Lon Kurashige, and Ben Labaree for their friendship.

At Yale University, my impractical research interests found a happy home
among a remarkable community of historians, friends, and activists. I owe an immense debt to my dissertation advisers William Cronon, David Montgomery, and
Howard Lamar, each of whom has exemplified the importance of writing history
with passion and conviction rather than dispassionate skepticism. William Cronon
has been of inestimable help in encouraging me to think creatively about the
writing of history and to tell narratives that move beyond academic boundaries.
David Montgomery's rare example of combining history teaching and writing
with a life of political activism has been a model and inspiration to myself and
many others. Finally, Howard Lamar has exemplified, with his remarkable warmth,
wit, and generosity, the humanism that inspires many of us to write history in the
first place.

I also learned a great deal from my dissertation study group and breakfast-at-
the-pantry cohort of Sylvie Murray, Lane Witt, David Waldstreicher, and Nikhil
Singh. Their insights and irreverence continue to strengthen my own. My friendships with Phil Deloria, Pamela Haag, Yvette Huginnie, Reeve Huston, Susan
Johnson, Maria Montoya, Jenny Price, Louie Warren, and Carl Weinberg not only
sharpened the insights of my dissertation but greatly enriched my experience in
graduate school. Special thanks go to Susan Johnson for her astute written comments on both the dissertation and the book. While performing dissertation
research in scattered archives, I also relied on the hospitality of both friends and
colleagues. I give heartfelt thanks to Lawrence Glickman, Zeese Papanikolas,
Susan Posner, Bruno Ramirez, Selene and Seymour Sheriff, Jeffrey Wells, and
especially to Helen and Nick Papanikolas, who literally opened their home and
community to me in Utah.

Transforming the dissertation into a book has been another journey all its own,
one made exciting and enjoyable by a fine group of colleagues at the University of
Texas at Austin. Jonathan Brown, Judith Coffin, Neil Foley, William Forbath,
Kevin Gaines, Kevin Kenny, Sandra Lauderdale, David Montejano, Robert
Olwell, Jim Sidbury, Mauricio Tenorio, and Penny Von Eschen each offered astute
comments on individual chapters that helped clarify several of my claims. Col-
leagues, family, and friends far and near – James Abbott, Eric Arnesen, Jeff
Cowie, Melvyn Dubofsky, Alicia Erian, Leon Fink, Carol Fox, Lucy Fox, Joshua
Freeman, Julie Greene, Alison Isenberg, Elizabeth Jameson, Hal Langfur, Bruce
Laurie, Georg Leidenberger, Andrew Neather, Demaree Peck, Nathan Peck,
Michael Staff, Robert Steinfeld, and Robert Tinkler – improved both the book and

the experience of writing it. I would also like to thank my graduate students at the University of Texas for their critical engagement with many of the issues in the book. Special thanks go to Ryan Carey for help preparing the bibliography and proofreading, to Joel Tishken for initial help with the index, and to Sara Pullum for expertise in preparing the maps and tables.

Portions of Chapters 1, 4, and 6 first appeared in the *Journal of American History* (December 1996) and were greatly improved by the close criticisms of David Thelen, Susan Armeney, and the journal's anonymous reviewers. Another portion of Chapter 6 appeared in the *Western Historical Quarterly* (May 1993) and received helpful advice from the dynamic trio of Clyde Milner, Anne Butler, and David Lewis. I thank both journals for permission to reprint portions of the articles. I would also like to thank my editor at Cambridge, Frank Smith, for his enthusiasm, support, and patience with this project as it has taken final shape. His comments, plus the rigorous reviews of Sarah Deutsch and David Emmons, have helped me rethink and extend the transnational implications of my book. I was fortunate to have Brian MacDonald as my production editor at Cambridge. His skills and good humor saved me from many mistakes and substantially improved the final product.

At every stage of writing and revision, finally, I have benefited enormously from the insights of David Waldstreicher. His intellectual rigor, political passions, humor, and shared enthusiasm for edifying conversation over pancakes have not only enriched the book but nearly exhausted my supply of home-made maple syrup. It's time, perhaps, to make a new batch.

To my parents, Russell and Ruth Peck, who taught me how to make maple syrup and to write, I owe incalculable intellectual and personal debts. They recognize, better than anyone, the homes in the disparate landscapes of Greece, Canada, and the West in this book. My sweet boys, Elijah and Gabriel, have been my constant companions on the journey of revision, reminding me, in their unique ways, how to imagine new stories and new homes. My closest navigator in the geography of freedom and home is Faulkner Fox. To her, I dedicate this book.

Introduction

In the winter of 1911, fifty Greek copper miners from Bingham Canyon, Utah, wrote an impassioned letter to the governor of Utah, William S. Spry, seeking his help and intervention against their padrone, Greek immigrant Leon Skliris, a man they nicknamed "the czar of the Greeks."

> Do you think this is right for Skliris to sell livelihoods to the poor workman at extortion 20 dollars and to thus suck the blood of the poor laborer? Where are we? In the free country of Amerika or in a country dominated by a despotic form of government? . . . Hoping you will liberat us from this padrone, who is ravaging the blood of the poor laborer.

For these highly mobile young men, the North American West, region of free labor and free men, appeared instead a mocking backdrop to their suffering. The labor contracts that Skliris provided Greek workers did not codify truly free labor relations, but instead sanctioned perpetual deductions of one dollar a month from their meager paychecks. As consumers, Greek workers also faced a grim choice: exorbitant prices at the Panhellenic grocery store, run by Leon Skliris's brother, or unemployment. Perhaps most onerous, Skliris charged his sojourning compatriots twenty dollars for the privilege of working at the Utah Copper Company, an "extortion" frequently assessed by periodically firing workers in order to get new fees.[1]

When Greek workers tried to escape Skliris's tributes by leaving the mining town of Bingham, Utah, economic necessities frequently compelled them to pay Skliris yet another round of job fees, as he controlled access to most unskilled mining, railroad, and construction jobs in Utah and many more in Colorado, Nevada, and Idaho. Mobility, whether between jobs or between states in the West, brought not freedom to these transient men but hardship and ever greater debts to the padrone. When Greek workers questioned Spry about the location of freedom,

---

[1] Fifty Greek and Crete men to Governor William S. Spry, February 12, 1911, William S. Spry Papers, Personal Correspondence Files, box 10, file "G," Utah State Archives, Salt Lake City, Utah.

they turned upside down what seemed a truism in the West and the nation: that open space and mobility defined freedom. Even satirists of American democracy found redemption through mobility in the West. When Huck Finn "lights out for the territories," Mark Twain connected, like many before and after, the themes of mobility and freedom.[2] Yet for these Greeks and thousands of other immigrants who paid tribute to their padrones in the early twentieth century, job mobility only fattened padrone earnings and confirmed the notion that "a despotic form of government" ruled the land.

Explaining the riddle that befuddled Greek immigrants in Utah in 1912 – how there could be so little freedom in so much space – is the first purpose of this book. Doing so requires taking workers' mobility seriously, considering how it brought padrones to power throughout North America in the early twentieth century. The geography of labor mobility that made Skliris rich at the peak of his power was not contained within Utah but stretched across the Atlantic Ocean directly to villages in the southern Peloponnese and the island of Crete where his agents mobilized men for work in the industrial West. The relationship between workers' mobility and padrone power was not defined purely by geographic distances, however, but also by cultural and political aspects of workers' transnational movement. Padrones gained power by their professed ability to traverse the legal, lingual, class, and racial boundaries that separated new immigrants from North Americans of many political and cultural outlooks. When immigrant workers needed assistance crossing international borders, padrones instructed them on how to evade immigration authorities. When their compatriots needed legal representation, padrones provided counsel. When immigrants needed to remit money to their families back home, padrones drafted bank orders and sent letters to and from mobile kin in North America. The tributes that padrones demanded for these services varied and changed over time, ranging from simple fees to more sophisticated forms of debt peonage in which all services were garnished directly from workers' wages. Padrones also exacted cultural fees that were not monetary but no less real, as when they claimed the assets of whiteness, manhood, and citizenship, gaining respectability in American eyes at the expense of their "unwashed" brethren who remained nonwhite, emasculated, and alien in the eyes of most native-born Americans. As professional middlemen, padrones not only created international labor markets but also mediated the ways both immigrant workers and native-born Americans created cultural hierarchies in North America.[3]

To gain a clear picture of the transnational mobility that brought padrones to power in the West, I examine the careers of three padrones and the immigrant

[2] Frederick Jackson Turner, "The Significance of the Frontier in American History" (1893), in Turner, *The Frontier in American History* (New York, 1920); Mark Twain, *The Adventures of Huckleberry Finn* (1884; New York, 1996), 366.

[3] On connections between padronism and capitalist economic development, see David Montgomery, *The Fall of the House of Labor: The Workplace, the State, and American Labor Activism, 1865–1925* (Cambridge, 1987), 75–78; and Robert Harney, "Montreal's King of Italian Labour: A Case Study of Padronism," *Labour/Le Travailleur* 4 (1979): 57–84.

workers they imported to North America. Italian entrepreneur Antonio Cordasco, known by many as the "king of the laborers," lived in Montreal, Canada, but from there sent Italians vast distances across the Canadian plains to British Columbia as railroad workers for the Canadian Pacific Railway. Greek businessman Leon Skliris lived on the top floor of the Hotel Utah in Salt Lake City and sent Greeks to jobs in coal and copper mines and railroads throughout Utah, Colorado, Nevada, and Idaho. Roman Gonzalez, a Mexican American ex-policeman, lived in El Paso, but from there sent migrant workers to railroad jobs in Kansas and to sugar beet fields in Minnesota, Nebraska, and North Dakota.[4] Cordasco, Skliris, and Gonzalez were not the most powerful or even typical padrones of their day in North America, but their locations on the borders of the North American West, a region stretching from northern Mexico through the western United States to northern Canada, highlight the importance of transnational boundaries in shaping padrone power and workers' resistance to it.[5]

Tracking the multinational passages of these diverse padrones and immigrant workers has led me to question the varied forms of exceptionalism that still pervade many narratives of U.S. immigration, western, labor, and legal history. Until recently, most immigration histories probed the experience and culture of separate national migrations in relative isolation from other groups on the move. Historical monographs of one ethnic group in single urban contexts have yielded indispensable insights into the complex ways immigrants adapted and transplanted aspects of their culture to North America.[6] But that monographic focus has also led historians to neglect the experience of transient immigrants who left a given urban neighborhood under study. Equally important, by highlighting the intrinsic aspects of identity formation – how immigrants themselves fashioned unique and often exceptional ethnic cultures in North America – immigration historians have paid

---

[4] On Cordasco's career, see Harney, "Montreal's King of Italian Labour," 57–84. On Skliris's career, see Helen Papanikolas, "Toil and Rage in a New Land: The Greek Immigrants of Utah," *Utah Historical Quarterly* 38 (Spring 1970): 100–204. On Roman Gonzalez's early career, see Mario T. Garcia, *Desert Immigrants: The Mexicans of El Paso, 1880–1920* (New Haven, 1981), 53–56; and Camille Guerin-Gonzalez, *Mexican Workers and American Dreams: Immigration, Repatriation, and California Farm Labor, 1900–1939* (New Brunswick, 1994), 38–41.

[5] My analysis of padrones as entrepreneurs who straddle the border between "core" and "periphery" is indebted to the work of Immanuel Wallerstein, especially *The Modern World-System: Capitalist Agriculture and the Origins of the European World-Economy in the Sixteenth Century* (New York, 1976). For an analysis of the "interdependent" relationship between the two, see William Cronon, *Nature's Metropolis: Chicago and the Great West* (New York, 1991).

[6] Of many fine monographs on Mexican, Italian, and Greek immigration, see Virginia Yans-McLaughlin, *Family and Community: Italian Immigrants in Buffalo, 1880–1930* (Ithaca, 1977); Humbert Nelli, *From Italy to San Francisco: The Immigrant Experience* (Stanford, 1982); Garcia, *Desert Immigrants*; Albert Camarillo, *Chicanos in a Changing Society: From Mexican Pueblos to American Barrios in Santa Barbara and Southern California, 1848–1930* (Cambridge, 1979); Papanikolas, "Toil and Rage"; Dan Georgakas, ed., *New Directions in Greek American Studies* (New York, 1991).

less attention to the externally imposed dimensions of immigrant experience. Ethnicity has frequently been narrated as a vehicle for resisting the homogenizing impact of U.S. culture, whereas extrinsic factors, such as racial ideology, cross-ethnic social relations, U.S. political culture, and nationalisms, have only recently become important subjects for research, comparison, and investigation. I build on that comparative work, not by ignoring the unique aspects of Mexican, Greek, and Italian ethnic cultures in North America, but by examining those cultures in the national and transnational political contexts that helped produce them.[7]

If immigration historians have tended to view ethnic groups in isolation, western historians have too often viewed western history in a nationalist vacuum, rarely comparing it with other regions or frontiers. Although many "new" and "old" western historians have called for a more comparative approach to the western past, few have actually attempted to decenter the U.S. West, however defined, within their narratives.[8] This is not surprising; the purpose of much western history has been to excavate the boundaries of what all would recognize as a unique, distinct, and, for many, exceptional region or process in U.S. national history.[9]

To confine the transient lives of Greek, Italian, and Mexican workers within the geographic and ideological boundaries of the U.S. West, however, distorts several aspects of their experience. Most of them did not initially travel to the North American West to stay, nor were their identities as men, citizens, or workers exclusively molded by institutions or ideas peculiar to the U.S. West. For Greek workers, Bingham Canyon was but a way station among many others in a hostile and exotic region, a stepping-stone that they hoped would ultimately bring them back to their home villages in Greece. Moreover, the West that transient workers and their

---

[7] On pathbreaking work that compares different national migrations, see Matthew Jacobson, *Special Sorrows: The Diasporic Imagination of Jewish, Polish, and Italian Immigrants* (Cambridge, 1995); Alejandro Portes and Robert L. Bach, *Latin Journey: Cuban and Mexican Immigrants in the United States* (Berkeley, 1985); John Bodnar, Roger Simon, and Michael Weber, *Lives of Their Own: Blacks, Italians, and Poles in Pittsburgh, 1900–1960* (Urbana, 1982). For studies that compare the experience of the same ethnic group in different countries, see Kevin Kenny, *Making Sense of the Molly Maguires* (New York, 1998); Susan Glenn, *Daughters of the Shtetl: Life and Labor in the Immigrant Generation* (Ithaca, 1990); David Emmons, *The Butte Irish: Class and Ethnicity in an American Mining Town, 1875–1925* (Urbana, 1989), and Donna Rae Gabaccia, *Militants and Migrants: Rural Sicilians Become American Workers* (New Brunswick, 1989).

[8] For a comparative history of the U.S. West, see Howard Lamar and Leonard Thompson, eds., *The Frontier in History: North America and Southern Africa Compared* (New Haven, 1981). For analyses that decenter the West, see David Gutierrez, *Walls and Mirrors: Mexican Americans, Mexican Immigrants, and the Politics of Identity* (Berkeley, 1995); and Neil Foley, *The White Scourge: Mexicans, Blacks, and Poor Whites in Texas Cotton Culture* (Berkeley, 1997).

[9] See Turner, *The Frontier in American History.* For Neo-Turnerian approaches to Western history that avoid his ethnocentric pitfalls, see William Cronon, "Revisiting the Vanishing Frontier: The Legacy of Frederick Jackson Turner," *Western Historical Quarterly* 18:2 (April 1987): 157–176. Turner's critics have rejected the frontier and his avowedly exceptional processes, but even his harshest critics have maintained a commitment to defining a unique western past, albeit one that "has learned to live with relativism." See Patricia Limerick, *The Legacy of Conquest: The Unbroken Past of the American West* (New York, 1987).

padrones briefly inhabited was not confined to the United States. Italian workers paying tributes to Cordasco typically began the work season in Boston or a small village in northern Italy but soon found themselves laying railroad track in British Columbia or northern Ontario before returning to friends in Boston or Italy the following winter. The Mexican workers that Gonzalez imported also worked and migrated with the seasons, laboring in northern Mexico, Arizona, Kansas, and even Minnesota in a single year. National boundaries proved difficult for these "birds of passage" to cross, creating a need for the padrone's services, but their perspectives on wage labor and free labor ideology developed primarily in transnational contexts.[10]

Labor and social historians have more explicitly considered the transnational dimensions of immigrant workers' lives. Capitalism, despite the variety of definitions assigned to it, has been correctly understood as an international phenomenon, one that has linked the experience of diverse immigrants and workers into a single holistic economic system. But although labor and social histories provide conceptual starting points for comprehending the dilemmas of working-class transience, they have only recently begun to examine that experience. One reason for this oversight is methodological. Case studies of workers have traditionally focused on fixed locales – the shop floor, the ethnic enclave, the residential community – and devoted much of their attention to persistent members of working-class communities.[11] Transient workers, by contrast, have received less sustained attention for the simple but important reason that tracking their lives across space is enormously difficult.

But conceptual predilections within labor and social history also account for the neglect of transient workers. Labor historians have focused their case studies primarily on questions of temporal transition, making distinctions between artisans and workers, working-class awareness and working-class consciousness, premodern and modern forms of protest. How class relations and class conflicts were spatially rather than temporally expressed and understood, by contrast, has,

---

[10] On the transnational nature of immigrant workers' experience, see Donna Roe Gabaccia, "Worker Internationalism and Italian Labor Migrating," *International Labor and Working-Class History* 45 (Spring 1994): 63–79; Michael Piore, *Birds of Passage: Migrant Labor and Industrial Societies* (Cambridge, 1979); John Bodnar, *The Transplanted: A History of Immigrants in Urban America* (Bloomington, 1985); Lucie Cheng and Edna Bonacich, eds., *Labor Immigration under Capitalism: Asian Workers in the United States before World War II* (Berkeley, 1984); Thomas Archdeacon, *Becoming American: An Ethnic History* (New York, 1983); Dino Cinel, *The National Integration of Italian Return Migration, 1870–1929* (Cambridge, 1991); and Guerin-Gonzalez, *Mexican Workers and American Dreams.*

[11] Among many studies examining the role of persistent communities and the shop floor in working-class mobilization, see Herbert Gutman, *Work, Culture, and Society in Industrializing America: Essays in American Working-Class and Social History* (New York, 1976); David Montgomery, *Worker's Control in America: Studies in the History of Work, Technology, and Labor Struggles* (Cambridge, 1979); Richard Oestreicher, *Solidarity and Fragmentation: Working People and Class Consciousness in Detroit, 1875–1900* (Urbana, 1986); James R. Barrett, *Work and Community in the Jungle: Chicago's Packinghouse Workers, 1894–1922* (Urbana, 1987); and Dorothy Sue Cobble, *Dishing It Out: Waitresses and Their Unions in the Twentieth Century* (Urbana, 1991).

as David Harvey and Edward Soja have suggested, received less sustained attention from social historians.[12]

U.S. labor historians have also been hampered, until recently, by national frames
of analysis that obscure the importance of transient workers and the transnational
paths they established. Even among historians who explicitly reject the exceptionalism of the U.S. labor movement, one finds little attention to transient workers or
the politics of their mobility. Sean Wilentz, for example, has brilliantly critiqued
the distortions of exceptionalism in U.S. labor history, but in his search to find an
indigenous American radicalism he nonetheless focused on an exceptional portion of the working class: skilled, persistent, native-born artisans who possessed a
passionate belief in the virtues of their republican inheritance. As Peter Way has
observed, the focus of new labor history on the republican rights of skilled workers has distorted how unskilled "common laborers" experienced class relations in
North America.[13] If Irish navvies experienced little affinity for an indigenous
working-class republicanism, that inheritance was even less accessible to Greek
muckers in Utah, Italian track laborers in British Columbia, and Mexican sugar
beet workers in Kansas. Indeed, it was one aspect of that same republican ideological inheritance – the assumption that free labor was somehow freer in the West –
that Greek workers questioned in their letters to Utah authorities in 1911.

Critical legal studies scholars have recently shed more light on the frustration
experienced by Greek workers by exploring how laws designed to secure free
labor relations in the United States sanctioned a great variety of coercions for
wage earners after 1863.[14] Their studies complicate the Whiggish narratives of

[12] On the neglected importance of space to social theory, see David Harvey, *The Condition of
Postmodernity: An Inquiry into the Origins of Cultural Change* (London, 1989); David Harvey, *The Urbanization of Capital: Studies in the History and Theory of Capitalist Urbanization* (Baltimore, 1985), 33; and Edward W. Soja, *Postmodern Geographies: The Reassertion
of Space in Critical Social Theory* (London, 1989). On critiques of Harvey and Soja, see Derek
Gregory, *Geographical Imaginations* (Cambridge, 1994), 217–226, 348–353, and 257–316
respectively. For histories of capitalist space in North America, see Mike Davis, *City of
Quartz: Excavating the Future in Los Angeles* (London, 1990); and David E. Nye, *Narratives
and Spaces: Technology and the Construction of American Culture* (New York, 1997). On histories of capital mobility, see Jefferson R. Cowie, *Capital Moves: RCA's Seventy-Year Quest
for Cheap Labor* (Ithaca, 1999).

[13] Sean Wilentz, *Chants Democratic: New York City and the Rise of the American Working Class,
1788–1850* (New York, 1984); Sean Wilentz, "Against Exceptionalism: Class Consciousness
and the American Labor Movement, 1790–1920," *International Labor and Working-Class
History* 26 (Fall 1984): 1–24; Peter Way, "Evil Humors and Ardent Spirits: The Rough Culture
of Canal Construction Laborers," *Journal of American History* 79:4 (March 1993):
1397–1428; Peter Way, *Common Labour: Workers and the Digging of North American
Canals, 1780–1860* (Cambridge, 1993).

[14] On coercions within contractual labor relations in the United States, see Amy Dru Stanley,
"Beggars Can't Be Choosers: Compulsion and Contract in Postbellum America," *Journal of
American History* 78:4 (March 1992): 1265–1270; Christopher Waldrep, "Substituting the
Law for the Lash: Emancipation and Legal Formalism in a Mississippi County Court," *Jour-
nal of American History* 82 (March 1996): 1425–1430; Pete Daniels, *The Shadow of Slavery:
Peonage in the South, 1901–1969* (Urbana, 1972). On similar complexities within the

much U.S. labor and political history by suggesting ways that men like Skliris and Cordasco could have used contracts to sanction coercive labor relations. Their analyses also illuminate the peculiar character of the U.S. labor movement by exploring its mutually defining relations with the U.S. legal system.[15] But like the U.S. labor historians they are in dialogue with, critical legal studies scholars have also adopted national frames of analysis that obscure the international contexts that created padrone power and produced resistance to it. Such an approach not only ignores the full sources of padrone power but also neglects how free labor ideology and wage labor relations shaped each other's evolution outside the United States.[16] Antonio Cordasco gained power as a padrone in Montreal not simply by evading U.S. immigration laws but also by circumventing laws in Canada and Italy.

Tracing the footprints of padrones and immigrant workers to and from the North American West has thus enabled me to bring immigration, western, labor, and legal history into productive collaboration across national boundaries. By exploring the mobility of immigrants through the region of the North American West, I consider some of the mutually defining and interrelated aspects of Canadian, United States, and Mexican history. Although I offer no systematic comparison of the social history of those nations, this study demonstrates the advantages that can be gained by seeing the North American West as one economic and cultural entity. The journeys of Greek, Italian, and Mexican immigrant workers to and from the West were individually unique, but they shared common experiences with labor scarcity and mobility, frequent border crossings, padrone exactions at every stage of their sojourns, and remarkably similar personal disappointments and frustrations. By examining the dilemmas and opportunities that transnational mobility posed, we can begin to understand the political battles that labor mobility has inspired throughout the continent. Understanding the frustrations of transient Greek workers in Utah not only puts class relations at the heart of any understanding of western history; it also transforms how and where social historians conceptualize class relations. For Italian track workers on the move in British

Caribbean after emancipation, see Mary Turner, ed., *From Chattel Slaves to Wage Slaves: The Dynamics of Labour Bargaining in the Americas* (Bloomington, 1995). For a more detailed discussion of contracts and the ideologies of them among middle-class reformers, padrones, and U.S. immigration officials, see Chapter 3.

[15] On critical legal studies scholars' engagement with the well-worn question of why no Socialism in the United States, see Chistopher L. Tomlins, *Law, Labor, and Ideology in the Early American Republic* (Cambridge, 1993); Victoria Hattam, *Labor Visions and State Power: The Origins of Business Unionism in the United States* (Princeton, 1993); and William Forbath, *Law and the Shaping of the American Labor Movement* (Cambridge, Mass., 1991).

[16] Throughout the book, I use the term free labor to describe the ideologies that people used to make sense of the varied obligations and coercions of wage work. By recognizing that free labor was a fiction rather than a "true" social reality, I do not mean to suggest that workers and others who embraced aspects of it suffered from false consciousness. Rather than search for one ideologically consistent and correct form of free labor ideology, I seek to illuminate the diverse and often contradictory meanings that it possessed for immigrant workers, padrones, corporate managers, bureaucrats, and reformers in North America.

Columbia, Mexican sugar beet workers traveling to Minnesota, and Greek miners seeking freedom in Utah, alienation did not begin and end on the shop floor or at points of production, but in the padrone's commodification of their mobility between jobs, between nations, and between cultures.[17]

In their diverse struggles to control mobility and curtail padrone power, immigrant workers used the same tools that had been deployed by padrones to exploit them. Rather than reject free labor, immigrant workers used it to justify their actions against padrones. Precisely what constituted free labor, however, was bitterly fought over by immigrant workers, their padrones, middle-class reformers, immigration officials, and corporate employers in North America between 1880 and 1930. Indeed, wage labor relations during this half century were not truly free but comprised a spectrum of consensual and coercive elements.[18] Because transient wage earners had few alternative means of survival, they were often compelled to accept whatever wage work they could find. For the unskilled, transient worker, the right to earn wages was as much a gamble as a promise, a chance to earn a livelihood but also the right to starve if one failed or was injured on the job.

Perhaps because of the insecurities and dependence intrinsic to unskilled industrial work, not all viewed wage earning as free or all wage earners as equal. Although juxtaposed to slavery rhetorically, free labor was in practice closely linked to notions of hierarchy and inequality. For some workers, free labor meant wage slavery, the coercive expropriation of their labor power by capitalist employers. To others, free labor was synonymous with white labor.[19] For most male

[17] On case studies that consider the relationship between workers' geographic mobility and class formation, see Gabaccia, *Militants and Migrants*; Sarah Deutsch, *No Separate Refuge: Culture, Class, and Gender on an Anglo-Hispanic Frontier in the American Southwest, 1880–1940* (New York, 1987); and David Montejano, *Anglos and Mexicans in the Making of Texas, 1836–1986* (Austin, 1986); Cindy Hahamovitch, *The Fruits of Their Labor: Atlantic Coast Farmworkers and the Making of Migrant Poverty, 1870–1945* (Chapel Hill, 1997); Gunther Peck, "Mobilizing Community: Migrant Workers and the Politics of Labor Mobility in the North American West, 1900–1920," in Eric Arnesen, Julie Greene, and Bruce Laurie, eds., *Labor Histories: Class, Politics, and the Working Class Experience* (Urbana, 1998), 175–200.

[18] On coercive aspects of free labor relations, see Robert Steinfeld, *The Invention of Free Labor: The Employment Relation in English and American Law and Culture, 1350–1870* (Chapel Hill, 1991); Stanley, "'Beggars Can't Be Choosers,'" 1265–1293. On the contested meanings of free labor after the Civil War, see William Forbath, "The Ambiguities of Free Labor: Labor and the Law in the Gilded Age," *Wisconsin Law Review* (1985): 767–809; Julie Saville, *The Work of Reconstruction: From Slave to Wage Laborer in South Carolina, 1860–1870* (Cambridge, 1994); and Waldrep, "Substituting the Law for the Lash," 1425–1451. On free labor ideology before the Civil War, see Eric Foner, *Free Soil, Free Labor, Free Men: The Ideology of the Republican Party before the Civil War* (New York, 1970); Tomlins, *Law, Labor, and Ideology*; and Jonathan A. Glickstein, *Concepts of Free Labor in Antebellum America* (New Haven, 1991).

[19] Of many books exploring ideological connections between whiteness and wage labor, see David Roediger, *The Wages of Whiteness: Race and the Making of the American Working Class* (London, 1991). One of the best case studies to assess connections between whiteness

workers, the freedom they sought in wage labor was based, in part, on maintaining control over the unpaid female labor of the family, which remained in their home villages.[20] In their quest to subvert padrone power, immigrant workers embraced these and other crosscutting aspects of free labor relations. In so doing, they did not redeem free labor any more than padrones had truly sullied it in the first place. Rather, free labor remained an unstable fiction in which numerous participants – employers and employees, padrones and immigrants, men and women, white and nonwhite workers, transient and persistent immigrants – attempted to reinvent its form to their advantage.

Those struggles did not take place on equal terms or even on the same political or cultural terrain. Although padrones successfully used the trappings of free labor ideology to acquire power, many of their coercive tributes existed without any legal sanction whatsoever. If much of the padrone's power was culturally and geographically derived rather than legally based, so too did immigrant workers find ways to resist padrone authority without legal doctrines or channels. For transient men, free labor comprised a group of powerful cultural assumptions about wage labor and its relationship to immigrants' changing racial, gender, and class status in North America. Free labor was as much an unfulfilled expectation as a formal legal doctrine, an imagined narrative of sojourners' lives and desires to become free men. Those expectations could be turned to strikingly different ideological purposes, stimulating one group of working-class men to demand collective emancipation with the abolition of "wage slavery," while motivating others to embrace Abraham Lincoln's Whiggish claim that "The man who labored for another last year, this year labors for himself, and next year ... will hire others to labor for him."[21] The informal meanings of free labor and the dispersed geographic contexts in which immigrants struggled to realize them both played key roles in how they perceived wage laboring and the authority of padrones, corporate managers, and immigration officials.

Researching the history of the padrone system and the diverse forms of mobility that brought it into being has been a challenging task. Padrones were expert at obscuring their tracks, while immigrant workers were almost continuously on the move and left even fewer traces of their sojourning presence. Fortunately, I located a substantial paper trail of documents on padrone business activities and their relations with both corporations and immigrant workers in local public records at El Paso, Texas, Salt Lake City, Utah, and Montreal, Canada. Court cases involving

and social context is Foley, *The White Scourge*. For a comparative discussion of whiteness among immigrant workers, see Chapter 5.

[20] On ideological connections between paid and unpaid labor, see Jeanne Boydston, *Home and Work: Housework, Wages, and the Ideology of Labor in the Early Republic* (New York, 1990). On the relationship between marriage and wage contracts, see Amy Dru Stanley, "Conjugal Bonds and Wage Labor: Rights of Contract in the Age of Emancipation," *Journal of American History* 75:2 (September 1988): 471–500.

[21] Roy F. Basler et al., eds., *The Collected Works of Abraham Lincoln* (New Brunswick, 1953), 2:364. Quoted in Foner, *Free Soil, Free Labor, Free Men*, 30.

battles between padrones and corporations, jealous immigrant elites, and disgruntled workers proved particularly helpful in exploring how padrones transformed the labor contract and the right to quit into sources of financial and cultural power. Legal records also illuminated how immigrant workers used the courts to their advantage.

But legal records have not shed light on the geographic and cultural contexts in which padrone-worker relations evolved in North America. Foreign-language sources, including Greek, Italian, and Spanish newspapers, church records, and letters between workers and their families have greatly enriched and expanded my narrative of the contentious relations between padrones, immigrant families, and their ethnic communities. The research files of undercover U.S. immigration agents, although often marred by nativist bias, likewise yielded a wealth of information on the relations between padrones and corporations, and the various strategies immigrant workers devised outside of the law to break free of padrone authority. Company records and union records have also amplified this story, as have oral histories of immigrant workers.

I use these sources to compare the rise and fall of padrone power at key stages of its evolution among Mexican, Italian, and Greek workers.[22] The first half of the book explores the creation of padronism in North America, examining in three separate chapters how padrones variously exploited labor mobility, corporations, and a variety of national legal systems to acquire control over the movement of their compatriots. The first chapter examines how padrones traversed and commodified the geographic spaces between sites of labor supply in Europe and Mexico and labor demand in the North American West. The second chapter considers the mutually defining relations between padrones and corporations in North America, focusing on how padrones took advantage of spaces created by corporate hierarchies to centralize their control over hiring and firing unskilled workers. The third chapter explores the symbiotic relationship between padrones and border bureaucrats in both North America and Europe. Whereas padrones used immigration laws of several countries to strengthen their niche in the international labor market, border officials from the United States to Bulgaria used nativist fears of the padrone to clarify the moral purpose of the laws they were creating and to justify expanding their own bureaucratic power.

After examining the creation of padrone power in the first half of the book, I consider in the second half its evolution and eventual disintegration at the hands of immigrant workers. Chapter 4 explores the complex relationship between immigrant workers' notions of manhood and padrone authority. Padrones initially gained power by mediating international kin connections and seeking to represent honorable forms of manhood in North America. But transnational mobility transformed how and where transient men defined manhood and honor in the North

---

[22] On the variety of coercive labor systems in the U.S. West, see Howard Lamar, "From Bondage to Contract: Ethnic Labor in the American West, 1600–1890," in Steven Hahn and Jonathan Prude, eds., *The Countryside in the Age of Capitalist Transformation: Essays in the Social History of Rural America* (Chapel Hill, 1985), 293–324.

American West, with explosive consequences for their padrones. If family ties and immigrant manhood proved unstable foundations for padrone power, so too were the boundaries of community – ethnic, national, and racial – that padrones attempted to define and mediate, the subject of the fifth chapter.

The manifold tensions within padrone-worker relations are brought to a dramatic climax in the final chapter, which analyzes how immigrant workers used both the practices and ideology of free labor to overthrow their padrones. Italian workers used the Canadian legal system to sue Cordasco for having violated their labor contracts and their newly realized rights as free laborers. Mexican workers resisted Gonzalez with their feet by quitting, making it nearly impossible for him or any labor agent to exploit their mobility. Greek workers, in turn, took over the local chapter of the radical Western Federation of Miners and went on strike to get rid of the czar of the Greeks.

From today's vantage point, the resistance immigrant workers generated appears neither consistent nor particularly "radical." Although immigrant workers rebelled against the padrone's exactions, they did not reject the language of contracts that sanctioned his authority. Although they succeeded in cutting through the padrone's manly representations, they by no means rejected patriarchy as a model of family relations. And although pathologized as nonwhite through much of their sojourns, immigrant workers did not reject whiteness as an identity. And yet to impose idealized expectations and definitions of resistance on immigrant workers diminishes their accomplishment in both sanctioning and destroying padronism. To understand the dilemmas immigrant workers faced, how they used the tools of padrone power to their advantage, let us examine how padrones first gained prominence in North America.

PART ONE

The World Padrones Made

CHAPTER ONE

Free Land and Unfree Labor

"Who do you live with?" asked Henry.

"With the *padrone*," replied Philippo.

"And who is the padrone?"

"He take care of me, – he bring me from Italy."

"Is he kind to you?"

Philippo shrugged his shoulders. "He beats me sometimes," he answered.

"*Beats* you? What for?"

"If I bring little money."

"Does he beat you hard?"

"Si, signore, with a stick."

"He must be a bad man," said Henry indignantly. "How much money must you carry home?"

"Two dollar."

"But it isn't your fault, if people will not give you money."

"Non importa. He beat me."

"He ought to be beaten himself."[1]

In the imagination of many Americans who read Horatio Alger's harrowing tale of childhood enslavement and exploitation, *Phil, The Fiddler; or, The Story of a Young Street Musician*, few figures possessed greater villainy than the padrone. Although the word denoted father in Italian, the padrone represented the antithesis of Victorian manhood to Alger, a figure who typified everything archaic, cruel, and un-American about the cultures of the nation's burgeoning immigrant ghettos. Alger's narrative was a shocking discovery to many readers, one that suggested the nation's cities were indeed replicating the oppressive social conditions of Europe. Here, in the subterranean recesses of New York City, the exotic and Old World padrone had found his niche.

---

[1] Horatio Alger Jr., *Phil, The Fiddler; or, The Story of a Young Street Musician* (Boston, 1872), 16–17.

Even more startling to middle-class reformers over the next half century, how-ever, was the padrone's proliferation beyond the circumscribed boundaries of immigrant ghettos in North American cities.[2] When Grace Abbott investigated padrone abuses within the Chicago employment district in 1908, she was most incensed by the tale of ten Polish workers sent to fictitious jobs in Wyoming. Stranded without enough money to purchase a return ticket, they walked back to Chicago along the same railway lines that had brought them West. Along the way, one of the men, "A bright young fellow of twenty-two," froze his foot and upon reaching Chicago had to have it amputated. Abbott used this story to justify her call for greater municipal regulation of urban labor markets and the padrones who profited from them. Key to her outrage was the padrone's corruption of that most sacred of U.S. national icons, the free land of the West. Abbott was hardly alone in condemning the padrone's outrages in rural North America. Morris Ernst, chair-man of the philanthropic City Club of New York, for example, discovered in 1912 that padronism was flourishing in upstate New York and that "almost six times as many contract laborers are sent to places outside of cities as within them" by their padrones. No landscape was safe it seemed from the reach of the cancerlike padrone, not the free lands of the North American West nor its vestiges in upstate New York.[3]

The discoveries of Abbott, Ernst, and municipal reformers like them highlighted not only how powerful padrones had grown in rural areas of the continent, but also how connected such regions were to urban labor markets. Yet these reformers had a great deal of difficulty locating the padrone's origins in North America. The question of the padrone's origins was, as most realized, an intensely political one; to acknowledge that padronism possessed New World origins cast doubt on the morally progressive features of immigration and capitalism itself. Most middle-class reformers and government investigators were consequently at a loss to explain the padrone's expansion throughout North America and his particular prominence in rural landscapes. How could the western landscape, in particular, with its abun-dance of undeveloped resources be fertile soil for the padrone? Where did padrones like Antonio Cordasco, Leon Skliris, and Roman Gonzalez come from?

New World Fictions

Middle-class reformers, dime novelists, and immigration authorities in the United States explained the padrone's presence in North America by severing, ironically,

---

[2] On the geographic expansion of the padrone, see the testimony of Herman Stump. Senate, *Congressional Record*, 53rd Congress, 2nd Session, 1894, Ex. Doc. 114; John Koren, *The Padrone System and Padrone Banks* (Washington, D.C., 1897).

[3] Grace Abbott, "The Chicago Employment Agency and the Immigrant Worker," *American Journal of Sociology* 14:3 (November 1908): 298–299; Morris L. Ernst, *Public Employment Exchanges: Report of Committee Appointed by the Trustees of the City Club of New York on December 17, 1913 "to inquire into needs of public employment exchanges in New York"* (New York, 1914), 12.

any links between padrones and the North American landscapes they inhabited. In *Phil, The Fiddler*, Horatio Alger portrayed the padrone as a Fagin-like villain whose economic practices were archaic and un-American. Phil not only had to give the padrone his daily earnings, he also was forbidden to spend money on the free market. When the padrone learned that Phil and his friend Giacomo had spent some of the money they had received during the day for food at a restaurant, for example, he whipped Giacomo forty times. If Phil's inability to spend money defined his slavery under the padrone, spending money and earning wages likewise served to liberate him. Phil managed to escape the padrone through the help of a street vendor named Paul, who lent him the money to buy his own fiddle and begin "earning" money rather than begging for it. Although Alger never clarified what distinguished begging from earning – Phil continued to play his fiddle – padronism and capitalism remained incompatible in *Phil, The Fiddler*, a message summarized by the chapter detailing Phil's emancipation: "Phil Finds a Capitalist."[4]

Subsequent narrative accounts of the padrone during the Progressive Era similarly portrayed him as an ahistoric personification of greed and primitive cruelty. In "The Biography of a Bootblack," an eight-page narrative published by the muckraking magazine, *Independent*, Italian immigrant Rocco Corresca recounted his adoption and enslavement by two padrones, one in Italy, the other in New York.[5] Rocco's padrone in Naples taught his adopted children to beg and steal from rich tourists, playing especially on the sympathies of rich women. When Rocco failed to bring in sufficient "earnings," his padrone decided he "should be made so that people would shudder and give him plenty of money." Hearing of the plan to maim him, Rocco and a friend stowed away on a steamship for America the next day. On their arrival, however, both were "adopted" by another padrone, this one named Bartolo who claimed to immigration authorities to be their uncle. Rocco and Francisco once again found themselves at work for a padrone, this time collecting junk from the streets of Brooklyn, "picking rags and bottles." The more seasoned of Bartolo's men were sent to dig a sewer in downtown Brooklyn, but they too "got little money after all."[6] Like the padrone in Naples and in Alger's fiction, Bartolo exercised strict control over their daily earnings, deducting from them the cost of all room and board. After a year of arduous work, Rocco managed finally to escape with Francisco, but only after Bartolo pursued them into New Jersey and threatened to send the local police magistrate after him.

But if "The Biography of a Bootblack" contained many of the same narrative sequences as *Phil, The Fiddler*, the biography also suggested some of the semantic changes padrones had undergone by 1900. Although the *Independent* editor presented Bartolo as a seamless extension of the culturally primitive Italian padrone, Bartolo's social relations revolved primarily around the wages his "boys" earned and his ability to provide them jobs as sewer workers. The junkyard and

---

[4] Alger, *Phil, The Fiddler*, 92, 122–131.

[5] Rocco Corresca, "The Biography of a Bootblack," *Independent* 5:4 (December 1902): 2863–2867.

[6] Ibid., 2865.

labor-contracting business that Bartolo supervised had no direct prototype in Italy, and though exploitative and unseemly to readers of the *Independent*, it was by no means antithetical to capitalism. To the contrary, Bartolo exemplified many of the virtues of capitalist success: energy, thriftiness, and punctuality. The "Biography of a Bootblack" likewise suggested that occupation-based definitions of the term had become increasingly problematic. Bartolo, after all, possessed a variety of jobs: labor contractor, boardinghouse keeper, junk collector, ragpicker, and gambler. What, then, made Bartolo a padrone? Was every immigrant junk dealer and boardinghouse keeper in Brooklyn a padrone?

In the eyes of many nativist Americans, virtually any middle-class immigrant was tainted with suspicion of being a padrone. In his pathbreaking articles on padronism, historian Robert Harney chronicled a list of jobs associated with the padrone that conveys some of the word's diverse usages by 1900: "Labor recruiters, immigrant bankers, steamship and travel agents, contractors, saloon keepers, boardinghouse proprietors, interpreters, private postal agents, food importers, ethnic newspaper publishers, foremen (work gang bosses), commissary and bunkhouse agents, and finally that most hated institution of the isolated worker, the company store." Because of the profusion of potential "padrones" in any given ethnic community, the word's precise occupational meaning had virtually vanished by 1900. Consequently, the most useful historical definition of the padrone's occupation remains ascriptive. As Robert Harney stated, the padrone was "a man whom other people called padrone."[7]

But if the padrone possessed no fixed occupational status, the figure retained a pejorative moral reputation and an exotic origin in the minds of most government investigators. In 1897 U.S. Labor Department researcher John Koren opened his study of the padrone system by stating that, "although the Italian Padrone discovered in the United States a field peculiarly suited to his activity, he must be considered a distinct product of European soil, however much he for a time prospered under American conditions."[8] Koren's assertion of the padrone's non-American origins had a long-lasting impact on government studies of the topic. In the Dillingham Commission's report on the Greek padrone system in 1911, government investigator Andre Seraphic defined the padrone as a preindustrial European phenomenon, despite his findings that the system flourished among Asian and Mexican immigrants as well. In 1921 government investigators once again described padronism as a form of serfdom that had been imported from abroad.[9]

Government investigators nonetheless had great difficulty making the empirical evidence conform to their explanations of the padrone's exotic origins. One such study was U.S. immigration commissioner Frank Sheridan's report of 1907,

[7] Robert Harney, "The Padrone and the Immigrant," *Canadian Review of American Studies* 5 (1974): 108, 110.

[8] Koren, *The Padrone System*, 1.

[9] Senate, *The Dillingham Commission: Immigrants in Industry*, vol. 2, 61st Congress, 1st session, 1911, S. Doc. 633, 396; House, *Report of the Committee on Immigration and Naturalization*, 67th Congress, 1st session, 1921.

which explored the variety of connections between padrones and railroad corporations in North America. Throughout, Sheridan remained confused over the padrone's precise economic nature. Initially, he recounted the origins of the "padrone system," then of the development of the "padrone commissary system," followed by descriptions of "padrone labor agents," and later "labor padrone agents." By the end of his report, Sheridan had dropped the word padrone altogether, calling merely for the abolition of the "commissary system." Sheridan's study drew intriguing parallels between padrones and railroad managers, but he nonetheless attempted to obscure them in his conclusions by suggesting that padrones, rather than corporations, were the real villains behind the commissary system:

In former years overcharges and extortions were deducted from the pay rolls without let or hindrance or with unavailing protests.... The padrone labor agents were called to offices of the companies and were emphatically told that there had to be radical changes made in their dealings with the laborers.

The result of the company's enlightened efforts, according to Sheridan, was that "conditions ... greatly improved" for immigrant workers. The problem had not been railroad managers but the immoral and inefficient padrone who remained an obstacle to the corporation's moral progress and economic modernization.[10]

Government investigators traveling to Europe experienced fewer frustrations than Sheridan, as they discovered a host of men who preyed on would-be emigrants and more closely resembled their image of the villainous and urban padrone. Seeking to find the origins of the padrone system in Europe, U.S. sociologist Broughton Brandenburg disguised himself and his wife in 1902 as Italian sojourners and traveled to and from Italy in steerage class among "common peasants." In Italy, Brandenburg was pleased to discover cities infested with "scoundrels" and "rogues" of every stripe who offered to "help" their migrating countrymen. One person who closely resembled the padrone of Brandenburg's imagination was known instead as the *sfruttatori*, a man who, as the *"mediazione* of labor"* charged emigrating peasants fees for getting jobs in Naples's nascent building trades. Far more ubiquitous, dangerous, and interesting to Brandenburg, however, were the numerous tricksters, gamblers, and criminals who stole the life savings of their greenhorn compatriots with considerable mirth and frequency.[11]

[10] Frank J. Sheridan, *Italian, Slavic, and Hungarian Unskilled Immigrant Laborers in the United States* (Washington, D.C., 1907), 435, 444, 445, 450, 482.

[11] Broughton Brandenburg, *Imported Americans: The Story of the Experiences of a Disguised American and His Wife Studying the Immigration Question* (New York, 1903), 1, 155, 170. Despite his moral judgments, Brandenburg himself used the services of as many "scoundrels" as he could find, paying one "rogue" several lira to get his luggage on board without a detailed inspection and another to acquire better food and beds within steerage class once on board. Brandenburg justified such actions by stating with no irony that "we had been parties to the fraud in order to catch the counterfeiters."

Had Brandenburg left Naples and headed for the surrounding countryside he might have enountered men who were indeed known as padrones in Italy. These men were anything but urban villains, however, but rather rural landowners who desired to keep their sharecropping tenants as closely tied to the land and as immobile as possible. Perhaps more akin to the padrones of Brandenburg's expectations were the *gabellotti*, men who served as crucial middlemen in an increasingly commercialized form of agricultural production, leasing the land from absentee landlords and arranging contracts with local peasants. Entrepreneurs in rural regions where the power of government was limited, gabellotti also provided peasants traditional forms of protection from brigands and other outlaws in return for tribute, usually a fixed percentage of the peasant's harvest. Working for the gabellotti were *soprastanti* (supervisors) and the *campiere* or field guards who made sure agricultural production proceeded apace on the peasant's land. Like the gabellotti, campiere played a crucial role as middlemen in the complicated social and economic hierarchy between peasant, gabellotti, and their absentee landlords, some of whom were known as padrones.[12]

Similar forms of patron-client relations characterized the forms of agricultural production in Mexico and Greece in the late nineteenth century. In Mexico, the landowner of a large estate or *hacienda* was known as the *hacendado*, a figure who, like the Italian padrone, desired to keep his work force immobile and tethered to the land through debt and intimidation. The Mexican hacendado likewise gained power from the relative weakness of the Mexican state in the late nineteenth century, offering "protection" to Mexican peons against the raids of social bandits and a variety of native peoples.[13] Greece, by contrast, did not possess large agricultural estates in the nineteenth century, but patron-clientelism nonetheless flourished in the countryside. The power brokers between town and country were not owners of large estates, but local political leaders and administrators who, as historian William McGrew put it, "served as influence brokers, regulating the villager's access to the powers and benefits of government." One of these benefits

---

[12] On Italian padrones in Italy, see David I. Kertzer and Dennis P. Hogan, *Family, Political Economy, and Demographic Change: The Transformation of Life in Casalecchio, Italy, 1861–1921* (Madison, 1989), 15, 46–47; Rudolph M. Bell, *Fate and Honor, Family and Village: Demographic and Cultural Change in Rural Italy since 1800* (Chicago, 1979), 160–161; Gabaccia, *Militants and Migrants*, 112–115; Luigi Graziano, "Patron-Client Relationships in Southern Italy," *European Journal of Political Research* 1 (1973): 9. On the role of gabellotti in the Italian countryside, see Anton Blok, *The Mafia of a Sicilian Village, 1860–1960: A Study of Violent Peasant Entrepreneurs* (New York, 1974), 33; John A. Davis, *Merchants, Monopolists, and Contractors: A Study of Economic Activity and Society in Bourbon Naples, 1815–1860* (New York, 1981), 63.

[13] On the complexities of social relations between hacendados and peons, see Friedreich Katz, "Labor Conditions on Haciendas in Porfirian Mexico: Some Trends and Tendencies," *Hispanic American Historical Review* 54:1 (February 1974): 1–47; Arnold Bauer, "Rural Workers in Spanish America: Problems of Peonage and Oppression," *American Historical Review* 59:1 (1979): 34–63, and his response, 478–485; John Tutino, "Agrarian Social Change and Peasant Rebellion in Nineteenth-Century Mexico: The Example of Chalco," in Friedreich Katz, ed., *Riot, Rebellion, and Revolution: Rural Social Conflict in Mexico* (Madison, 1988), 95–146.

was controlling the taxation system that applied to all public lands, the government's primary instrument for extracting whatever small agricultural surpluses developed in the Greek countryside. Like the hacendado, the Greek *dimarhos*, or local mayor, mediated the political distance between Athens and villages in the Greek countryside.[14]

Patron-client relations extended from the organization of political power and agricultural production in Greece, Italy, and Mexico to rural family life as well, where godparenthood served as an institution of central importance. Known as *koumbaria* in Greek villages, *compadres* or *padrinos* in Mexican villages, and *padrones* in Italian villages, godparents were chosen by parents at a child's First Communion and were supposed to serve as the child's sponsor later in life, giving advice and helping him or her secure a job or even a marriage partner. Godparents most often were well known by the family, though strategic financial and political considerations often played a role in the selection of a godparent.[15]

But the prominence of these patrons and their similiarities to patrons of immigrants in North America should not obscure the important point that padronism, as it evolved in North America, possessed no single or clear antecedent in the countryside of Italy, Greece, or Mexico. Cordasco, Skliris, and Gonzalez were each entrepreneurs who made money from the mobility of their compatriots, in sharp contrast to traditional patrons who sought to immobilize local work forces. Moreover, the word padrone was unknown to Greek and most Mexican immigrants before emigrating, possessing instead a pluralistic and cross-ethnic usage in North America.[16] Andre Seraphic, congressional investigator for the Dillingham

[14] William McGrew, *Land and Revolution in Modern Greece, 1800-1881: The Transition in the Tenure and Exploitation of Land from Ottoman Rule to Independence* (Kent, Ohio, 1985), 217–218, 221. On Greek political development, see Constantine Tsoucalas, "On the Problem of Political Clientelism in Greece in the Nineteenth Century," *Journal of Hellenic Diaspora* 5:1 (1978): 5–15; and Iannis Mavrogordatos, *Still-Born Republic: Social Coalitions and Party Strategies in Greece, 1922–1936* (New York, 1985).

[15] On Mexican godparenthood, see Vicki L. Ruiz, *Cannery Women, Cannery Lives: Mexican Women, Unionization, and the California Food Processing Industry, 1930–1950* (Albuquerque, 1987), 140, n. 17; Richard Griswold del Castillo, *La Familia: Chicano Families in the Urban Southwest, 1848 to the Present* (Notre Dame, 1984), 43; Deutsch, *No Separate Refuge*, 49. On Greek godparenthood, see Paul Sant Cassia with Constantine Bada, *The Making of the Modern Greek Family: Marriage and Exchange in Nineteenth Century Athens* (Cambridge, 1992), 155–163; John K. Campbell, *Honour, Family, and Patronage: A Study of Institutions and Moral Values in a Greek Mountain Community* (New York, 1964), 257–259. Perceptions of godparenthood remain heavily influenced by fictional accounts of the mafia, which dwell on the exotic origins of Italian-American family structure and the mafia itself. See Mario Puzo, *The Godfather* (New York, 1969). On critiques of that exoticism, see Thomas J. Ferraro, "Blood in the Marketplace: The Business of Family in the Godfather Narratives," in Werner Sollors, ed., *The Invention of Ethnicity* (Oxford, 1990), 176–207; Marco Morrone, "The Making of an American Mafia: Italians in New Orleans, 1890–1910" (M.A. thesis, University of Texas at Austin, 1998).

[16] Historians of Italian emigration consider the padrone an American phenomenon. See Bell, *Fate and Honor, Family and Village*, 160–161; William A. Douglass, *Emigration in a South Italian Town: An Anthropological History* (New Brunswick, 1984).

Commission, expressed this tension well in 1911 when he reported that the padrone system was an un-American and archaic system of coercion that had originated in Italy, but also flourished among Italian, Greek, Syrian, Bulgarian, Turkish, Japanese, and Mexican immigrants. If the Americanness of the word was lost upon U.S. immigration officials, it was more plainly apparent to immigrant workers. For Greeks in Utah the word "padrone" was one of the first English words they used in describing Leon Skliris to the governor of Utah in 1911.[17]

Even in Italy, where the word padrone had a clear etymological and social history, very few similarities existed between American and Italian uses of the word. Newly arrived Italian immigrant Constantine Panunzio expressed some of the semantic confusion Italian immigrants experienced upon hearing the word in its North American context. Panunzio recalled his first encounter with a padrone in Boston in his memoir *The Soul of an Immigrant*:

One morning we were standing in front of one of those infernal institutions which in America are permitted to bear the name of "immigrant banks" when we saw a fat man coming toward us.... "Buon giorno, padrone," said one of the men. "Padrone?" said I to myself. Now the word "padrone" in Italy is applied to a proprietor, generally a respectable man, at least one whose dress and appearance distinguish him as a man of means. This man not only showed no signs of good breeding in his face, but he was unshaven and dirty and his clothes were shabby. I could not quite understand how he could be called "padrone."[18]

Panunzio was baffled among other things by the "shabby" working-class appearance of this Boston padrone. From Panunzio's perspective, the "unshaven and dirty" Italian banker was not a landlord and had thus appropriated his title of respect. Yet he ignored how the new padrone's power reflected his ability to represent and provide services to what was an overwhelmingly working-class constituency in Boston.

Perhaps the closest prototype for the actual padrones discovered in North America was not the traditional landowner but a European steamship agent. Between 1908 and 1910, U.S. immigration inspector John Gruenberg sought, like others before him, to find the origins of the padrone system in Europe. Instead, he discovered hundreds of steamship companies and individuals engaged in financing, outfitting, and transporting emigrants to the United States. The most "extensive and systematic" of these exporters was a German agent named Frank Missler, who through the North German Lloyd and Austro-American steamship lines organized the emigration of some three hundred thousand central and eastern Europeans to the United States in 1907 alone. His subagents scoured villages in Hungary, Austria, Bulgaria, Serbia, Turkey, and Greece, armed with circulars advertising wage rates in both North and South America and guaranteeing entry into

[17] Fifty Greek and Crete men to Governor William S. Spry, February 12, 1911, file "G," box 10, William S. Spry Papers.
[18] Constantine Panunzio, *The Soul of an Immigrant* (New York: 1921), 78–79.

the United States should they pay their commissions. Working with Missler's subagents were numerous moneylenders who lent emigrants the money for their transportation to North America, but at extraordinarily high interest rates, often twice the actual cost of a steamship ticket.[19] Gruenberg suggested that Missler and similar European steamship agents were indeed "unscrupulous," but he refused to describe Missler as a padrone. To do so would acknowledge the figure's modernity, a disquieting task from which even the most studious immigration inspector recoiled. As long as padrones remained archaic, North America's political economy remained progressive, its system of wage labor relations truly free.

The plethora of connections between padrones and modern economic practices in North America suggests one reason they remained persistent figures in the cultural landscape of both North American city and countryside after 1870. Padrones were threatening to Sheridan, Brandenburg, and Gruenberg not because they were preindustrial but precisely because they were not. The anxieties and dilemmas produced by North America's rapid industrial and urban growth were profound and enduring, ones not solved by the teleological narratives of progress or modernization. The Thirteenth Amendment may have officially ended all forms of slavery and coercive labor in the United States, but it did little to secure the precise meaning of wage labor for growing numbers of newly dependent wage earners.[20] For middle-class reformers, the distance between free and unfree labor had to be constantly reaffirmed and made visible, a task for which the padrone seemed eminently suited.

But if the reports of government investigators and reformers unwittingly highlight the modernity of padrones in North America, they do not reveal why rural landscapes became arenas for padrone power. Rather than reconsider whether "free land" actually liberated the wage earner, reformers and government investigators alike continued to view city and countryside as antithetical places and thus saw in the land a solution to the urban pathologies of both padronism and unemployment. "The characteristic feature of unemployment in New York State," wrote reformer Morris Ernst in 1912, "is congestion in New York City and great areas of untilled soil up the state." Free, uncultivated land, whether in the West or in the Adirondack Mountains, would function they hoped as it always had: as a safety valve to oppressive urban social conditions. Despite their evidence to the contrary, these reformers continued to view the padrone as an urban problem, whether in Naples or New York. There simply existed no room in their romantic vision of rural landscapes for anyone so exploitative as the padrone.

Romantic renderings of the relationship between land and labor were pervasive

[19] John Gruenberg to the Immigration Commission, November 10, 1910, 61, 70, Records of the Bureau of Immigration, Immigration Subject Correspondence, file 52066/A, box 79, RG 85, National Archives, Washington, D.C.; John Gruenberg to Daniel J. Keefe, December 18, 1908, 2, file 52066/1, ibid.

[20] On the contested meanings of free labor after the Civil War, see Forbath, "The Ambiguities of Free Labor," 767–780; Saville, The Work of Reconstruction; Waldrep, "Substituting Law for the Lash," 1425–1435; Stanley, "'Beggars Can't Be Choosers,'" 1265–1275.

during the Progressive Era, reflecting the popularity of the ideas of Frederick Jackson Turner Jr., who explicitly linked the existence of "free land" to the development of free labor relations on the frontier. One measure of the popularity of his thesis was that even labor historian John R. Commons, who disagreed with Turner's sanguine portrayal of democracy and individualism, agreed that a frontier of free land had historically muffled industrial and urban conflicts in eastern cities.[21] The proliferation of padrones on or near the edges of settlement and economic development, however, remained an unexplained phenomenon. To understand how padrones became powerful in the West and North America more generally, how they took advantage of the numerous opportunities this labor-scarce region offered, let us turn to the lives and careers of Antonio Cordasco, Leon Skliris, and Roman Gonzalez.

The King of the Laborers

On January 23, 1904, over two thousand Italian men marched down the main business streets of Montreal chanting "Viva Edouardo VII! Viva Le Canada! Viva Antonio Cordasco! Viva Le Canadian Pacific Railway!" Walking in rows ten abreast, the militant-looking laborers were not on strike, or soldiers on their way to war, but seasonal railroad workers gathered to honor their padrone, Antonio Cordasco, who had secured them jobs with the largest corporation in Canada, the Canadian Pacific Railway (CPR). At the end of the procession, as Cordasco later recalled, two of his Italian foremen presented him with "a very elegant crown, gilded, and a very artistic basket of flowers," while pronouncing him "king of the labourers," amid cheers from the assembled workers. A few weeks later, Cordasco's foremen threw a banquet in his honor, attended by CPR superintendents, Cordasco's family members, and his *caposquadri*, or personal deputies. All invitations arrived in envelopes embossed with Cordasco's title and insignia closely resembling the "royal crest of Italy."[22]

Cordasco's conspicuous coronation invited a hostile reaction from Montreal's native-born residents, many of whom saw in his parade evidence of the undemocratic, archaic, and corrupt nature of Italian culture. Cordasco's royal insignia to

---

[21] Turner, *The Frontier in American History*, 23; John R. Commons, *A History of Labor in the United States*, vols. 3 and 4 (New York, 1935), xiii. New western historians and new labor historians have both debunked Turner's notion that the West acted as a safety valve, with labor historians noting how militant and radical western workers were and western historians suggesting that the "free" lands of the region were not free but taken. But both groups have neglected the precise relationship between the region's taken lands and its labor relations, perhaps because of apparent connections to Turnerian formulations of western history.

[22] Much of my knowledge of Cordasco's career has been gleaned from the rich investigation of his business practices by the Canadian government in the summer of 1904. See Canadian Department of Labor, *The Royal Commission Appointed to Inquire into the Immigration of Italian Labourers to Montreal and the Alleged Fraudulent Practices of Employment Agents* (Ottawa, 1905), 86, 163, 167; Harney, "Montreal's King of Italian Labour," 57; A. Cordasco to Dear Friend Raffaele, March 12, 1904, Microfiche 3473, RG 33/99, Canadian National Archives, Ottawa.

the contrary, he was not an ethnic leader with deep roots in Old World hierarchies or political privileges. Indeed, not much is known about Cordasco before his arrival in Montreal. Born into a small landowning family in the northeastern province of Veneto during the 1860s, he was not a local notable or a landlord of any significance. Nor was he among the pioneers of the Italian migration to North America, who emigrated before the upsurge in Italian migration during the 1890s. Rather, Cordasco emigrated with thousands of his compatriots to New York in 1894, where he began learning English and looking for work. He moved to Montreal in 1897, thirty years after the first Italians had settled there.[23]

But if Cordasco was not the first Italian to establish himself in Montreal, his timing could not have been more opportune. In 1897, Montreal stood on the threshold of a dynamic period of economic growth and urban expansion. Between 1900 and 1910, the city's manufacturing output more than doubled, while its population grew by nearly 80 percent (see Table 1.1 in Appendix A).[24] This dramatic growth was not fueled by the city's proximity to water on the St. Lawrence River, but by its rapidly expanding inland transportation system. As the eastern hub for all three of Canada's railroads – the Canadian Pacific, the Great Northern, and the Grand Trunk Line – Montreal became an ideal location for manufacturing the vast array of raw goods that began moving east along steel rails.

Much of Montreal's growth was highlighted by the expanding fortunes of Canada's greatest railroad, the CPR. Although it completed its first transcontinental line in 1885, the amount of freight the company hauled remained relatively small throughout the depression-ridden 1890s. The central challenge the company faced was to find ways to liquidate its chief asset: land. Granted over twenty-five million acres by the Canadian government along both sides of its entire transcontinental route in 1886, the CPR found that there were as yet few farms or towns producing anything of value to haul. Beginning in 1901, however, the CPR began an aggressive campaign to sell off its remaining seventeen million acres (see Figures 1.1 and 1.2).[25] "Get your Canadian Home from the Canadian Pacific," began one CPR advertisement, "the Home Maker. We will make you a long-time loan . . . and your Canadian farm will *make you independent*." In offering cheap credit to families and appealing to the same ideals of free labor that had settled the U.S. West, the CPR succeeded not only in selling off millions of acres but also increased the value of its remaining land holdings as shown by the escalating prices it charged per acre.[26] The growth of farms and small towns along its routes

---

[23] Charles Catelli, for example, president of Montreal's Italian Immigration Aid Society, emigrated to Montreal in 1866 and was one of the Italian community's richest and most established members. See testimony of Catelli, *Royal Commission*, 126.

[24] Figures were gleaned from Benjamin Higgins, *The Rise and Fall? of Montreal: A Case Study of Urban Growth, Regional Expansion, and National Development* (Montreal, 1986), 44.

[25] Compiled from *The Annual Reports of the Canadian Pacific Railway Corporation* (Montreal, 1894–1912).

[26] On the CPR's role in settling the Canadian plains, see John W. Bennett and Seena B. Kohl, *Settling the Canadian-American West, 1890–1915: Pioneer Adaptation and Community Building: An Anthropological History* (Lincoln, 1995), 19; John A. Eagle, *The Canadian Pacific Railway and the Development of Western Canada* (Montreal, 1989), 185; William Kaye

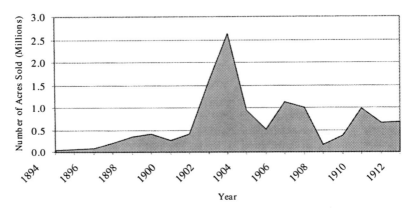

Figure 1.1. Canadian Pacific Railway land sales, 1894–1912: Total acreage (*Source*: CPR annual reports)

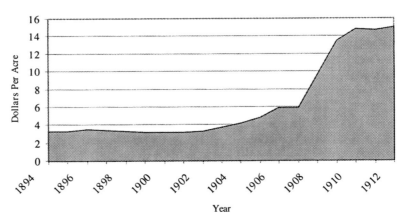

Figure 1.2. Canadian Pacific Railway land sales, 1894–1912: Price per acre (*Source*: CPR annual reports)

likewise expanded the amount of freight the line carried. Although the number of track miles the CPR operated increased roughly 40 percent between 1900 and 1910, the volume of freight swelled over 300 percent in the same period. Much of this new freight comprised grain, helping make Montreal the biggest cereal processing and grain exporting city in the world by the 1920s.[27]

If Canada's railroads transformed Montreal's economy by opening up a vast hinterland of goods and markets for its own manufactured goods, they also transformed the shape and structure of the labor market in both Montreal and western

Lamb, *History of the Canadian Pacific Railway* (New York, 1977), 440, 446; and James B. Hedges, *Building the Canadian West: The Land and Colonization Policies of the Canadian Pacific Railway* (New York, 1939).

[27] Higgins, *The Rise and Fall? of Montreal*, 45.

Canada. As thousands of workers moved west either to settle land or work on the CPR each spring, labor in Montreal became much scarcer and had to be replaced by workers from outside the city – first from the countryside of Quebec and Ontario, then the cities of New York and Boston, and eventually villages of northern Italy. In so doing, Canada's railroads greatly expanded the regions that reciprocally influenced each other within Montreal's labor market.[28]

Standing astride these evolving boundaries between city and country, Antonio Cordasco played a key role in expanding the geographic dimensions of Montreal's labor market. In his scramble to become established between 1897 and 1901, Cordasco aggressively developed connections with Italian communities throughout the northeastern United States. These ties served him well in the summer of 1901. When over two thousand Irish and Scottish track workers went on strike in Vancouver in the spring of 1901, CPR manager George Burns decided to give the unknown Cordasco a try at recruiting strikebreakers. Burns never had to look further that summer.[29] On July 7, Cordasco began making regular shipments of one hundred men from Boston and New York to Montreal. Over the course of the summer, Cordasco supplied the CPR with more than two thousand strikebreakers, all of them Italians from Boston and New York. His accomplishment greatly impressed special agent Burns and his superiors at the CPR. Cordasco's efforts not only broke the strike but earned him the enviable position of sole Italian labor agent.[30] Henceforth, only he could recruit, hire, and fire Italian workers on the CPR, giving him control over one of the most lucrative sites of labor demand in North America.

Cordasco used his control over labor demand to exploit as much of the vast space between Montreal and the countryside of Italy and western Canada as possible. In the spring of 1902, he began charging all Italian workmen one dollar for the cost of transporting them to their jobs in the Canadian West. This fee came on top of a two dollar fee for each job in Canada. Cordasco also extended the geographic distances his countrymen traveled each season under his control. During the strike of 1901, Cordasco imported virtually all of his Italian workers from New York and Boston. By the spring of 1903, he was corresponding with Italian padrones in over a dozen North American cities and importing workers from Buffalo, Columbus, Baltimore, Detroit, Philadelphia, Chicago, and St. Louis.[31] In addition, nearly 40 percent of the thirty-one hundred Italians hired by the CPR in 1903 came to Montreal directly from Italy.[32] Having exhausted the ready supply of

---

[28] On the geography of urban labor markets, see Harvey, *The Urbanization of Capital*, 128–135.

[29] For an account of the 1901 strike, see Joseph Tuck, "Canadian Railways and the International Brotherhoods: Labour Organization in the Railway Running Trades in Canada, 1865–1914" (Ph.D. diss., Western Ontario University, 1975), 191–196; Joseph Tuck, "The United Brotherhood of Railway Employees in Western Canada, 1898–1905," *Labour/Le Travailleur* 11 (Spring 1983): 65.

[30] Testimony of George Burns, *Royal Commission*, 41.

[31] See Cordasco's address lists, Records of the Royal Commission's Investigation, Microfiche 3473, RG 33/99.

[32] Testimony of George Burns, *Royal Commission*, 44.

transient Italians in the labor markets of eastern U.S. cities, Cordasco looked to the Italian countryside for more recruits and for greater profits created by the longer migration under his control. In the fall of 1903, Cordasco traveled to New York City with Burns, where they persuaded several major steamship lines to make Cordasco their official representative in North America. Such efforts paid off handsomely. In the spring of 1904, Cordasco registered thirty-nine hundred Italians in Montreal, an all-time record, with over 60 percent coming directly from Italy.[33]

Cordasco attempted to regulate the flow of his compatriots with a registration system that protected the jobs of more experienced workers. Foremen were required to send Cordasco the names of their section gang members, plus a fee of one dollar a man and ten dollars for the foreman himself. Cordasco's bookkeeper, Antonio Ganna, recorded their names and then provided them with jobs that spring in the original order they paid their job fees. Experienced workers were thus first in line for the longer and steadier positions on the CPR that summer.[34]

Cordasco's registration system not only protected his loyal customers, but minimized the time Italian workers were concentrated in Montreal. The constant mobility and isolation of Italian workmen created tremendous profits for Cordasco, who made almost as much from his commissary business as from his job and travel fees. With the help of Burns in the spring of 1902, Cordasco began supplying food – mostly sardines and bread – to the CPR's Italian and Chinese employees. Cordasco charged handsome markups on these items – usually between 60 and 100 percent – and the costs of these necessities were deducted directly from workers' wages.[35] In 1903, nearly 40 percent of the fifteen thousand dollars Cordasco earned as labor agent came directly from sales of food purchased by Italian and Chinese workers.[36] Cordasco's migration system created truly international labor markets not by annihilating space but by commodifying it, a transformation dearly understood by Italian workers whose job and transportation fees and commissary expenses made Cordasco rich.

Yet if Cordasco's tribute system exploited an almost continuous movement of Italian workers, the evolution of his migration system was still very much rooted in the land and its relationship to urban labor markets. During the 1903 work season, the CPR's demand for unskilled Italian labor was directly related to the booming demand for "free" land on the Canadian prairies (see Figure 1.1). The great land rush produced an acute labor shortage in the West during the summer of 1903, as thousands of CPR track men, most of them French Canadians and English-speaking immigrants from Ireland and Scotland, left their jobs in order to bring in the new wheat harvests during the summer and to settle their own plots of land. Given the choice between earning CPR wages of $1.50 a day and buying

[33] Testimony of Antonio Cordasco, ibid., 101, 128.

[34] Ibid., 88.

[35] On similar markups among Italian padrones in the United States, see Sheridan, *Italian, Slav, and Hungarian Unskilled Immigrants*, 454.

[36] According to the CPR, Cordasco made $3,800 in 1903 from selling food to Italian and Chinese laborers. Testimony of John Skinner, *Royal Commission*, 166.

CPR land at $3.67 an acre in 1903, thousands of track workers chose the company's latter offer. The Italians were subsequently brought in, as special agent Burns explained, "to replace those men in the North-West Territories who have been employed earlier in the season and ... who jump their jobs." Burns relied on Cordasco's Italians because they represented the most readily available labor supply and because, as Burns stated, "we had to rely on anything we could get." The result of the CPR's land rush was thus a bonanza for Cordasco, as the CPR not only sold a record number of acres in 1903, but also employed a record number of Italian workers.[37]

Cordasco's profits would have been considerably smaller had his Italian workers quit their jobs on the CPR as the Irish, Scottish, and French Canadian workers did each summer work season. The mobility of Italian workers through space had to be controlled to be profitable. Cordasco had no formal mechanism for keeping Italian workers from "jumping" their jobs, but benefited instead from Italian workers' familial obligations. Unlike the many Irish, Ukranian, and French Canadian workers who were either single or whose families resided nearby, Italian laborers were primarily married sojourners who were keen on returning to families in the off-season. Although family connections facilitated and subsidized the Italian worker's travel to North America, they also functioned to keep him quite literally on track during his brief sojourn in North America.

The strength of Italian family ties and the great abundance of cheap and uncultivated land in the Canadian West at the turn of the century, then, did not so much create a system of free labor relations as a range of coercive practices. This was an old story in the labor history of the North American West. Abundant cheap land on the frontier and the resulting scarcity of labor had produced sharply different labor systems, often within the same geographic space and time.[38] If the scarcity of labor drove the wages of certain laborers up on the California mining frontier in the 1850s, for example, it also justified the development of coercive labor systems involving nonwhite peoples, principally Chinese immigrants, African American slaves, and certain of California's Indian populations. In western Canada in 1900, free land and unfree labor once again developed not coincidentally, but rather helped bring each other into being. The recently settled Canadian farmer who jumped his contract in order to become a free laborer harvesting his own wheat could not have brought his crop to market in the fall of 1903 were it not for Cordasco and thousands of Italian laborers laying track between numerous boomtowns in the Canadian West.[39]

---

[37] Testimony of George Burns, ibid., 52. According to CPR labor agent John Skinner, the Italians "stuck to their contracts quite well," ibid., 22.

[38] Lamar, "From Bondage to Contract," 320–324.

[39] On the complexity of social relations among different groups of immigrant farmers in the Canadian West, see Bennett and Kohl, *Settling the Canadian-American West*, 27–39. On the impact of westward conquest on Canadian national identity, see Walker D. Wyman and Clifton B. Kroeber, *The Frontier in Perspective* (Madison, 1957); J. M. S. Careless, *Frontier and Metropolis: Regions, Cities, and Identities in Canada before 1914* (Toronto, 1989).

But if the land helped swell Cordasco's pockets during the summer of 1903, it also contributed to his crisis in the summer of 1904. The seasonal employment of Italian workers typically began in late March as the Canadian winter slowly subsided, enabling laborers to return to the West and begin laying track until October when snow and cold once again put a stop to their arduous work. The spring of 1904 threw a wrench into this pattern. Put simply, the thaw came late, with the beginning of May finding frozen ground across much of western Canada. Only in June did the season's track work begin in earnest, and then on a reduced scale. Because the late thaw contributed to a sharp reduction in the sale of new lands as well as to a smaller harvest, more French Canadian, Irish, and Scottish farmers were available for work on the CPR. The consequences for Italian workers – traditionally last hired and first fired – were devastating. By mid-July, the CPR had employed just 700 Italians, down considerably from the 3,200 it had employed the previous season, and dramatically less than the 10,000 men Cordasco hoped would be hired in 1904.[40]

When it became apparent that the season's work would start much later, Cordasco tried to slow the ongoing Italian migration to Montreal by writing letters to his agents in New York and Italy. But he could not stop the flow of his countrymen so late in the season, for most had already sent their fees and embarked on their journeys. Equally maddening to Cordasco, many more Italians arrived in Montreal than were registered. Of the 877 Italians who arrived in Montreal from the United States in the spring of 1904, for example, 40 percent had made no prior arrangements with Cordasco's agents in New York, Boston, or Chicago.[41] Nor had many of the Italians arriving from Italy, a situation that prompted Cordasco to write an angry letter to his agent Antonio Paretti of Udine, Italy, on April 26, 1904:

Many immigrants from the Venetian provinces come to me declaring they were sent by you, but without any card of recognition.... I don't wish to blame you for that ... but it is absurd to expect that I am to give employment tomorrow to a man who applies today to my office. I could not put him before the others.... You will understand how this all annoys me. I am not responsible for the extremely cold season that prevents the companies from starting work.

Cordasco's anger reflected the barrage of criticism that was being directed against him by Italian workers, who increasingly felt betrayed and angered by Cordasco's hollow promise to give "employment to all Italians who come to me."[42]

For Cordasco, the success of his recruitment overseas combined with the Canadian snows to produce a scenario of truly nightmarish proportions. His ability to gain power by exploiting the mobility of his compatriots had, in the passing of a

[40] Testimony of John Skinner, *Royal Commission*, 23.
[41] Testimony of Antonio Cordasco, ibid., 128.
[42] Antonio Cordasco to Antonio Peretti, April 26, 1904, ibid., 81–82; Antonio Cordasco to Antonio Paretti, March 1, 1904, ibid., 80.

snowstorm, abruptly vanished. The only place Cordasco still controlled was his office, but here he found headache and frustration, as first a few, then dozens, and finally hundreds of Italian laborers visited him daily, demanding immediate employment or their money back. Cordasco refused to refund any of his clients, insisting that work would begin any day. But the number and anger of immigrant workers only grew as time passed, leading many to testify against him in the Canadian government's Royal Commission investigating "the fraudulent practices of labor contractors."[43]

The rebellion of Italian workers against Cordasco and the widespread publicity of the government's investigation severely damaged his reputation and his international business operations. His contact in Italy, Antonio Paretti, also suffered because of the unusual bottleneck of workers in Montreal and had no business dealings with him thereafter. Other labor agents in Montreal, notably Alberto Dini, stepped into the momentary vacuum created by Cordasco's troubles and established their own contacts with steamship agents in Italy, some of them Cordasco's former associates.[44] But Dini would never become the *sole* labor agent for the CPR. The company's experience with a single immigrant labor agent had soured badly.[45] Although the favorable geographic location that Cordasco enjoyed in Montreal – working at a great distance from both sites of labor supply and labor demand – was not destroyed as a result of the Royal Commission's findings, never again would any single individual establish a choke hold over Italian migration to Canada. Indeed, between 1904 and 1907, the percentage of Canada-bound Italians listing Montreal as their final destination dropped from 80 to less than 20 percent (see Maps 1.1A and 1.1B).

The Czar of the Greeks

Like Cordasco, Leon Skliris seemed an unlikely candidate to become a king or a "czar" to his ethnic compatriots. Born in the small village of Vresthena in the Peloponnese in 1880, he emigrated to the United States at the age of seventeen.[46] Leon undoubtedly learned something about patron-client relations from his father, who as Vresthena's mayor mediated the interests of his fellow villagers and the Greek state. But this experience gave him little help in America, for he arrived in New York, like most Greek immigrants, with no money and few skills. Skliris spent his first years working as a peddler, selling violets and carnations to businessmen on Wall Street, where he learned some of the mores of American corporations. In 1901 he went to work for the Illinois Central Railroad as a track foreman, where he

---

[43] Testimony of Pietro Bianco, *Royal Commission*, 67; Testimony of Giovanni Morillo, ibid., 68. See also *Guiseppe Teolo vs. Antonio Cordasco*, Case 990, 1905, Records of the Superior Court, District of Montreal, Canadian National Archives, Montreal.

[44] Corecco and Brivio to Mr. Alberto Dini, May 7, 1904, *Royal Commission*, 50.

[45] Report of Judge John Winchester, ibid., xxxviii.

[46] Salt Lake County, Naturalization Files, Gust Skliris, August 7, 1905, Utah State Archives, Salt Lake City, Utah.

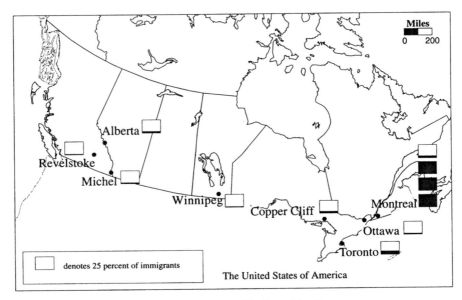

Map 1.1A. Final destinations of Canada-bound Italians, March 1904

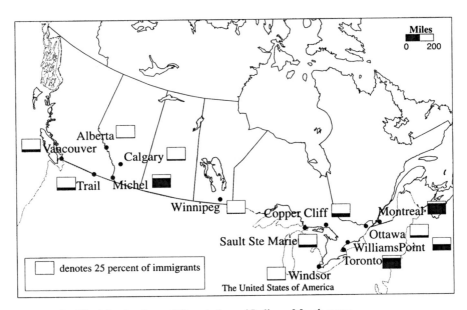

Map 1.1B. Final destinations of Canada-bound Italians, March 1907

supervised a group of thirty Greek laborers. Work in Illinois was seasonal, even as a foreman, and Skliris continued his journey, traveling to Salt Lake City in the fall of 1902 at the request of Greek labor agent and childhood friend, William Caravelis. With his encouragement, Skliris decided to stay put, having sized up his opportunities by "making a study of the problem of employing laborers on railroads," as he later recalled.[47]

Skliris's timing could not have been better. In 1902, Salt Lake City and its outlying periphery, the Jordan Valley, stood on the brink of a mighty and dramatic economic expansion. Since the 1890s, when the Mormon Church modified its hostility to industrial pursuits, coal mining had been booming in Utah and copper production in Bingham Canyon was just beginning to expand. Thousands of miles of new railroad track would be laid in the intermountain West between 1900 and 1910 to accommodate these new enterprises. Although the Mormon commonwealth remained officially committed to agriculture, Salt Lake City had by 1900 emerged as a regional center for industrial growth, serving as the hub for the Union Pacific and the Denver and Rio Grande (D&RG) railroad companies, and several growing smelting and refining industries.[48]

The rapid growth of mining and railroad enterprises in Utah did not alter the acute shortage of labor that had been the defining feature of the region's labor market during the nineteenth century. Labor remained scarce in Utah in part because of the continuing abundance of cheap land, which drained any potential surplus in Salt Lake's urban labor market. Salt Lake City faced a predicament similar to the CPR's: how could it turn the region's principal asset – cheap and undeveloped resources – into useful commodities, be they farmland or copper mines? During the nineteenth century, both Mormon Church leaders and urban boosters actively promoted the emigration of farmers to Utah, many of them Swedish and Norwegian immigrants.[49] This organized importation transformed the landscapes of both Salt Lake City and the Jordan Valley in the nineteenth century, making the temple city swell and its surrounding desert bloom.

Yet it would take far more than Norwegian and Swedish farmers to satisfy the demand for labor in Utah as the state's industrial output more than doubled between 1900 and 1910.[50] Beginning in the 1890s, a series of "new" immigrants began emigrating to Utah to perform the expanding number of unskilled jobs, most of them from southern and eastern Europe. Finnish miners were some of the first to arrive, settling mostly in the silver mining regions around Park City and Bingham Canyon. Italians followed soon after, many of them as strikebreakers in

---

[47] *Eastern Utah Advocate*, April 9, 1915, 1; *Salt Lake Tribune*, April 6, 1915, 3.
[48] On Salt Lake's early urban history, see Edward W. Tullidge, *The History of Salt Lake City and Its Founders* (Salt Lake City, 1896). See also Vernon Jensen's analysis of Mormon debates about mining in *Heritage of Conflict: Labor Relations in the Nonferrous Metals Industry Up to 1930* (Ithaca, 1950), 257–259.
[49] Tullidge, *The History of Salt Lake*, 697–699.
[50] Papanikolas, "Toil and Rage," 112.

the coalfields of Carbon County.[51] Other Italians, along with numerous Basque immigrants from Spain, came to work as cattle and sheep ranch hands in the Wasatch Mountains east of Ogden and Provo, Utah. The Italians were, in turn, followed by "Austrians" – primarily Serbians, Croatians, and Slovenians – who found work in the smelters of Magna, Garfield, Midvale, and Murray, each located on the southwestern periphery of Salt Lake City. Finally came Japanese and Greek immigrants who found work initially on the railroads and later in the mining communities of Carbon County and Bingham Canyon.[52]

The vast majority of these immigrants did not find their way to Utah's mining towns and railroad lines as individuals but within organized migration networks. Many connections were informal, consisting of family relations or friends who already worked in Utah and who sent information about job openings to their home villages.[53] But many connections were more formally organized by immigrant labor contractors, of whom Leon Skliris was just one in 1902. Italian immigrants, for example, found their way to Utah through the business connections of Moses Paggi, who provided his countrymen jobs building dams and laying electrical wire for the Utah Power and Light Company. Japanese workers likewise paid tributes to their labor agent, Edward Daigoro Hashimoto, who found them jobs on Utah's railroads and mines and in digging irrigation ditches across much of the state. Basque sheepherders and ranchers traveling to the mountains around Ogden, in turn, depended upon Pedro Altube of Elko, Nevada, who found them positions in the increasingly competitive sheep and cattle ranching business.[54] In return for their "help," immigrant workers paid them a variety of tributes throughout their sojourns in North America.

As in the Canadian plains, free land played an important role in shaping the evolution of these systems of unfree labor.[55] For Pedro Altube, the abundance of free public land in the intermountain West helped bring his system of unfree labor

---

[51] Ibid., 109.
[52] On the experience of varied ethnic groups in Utah, see Helen Papanikolas, ed., *The Peoples of Utah* (Salt Lake City, 1976).
[53] On informal methods of controlling the supply of labor within immigrant communities, see John Bodnar, *The Transplanted: A History of Immigrants in Urban America* (Bloomington, 1985), 57–60.
[54] On Paggi's business dealings as a padrone, see *Paggi vs. Skliris*, State of Utah, Records of the Utah Supreme Court, March 12, 1919, Case 3216, Utah State Archives. *Moses Paggi vs. G. Milana*, Salt Lake County, Records of the 3rd District Civil Court, April 23, 1915, Case 19657, Utah State Archives. On Hashimoto's business activities, see *E. D. Hashimoto vs. Showell Brothers*, Salt Lake County, Records of the 3rd District Civil Court, November 19, 1906, Case 8641, Utah State Archives. On the Japanese labor-contracting system in Utah, see Yuji Ichioka, *The Issei: The World of the First Generation Japanese Immigrants, 1885–1924* (New York, 1987), 60–61. On Pedro Altube's career, see Jon Bilbao and William A. Douglass, *Amerikanuak: Basques in the New World* (Reno, 1975), 256–259.
[55] Systematic comparisons of the Canadian and U.S. Wests are lacking, but some fine comparative work exists in case studies of agricultural settlement and western labor struggle at the turn of the twentieth century. See Bennett and Kohl, *Settling the Canadian-American West*, 9–10, 259; and Carlos Schwantes, *Radical Heritage: Labor, Socialism, and Reform in Washington and British Columbia, 1885–1917* (Seattle, 1979).

into existence in the late nineteenth century. He built a tribute system spanning four states by importing his countrymen to herd large flocks of sheep across thousands of acres of public land. When the supply of public land was abundant, all profits of the sheep operations went to Altube who provided food and lodgings to his imported countrymen. Altube, did not pay his men wages, but instead promised them livestock at the end of their work contracts, typically ranging from two to three years.[56] By 1900, however, with the supply of public land becoming ever more constricted, Altube began paying his imported countrymen wages for their labor instead of sheep. The transition to wage labor was quickened by the federal government, which restricted the lands available to Basque sheepmen in creating the nation's early national parks system.[57] For Basque sheepherders, it was not a frontier of free public lands but rather the creation of another national commons that ironically led to the adoption of wage labor in their community.

For Leon Skliris, in turn, it was not free land itself but the scarcity of labor in the resource-rich great basin that brought him power as a padrone. Although there remained arable land uncultivated in Utah in 1902, most of the state's potential labor supply was simply not available for hire year round.[58] The scarcity of labor became especially acute during planting and harvest seasons, when every free hand was needed to secure the crops. Typically, this timing coincided with the railroad's need for extra workmen, thus exacerbating the seasonal shortage of labor.[59] To meet these demands, Skliris visited Greek coffeehouses from Chicago to San Francisco in the off-season, discussing the work opportunities in Utah with local Greek workers, saloon owners, and coffeehouse proprietors. These early connections served Skliris well for in 1904, the D&RG made him one of its chief labor agents for Utah and Colorado. Skliris spent much of 1904 "on the line," supervising the movement of Greek workers along D&RG tracks in Colorado and Utah.[60] This work was immensely profitable as he charged all workers fees of between five and ten dollars to get a job and an additional dollar a month to keep it.

Like Cordasco, Skliris's success in establishing control over one source of labor demand in North America enabled him to reach back to sites of labor supply in Greece. When Skliris became the D&RG's labor agent in 1904, nearly all of his recruited workers came from coffeehouses in North America. By 1907, however,

[56] For a description of such contracts, see Douglass, *Amerikanuak*, 225–226, 232–233.

[57] Ibid., 285–287. On social conflict engendered by the creation of a national parks system, see Louis Warren, *The Hunter's Game: Poachers and Conservationists in Twentieth-Century America* (New Haven, 1997).

[58] The relationship between free land and padronism was not fixed, as landholding could also subvert padrone authority. For the Japanese immigrant worker, owning land became one means of breaking free from the power of labor contractors, as thousands of Japanese immigrants began buying farmlands in the early twentieth century. See Ichioka, *The Issei*, 153.

[59] On the seasonality of labor markets, see Donald D. Lescohier, *The Labor Market* (New York, 1923). For a more sophisticated and recent examination, see Claudia Goldin and Stanley Engerman, *Seasonality in Nineteenth Century Labor Markets* (Boston, 1990).

[60] See *Walker Brothers vs. Caravelis & Company*, Case 1938, 67–68, State of Utah, Records of the Utah Supreme Court. For an abstract of the case, see *Utah Reports* (Salt Lake City, 1908), 353–368.

a well-organized flow of immigrants came to Utah directly from Greece. Like
Cordasco, Skliris sought a ready supply of transient workers, one that was not
available in the competitive urban labor markets of Denver and other western
cities. An examination of the manifest lists of all Greek passengers arriving in the
port of New York in the month of March in selected years reveals that 125 Greek
immigrants listed Utah as their final destination in March 1912, up from just 6 in
March 1904.[61] The vast majority of the 1912 immigrants – 120 of them – possessed railroad tickets directly to towns in Utah. It is difficult to determine what
percentage had been recruited by Skliris's agents, but a significant portion listed
common addresses in Salt Lake City, Bingham Canyon, and Castle Gate, Utah. Of
50 Greeks listing Salt Lake City as their final destination in 1907, for example,
21 were destined to Skliris's office or the saloon that he owned next door in Salt
Lake City's Greek quarter.[62]

Several factors placed limits on Skliris's modest business successes in Utah and
Greece in 1907, however. Unlike Cordasco, Skliris had a great deal of difficulty
controlling or profiting from the mobility of Greek workers in Utah who frequently quit their positions on the D&RG. Greek mobility between jobs reflected
two circumstances. First, in contrast to the Canadian Rockies, there existed
numerous alternative job possibilities for the Greek railroad worker in Colorado
and Utah's burgeoning mining and construction industries. Quitting one's job only
made sense when alternatives existed. Equally important, Greek workers were
predominantly young, single, and less encumbered by family obligations than
their married counterparts on the CPR. Consequently, Greek workers were far
more likely than married Italians to "bounce" between jobs. The impact of such
mobility on Skliris, initially, was to weaken his ability to profit from the railroad
commissary.

Because of the footloose behavior of Greek workers, Skliris also experienced
terrific competition from other Greek padrones who, like him, established control
over one site of labor demand. Skliris's influence in 1907 was circumscribed by a
variety of Greek entrepreneurs. To his north, onetime partner William Caravelis of
Pocatello, Idaho, supplied all Greek labor for the Oregon Short Line Railroad
Company, which ran from Salt Lake City north through Idaho's central valley.
Farther north still, Pericles Skarlatos supplied Greek laborers to railroad and
construction companies in Oregon and Washington.[63] To Skliris's west, Louis Cononelos controlled the hiring of Greek laborers in the rapidly expanding copper-
mining communities of Ely and McGill, Nevada. To the east in Wyoming,
Nicholas Meindaris "placed laborers for the Union Pacific" and operated both a

---

[61] See Table 1.3, Appendix A. Steamship manifest lists, Port of New York City, March 1907,
March 1910, March 1912, and March 1914, U.S. Department of Immigration and Naturalization, RG 85, National Archives, Washington, D.C.

[62] Ibid.

[63] For evidence of Skarlatos's business dealings, see *Skarlatos vs. Brice*, State of Washington,
Records of the Washington Supreme Court, May 9, 1917, Case 13533, cited in *Pacific
Reporter* (Seattle, Wash.), 164, (1917): 939–940.

labor agency and a saloon in Cheyenne. Born in Arahova, a village near Skliris's hometown of Vresthena, Meindaris brought over one hundred of his fellow villagers to work on a Union Pacific track gang in 1900 and served as "one of the first interpreters" on the western railroads.[64]

But if Skliris remained constrained by Greek and Italian competitors in 1907, he soon positioned himself to take best advantage of Greek workers' remarkable mobility between jobs. He did so by expanding the number of companies he provided unskilled labor for, making it increasingly difficult over time for his compatriots to find any unskilled work in Utah, Colorado, or Nevada without first coming to him or one of his lieutenants. By 1912, Greek workers could no longer escape Skliris's tribute system simply by quitting their jobs and moving on to a new industrial outpost in Utah. With labor on over a dozen mining and railroad companies in Utah, Colorado, Idaho, and Nevada under his control, the mobility between jobs that had recently hampered his prestige and profits as a labor agent for the D&RG was now transformed into a source of tremendous revenue. Every time a Greek worker quit his job and sought a new one he paid Skliris ten dollars. The more Greek workers changed jobs and remained within the region, the more money Skliris made. Greek immigrant Jack Tallas explained the relationship between job turnover and Skliris's power in a 1971 oral history:

The biggest trouble was Louie Skliris. Kennecott had him bring in labor, cheap labor. As they were coming from Greece, he sent them up there and charge them $10 to get job.... And they put you to work about twenty days and then they fire you and hire somebody else. In other words just to make money. And you couldn't get a job unless through Skliris.[65]

Protesting with your feet by quitting only fattened Skliris's profits.

Key to the expansion of Skliris's power was his relationship to the Kennecott Corporation, known initially as the Utah Copper Company.[66] Between 1907 and 1910, Skliris regularly supplied the company with Greek workers for its expanding open-pit mining operation, the first of its kind in North America. He was not the sole labor agent of the Utah Copper Company, but during the winter of 1910 the company sought to streamline its hiring system by making him their chief labor agent for hiring all Greek workers. Skliris's new position greatly improved his visibility among businessmen throughout the United States and helped him better exploit the mobility of his countrymen both through space and between jobs. In 1912 he formalized his connections to the labor markets of New York,

[64] Greek fraternal lodge records of the Adelphotis Arahoviton in *The Adelphis Arahoviton "Karyae"* (New York, 1951), 422, cited in Cononelos, "Greek Immigrant Labor" (M.A. thesis, University of Utah, June 1979), 247–248. On Meindaris's career, see Records of the Bureau of Immigration, Immigration Subject Correspondence, file 51747/11, box 54, RG 85.

[65] Jack Tallas interview by Theodore Paulos, Salt Lake City, January 18, 1971, Greek Archives, University of Utah, Salt Lake City.

[66] On the history of the Utah Copper Company, see Leonard Arrington, *The Richest Hole on Earth: A History of the Bingham Copper Mine* (Logan, 1963).

Chicago, and San Francisco by opening branch offices for business in each of these cities.[67]

These changes were reflected in the growing strength of Bingham Canyon and Skliris's Panhellenic Grocery Store as magnets of Greek migration. In March 1910 just thirteen men gave Bingham as their final destination, but in March 1912 fully seventy-three listed Bingham (see Map 1.2A). Most of these immigrants – fully 71 percent – were booked to the address of Skliris's Panhellenic Grocery Store.[68] As the destinations of Utah-bound Greeks became concentrated in the town of Bingham Canyon in 1912, the birthplaces of these new arrivals became more dispersed in Greece. A substantial number of immigrants continued to arrive from villages such as Megara, but a larger number of Greeks now hailed from the island of Crete and more remote islands such as Samos and Lesbos. These patterns suggest that, as Skliris's need for Greek workers increased in 1911, he was compelled to search far more broadly in Greece and to rely more heavily on the labor markets of Athens, which drew Greeks from every quarter of the eastern Mediterranean. Most of these new arrivals had little if any personal connection to Skliris and heard about him through newspapers and hired agents rather than family and friends.[69]

Both of these geographic changes – the concentration of Greeks working in one location in Utah and the growing spatial dispersion of their origins in Greece – had a destabilizing impact upon Skliris's migration business. Not only did the growing minority of men from Crete view Skliris as something of a foreigner, but they were concentrated together in Bingham Canyon. The mobility of Greek railroad workers compounded the difficulties of organizing any unified response to the conditions and terms of their work; however, for the nearly two thousand Greek laborers living and working in Bingham and its nearby smelter towns – Magna and Garfield – year round by 1912, the possibilities for collective mobilization against Skliris began to multiply.

Greek workers created a dramatic opportunity for resisting Skliris in the fall of 1912 when they led an impassioned multiethnic strike movement against the Utah Copper Company, demanding union recognition and the abolition of padronism. Their militancy forced Skliris to resign from his privileged position as the Company's sole Greek labor agent. Although the Bingham strike did not put Skliris out of business, it did destroy the gem of his international migration network, a loss from which he never fully recovered. The clearest measure of this was manifest in the changing geography of Greek migration to Utah. In March 1914, the number of Greeks bound to Utah fell to just 66, down from 216 two years earlier. Perhaps more significant, virtually none of these immigrants were now bound for

---

[67] *New York Call*, October 3, 1912, 3.

[68] Thirty-nine of fifty-five Bingham-bound Greeks in March 1912 were sent to the Panhellenic Grocery Store in Upper Bingham. By contrast, in March 1907, only three of thirty-one Bingham-bound immigrants listed the same address. Steamship manifest lists, Port of New York, March 1907, March 1912.

[69] Ibid.

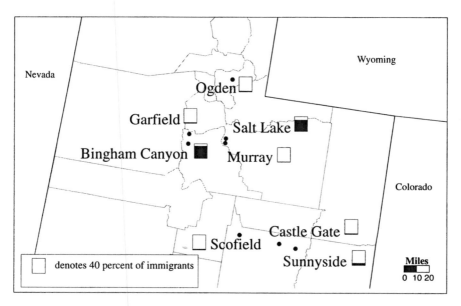

Map 1.2A. Final destinations of Utah-bound Greeks, March 1912

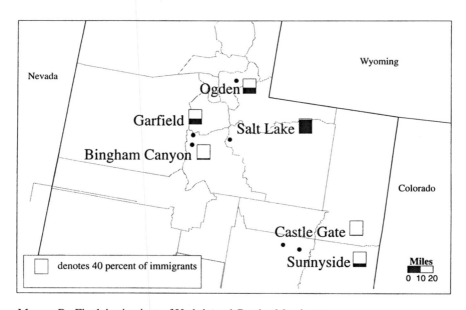

Map 1.2B. Final destinations of Utah-bound Greeks, March 1914

Bingham[70] (see Map 1.2B). No longer did Skliris's connections span the Greek diaspora, the Atlantic Ocean, and the North American continent. Instead, he operated within a fragmented and truncated space between Denver, Chicago, and Salt Lake City. Having lost control of the biggest and most lucrative site of labor demand in Bingham, he could no longer exploit the great distance between it and sites of labor supply in Greece. Nor could he effectively tax Greek workers' mobility between jobs in Utah as he once had. Skliris continued to connect urban and rural labor markets in the United States, but his close proximity to Utah's mining towns and the fierce resistance he encountered there prevented him from regaining the international power he had enjoyed before the 1912 rebellion.

El Enganchado

When Roman Gomez Gonzalez opened his first labor agency in El Paso, Texas, in 1905, he stood on the brink of one of the longest and largest migrations to the United States in its history. Although precise estimates are difficult to make given the incomplete nature of immigration records on the U.S.-Mexican border, at least 1.5 million emigrants passed through El Paso to the United States between 1885 and 1930. During this time, El Paso and its sister city across the Rio Grande, Ciudad Juarez, were transformed from sleepy border towns into a single industrial metropolis that served as the principal port of trade and commerce between the United States and Mexico. This urban growth was fueled almost entirely by railroads. Three major lines used El Paso as a major transportation hub in the early twentieth century: from the south the Mexican National Railway, and from the east, west, and north the Southern Pacific Railway (SP), and the Atchison, Topeka and the Santa Fe Railway (AT&SF). As in Utah, railroads spurred economic development of vast stretches of countryside in both northern Mexico and the southwestern United States. Railroad companies remained the single largest employer of El Paso's residents in 1900, followed by the El Paso smelter, which concentrated many of the ores flowing on steel rails from Chihuahua and Sonora, Mexico, and from Arizona and New Mexico.[71]

As in Salt Lake City and Montreal, railroads dramatically expanded El Paso's labor market, connecting it directly to a vast geographic hinterland. Mexican immigrants primarily found jobs as railroad workers in El Paso, but many subsequently quit their jobs to find work in manufacturing centers across the U.S. industrial heartland. This expansion, in turn, only increased the demand for Mexican labor as a variety of U.S. companies became interested in Mexican workers as a

[70] The decrease in Greek migration to Utah reflected an overall decline in Greek migration precipitated by the outbreak of the Balkan War, a topic we return to in Chapter 6. The number listing Bingham as their point of final destination dropped from seventy-three in 1912 to just three in 1914, ibid.

[71] On Mexican emigration to the United States, see Lawrence Cardoso, *Mexican Emigration to the United States, 1897–1931: Socio-economic Patterns* (Tuscon, 1987). On the role of railroads in El Paso's urban history, see Garcia, *Desert Immigrants*, 9–32.

source of cheap labor. L. G. Burnett, a company official of the Carnegie Steel Company, captured the sequence of events in an interview with sociologist Paul Taylor in 1926. "The railroads first brought Mexicans to this locality. The Mexicans quit the railroads and went to work for us. After the railroads quit bringing them in we sent men to Texas and shipped up a large number beginning in 1921."[72] Although several U.S. cities became centers for distributing and recruiting Mexican labor by the 1920s, El Paso remained the most important primary labor market for recruiting Mexican industrial labor in North America throughout this period, shaping the supply of secondary Mexican labor markets throughout the U.S. Midwest, East, and West.[73]

El Paso likewise functioned as the primary labor market for organizing agricultural labor in the U.S. Southwest and Midwest during the early twentieth century. The rapid growth of the sugar beet industry after 1900 illustrates El Paso's importance in transforming the organization and structure of midwestern agriculture. Initially, sugar beet growers struggled to secure a labor force that would perform the arduous seasonal work of cropping, thinning, and harvesting sugar beets. Many companies imported immigrants from the Ukraine, but these families soon began buying their own land as many had in Canada, removing themselves at least temporarily from the agricultural wage labor market.[74] During World War I, growers looked of necessity south rather than east for labor, and Mexican workers quickly became crucial to the growth of the industry. As one beet grower in Kansas succinctly put it in 1928, "the business of making sugar out of beets ... owes its development and prosperity to Mexican Labor."[75] As with track workers, the majority of sugar beet workers were recruited out of El Paso.

The sugar beet industry's rapid growth seems at first to suggest a different relationship between land and labor than developed in the Canadian Rockies or in the Great Basin. By 1910 the supply of free land had long since vanished in western Kansas and Nebraska, and no padrone systems had taken root there. But the scarcity of labor, which had defined the frontier in Utah and western Canada, remained the central problem that beet growers confronted in trying to expand production during the first decade of the twentieth century. The scarcity of labor had in fact never been greater in Nebraska and Kansas than in the early 1910s. The solution to the beet growers' labor "problem" was to import Mexicans to the beet fields for the duration of the beet season and export them after the harvest was completed in October. Because of Mexican workers' transience and relative

---

[72] George L. Edson, "Mexicans in the Pittsburgh, Pa., District," September 10, 1926, 15, "Interviews with Labor Contractors" file, BANC-MSS-74/187c, Paul S. Taylor Papers, Bancroft Library, University of California at Berkeley.

[73] Garcia, *Desert Immigrants*, 57.

[74] Dennis Nodin Valdes, *Al Norte: Agricultural Workers in the Great Lakes Region, 1917–1970* (Austin, 1990).

[75] George L. Edson, "Mexicans in Sugar Beet Work in the Central West: A Summary of Local Reports," 1926, 1, "Interviews with Labor Contractors" file, BANC-MSS-74/187c, Paul S. Taylor Papers.

isolation in the midwestern countryside, sugar beet companies created a commissary system that kept many beet workers in a state of virtual debt peonage.[76] The frontier of free land may have officially passed thirty years earlier, but the acute seasonal demand for sugar beet labor helped produce a new, though familiar system of coercive labor in the isolated regions where sugar beets grew.[77]

Given the massive scale of Mexican migration through El Paso between 1905 and 1925, Roman Gonzalez seemed perfectly poised to become the most powerful padrone in North American history. Between 1905 and 1909, he made great strides toward that mantle. The number of Mexicans he provided jobs for skyrocketed from seventy-five in 1905 to thirty-five hundred in 1907 to just under six thousand in 1909.[78] Most of these men were sent to Kansas and Oklahoma as track workers for the AT&SF railroad, which was upgrading its lines from narrow to standard gauge. In addition to the three dollar job fee that all Mexican workers paid him, Gonzalez received a one dollar commission from the railroad for every worker he supplied. Although he did not control the AT&SF's commissary, Gonzalez operated two boardinghouses, one in El Paso the other in Ciudad Juarez, which provided new Mexican recruits with room and board while waiting for their job assignments.[79]

Like Skliris and Cordasco, Gonzalez could bring workers directly from Mexican villages to El Paso because of his growing control over sources of labor demand. Only after Gonzalez secured work for thirty-five hundred railroad workers in 1907, most of them recruits from across the river in Ciudad Juarez, did he hire agents to comb the countryside of Mexico, dispersing his business card as they went. These hired agents helped expand the geography and efficiency of Gonzalez's business. In 1909, they succeeded in raiding a mining operation in Chihuahua and collected over two hundred men to help fill Gonzalez's contract with the Colorado Iron and Fuel Company. Gonzalez's agents even completed business deals for him entirely on the Mexican side of the border. When two hundred Mexicans were disbarred at the El Paso border in the spring of 1909, Gonzalez's agents found them jobs as track workers on the Mexican Central Railway in southern Mexico.[80] Neither Skliris nor Cordasco ever experienced such

---

[76] Ibid., 2; American Sugar Beet Company, "Agreement for Hand Labor on Sugar Beets for the Year 1926," Z-4-R, ibid.

[77] On the growth of the sugar beet work force in the northern Midwest, see Dennis Nodin Valdes, "Betabeleros: The Formation of an Agricultural Proletariat in the Midwest, 1897–1930," *Labor History* 30:4 (Fall 1989): 536–562.

[78] *El Paso Times*, February 6, 1907, 5; U.S. Bureau of Immigration, *The Stone Report*, table B, Immigration Subject Correspondence, file 52546/31, box 125, RG 85, National Archives, Washington, D.C. On Gonzalez's career, see Garcia, *Desert Immigrants*, 53, and Guerin-Gonzalez, *Mexican Workers and American Dreams*, 32–40.

[79] On Gonzalez's boardinghouse in Ciudad Juarez, see *Stone Report*, 35–41. On his boarding operations in El Paso, see *The State of Texas vs. R. G. Gonzalez and the Sultana Athletic Club*, El Paso County, Records of the 65th District Civil Court, Case 13458, El Paso County Courthouse, El Paso, Texas.

[80] *Stone Report*, 6, 19.

control over both sides of the U.S. border. Indeed, the geographic scope of Gonzalez's migration network rivaled that of Cordasco's, as he succeeded for a time in placing thousands of Mexicans on sugar beet farms in Michigan and the Dakotas, and thousands more as track workers in Kansas, Texas, and even central Mexico.[81]

And yet for all of the territory Gonzalez covered and the thousands of men he transported, he never became a "king" or a "czar" to the Mexican laborer. Instead, Gonzalez spent much of his long career in financial difficulties and on the margins of what was one of the largest internal migrations in the history of North America. The nearly six thousand workers he found jobs for in 1909 exceeded Cordasco's highest totals in 1904, but that represented only a small portion – just 14 percent – of the much larger migration through El Paso that year. Two years later, Gonzalez was nearly bankrupt and unable to pay his property taxes. Over the next eight years he managed to stay in business, despite the disruptions to migration created by the Mexican Revolution. In 1921, he reorganized his business under a new title and exported over five thousand Mexicans to the upper Midwest in his first year of business. But Gonzalez went bankrupt six years later, even though thousands of Mexicans continued to stream north every spring.[82]

Gonzalez's repeated failures and remarkable tenacity did not reflect any lack of business skill or acumen but rather highlighted the critical importance of Mexican family relations and geography in defining the development of padronism in North America. Like Greeks in Utah, the vast majority of Mexicans traveling through El Paso were "solos" – young, single men who frequently quit their jobs to find better work conditions or to return to their home villages in central Mexico in the off-season. Indeed, the proximity of Mexican villages to the labor market of El Paso meant that even married Mexicans were likely to "jump" their job if it meant a quick reunion with family and friends. Although El Paso remained isolated because of its surrounding deserts, the countryside of central Mexico was heavily populated by farmers and peasants in the late nineteenth century. The relative proximity of a large pool of Mexican labor to El Paso meant that American corporations could recruit their own workers directly from El Paso without the help of an intermediary such as Gonzalez. The control that Skliris and Cordasco held over far distant sites of labor supply in the Mediterranean countryside simply did not exist for Gonzalez or any labor agent in El Paso. Although the spaces between El Paso and the sites of labor demand in the United States were large, there was in fact little space between El Paso and its supply of labor to be exploited. Equally important, labor agents had a great deal of difficulty regulating or commodifying the mobility of Mexicans once in the United States, as their mobility foiled the best attempts to build successful commissary businesses.

For Gonzalez and all of El Paso's labor agents, geography and the mobility of

---

[81] On Gonzalez's career in the 1920s, see Robert Zarate interview with Paul Taylor, 1929, doc. no. 17-189, BANC-MSS-74/187c, Paul S. Taylor Papers.

[82] Ibid.

Mexican solos meant that El Paso's labor market was characterized by extreme competition, as agents of U.S. railroads, private labor agencies, and Mexican labor contractors all directly competed with one another for Mexican laborers. This competition produced moments of almost ludicrous struggle over the very bodies of immigrants, as happened in the summer of 1907 when eleven employment agents descended upon twelve workers who had just crossed the bridge into El Paso:

Each agency seized on his victim. One tried to pull his laborer one way and another another. One had a laborer by the coat, another by the sleeve, and another by his hair, each voicing in loud tones, with a noise like a rough house, the advantages of his particular agency. In a compact mass the group swayed back and forth, completely blocking the sidewalk on south El Paso street, and stopping passengers as well as attracting quite a crowd.[83]

The struggle was settled before the police could break up the "compact mass" after "reinforcements" from Holmes Supply Agency arrived and succeeded in cor- ralling the laborers into their office. The moment of entry at the bridge was usually not so violent, but such happenings demonstrated the aptness of the Spanish words for labor agent and the immigrant worker who signed his contracts – el enganche, meaning "the hook," and el enganchado, meaning "the hooked one."[84]

The constant and often bitter competition within El Paso's labor market pro- duced a high failure rate among labor agents, who came and vanished with remark- able frequency. Between 1905 and 1920, nine different Mexican-owned employ- ment offices opened in the city of El Paso. Of these, only two, the Zarate and Avina Labor Agency and Roman G. Gonzalez, remained in business longer than 3 years.[85] The other seven agents stayed in business an average of just 1.4 years. Anglo-American employment agencies fared little better. Between 1905 and 1920, twenty-six opened their doors for business but only two stayed open longer than a decade. The remaining twenty-four agencies stayed in business an average of just 1.9 years; nearly 60 percent of them folded the same year they opened.[86]

Such high turnover rates among El Paso's labor agencies suggest that Gonzalez's failure to become a "king" or a "czar" may be the wrong yardstick for measuring his career. His longevity within El Paso's competitive labor agent community suggests asking instead why he managed to stay in business so very long. The answer lies in a closer examination of the urban geography of El Paso itself. Throughout his long and checkered career, Gonzalez had one important advantage over his numerous competitors that helped keep him in business if only marginally:

---

[83] *El Paso Times*, September 14, 1907, 1.

[84] Paul S. Taylor, *Mexican Labor in the United States: Chicago and the Calumet Region*, vol. 2 (Berkeley, 1928), vii.

[85] The first Mexican labor agent in El Paso was in business for about three months in 1891. See Ochoa's advertisement and Aurelio Perez's poem to "Los Pobres" in *El Latino Americano*, March 21, 1891, 3, Southwest Collection, El Paso Public Library.

[86] El Paso, *City Directory*, 1890–1930, ibid.

his intimate knowledge of El Paso's Mexican barrio, Chihuahuita. Gonzalez arrived there in 1883 as a nine-year-old boy. Unlike most residents, he arrived before the railroad turned the city into a boomtown in 1885. Gonzalez attended English-language public schools long enough to learn English, a skill that gave him an advantage over the many thousands of emigrants who arrived later. Much of his education also took place in his father's grocery store, located in the middle of Chihuahuita. Here Gonzalez met people of all stripes in the community – businessmen, workers, and older residents of the barrio, as well as its newer transient arrivals. After a decade of work in his father's store, Gonzalez experimented with work as a plumber at the age of twenty-four and a year later began working as a blacksmith's helper on the Gulf, Colorado, and Santa Fe Railroad, where he made friends and contacts that would serve him well five years later.[87]

But perhaps the best preparation Gonzalez received for his career as a labor agent were his years as a policeman in Chihuahuita. Gonzalez became El Paso's first Mexican American policeman amid a municipal crisis in the spring of 1901, when hundreds of Mexican immigrants were pouring into the city every week and crowding the city's already crowded Mexican neighborhoods and public parks. The day before Gonzalez was sworn into office, a police committee for the El Paso City Council summarized the problem that Gonzalez was meant to address: "The considerable increase in population and rapid extension of the building limits render necessary public supervision over a large territory heretofore unpatrolled." Gonzalez's appointment the next day was not so much an act of affirmative action or power sharing as one of social control. So eager were municipal authorities to hire a Mexican who could police the streets of the barrio that they allowed Gonzalez to skip the normal procedure of posting a five hundred dollar bond for his time in office. Gonzalez's territory was, not surprisingly, the neighborhood he had grown up in, Chihuahuita.[88]

Gonzalez's official duty as a patrolman was to "keep the peace" in Chihuahuita, but in practical terms this meant keeping new immigrants off the city's more traversed streets and out of its public spaces. A series of public ordinances passed during his first year and a half as a police officer highlights the importance of this task. In January 1902 the El Paso City Council authorized the chief of police, James H. White, to "arrest any and all persons ... obstructing the streets." Eight months later the City Council passed a more explicit resolution, declaring it "unlawful for any number of persons to collect or assemble, or gather together, on or upon any street or sidewalk ... so as in any manner to obstruct or delay free passage ... of persons in passing along the same." To increase his ability to disperse crowds quickly, Gonzalez soon acquired a deputy, Mexican American Cruz Ortiz, and was designated a "mounted policeman," a position of greater prestige.[89]

[87] Ibid., 1895–1915.
[88] El Paso, City Council Minutes, May 23, 1901, 181, ibid.; April 29, 1903, 309, ibid.
[89] January 30, 1902, 511, ibid.; September 11, 1902, 60, ibid.; June 18, 1902, 7, ibid. On tensions between Mexican Americans and Mexican immigrants in the U.S. Southwest during this period, see Gutierrez, *Walls and Mirrors*, 39–68.

Police Chief James White and officer Roman Gonzalez soon discovered that the most effective way to address the anxieties of city councilmen was to expedite the passage of the city's new arrivals out of El Paso to sites of work on railroad lines. This solution could also be profitable.[90] In 1905 Gonzalez resigned from the police force and immediately opened a full-time labor agency, one that capitalized on his intimate knowledge of El Paso's vagrancy laws. He was joined in this line of work by his former police chief, James White, who himself became a labor agent after resigning from the force in 1905.[91]

Gonzalez's control over one urban space in the Mexican barrio gave him tremendous staying power in the labor-contracting business over the next twenty years. Yet, it also explains why he never achieved a tight choke hold on the migration of his compatriots. Like all labor agents in El Paso, Gonzalez possessed little control over the supply of Mexican laborers streaming north to El Paso. As a policeman, he possessed some informal authority over the labor supply of Chihuahuita, a control that the municipality of El Paso encouraged and sanctioned. By the 1920s, however, the political influence that Gonzalez formerly enjoyed in the barrio had disappeared. With the retirement of James White, Gonzalez had few if any champions in El Paso's municipal government. Longtime rival Isaac Avina meanwhile had become El Paso's county probation officer, a position of power similar to that once enjoyed by Gonzalez.[92] When three of Gonzalez's clients complained to the El Paso police about their treatment during the winter of 1922, municipal authorities jumped at the opportunity to put Gonzalez out of business. Although 1923 represented a good business year, the legal actions of these former clients further weakened Gonzalez's reputation in both Chihuahuita and the city's business community. The geographic space that Gonzalez had formerly controlled in Chihuahuita, small though it had been, would soon disappear entirely.[93] In 1927, Gonzalez went bankrupt and, at the age of fifty-seven, began earning wages as a night watchman.

Entrepreneurs of Space

Although Antonio Cordasco, Leon Skliris, and Roman Gonzalez may have aspired to wear the garb of kingly or despotic power, these men were not in fact primitive or archaic figures as depicted by middle-class reformers. Their power did not originate in the premodern European or Mexican countryside, but in the

[90] In 1905, the El Paso *City Directory* listed Gonzalez as a full-time "labor agent," but records of the City Council and police department reveal that he did not leave the police force until October 17, 1906. El Paso, City Council Minutes, October 17, 1906, 562; El Paso, *City Directory*, 1905.

[91] El Paso, *City Directory*, 1903–1908.

[92] Ibid., 1924

[93] *Willie Kimble vs. R.G. Gonzalez*, El Paso County, Records of the 65th District Civil Court, Case 22567, El Paso County Courthouse; *The City of El Paso vs. Roman G. Gonzalez*, Case 22687, ibid.

dynamic and expanding connections between city and countryside in North America that transformed both landscapes in the late nineteenth and early twentieth centuries. Cordasco, Skliris, and Gonzalez first tasted financial success as labor agents in the urban labor markets of Montreal, Salt Lake City, and El Paso and only later attempted to reach back to their homelands to recruit workers. Along the way, they encountered agents recruiting workers from the countryside, entrepreneurs like them who made money from the commerce of migration.

For Gonzalez, Skliris, and Cordasco, the control of geographic space was critical to whatever success they enjoyed as padrones. The longer the distance between sites of labor supply and labor demand and the more frequently their compatriots had to cross the political, cultural, and economic portals they controlled, the greater their potential profits and power. By linking diverse and isolated sites of labor demand such as Kootenay Landing, British Columbia, Bingham Canyon, Utah, and Minnesotan sugar beet fields with equally isolated sites of labor supply in the countryside of Italy, Greece, and Mexico, they helped build truly international labor markets. In so doing, Cordasco, Skliris, and Gonzalez did not annihilate space but rather commodified it in the form of tributes from their compatriot customers. The cost to workers of moving across the geographic and cultural spaces that Cordasco, Skliris, and Gonzalez mediated was not tallied in a single sum but took numerous forms, including job fees and commissary expenses. For these entrepreneurs of the international labor market, all tributes were monetized: space, rather than time, was money.

Understanding how padrones could make worker mobility both through space and between jobs profitable illuminates why the North American West could become a bastion of coercive labor relations in the early twentieth century. With its vast expanses of sparsely populated geography and enduring labor scarcities, the region contained remarkable potential for middlemen who could traverse those spaces and regulate the geographic mobility of workers. The ability of padrones to make money from worker mobility did not make the North American West exceptional. What Skliris, Cordasco, and Gonzalez accomplished was not fundamentally different from what padrones did in the migrant labor camps of upstate New York, where they remained "all powerful" according to municipal authorities in 1912.[94] The exploitation of workers' mobility was not exceptional to the West but rather unique in its intensity and visibility.

If the connections between city and countryside that padrones made each spring perverted the noble meaning and purpose of the North American landscape to reformers such as Grace Abbott, they also illuminated many of the paradoxical connections between free land and coercive labor relations in the continent. For it was the scarcity of labor as much as the "hither edge of free land" that defined the shape of labor relations on Frederick Jackson Turner's celebrated frontier. This scarcity endured well beyond the frontier's official closing in 1893, for much of the West's resources remained to be discovered and exploited. With the discovery of

[94] Ernst, *Public Employment Exchanges*, 12.

each new commodity in the land – be it copper or sugar beets – the problem of the frontier was confronted anew: how should one assemble a labor force in a remote and relatively unpopulated countryside?

The answers that padrones provided to this question helped them achieve remarkable financial success, but geographic conditions alone did not bring them power. For Cordasco, Skliris, and Gonzalez, success as a padrone was not guaranteed by the sheer size of the urban labor markets they mediated or the territories their migration systems encompassed. Crucial to making workers' mobility through space and between jobs profitable was the padrone's relationship with the corporations in North America that so desperately needed cheap labor, the subject of the next chapter.

CHAPTER TWO

Padrones and Corporations

When John D. Rockefeller visited the new, open-pit mining operation of fellow industrialist Daniel J. Guggenheim in Bingham Canyon, Utah, in 1910, he declared with genuine envy and admiration, "it's the greatest industrial sight in the whole world." What most impressed Rockefeller were the massive steam shovels that had revolutionized the process of copper extraction by enabling firms to mine and smelt tons of previously worthless low-grade copper ore. Equally impressive, where skilled American miners had very recently toiled underground in search of rich veins of copper, unskilled immigrants now worked above ground, loading tons of newly blasted copper ore onto train cars. Rockefeller was not alone in expressing wonder at this new man-made marvel. Hundreds of sight-seeing tourists also traveled to the open pit by train each week to experience the thrill of industrial America's newfound ability to move mountains. Like Rockefeller, they saw nothing but progress and modernity in the great open-pit mine.[1]

It thus came as a shock to many when they learned in the fall of 1912 that the "greatest industrial sight in the whole world" had been using a seemingly primitive form of labor recruitment and management, the ethnic padrone system. Here, suddenly visible to middle-class onlookers, were immigrant men who toiled at the bottom of the open pit with no instruments but their arms and backs, paying job fees and tributes to their padrones in a system that seemed as old and timeless as the pyramids. The raw and harsh nature of this backbreaking work and the padrones' exactions hardly evoked the "simplicity" of Frederick Jackson Turner's western frontier life, much less the modernity of the civilization that was supposed to have replaced it. Most onlookers were thus befuddled by their discovery. Put simply, how could padronism be thriving at the most modern mining operation in North America?

Answering this question requires examining not only the particular relationships that corporations had with men like Cordasco, Skliris, and Gonzalez, but

---

[1]Arrington, *The Richest Hole on Earth*, 8; Harvey O'Connor, *The Guggenheims: The Making of an American Dynasty* (New York, 1937), 269; Will Higgins, "Tearing Down Mountains at Bingham," *Salt Lake Mining Review*, July 30, 1908, 1.

also their alternatives to the padrone system. Why did padrones become so attractive for companies in the West at the turn of the century? How had railroad, mining, construction, and agricultural companies previously recruited a work force in a region defined by acute labor scarcities and isolated work sites?

Corporate Antecedents

Antonio Cordasco, Leon Skliris, and Roman Gonzalez were hardly the first to import immigrant workers to remote areas of the North American West. Before the Thirteenth Amendment to the U.S. Constitution formally abolished slavery and indentured servitude in 1865, hundreds of African Americans were brought to the trans-Mississippi West as slaves by individual miners, mining companies, and other business enterprises. Such coerced labor ostensibly solved two of the greatest challenges that had long confronted entrepreneurs in the New World: recruiting a labor force in a labor-scarce region and controlling the mobility of that work force once assembled. The North American West, despite its potent symbolism, was no exception to this pattern throughout its long history, with systems of slave, indentured, and "free" labor coexisting in close proximity to one another, as historian Howard Lamar has suggested.[2]

Although slavery was no longer an option for western companies after 1865, contract labor, whereby immigrants worked under contract for a specific period of time to pay off the costs of passage and room and board in North America, initially seemed a promising alternative. Not only was contract labor being used by several Central and South American nations in the wake of slavery's abolition, but contract labor was legalized and encouraged in 1864 by an act of the U.S. Congress seeking to alleviate its wartime labor shortages. But contract labor never became viable for U.S. companies because imported workers could and did quit before their work terms had expired with few individual consequences. When contract laborers broke their work contracts in Brazil, Cuba, Peru, or Australia, criminal penalties were levied against the "runaway" workers.[3] In the United States, by contrast, workers had since the 1830s successfully quit their jobs without criminal penalties. More often than not they simply escaped their employer's purview entirely.[4]

The difficulties that U.S. companies faced in using contract labor were illustrated

[2] Lamar, "From Bondage to Contract," 295–296.

[3] On Chinese contract labor migrations to Latin America and Australia, see Kil Young Zo, "Chinese Emigration to the United States, 1850–1880" (Ph.D. diss., Columbia University, 1971), 35–55; Sing-Wu Wang, *The Organization of Chinese Emigration, 1848–1888: With Special Reference to Chinese Emigration to Australia* (San Francisco, 1978), 39–87; Stewart Watt, *Chinese Bondage in Peru: A History of the Chinese Coolie in Peru, 1849–1874* (Durham, 1951); Edward Wybergh Docker, *The Blackbirders: The Recruiting of South Seas Labour for Queensland, 1883–1907* (Sydney, 1970), 167–168; Kay Saunders, *Workers in Bondage: The Origins and Bases of Unfree Labour in Queensland, 1824–1916* (St. Lucia, 1982); David Northrup, *Indentured Labor in the Age of Imperialism, 1834–1922* (Cambridge, 1995).

[4] Steinfeld, *The Invention of Free Labor*, 160–163.

well by the failure of the American Emigrant Company. Founded in 1864, the company sought to furnish both skilled and unskilled workers from Europe directly to North American companies with labor shortages. Yet it never succeeded in attracting more than a few thousand workers. Most European workers were not impressed by the long length of service demanded by the work contracts – usually at least one year – and preferred to make their own travel arrangements to North America. Those that did sign contracts often "jumped" their jobs at the first opportunity, making it even less likely for American companies to profit from the emigrant company's services. In 1866, company president John Hooker demanded that Congress stiffen penalties against such "runaway" contract workers, calling for the right to seize twice the amount of a worker's unpaid passage debts from their wages. Some Radical Republicans were sympathetic to Hooker's pleas, but confusion reigned as to which contracts legislators should protect: those of the American Emigrant Company or the new employer. Congress ultimately refused to criminalize violations of the original work contract or to impose harsh penalties on those who quit. Doing so in Connecticut would have made it more difficult for Radical Republicans to roll back the Black Codes in Louisiana and other southern states in 1866, a key part of their political agenda. Quitting one's job was deemed an inalienable aspect of the wage laborer's condition, the right that made wage labor truly free. The American Emigrant Company's fortunes thus continued to sputter, particularly in cities where most of its contracts originated and where opportunities for alternative job prospects were numerous. By 1870, it was bankrupt.[5]

But the failure of contract labor to take hold in the United States did not prove that its labor relations were truly free or exceptional. The American Emigrant Company might have fared better had it sought to import unskilled workers who were unfamiliar with the English language and sent them to job sites that were isolated and remote. Indeed, to many observers, this was precisely what a group of Chinese merchants, known as the Six Companies, accomplished in supervising the emigration of some 180,000 Chinese nationals to the North American West between 1849 and 1882. Founded and operated in San Francisco, the Six Companies controlled a vast network of intermediaries in both China and California and possessed a virtual monopoly on the migrations of nearly all U.S.-bound Chinese immigrants.[6]

Although popularly known as "coolies" and contract laborers, Chinese immigrants bound for the United States had not in fact signed employment contracts in China specifying the length of time and service, unlike their sojourning counterparts in Brazil, Hawaii, Peru, and Mexico.[7] Rather, the Six Companies used the

---

[5] On the free labor ideologies of Radical Republicans, see David Montgomery, *Beyond Equality: Labor and the Radical Republicans, 1862–1872* (New York, 1967); Eric Foner, *Nothing but Freedom: Emancipation and Its Legacy* (Baton Rouge, 1983). On the weakness of the contract-labor system in the United States, see Charlotte Erickson, *American Industry and the European Immigrant, 1860–1885* (Cambridge, 1957), 9–29, 46–50.

[6] Wang, *The Organization of Chinese Emigration*, 313.

[7] Ibid., 105–107.

credit-ticket system, whereby Chinese workers signed contracts only after they had arrived in North America and accumulated substantial debts to a particular Chinese company. The Six Companies did not themselves compete for business but rather split up the countryside of China into discrete regions of control and recruitment, thus strengthening each company's local monopoly over the migration of their compatriots. On arriving in San Francisco, Chinese workers signed contracts, under the supervision of an agent for the Six Companies, with an American corporation for a specific period of employment, during which time the emigrant's ticket costs and passage debts to the Six Companies were garnisheed from their wages.[8] The costs of food and other items purchased on the job in North America were also deducted from their paychecks, leaving workers with little but debt when they completed their contracts. As historians Gary Okihiro and Sucheng Chan have suggested, the credit-ticket system was every bit as effective as long-term contracts in exploiting Chinese sojourners.[9]

Yet the credit-ticket system and the Six Companies' control over it were short-lived solutions to the problem of labor scarcity in the western United States. The power of the Six Companies was undermined not by changes in the Chinese countryside but by changes at sites of labor demand in the United States. As railroad and mining corporations quickly discovered, hiring Chinese workers involved many unforeseen costs. First, Chinese workers proved themselves capable of remarkable militance against their employers, despite their status as tractable workers. Perhaps the most dramatic mobilization occurred in Utah in 1868 when thousands of Chinese workers struck the Union Pacific Railroad for better pay and the abolition of coercive work disciplines such as whipping. But even where Chinese workers did not work in concentrated numbers, they proved themselves capable of daring and costly mobilizations, going on strike against companies and labor contractors in the West, South, and even Pennsylvania in the 1870s, wherever, in short, Chinese workers were employed.[10] Equally important, their presence or rumored arrival stimulated white workers throughout the nation to join unions and to exclude Asians from their ranks. Indeed, as Alexander Saxton has ably demonstrated, white workers fueled the growing political pressure to exclude Chinese from the United States altogether, a task begun in 1882 with the

[8] The Six Companies did much of its business with local construction firms in San Francisco such as the Tideland Reclamation Company, which needed Chinese workers for building "dikes, gates, and ditches" along the Sacramento and San Joaquin Rivers. See *Report of the Joint Special Committee to Investigate Chinese Immigration*, 44th Congress, 1st session, 1877, 436–437.

[9] See Gary Okihiro, *Margins and Mainstreams: Asians in American History and Culture* (Seattle, 1994); Suchen Chan, *Asian Americans: An Interpretive History* (Boston, 1991), 4. For a description of the credit-ticket system, see Wang, *The Organization of Chinese Migration*, 93–97; Zo, "Chinese Emigration to the United States," 91–103.

[10] Montgomery, *Fall of the House of Labor*, 67–68; Lucy M. Cohen, *Chinese in the Post-Civil War South: A People without a History* (Baton Rouge, 1984), 105–132; Edward J. M. Rhoads, "Asian Pioneers in the Eastern United States: Chinese Cutlery Workers in Beaver Falls, Pennsylvania, in the 1870s," *Journal of Asian American Studies* (forthcoming).

passage of the Chinese Exclusion Act. The law did not forbid the hiring of Chinese workers, but forbid any further immigration, thus weakening the Six Companies' control over sites of labor supply in China.[11]

The Chinese Exclusion Act did not apply to Canada, however, whose companies continued to seek Chinese workers to help fill dire labor shortages. The greatest importer of Chinese workers was Cordasco's future sponsor, the Canadian Pacific Railway (CPR), which hired some seventeen thousand Chinese men to complete its first transcontinental line in 1885. Many of these desperately needed workers were recruited from the western United States, but ten thousand came directly from Asia when the CPR contacted agents from one of the Six Companies in Washington.[12] Like their Chinese counterparts in the United States, all of these men arrived in Canada under the credit-ticket system, whereupon they signed work contracts with the CPR and began attempting to pay off their debts.

Unlike most U.S. companies, the CPR used its steamship service to Asia to recruit unskilled labor for its railroad and mining enterprises in the 1890s and 1900s. Steamship lines to Japan, China, and India complemented the CPR's existing steamship lines to Europe, particularly England, France, Russia, and Scandinavia. Although the bulk of its Asian passenger traffic did not come to the North American West under the credit-ticket system, the CPR did fill many of its own labor needs through such means, bringing several thousand workers from India in a credit-ticket system between 1904 and 1907. The CPR possessed no monopolies on passenger traffic for its far-flung transportation routes, but it helped transport a large portion of the one million immigrant farmers who came to Canada between 1896 and 1914.[13] Whether farmers buying land along CPR lines or industrial workers building new feeder lines across the Canadian prairies, these immigrants helped make the CPR one of the most powerful international transportation companies on the globe by 1900. The aphorism that the sun never set on the British Empire could almost be applied at the turn of the century to the CPR, whose transportation lines traversed three-quarters of the planet.

In the U.S. West, by contrast, no well-organized system of labor migration immediately took the Six Companies' place after 1885. The Chinese Exclusion Act deterred corporations from organizing recruitment efforts in Asia, though most such ventures had already proved costly and unsuccessful. The Union Pacific Railroad attempted briefly to establish its own labor agencies in Asia in the 1860s with little success. Consequently, the company was ill-equipped to step into the

---

[11] On grass-roots movements to exclude Chinese immigrants, see Alexander Saxton, *The Indispensable Enemy: Labor and the Anti-Chinese Movement in California* (Berkeley, 1971). On the passage of the Foran Act, see Erickson, *American Industry and the European Immigrant*, 164–168, and Gwendolyn Mink, *Old Labor and New Immigrants in American Political Development: Union, Party, and State, 1875–1920* (Ithaca, 1986), 108–110.

[12] Harry Con, *From China to Canada: A History of the Chinese Communities in Canada* (Toronto, 1982), 21–22.

[13] Donald Avery, *Reluctant Host: Canada's Response to Immigrant Workers, 1896–1914* (Toronto, 1995), 24, 46–47.

vacuum created by the Six Companies' demise. Equally important, the United States passed the Foran Act in 1885, which explicitly forbade U.S. companies from importing workers of any nationality into the United States under contract, a topic we explore further in Chapter 3. The Foran Act increased the political price that U.S. corporations faced in recruiting their own labor supply directly from overseas, a circumstance that helped keep much hiring in the United States decentralized arenas of corporate activity.

The ad hoc nature of corporate hiring practices in the United States had less to do with legal barriers against contract labor or Chinese immigration than with the fact that corporations in the East did not need to "organize the immigrant labor market," as Charlotte Erickson has suggested.[14] Chain migrations within new immigrant communities and the steady influx of European immigrants to northeastern cities kept the unskilled labor market full throughout much of the early twentieth century. Most corporations operating on the East Coast such as the giant factories in Amoskeag, Delaware, did not need overseas labor recruiters, but looked only to domestic labor agencies when chain migrations did not meet their demand for unskilled work. Occasionally, informal systems of labor recruitment were sufficient to maintain a stable work force in the North American West as well. As David Emmons has demonstrated, Irish residents of Butte purchased train and steamship tickets for male family members whenever positions opened up at the great Anaconda copper works, often with the help of Irish business leader Marcus Daly.[15] Irish chain migrations were remarkably effective in maintaining a supply of labor in Butte throughout its heyday as one of the most prosperous mining communities in North America.

Most corporations in the U.S. West had a much harder time assembling work forces by relying on kinship networks and local labor agencies, however. Yet corporate attempts to re-create after 1885 the tightly organized labor migrations of the Six Companies or to imitate the CPR's far-flung connections between Europe and Asia met with only mixed success. Consider, for example, steamship agent Frank Missler's spectacular failure to organize the West's immigrant labor market. Beginning in 1907, Missler sought a direct route to the region by sending hundreds of Serbian, Croatian, Polish, and German emigrants to Galveston, Texas, "one of the ports through which the emigrant is most sure of admission." From there, Missler asserted in his circulars, prospective emigrants were closer to "the richest states in America.... In the states of Texas, Colorado, and California, labor is paid the highest, because in these states workmen are scarce." Missler portrayed the West, as other labor recruiters had before him, as a place of unrivaled opportunity for the industrious emigrant. "It is rightly said," Missler began another circular, "that Texas is the paradise of the laborers."[16]

[14] Erickson, *American Industry and the European Immigrant*, vii.
[15] Emmons, *The Butte Irish*, 25–29. On similar recruitment strategies in eastern factories, see Tamara K. Hareven and Randolph Langenbach, *Amoskeag: Life and Work in an American Factory-City* (New York, 1978), 19–20; Walter Licht, *Getting Work: Philadelphia, 1840–1950* (Cambridge, 1992).
[16] Bogomir Jakich, "Information and Directions for Those Intending to Go to American or Other

To substantiate these promises, Missler's agent in Texas, Mr. Lenkenau, secured employment for everyone on the first shipment of emigrants to Galveston. Ten went to Durant, Oklahoma, as track workers at the modest wage of $1.75 a day, twenty-three became coal miners for the Rock Island Railroad Company in Glenham, Texas, and thirty-five more found jobs with the Colorado Iron and Fuel Company in Trinidad, Colorado, at $1.95 a day. As word spread of Mr. Lenkenau's activities, work orders poured into his Galveston office and were forwarded to Missler and his agents in eastern Europe for advertising purposes. One such ad in 1908 quoted the Rock Island Railroad's call for twenty-five hundred immigrants for work in "the coal fields of the Southwestern states," copied on company stationery as proof of the job openings. But problems for Missler arose shortly after he began supplying companies with workers. Six months after hiring two hundred of Missler's emigrants, lumber company president V. H. Montgomery of Emory, Texas, wrote a letter stating that "the last lot you sent me were very unsatisfactory and have now become indebted to me in quite an amount and some are talking of leaving." Many of these lumber workers subsequently fled the camp, leaving both Montgomery and Missler stuck with large unpaid debts. Although Missler still possessed connections to emigrant workers' families, he had little power to control their mobility in North America. By early March of 1908, with a depression in high gear, Mr. Lenkenau reported placing only thirteen emigrant workers with jobs, in sharp contrast to his earlier successes.[17] By 1909 he had abandoned his attempts to control sites of labor demand in the United States and had refocused his energies on what he did best: organizing the supply of unskilled labor in eastern Europe.

Missler's difficulties were not simply about timing, but also reflected the geography of his business efforts. Unlike the CPR or the Six Companies, he never established control over sites of labor demand in the region. Missler might have offset such obstacles had he been able to control workers' mobility once they arrived in the Southwest, as CPR officials did along remote track lines in British Columbia. But even if Texas was no worker's "paradise," it was better connected to alternative job markets than the remote regions of western Canada where Chinese and later Italian workers toiled. Consequently, Missler's dreams of establishing a new gateway to the West, with his logo stamped on the engine passing through, never materialized.

Perhaps the best-organized labor migration to develop in the western United States between 1885 and 1905 involved Japanese labor contractors who, unlike Missler, gained control over sites of labor demand and then built international connections to sites of supply in Japan. One of the most powerful, Ban Shinzaburo of Portland, Oregon, supplied the Southern Pacific Railway, the Chicago, Burlington, and Quincy Railway, the Astoria and Columbia River Railway, and the Oregon Railway and Navigation Company with Japanese track workers throughout the

Ports of the World," file 52066/A, circular 3, p. 6, box 79, Records of U.S. Bureau of Immigration, Immigration Subject Correspondence, RG 85; Exhibit 4, ibid.
[17] Exhibits 4, 5, 9, 13, 15, ibid.

1890s. To meet his expanding labor needs, Shinzaburo began importing workers directly from Japan, advancing emigrants passage fares and "show money" to persuade immigration officials they were not indigent. At its peak, Shinzaburo's credit-ticket system was quite similar to that used by the Six Companies and other labor market entrepreneurs of the North American West.[18]

Shinzaburo and other Japanese labor contractors received a dramatic boost in 1900 when the United States annexed the Kingdom of Hawaii. Suddenly available for exportation were some thirty-four thousand Japanese plantation workers who had been imported to Hawaii under contract before the Spanish-American War. As residents of a new U.S. territory, these workers were not subject to the perils of crossing a U.S. border under contract, but could move freely anywhere in the continental United States. Shinzaburo and others capitalized on this opportunity, despite the protests of local planters in Hawaii, and succeeded in exporting nearly thirty-two thousand Asian workers to the U.S. mainland between 1901 and 1906.[19] Most of these men worked on western railroads, mines, and agribusinesses. For the first time since the 1870s, a system of labor migration thrived in the western United States in which sites of labor supply and labor demand were directly controlled by a single group of individuals.

Yet the power established by men like Shinzaburo proved to be fleeting as well. Competition among Japanese labor contractors was intense, especially in agricultural work where bidding wars drove down contractors' commissions and the wages of Japanese workers.[20] Shinzaburo was one of the most successful Japanese contractors because he expanded beyond his labor-contracting business, founding three Asian department stores in Wyoming, Oregon, and Colorado and supplying them with produce from his own sugar beet and dairy farms. But even his diversified forays into the commerce of migration could not stave off financial crisis when the Gentlemen's Agreement between Japan and the United States in 1908 virtually eliminated all new Japanese migration to the United States. Like the Six Companies, Japanese labor contractors began competing over a rapidly dwindling pie of workers, many of whom returned to Asia or left the ranks of industrial labor.

In the North American West, then, a variety of recruitment systems sporadically flourished for unskilled immigrants after 1865, each of them compromising workers' freedoms with debts, contracts, and geographic isolation. The instability of each entrepreneur's choke hold over migration to the region did not so much vindicate the progressive meaning of the West's labor relations as suggest the enduring hazards that unskilled immigrants faced in finding work there. If notions of western exceptionalism shed little light on the region's coercive labor relations or the transnational context that produced them, neither do they explain variations within the North American West. Whereas peonage and forms of coerced labor

---

[18] Ichioka, *The Issei*, 58–59, 63.
[19] Ibid., 65; Alan Takeo Moriyama, *Imingaisha: Japanese Emigration Companies and Hawaii, 1894–1908* (Honolulu, 1985), 134–135.
[20] Ichioka, *The Issei*, 81.

were far more common in the southeastern United States than in the Northeast, no such north-south variation existed within the North American West. If anything, the opposite pattern was true. The CPR's labor recruitment efforts were far better organized and more coercive in the northern plains than were the efforts of Frank Missler in Texas, who struggled to maintain any leverage over his mobile workers. Moving north was anything but a journey to greater freedom.

In the first decade of the twentieth century, as all manner of industrial developments boomed across the North American West, many corporate managers in the region were in a quandary over how to solve the perennial problems of labor scarcity and labor mobility. The Gentlemen's Agreement left many companies, including the Utah Copper Company, with a diminishing supply of Japanese workers and few clear alternatives. Some corporate hiring managers in the U.S. West began looking south to Mexico as railroads opened up vast sections of that nation's interior, but to many the supply of Mexican labor still seemed remote. In Canada, meanwhile, the passage of anti-Chinese immigration legislation in 1901 and again in 1904 confronted the CPR and other industrial employers with their first legal obstacles to labor recruitment. Never again would the CPR be able to rely heavily upon Chinese immigrants. Like companies in the U.S. West twenty years earlier, CPR managers began looking for alternative supplies of unskilled labor. But who would create such alternatives at the turn of the century, either in Canada or the United States? What would the precise relationship be between these new labor recruiters and the increasingly complex world of corporate management in North America?

The Canadian Pacific Railway

When Antonio Cordasco became sole Italian labor agent for the CPR in the fall of 1901, he set in motion a complicated transformation in the way the company recruited an unskilled and seasonally disposable work force. The precise nature of that change would be fiercely debated by Cordasco and the CPR after he sued the railroad in 1905 for having "maliciously and in bad faith" reneged on its contractual obligations to hire four thousand workers during the spring of 1904. Cordasco claimed that he had been a CPR employee, whereas his former boss, George Burns, head of the CPR's Special Service Department, contended "I have never regarded Cordasco as an employee of the company." When asked by lawyers to explain how the business relationship between them had developed, Burns stated "We simply engaged him as an employment agent, and it was his own business; he could collect whatever fees he liked from the men."[21]

Although the Montreal judge ultimately accepted Burns's claims, both men had a point. Cordasco was in fact both an entrepreneur and an employee, and it is only

---

[21] *Antonio Cordasco vs. Canadian Pacific Railway Company*, Case 2195, July 20, 1905, 5, Records of the Superior Court, District of Montreal; Testimony of George Burns, *Royal Commission*, 61; *G. Teolo vs. Antonio Cordasco*, Case 990, May 5, 1904, 9, Records of the Superior Court, District of Montreal.

by placing these roles side by side that we can discern how he helped reshape the CPR's methods for recruiting and maintaining an unskilled work force in the North American West. George Burns's claim that Cordasco ran "his own business" was in fact substantially correct. Although Cordasco made an agreement with George Burns in November 1901 to give the CPR "first crack" at the men he imported, he did not supply men exclusively to the CPR. Between 1901 and 1904, he provided laborers to several Canadian clients in Montreal, most notably the Dominion Coal Company, the Canadian Northern Railway Company, and the Canadian labor contractor, H. J. Beemer, who in turn supplied laborers to the city of Montreal for building its sewer and subway lines. The CPR, by contrast, relied entirely upon Cordasco for its Italian employees, hiring nearly twelve thousand of them between 1901 and 1904.[22]

Cordasco's relationship with Italian workers likewise approximated that of an employer. Although most Italian workers earned wages directly from the CPR, they had no hope of being hired by the company without first putting their names on Cordasco's registration list. Occasionally, Cordasco actually collected workers' wages himself and "paid" them after deducting the cost of their food and transportation.[23] Cordasco also controlled any job advancements among Italian sojourners, determining who became a foreman and how much power he would amass in so doing. Even the most experienced foremen waited for Cordasco's permission before recruiting a work gang. Pompei Bianco, for example, had served as Cordasco's foreman for three consecutive years, supervising some of the largest single work gangs on the CPR, but he always waited until Cordasco "told me to make up a gang" before signing up his men. If Cordasco made experienced foremen wait, he could also create foremen almost instantly from the pool of Italian laborers. Consider the testimony of Giuseppe Mignella to the Royal Commission:

Q: Cordasco asked you to make up a gang?
A: Yes.
Q: Have you had experience for some years?
A: No, none.
Q: What conditions did Cordasco make, what did he tell you?
A: He says make up a gang.
Q: And did you?
A: Yes, and I gave money to him.

Indeed, most Italian foremen quite properly considered Cordasco rather than CPR officials to be their immediate employer. This sentiment was captured by the testimony of foreman Rafaele di Zazza, who stated "I always worked for Cordasco since I have been in Canada, the last five years."[24]

---

[22] Testimony of George Burns, *Royal Commission*, 43; *Antonio Cordasco vs. Canadian Pacific Railway Company*, 1, Records of the Superior Court, District of Montreal.

[23] Affidavits by Antonio Salvatore and Vicenzo Loronzo, November 4, 1903, Montreal, *Royal Commission*, 116–117.

[24] Testimony of Giuseppe Mignella, ibid., 31; Testimony of Rafaele di Zazza, ibid., 33.

Yet if Cordasco's ability to hire and fire Italian laborers and foremen seemed to make him more of an employer than an employee, his "business" was in crucial respects sanctioned and organized by CPR officials. At its peak, Cordasco's labor contracting business resembled nothing less than a division within the CPR's own Special Services Department. A February issue of the newspaper *Corriere del Canada* presented a composite portrait of Cordasco's organization the day after two thousand Italian workmen and twenty-five foremen crowned him "king of the laborers." Dressed in a suit and holding a gold-chained watch, Cordasco looked more like a timekeeper or a corporate executive than a "king." Immediately surrounding Cordasco were the festival's five organizers and two grand marshals, two vice marshals, and its president and vice-president. All twenty-five foremen wore white shirts and ties and each had "Foreman della C.P.R. Co.," under their names. Only one foreman, Luigi di Carlo, was not wearing a businessman's clothing, appearing instead on a bike along a railroad track.[25]

The relationships between Cordasco and his foremen were not so much localistic, familial, or preindustrial, but rather reflected their respective positions as CPR employees. Job fees and tributes were not archaic but intrinsic to how foremen organized work gangs in factories, railroads, and mines throughout North America.[26] According to a 1914 article in *Engineering Magazine*, nearly every factory worker "pays some sort of tribute to his foreman. The tribute is usually in the form of money or service, but there are cases where the tribute is of a nature which cannot be mentioned in an open paper." George Burns's predecessor in the Special Services Department, Mr. Guertin, actively benefited from the "custom" of accepting fees for providing jobs to workers. Cordasco himself regularly paid Guertin fees to procure jobs for his compatriots before becoming the CPR's sole Italian agent.[27]

The compatibility between Cordasco's padrone system and the CPR's bureaucracy becomes even more apparent when one considers the company's role in creating Cordasco's power. Initially he received no commission from the CPR for the strikebreakers he provided them. But as new immigration restrictions on Asian immigration took effect in 1901, Burns made a "verbal agreement" to pay Cordasco five dollars a day in return for his continued services "drumming up men." Burns left Cordasco free to charge Italian workmen fees for finding them jobs, but also put him in charge of supplying and provisioning all of the CPR's Italian and Chinese employees. As Burns later explained, "I made a proposition to Cordasco and asked him to undertake to feed all Italians who went, selling them the necessary food.... He agreed to do that, provided I saw that his bills were

---

[25] *Corriere del Canada*, January 23, 1904, microfiche 3473, RG 33/99.

[26] See Sanford Jacoby, *Employing Bureaucracy: Managers, Unions, and the Transformation of Work in American Industry, 1900–1945* (New York, 1985), 16–18; and Daniel Nelson, *Managers and Workers: Origins of the New Factory System in the United States, 1880–1920* (Madison, 1975), 81–82.

[27] C. J. Morrison, "Short-Sighted Methods in Dealing with Labor," *Engineering Magazine* 46 (January 1914): 568; Testimony of Antonio Cordasco, *Royal Commission*, 149.

collected."[28] In addition to garnishing workers' debts directly from their pay-checks, Burns furnished him an office on the first floor of the CPR's main office building in Montreal.

This verbal agreement did not make Cordasco a CPR manager, but he clearly enjoyed a privileged position within the Special Services Department. Burns later justified his arrangement with Cordasco between 1901 and 1903 by emphasizing how important his profit-making abilities were to the company: "I did not want anybody to go into this business without making money, as I was quite aware that unless inducements were offered we would not have any guarantee that the gentle-men employed would be absolutely straight, and it was my desire that there should be money in the offer."[29] For Burns, being "straight" meant having a streamlined system of job fees in which all Italian workers participated on equal terms and in which Cordasco prevented smaller fry – upstart foremen or small contractors – from abusing the system. The "inducements" Burns offered Cordasco were in his mind perfectly legitimate. Burns gave them not merely to reward Cordasco but also to control the variety of tribute systems and illegal fees that had previously flour-ished among railroad work gangs.

The result of Burns's innovations was that Cordasco soon possessed more power even than the CPR's official labor agent, John S. Skinner. When an Italian foreman, Fonnerro, began collecting job fees from Italian track workers in Win-nipeg during the spring of 1903, Cordasco managed to get both Fonnerro and his old boss, Mr. Guertin, now a company superintendent, dismissed from the CPR.[30] In March 1904 Cordasco also blocked the attempt of two Italian labor contractors in Boston to usurp his business, writing them a letter even as Italians were piling up in Montreal's streets:

I was told that in your bank you hire men to go and work for the CPR in British Columbia, paying one dollar each. Really this is very strange news, because I am sole agent for sup-plying men to the CPR, and I did not give any order to anybody to hire men. If I had to give such an order for Boston, messrs. Stabile and Company are my sole agents.[31]

Now that he was sole Italian agent, Cordasco saw it as his right to determine who could be his sole procurers of Italian labor in labor markets throughout North America. Although Burns would later contest Cordasco's claim to be "sole agent," Burns in fact helped devise this arrangement with Stabile and Company and paid for advertisements in the *Corriere del Canada*, which stated Cordasco was "sole Italian labor agent of the CPR."[32] Far from being archaic or outmoded, CPR

---

28 Testimony of Antonio Cordasco, *Royal Commission*, 74; Testimony of George Burns, ibid., 42–43; Testimony of John S. Skinner, ibid., 23; Testimony of George Burns, ibid., 62.
29 Testimony of George Burns, ibid., 42.
30 Guertin was fired not because job fees were against CPR policies, but because of a conflict over the jurisdiction of such fees. See testimony of Antonio Cordasco, *Royal Commission*, 152.
31 Cordasco to M. Torchia, March 12, 1904, ibid., 75.
32 Testimony of George Burns, ibid., 41.

managers considered Cordasco's padrone system to be "in vogue," as Burns put it, the cutting edge of corporate hiring and labor recruitment: it had eliminated the worst cases of extortion among foremen within the company, improved the efficiency of labor recruitment in general, and helped keep the company's unskilled workers union-free.

But if Cordasco remained "in vogue" among CPR officials during the spring of 1903, developments during the following summer and fall led them to reconsider their faith in him. Despite his best efforts in the spring of 1903, Cordasco simply could not meet all of the CPR's demand for unskilled labor. In 1902 three thousand men had been more than enough for the work available, but in 1903 a massive strike among railroad workers in Winnipeg combined with huge agricultural harvests meant that even six thousand Italians did not meet the CPR's labor needs. Burns responded to this shortfall with a two-pronged strategy. First, he sought better mechanisms within the CPR's internal bureaucracy for estimating its labor needs in advance, asking all superintendents "to state exactly how many men stayed with the company and did not jump their contracts" in 1903. Burns also sought to improve Cordasco's ability to import Italian workmen. Recalled Burns, "I took some steps to get these agencies for him," including making a trip with Cordasco in November 1903 to meet representatives of the major Mediterranean lines in New York City and to persuade them to make Cordasco their official agent in Montreal.[33]

Burns experienced mixed results in his endeavors to streamline the CPR's employment needs. His attempt to establish precise estimates of labor demand from the information provided by superintendents proved, by his own reckoning, to be "fruitless." As Burns recalled, "some superintendents did not give correct information, some delayed answering so long that the spring . . . was far advanced." Ultimately, "there was no estimate" made of the number of laborers needed for the summer work season.[34] Burns was far more successful in helping Cordasco mobilize thousands of Italian workers to Canada. The endorsement of several steamship lines in New York enabled Cordasco to gain the cooperation of prominent agents in Italy such as Frank Ludwig. Initially skeptical of Cordasco's abilities, Ludwig soon gave him begrudging support:

If I see that you act as an honest man, I shall give your address to all the passengers who go to Montreal. What I especially recommend to you is not to change your residence every moment like a wandering merchant. . . . You must be satisfied with a modest commission and Alberto Dini, with whom I worked until now, placed my passengers without any commission, and I never had a complaint against him. We shall see then if you work with the same conscience and punctuality.[35]

Ludwig's doubts aside, Cordasco's success in besting his rival Alberto Dini represented an organizational coup, one that further strengthened his ability to transport thousands of men directly from Italy to western Canada.

[33] Ibid., 41, 44.
[34] Ibid., 51.
[35] F. Ludwig to Antonio Cordasco, November 27, 1903, ibid., 81.

Unfortunately for both Cordasco and Burns, it was the efficiency of these international connections that led to an acute overabundance of Italians in the streets of Montreal the following spring. But the subsequent rupturing of Cordasco's relationship with the CPR was not caused by this sheer number of Italian workmen. Rather, it stemmed from a slowly emerging conflict between Burns and Cordasco over who would control the far-flung and profitable Italian migration system that both of them had created.

The first signs of strain involved the CPR's official labor agent, John S. Skinner. As part of his attempt to consolidate the CPR's labor recruitment efforts in the winter of 1904, Burns made Cordasco a subordinate of Skinner, who now possessed jurisdiction over all Italian employees, although, as Skinner admitted, Cordasco's "negotiations with his laborers were all carried on in Italian behind closed doors." Unable to speak Italian, Skinner initially retained only nominal power over Cordasco and the CPR's Italian workers. In January 1904, Skinner began "cutting" some of the hours that Cordasco had claimed were spent working for the CPR. The twenty-seven dollars – or five and a half days of work – in late December that Skinner deducted was a paltry sum, but it led Cordasco to write a series of furious letters to Burns. As Cordasco later recalled, "I was looking out for my rights," but the exasperated Burns gave all of his support to Skinner.[36]

Just what rights Cordasco possessed in the CPR became extremely contentious during the early months of 1904. Although several important CPR officials attended Cordasco's coronation in what seemed to be a show of harmony, Burns was already making plans to reform further Cordasco's relationship to the CPR. Much of this pressure was generated by a court case in the Superior Court of Montreal in January 1904 involving six Italian laborers who successfully sued the CPR for the reimbursement of job fees paid to Cordasco the previous fall. The decision and negative publicity led Burns "to change the arrangements so that it could not be said that the CPR had accepted any fees" from its employees. On April 23, 1904, Burns met with Cordasco and informed him that henceforth all business relations would be spelled out in "a regular written contract agreement," which the CPR's lawyers were preparing. Until then, the CPR "would pay him one dollar per head with the understanding that he would collect nothing from the men."[37]

From the CPR's perspective, making Cordasco more like a regular CPR employee seemed the best way of controlling any negative publicity generated by his contentious relations with Italian workmen. Although establishing better estimates of labor demand had failed, Burns could at least establish closer supervision over how Cordasco hired and fired Italian workers. Cordasco, however, did not share Burns's enthusiasm for bureaucratic reform. Rather than simply accept the new written agreement, he insisted first that his registration system be preserved for the current work season. More important, Cordasco never accepted the basic

---

[36] Testimony of John S. Skinner, ibid., 165; Testimony of Antonio Cordasco, ibid., 75.

[37] *Vaccha vs. The Canadian Pacific Railway*, Case 1067, January 15, 1904, Records of the Superior Court, District of Montreal; Testimony of George Burns, *Royal Commission*, 42–43.

premise of the April 1904 agreement, that he be paid by the CPR rather than Italian workers for services rendered to the company. The new arrangement not only reduced his earnings from three dollars per man to one, but compromised his authority over Italian sojourners. Consequently, he continued to charge Italian workers fees throughout the summer of 1904, even though few jobs materialized. Cordasco defended his actions by insisting the new agreement was not "in black and white. . . . I agreed to it in my own way."[38]

Much of what made Cordasco's resistance so troubling to CPR managers was not his "inefficiency," but his control over a remarkably large flow of unskilled workers to Montreal. The conflicts between Burns and Cordasco in the spring of 1904 were exacerbated by a late thaw, an oversupply of Italian workmen, and growing public resentment toward both Cordasco and the CPR. But at its heart the conflict was a struggle for power and authority between the two men. Ultimately, Cordasco lost. Three days after the Canadian government opened its investigation of "the alleged fraudulent practices of employment agencies," the CPR dismissed Cordasco permanently from its employ. Although CPR managers had only recently attempted to make Cordasco a better employee, they now denied he had ever been one. Cordasco, by contrast, strenuously sought to prove in court his status as a legitimate player within CPR's management, one whose rights and contracts with the company had been "maliciously" violated. But the verbal and flexible nature of Cordasco's contractual relations with the CPR before 1904 proved a weak foundation for his legal demands to receive nearly thirty thousand dollars in damages from the CPR in 1905.[39] The final judgment against Cordasco took four years to reach in Montreal's Superior Court, but his most humiliating and costly moment came just days after he was fired as the CPR's labor agent when the company hired nearly thirty-five hundred Italian laborers, most of them Cordasco's former "subjects."

Although George Burns minimized Cordasco's role in the CPR after the fact, Cordasco left an enduring imprint on the company's hiring and management of unskilled workers. His departure did little to dampen the enthusiasm of CPR managers for Italian workers, who continued to be hired in substantial numbers over the next decade and charged high prices for food in company commissaries. The problem that Cordasco's tenure emblematized to CPR officials was not that job fees and commissary privileges were bad, but that bottlenecks of transient immigrant workers had to be avoided with better estimates of seasonal labor demands and labor supply. Indeed, the work that Cordasco had performed in centralizing the company's control over hiring and firing of unskilled workers was preserved and expanded under the office of the new labor superintendent, John Skinner. In part because of Cordasco's accomplishments, the CPR became even

[38] Testimony of Antonio Cordasco, *Royal Commission*, 76.
[39] Cordasco sued the CPR for a total of $29,520. See the original judgment and Cordasco's failed appeal in *Registre des Jugements de la Cour Superieure*, March 3, 1909, vol. I, 577, Records of the Superior Court, District of Montreal; ibid., May 11, 1906, vol. II, 515.

more efficient in administering and profiting from its commissary system, to the great chagrin of many transient workers who complained mightily about living conditions throughout the ensuing decade, a story we briefly return to in Chapter 6. Moreover, the CPR also became ever more proficient in mobilizing workers from overseas directly to the Canadian West in moments of acute labor needs, bringing Japanese and East Indian men, for example, directly to British Columbia in 1907 when strikes disrupted the lines. Never again did a single immigrant labor agent become "sole" contractor for his compatriots.[40] The risks – and the profits – that such centralized power created would henceforth remain within the CPR's own labor recruitment bureaucracy.

The Utah Copper Company

Although the Utah Copper Company greatly increased Leon Skliris's earnings as a padrone, he was by no means solely dependent on the company for his livelihood. If Cordasco's fame and fortune were directly tied to one company, Skliris created a sophisticated padrone system well before he became the Utah Copper Company's sole Greek labor agent in November 1910. Skliris's career in fact encompassed a variety of economic roles – laborer, foreman, labor agent, and entrepreneur – and included stints with a variety of companies. At first glance, his success makes him appear an embodiment of Abraham Lincoln's classic vision of free labor, that today's wage earner is tomorrow's boss. Skliris rose from the ranks of child laborer to railroad worker, interpreter, section foreman, and finally labor agent for the Denver and Rio Grande Railroad Companies (D&RG) and a dozen railroad and mining companies in Utah. Yet, Skliris's position at the D&RG was not as secure or formal as Cordasco's place within the CPR.[41] Initially, much of Skliris's work for the D&RG was arranged on an ad hoc basis. Most arrangements for extra work gangs were made by the subcontractors to whom the D&RG had farmed out its new construction projects. Unlike Cordasco, Skliris spent much of his time "out on the line," overseeing the extra work and provisioning Greek workers. Skliris was the principal labor agent for Greek track workers in Colorado, but the D&RG's labor department was even less centralized than the CPR's. Few formal hiring policies existed for unskilled workers and authority remained concentrated in the foreman and labor agents' hands.

Skliris nonetheless made considerably larger sums of money from his work than did Cordasco, clearing more than fifty thousand dollars in 1905, fully five years before he became Utah Copper's labor agent.[42] Skliris's financial success

---

[40] Avery, *Reluctant Host*, 47, 48.

[41] The bulk of most padrone "earnings," according to Frank Sheridan, came from selling provisions and supplies to railroad workers. See Sheridan, *Italian, Slavic, and Hungarian Unskilled Immigrants*, 446–448.

[42] In the fall of 1906, Steve Skliris sued his brother for approximately half of his earnings as a labor agent, or $25,600. See *Steve Skliris vs. Leonidas Skliris*, Case 8637, November 6, 1906, Salt Lake County, Records of the Third District Civil Court.

did not stem from his being a better employee than Cordasco or someone who had extracted a sweeter deal from company managers. Rather, his wealth was created by the distinctly entrepreneurial features of his padrone business and the way he organized it within the D&RG and other mining and railroad companies in Utah. Whereas Cordasco's men paid roughly three dollars to get a job, Greeks in Colorado and Utah paid from ten to twenty-five dollars for their positions. Skliris was not beholden to any previous company policy or tradition about how much immigrant workers could be charged. That independence was exemplified in the contracts that all Greek railroad workers signed:

I, _____, for myself, my heirs, executors, administrators, and assigns, do hereby irrevocably assign and set over to L. G. Skliris, of the city and County of Salt Lake and State of Utah, the sum of One Dollar ($1.00) per month out of wages earned or which may hereafter be earned by me in the employment of _____ and I hereby irrevocably authorize, empower, and direct said Railroad Company to deduct said amount ... and to pay same to L. G. Skliris.[43]

Skliris no doubt found models for this contract while working as a section foreman in Indiana. Indeed, his contract closely resembled what government investigator Frank Sheridan described in his national study of the "Padrone Commissary system" in 1897.[44] Skliris's contracts were not minted by a particular corporation, however; they worked for any railroad company that Greek workers encountered. They suggest the degree to which Skliris, rather than any company officials, dictated the terms of Greek workers' employment.

But if Skliris's contracts highlight the independence of his business operations, they do not explain why Greek workers would have signed them. Here we need to consider the importance of Skliris's agents and sub-bosses throughout Utah and Colorado. As for Cordasco, foremen were crucial intermediaries within Skliris's padrone system, collecting job fees from new workers and acquiring their signatures for the monthly deductions. Smelter worker John Kotsovos recalled that Skliris's agents "used to sit in the hiring office near the plant and indicate which Greeks the company should hire or fire."[45] Greek workers had little choice, it would seem. Nor for that matter did the management of the United States Smelting and Refining Company, where Kotsovos worked. It had not formally hired Skliris or his subagents, but Skliris managed to control the hiring and firing of Greek workers all the same by cajoling Greek foremen and bribing company superintendents.

[43] Unsigned labor contract of L. G. Skliris, straight numerical file 161414, box 1384, Records of the U.S. Department of Justice, RG 60, National Archives, Washington, D.C.

[44] Sheridan, *Italian, Slavic, and Hungarian Unskilled Immigrants*, 451–453. Not only did these Italian contracts "authorize" monthly deductions, but they also established where Italian workers should shop, cook, and board, and the fines to be levied for noncompliance.

[45] John Kotsovos interview by Louis Cononelos, Salt Lake City, September 19, 1974, American West Center, University of Utah.

As the official labor agent for the Utah Copper Company and the D&RG Railroad Companies, by contrast, Skliris administered his job fees and monthly pay tax with the apparent blessing of corporate managers. In Bingham, Skliris took full advantage of the free reign Utah Copper officials gave him by transforming the Panhellenic Grocery Store into a commissary for the company's Greek employees. The Utah Copper Company did not grant Skliris any formal commissary privileges, but neither did it object to his creation of what looked like a company store. That the "company" was Leon Skliris and not Utah Copper was fine as long as Greeks remained steady and tractable workers.

Like Cordasco's Italian foremen, Greek foremen in Utah's mines and railroads played critical roles in enforcing Skliris's power as a padrone. Unlike Cordasco, however, Skliris did not have the power to determine who became a foreman for the companies he serviced. Consequently, many foremen at the D&RG and the Utah Copper Company were not directly connected to Skliris's hierarchy and did not necessarily obey his decisions about hiring and firing unskilled Greeks. Consider, for example, the case of Dimitris Brousalis, a Greek foreman at the Yampa smelter in Bingham Canyon. According to the Greek newspaper *Ergatis* in 1908, Brousalis "managed, through a company secretary, to get twenty to fifty dollars from every Greek who wanted a job. And every month he taxed them two and half dollars each." Whereas Cordasco relied on George Burns to back him up in enforcing his control over Italian employment, Skliris had no such leverage with managers of the Utah Copper Company in 1908. Instead, he had to pressure Brousalis directly with the help of his agents and foremen who also worked at the Utah Copper Company. The result was nothing less than a pitched battle in which Brousalis's "house soon became full of holes and a mailbox was ruined from the numerous bullet holes."[46] Brousalis found such actions persuasive and joined Skliris's tribute system, but only after he agreed to give Skliris most of the more modest job fees he collected.

Bribes and violence did not make Skliris's tribute system preindustrial or primitive, for such practices were endemic to social relations between foremen and immigrant workers throughout North America at the turn of the century. Just as Cordasco was not the first CPR hiring agent to receive tributes, neither were Skliris and his agents the first to demand job fees and monthly pay deductions from immigrant workers. For many Greek laborers, the demands of the American boss were just as onerous or worse than Skliris's exactions. In Carbon County, Utah, Greek coal miner Jim Galanis recalled the exactions of his American boss: "I was offered a job at the coke ovens, provided I paid $20 commission for the boss and his gang. When I reported to work, as agreed, the boss told me that somebody else had bid the job with $10 more and since I had no more money, I lost the job plus the $20 commission."[47] Jobs to the highest bidder with no refunds – this was

[46] *Ergatis*, February 29, 1908, 3; ibid., May 17, 1908, 5. Translated from Katharevousa Greek to English by the author with the help of Lena Nikolaou.
[47] Jim Galanis interview by Louis Cononelos, Salt Lake City, September 1974, American West Center. Also cited in Cononelos, "Greek Immigrant Labor," 177.

hardly the "free" market of Horatio Alger's fiction or one that most immigrant workers anticipated finding in North America. Dimitris Brousalis may have charged workers exceptionally high fees in his wildcat tribute system, but the practice among unskilled workers within corporations was typical rather than exceptional.

"Padronism," then, was intrinsically related to the organization of unskilled work and corporate hiring practices in North America at the turn of the century. Foremen of all stripes possessed considerable authority in making most hiring and firing decisions. Although social critics viewed foremen who accepted or demanded "fees," "bribes," or "extortions" as immoral, such hiring practices reflected the decentralized nature of most corporate hiring decisions throughout the North American West, even in Canada where the CPR possessed superior links to overseas labor markets. As George Burns discovered to his chagrin in 1903, the CPR's hiring policies remained ad hoc affairs despite his best efforts, pulled together in response to emergencies and the vagaries of the weather. For the CPR, a late thaw, an unusually successful wheat harvest, a sugar beet blight, and several labor strikes dramatically altered the number of "extra" men needed and available for seasonal work on the CPR. Making systematic plans for such a variable work force was difficult work. Most unskilled immigrant workers consequently remained excluded from corporate welfare policies, despite the growing enthusiasm some industrial firms possessed for new forms of "scientific management." Amenities such as hot showers, company-run boardinghouses, and baseball leagues were developed primarily for skilled workers, such as the steam shovel operators in Bingham Canyon. Although corporations desired a ready supply of unskilled labor for extra work or a large strike, they did not want to be held responsible for its upkeep and general welfare. Better to have a disposable work force than one idled, demanding privileges and rights. The rise of padronism in the North American West reflected the highly variable labor market needs of the region's and the continent's most modern corporations.[48]

[48] On studies of industrial paternalism that emphasize its modern origins in labor market circumstances and the ideological needs of managers, see Gunther Peck, "Divided Loyalties: Immigrant Padrones and the Evolution of Industrial Paternalism in North America," *International Labor and Working-Class History* 53 (Spring 1998): 49–68; Douglas Flamming, *Creating the Modern South: Millhands and Managers in Dalton, Georgia, 1884–1984* (Chapel Hill, 1992), xxvii–xxviii; David Crew, *Town in the Ruhr: A Social History of Bochum, 1860–1914* (New York, 1979), 147–157; Jacoby, *Employing Bureaucracy*, 39–64; and Sanford Jacoby, *Modern Manors: Welfare Capitalism since the New Deal* (Princeton, 1997); Andrea Tone, *The Business of Benevolence: Industrial Paternalism in Progressive America* (Ithaca, 1997). On industrial paternalism as a "transitional" phenomenon originating in traditional values, see Gerald Friedman, "The Decline of Paternalism and the Making of the Employer Class: France, 1870–1914," in Sanford Jacoby, ed., *Masters to Managers: Historical and Comparative Perspectives on American Employers* (New York, 1991), 153–172; Way, *Common Labour*, 263; Shearer Davis Bowman, *Masters and Lords: Mid-19th-Century U.S. Planters and Prussian Junkers* (New York, 1993), 166; Mary Wingert, "Rethinking Paternalism: Power and Parochialism in a Southern Mill Village," *Journal of American History* 83 (1996): 872.

And yet padrones also led the effort to transform the distance that separated most unskilled immigrants from corporate managers. Cordasco took full advantage of the opportunities that Burns delivered to him, not only making three times what Burns had anticipated but maintaining tightfisted control over the hiring and firing of Italian workers, an unprecedented accomplishment in the CPR's history. The Utah Copper Company granted Skliris few of the same powers, but only because it did not need to. Skliris had already organized and streamlined the collection of fees between foremen and workers well before he became the company's official labor agent. The Utah Copper Company did not "offer additional inducements" to Skliris, as Burns had for Cordasco, because the company had few inducements left to give him. Although officially an employee of Utah Copper, Skliris was in key respects an entrepreneur. As Greek miner Steve Kalaides recalled, "The companies recruited Skliris for help; he didn't seek work from them."[49]

Skliris's entrepreneurial accomplishments were not lost on Daniel Jackling, general manager of the Utah Copper Company between 1903 and 1912 and future company president. Indeed, Skliris's success encouraged Jackling to solidify and expand padronism among other groups of immigrant workers, sponsoring the business endeavors of Italian labor agent Moses Paggi and Japanese labor contractor Edward Daigoro Hashimoto. Like Skliris, Paggi grew rich from the job fees that newly imported Italian employees paid him as well as the dollar a month deduction from their wages. Hashimoto also prospered under Jackling's watch, bringing several hundred Japanese workers from California to Bingham Canyon after 1910. Hashimoto established even tighter control over the domestic lives of Japanese workers than did Skliris among his Greek compatriots, building a dormitory in Bingham where all two hundred Japanese employees were housed, fed, and clothed under his immediate supervision.

Skliris's tenure as sole labor agent was short, but he had an enduring impact on the way the Utah Copper Company organized its recruitment and management of unskilled immigrant workers. When Jackling compelled Skliris to resign during the 1912 strike, Jackling nonetheless began considering how his company might build and manage its own company town for skilled and unskilled workers, a plan that reached fruition a decade later in the completion of Copperton near Bingham Canyon. Replete with its own company stores like the Panhellenic Grocery Store and boardinghouses like the one built by Hashimoto, Copperton was only one of several company towns built under Daniel Jackling's supervision in the late 1910s and 1920s.[50]

Jackling had numerous prototypes upon which to base his plans for a company town. The regional features of his corporate welfare efforts, however, recalled Skliris's success in exploiting labor mobility between several job sites simultaneously. In the spring of 1912, Jackling began investing Utah Copper

[49] Steve Kalaides interview by Helen Papanikolas, Salt Lake City, March 22, 1973, Greek Archives.
[50] On Copperton's history, see Arrington, *The Richest Hole on Earth*, 82.

capital in the Garden City Sugar Company of Kansas, an operation that grew sugar beets and a variety of other vegetables with imported Mexican labor in western Kansas and Nebraska. Jackling's intentions became clear in 1920, when the sugar beet company began selling its abundant crops to store managers in the new company towns of Hurley, New Mexico, Ray, Arizona, and Copperton, Utah, all of them owned by Kennecott, Utah Copper's new parent corporation. Like Greek workers in Bingham or Italians in western Canada, Mexican sugar beet workers and copper miners generated revenues interchangeably as producers and consumers. Like Skliris, Jackling extended his control beyond one site of labor demand and consumption, making it harder for Mexicans to escape Kennecott's interlocking network of farms, mines, and towns in the Southwest. Although Leon Skliris had left Utah by 1920, he would have been proud and perhaps jealous of what Jackling had made of "the greatest industrial sight on earth."[51]

El Paso's Octupi

If Skliris's entrepreneurial accomplishments demonstrate how padrones shaped corporate hiring practices, the lives of Roman Gonzalez and fellow Mexican labor agents in El Paso underscore how instrumental corporations remained in defining padrone opportunities. Gonzalez's failure to become El Paso's "king of the peons" was not merely an accident of geography but a reflection of the particular hiring policies of El Paso's railroad corporations. Like the D&RG, the Southern Pacific (SP) and the Atchison, Topeka and the Santa Fe (AT&SF) lines subcontracted much of their work to local construction companies.[52] A great variety of hiring practices along different sections of the SP's and AT&SF's railroad lines emerged, as labor agents for both the railroads and their subcontractors adopted different hiring methods even while competing for the same men.

The fragmented nature of labor recruitment was intensified by each company's bureaucratic structure. The AT&SF was divided into three different divisions in 1910, the western, the eastern, and the "coast lines," each managed by a different superintendent who recruited distinct groups of unskilled workers, depending on the local labor supply.[53] J. E. Hurley, general superintendent of the Kansas

[51] C. F. Jennings to Daniel Jackling, November 19, 1920, box 35, folder 5, Daniel Jackling Papers, Special Collections, Stanford University Archives, Palo Alto, California; Ino Sully to Daniel Jackling, November 9, 1920, ibid.; L. S. Cates to Daniel Jackling, November 14, 1920, ibid. On western company towns, see James B. Allen, *The Company Town in the American West* (Norman, 1966). On company towns throughout the United States, see Jacquelyn Hall et al., *Like a Family: The Making of a Southern Cotton Mill World* (Chapel Hill, 1987); Daniel Walkowitz, *Worker City, Company Town: Iron and Cotton-Worker Protest in Troy and Cohoes, New York, 1855–1884* (Urbana, 1978); and Gerald Zahavi, *Workers, Managers, and Welfare Capitalism: The Shoeworkers and Tanners of Endicott Johnson, 1890–1950* (Urbana, 1988).

[52] *Stone Report*, 91; For corporate histories, see Frank J. Taylor and Neil C. Wilson, *Southern Pacific: The Roaring Story of a Fighting Railroad* (New York, 1952), 49; and Don Hofsommer, *The Southern Pacific, 1901–1985* (College Station, 1986).

[53] *Stone Report*, 84.

City–based eastern division, informed U.S. immigration inspector Frank Stone in 1910 that he had employed "Slavs, South Italians, and Greeks," as well as Mexicans as track laborers over the past decade, most of them recruited from the local labor market in Kansas City. R. J. Parker, general superintendent of the Western Grand division, in turn, informed Stone that his Los Angeles–based division had hired Chinese, Japanese, and Mexican track workers and more recently employed a "small number of Mojave Indians" in California, Navaho Indians in New Mexico and Arizona, and "some Lagoona Indians (Pueblo Tribe)" in Colorado. The Southern Pacific likewise hired whatever "local" workers were already present in the cities and countryside it traversed in the U.S. Southwest, starting with Chinese and Irish track laborers in the 1880s, moving to Italians, Greeks, and Slavs in the 1890s, and Japanese and Mexicans by the early 1900s. Like the AT&SF, the SP employed Native Americans, particulary Yuma Indians from Colorado and Yaqui Indians from Mexico.[54]

Such diversity served company interests in maintaining an ethnically and racially divided work force, but it also reflected the localistic nature of hiring on the SP and the AT&SF. Most recruitment was not conducted by designated labor agents but by section foremen, who not only hired and fired members of their gang but had to recruit them in the first place. Consider, for example, the frustrations of section foreman John Sullivan who worked on the AT&SF's eastern division at Stafford, Kansas. In the winter of 1909 he sent a letter to Delphino Garcia, a former track worker residing in Chihuahua, Mexico, promising him work the following spring. Sullivan's letter included fourteen transportation passes for able bodied fellow villagers. Sullivan's plan would have worked had Delphino not been stopped by U.S. immigration officers at El Paso, who were concerned by the small amounts of money each possessed – between twenty cents and two dollars.[55] Most foremen were more careful in their recruitment efforts, instructing workers to bring at least enough "show money" to avoid hassles at the border. Sullivan learned a hard lesson as Delphino and his compatriots were deported as aliens likely to become "public charges."

One clear consequence of the SP and AT&SF's recruitment practices was that both companies were perennially short of labor at crucial moments of the work season, as subcontractors throughout the region competed for scarce workers. Both railroads sought to redress this problem by affiliating themselves with commissary companies in El Paso that recruited workers for them free of charge in exchange for the opportunity to feed these workers on the move. Between 1885 and 1903, the SP relied on the Norton-Drake Company, headed by Anglo businessman John G. Maxwell, to organize the commissary privileges for its employees. The AT&SF, meanwhile, relied on the Hanlin Supply Company to feed Mexican workers on its eastern division and the Holmes Supply Company for feeding them on its western division.[56]

[54] Ibid., 73–75, 84–85.
[55] Minutes of the Special Board of Inquiry, May 13, 1910, Exhibit 16, ibid.
[56] Testimony of George H. Mauser, April 13, 1910, Exhibit 3, ibid.

Here were many of the same privileges that Cordasco enjoyed as the sole Italian labor agent for the CPR. The Holmes Supply Company's policies toward immigrant railroad workers closely resembled the tribute system that Cordasco and Skliris organized in Utah and Montreal. Mexican workers were compelled to pay a dollar in order to secure their position and were subsequently required to use the boardinghouses and food that the Holmes Supply Company provided. The costs of board and food were deducted from immigrant workers' wages under the watchful eye of the local section foreman, who supervised the arrangement. The remaining balances of workers' wages were reserved in credit at any of their stores in "El Paso, Texas, Isleta, New Mexico, Winsor and Williams, Arizona, Needles, Barstow, Fresno, Richmond, San Bernardino, and Los Angeles, California."[57]

But unlike the CPR, railroad managers for the SP and AT&SF did not grant the commissary companies the sole right to recruit workers for their railroads. Nor for that matter did they prevent the commissary companies from doing business with other railroad lines. Indeed, both the railroads and their favored commissary companies did business with a great variety of companies and individuals. In 1909, for example, the AT&SF acquired numerous Mexican workers from the L. H. Manning Company, while the Holmes Supply Company provided Mexicans jobs with the SP and the Rock Island Railroads. Competition among the commissaries and within El Paso's labor market worked against the creation of exclusive contracts between labor agents and the railroads.

Yet the competitive and decentralized nature of the SP's and AT&SF's hiring practices does not explain why Gonzalez did not become a king of the Mexican peons, particularly when the same conditions fueled Leon Skliris's rise to power in Utah. Why, put simply, were Mexican labor market entrepreneurs in El Paso less successful than their Japanese, Greek, and Italian counterparts in the West? Racial prejudices among corporate managers and Anglo-run commissary companies toward their Mexican employees undoubtedly hurt the ability of men like Gonzalez to profit from the commerce of migration.[58] One Mexican employee of the Norton-Drake Company, for example, Paromino Contrara, briefly gained notoriety by regularly sending agents into northern Mexico to recruit workers, promising men "all the work they need at a dollar and a quarter a day," as well as free passage to and from work sites. At first glance, his position resembled that of Skliris and Cordasco: all three were employed by corporations to recruit a work force and to

---

[57] Ibid.; W. H. Talbot interview by Paul Taylor, 1928, doc. no. 56–61, Paul S. Taylor Papers; J. R. Silva interview by Paul Taylor, 1928, doc. no. 103–107a, ibid.

[58] The five managers of the L. H. Manning Company that Paul Taylor interviewed in 1928 were all Anglo-Americans. Only one of them, L. H. Manning, possessed any clear knowledge of Spanish. See W. H. Talbot interview by Paul Taylor, doc. no. 56-61, BANC-MSS-74/187c, Paul S. Taylor Papers; Mr. Clark interview, doc. no. 17-189, doc. no. 316-487, ibid.; Mr. Johnson interview, doc. no. 102-107, ibid.; G. A. Hoff interview, doc. no. 39-44, ibid.; L. H. Manning interview, doc. no. 40-45, ibid. On racism against Mexican labor agents in El Paso, see Guerin-Gonzalez, *Mexican Workers and American Dreams*, 38–41; and George Sanchez, *Becoming Mexican American: Ethnicity, Culture, and Identity in Chicono Los Angeles, 1900–1945* (New York, 1994), 51–54.

bridge the boundary between the corporation and the unskilled immigrant worker. Contrara, however, was paid only two and a half dollars a day and was not allowed to charge Mexican workers any job fees. His pay was more a wage than a salary, one that he earned only "from time to time," according to Contrara, when he was actually in Juarez rounding up work gangs.[59]

But was it racism alone that kept Contrara a part-time and underpaid employee? Racism had not prevented the Six Companies from amassing considerable power during the 1870s, after all, nor did Japanese labor contractors suffer from the racial exclusion of their compatriots. To the contrary, they may have gained from the racial distance between their compatriots and white Americans, being the only ones willing to provide commissary "privileges" to their shunned compatriots. That was certainly the case for Japanese workers in Bingham, Utah, whose padrone, Edward Hashimoto, not only charged them job fees but also made additional profits by boarding and feeding all of them in a single boardinghouse.[60]

Racial prejudice had not kept individual Mexican Americans from becoming very wealthy in El Paso either. Felix Martinez was perhaps the richest Mexican American in El Paso between 1900 and 1910 and enjoyed a comparatively rare level of acceptance within El Paso's Anglo-American community. Like Mexican entrepreneurs in Los Angeles twenty years later, Martinez seemed well positioned to lay claim to at least a portion of the lucrative labor-contracting business in El Paso in 1900 if he had so desired. Other Mexican businessmen before him had certainly tried for a combination of philanthropic and financial incentives. Between 1891 and 1893, Juan Ochoa, a newspaper editor in El Paso, sought to "aid the poor and destitute" by finding them jobs. But after Ochoa's newspaper folded, he never again sought to profit from the commerce of migration.[61]

One reason Mexican entrepreneurs may have avoided the labor-contracting business in El Paso before 1905 was the extraordinary competition that flourished within the business as well as the conspicuous advantages that official commissary companies possessed. Trying to compete with the Norton-Drake Company, whose company stores traversed three states, seemed a risky endeavor indeed. Equally important, the key building block of padrone power in other contexts – immigrant foremen – was largely absent among Mexican sojourners in El Paso. Not only were there fewer Mexican foremen than the number of unskilled Mexicans warranted, but few Mexican labor agents built their businesses around a successful coterie of them. If immigrant foremen occupied indispensable roles within

---

[59] *El Paso Times*, October 28, 1894, 6; ibid., January 24, 1900, 7.

[60] On Hashimoto's career, see Ichioka, *The Issei*, 60–61. For evidence of the shared living-arrangements of Japanese workers under Hashimoto, see U.S. Bureau of the Census, *Thirteenth Census of the United States, 1910. Population Schedules*, Salt Lake County, election districts 80 and 81, Bingham Canyon, Utah.

[61] On the career of Felix Martinez, see Mario Garcia, *Desert Immigrants*, 82–83. On Mexican American entrepreneurs in Los Angeles, see Sanchez, *Becoming Mexican American*, 174–175; Testimony of William Henry, May 14, 1910, Exhibit 6, *Stone Report*, 5.

Cordasco's and Skliris's respective tribute systems, Mexican foremen remained largely insignificant to the business endeavors of Gonzalez and his competitors. Gonzalez was hardly exceptional in that regard. None of the American labor agencies attempted to organize the foremen who worked on the SP and AT&SF railroads either.

The comparative scarcity of Mexican foremen reflected not racial prejudice alone, but also the remarkable mobility of Mexicans between jobs. Anywhere from one-half to two-thirds of every shipment that Gonzalez and the Manning Supply Company shipped out of El Paso between 1905 and 1925 deserted the train before arriving at the intended job. Mexican foremen, it would seem, proved no better able to control the mobility of their compatriots than the railroad companies and consequently accrued little influence among corporate managers. More often than not, entire Mexican work crews jumped ship together with their foreman. Given the mobility of Mexican foremen, their disorganized status within corporations, and the pervasive racial discrimination against Mexicans seeking profits from the commerce of migration, what seems remarkable is that any successful Mexican labor agents emerged in the early twentieth century at all.

When the Norton-Drake Company reorganized itself as the L. H. Manning Supply Company in 1903 and hired two Mexican American clerks, Robert Zarate and Isaac Avina, few expected them to become entrepreneurs of the migration business. But Zarate and Avina proved to be quick learners and, like Skliris in Utah, made a quick study of their company's labor recruitment methods before quitting their jobs and opening the Zarate-Avina Company in 1904. Success did not materialize overnight but grew steadily. In their first year of business, Zarate and Avina "shipped six or seven hundred Mexicans" to Kansas, while a year later they shipped thirteen hundred laborers to Missouri, on both occasions for the SP. Zarate and Avina's contacts with the railroad, forged while working at the SP's commissary, had paid off handsomely for their fledgling business. Yet their success in 1905 was overshadowed by the dramatic entrance of Roman Gonzalez into El Paso's competitive labor-contracting community. In his first full season, Gonzalez shipped nearly three thousand Mexicans to Kansas on the AT&SF. Although Gonzalez had never worked as a clerk in a labor agency, he had worked as a mechanic for the railroad before becoming a policeman, a connection that helped him secure his railroad contracts.[62]

But the modest success of both Gonzalez and the Zarate-Avina labor agencies raises an intriguing question: why would the SP and the AT&SF railroad companies create their own labor agencies and promptly give their business to renegade competitors? The answer here lies in understanding the impact of seasonal fluctuations in labor demand on El Paso's labor-contracting businesses. In 1904 and

[62] El Paso, *City Directory*, 1903–1904, Southwest Collection; Robert P. Zarate and personnel of Zarate-Avina Labor Agency interview, El Paso, 1928, doc. no. 110-114, doc. no. 17-189, BANC-MSS-74/187c, Paul S. Taylor Papers; *El Paso Times*, February 6, 1907, 5.

1905, an acute shortage of labor during the summer work seasons quickly exhausted all that the L. H. Manning and the Holmes Supply companies had to offer their affiliated railroads. In such periods of intense demand, railroad companies of necessity looked beyond their affiliated companies to recruit workers. Consequently, the number of labor agencies in El Paso mushroomed from five to seventeen between 1904 and 1906.[63] But such periods of prosperity for independent contractors were fleeting. An economic slowdown in 1908 put nearly a third of El Paso's labor agencies out of business and placed a tremendous financial burden on unaffiliated contractors such as Gonzalez and Zarate and Avina, whose contracts with railroad companies slowed considerably.

When demand for track workers boomed in 1909, Gonzalez and Zarate again benefited from the spillover business of the major railroad lines, evident in the late timing of their shipments during the 1910 work season. According to figures compiled by immigration inspector Frank Stone, June was Gonzalez's busiest month when he shipped 898 Mexicans to Oklahoma and Kansas on the AT&SF. Zarate's busiest months comprised the June, July, and August period when he shipped over 500 workers each month to Kansas, Missouri, Illinois, and Iowa, on both the AT&SF and the SP railroads. These peak months contrasted sharply with the L. H. Manning and Holmes Supply companies whose best months ran from January through April, when both companies supplied from 1,300 to 1,800 workers each month to El Paso's two major railroad lines. These were the "fill-up" months, when each railroad's section work was organized and outfitted. Summer months, by contrast, were the times for recruiting "extra" gangs, men who would supplement the main work of the section gangs as needed. The section work tended to be more reliable, while "extra" gangs, the lifeblood of Gonzalez's and Zarate's contracts, were far more temporary in nature.[64]

If El Paso's labor agencies mobilized workers at quite distinct times of the year, they also recruited track workers for particular regions of the nation. Gonzalez and Zarate not only recruited a higher number of "extra" gang workers but also sent a higher percentage of their workers to northern areas of the Midwest. Gonzalez, for example, shipped out 90 percent of all Oklahoma-bound Mexicans from El Paso, while Zarate provided jobs to 75 percent of all Illinois-bound track workers. The Holmes and Manning Supply companies, by contrast, shipped most of their men in the winter to the arid and warmer Southwest, especially California. The L. H. Manning Company, for example, handled over 60 percent of all of the Arizona-bound track workers, whereas the Hanlin Supply Company sent 80 percent of the track workers to Colorado. This variegated geography was produced by many individual contracts struck between regional managers and competing labor agencies during the previous spring and summer work seasons.[65]

Although the geographical control of El Paso's labor agencies recalled the

[63] El Paso, *City Directory*, 1904–1906, Southwest Collection.
[64] Table B, *Stone Report*.
[65] Table C, ibid.

regional monopolies created by the Six Companies, their control was nonetheless highly unstable, as each labor agency sought to win control over its competitor's turf. After the "crash" of 1908, the commissary companies tried to eliminate Gonzalez by redrawing the boundaries around the SP's and the AT&SF's labor needs. Gonzalez, who advertised on his business card that he shipped to "Illinois, Iowa, Missouri, Oklahoma, and Kansas," received no territory in this new arrangement, which eliminated his prior control over Oklahoma-bound Mexicans. Zarate-Avina, by contrast, received a small chunk of railroad territory in these "Mexican Agreements" as they became more formally known. As Zarate later recalled to Paul Taylor in 1928, "In 1909 the Hanlin Supply Company took over the lines from El Paso to Kansas City and the Zarate-Avina Labor Agency was given the territory from Newton, Kansas to Chicago, including Oklahoma and southern Kansas." But even the tenuous acceptance that Zarate and Avina enjoyed was short-lived. Collusion against both Gonzalez and Zarate resumed in 1910 when the Holmes, Hanlin, and Manning companies formed "an association" called the National Supply Company, which explicitly excluded both the Zarate-Avina Labor Agency and Gonzalez from any and all territory. As Avina stated to inspector Stone just after the association had been formed, "they ignored us completely."[66]

Gonzalez and Zarate-Avina retaliated by forming their own combination, the Mexican Labor Supply Company, in the spring of 1910. Its purpose was to commandeer the bulk of the subcontracted railroad business they believed remained up for grabs, or, as Avina stated to Stone in 1910, "to supply labor to the contractors." This was smart strategy for Gonzalez and Zarate-Avina because it built on their previous success in supplying hundreds of Mexican workers to construction firms, such as the C. H. Sharp Company of Kansas City and the Grant Brothers of Arizona. Gonzalez and Zarate-Avina also attempted, like Frank Missler before them, to acquire their own corporation-sponsored commissary privileges with two smaller railroads recruiting in El Paso, the Texas-Pacific and the Rock Island railroads, whose combined business comprised roughly 15 percent of the total migration out of El Paso.[67]

Unfortunately for Gonzalez, Zarate, and Avina, their gamble went belly-up almost before it started. During its one-month existence, the Mexican Labor Supply Company received just one order from a subcontractor named Mr. McFarland for five hundred men. No sooner had McFarland acquired the men than, as Avina stated, he "turned the business over to this Mr. Clark, representing the L. H. Manning and the Hanlin Supply Company, and they got it."[68] The attempts to garner a written contract with the Rock Island Company and the Texas-Pacific also failed to materialize. Having been excluded from their former territory by the National

[66] Business card of Roman Gonzalez, Exhibit 12, ibid.; Robert Zarate interview by Paul Taylor, 1928, doc. no. 110-114, BANC-MSS-74/187c, Paul S. Taylor Papers; Statement of I. Z. Avina, April 29, 1910, Exhibit 10, 13, *Stone Report*.

[67] Statement of Roman G. Gonzalez, April 28, 1910, 2, Exhibit 9, *Stone Report*; Statement of I. Z. Avina, April 29, 1910, 7, Exhibit 10, ibid.

[68] Statement of I. Z. Avina, April 29, 1910, 3–4, Exhibit 10, ibid.

Supply Company and with no orders coming in, the businesses of Gonzalez and Zarate-Avina looked to be in dire shape in the spring of 1910.

That Gonzalez and the Zarate-Avina Labor Agency did not go bankrupt underscores not only their financial dexterity, but also the limits of any labor agency or combination in dividing up El Paso's labor-contracting territory by itself. Despite the National Supply Company's grand plans, the SP and the AT&SF continued doing business with both Gonzalez and Zarate-Avina, over the objections of their respective commissary companies. When asked by immigration investigator Frank Stone about his relationship with the AT&SF railroad in June 1910, Gonzalez stated confidently that "My business is on the Middle Grant Division, which takes in part of the state of Kansas and part of Oklahoma." When Stone inquired who supported this arrangement, Gonzalez replied that W. H. Sharp, general superintendent of the Eastern Division, had recently granted him a contract to supply this portion of the railroad with both extra and section gang labor, though it was "just a verbal agreement." Although Gonzalez did not acquire commissary privileges for the workers on the job, he was reimbursed by the AT&SF for the room and board he advanced to Mexican workers while they waited to be shipped out.[69]

Gonzalez's business agreement with the AT&SF did not stem from any racial enlightenment or tolerance on the part of railroad superintendent W. H. Sharp but rather reflected his pragmatic assessments of how best to fill his company's variable and vast labor needs. The instability of Gonzalez's relationship with corporations in El Paso led him to state almost defiantly to Stone in 1910 that "I am not connected with any corporation.... I am alone, all by myself." But in proclaiming himself an entrepreneur, Gonzalez ironically highlighted his continuing dependence on a tenuous supply of verbal agreements from a variety of corporations during flush times. In truth, Gonzalez and Zarate survived by a combination of wits and the indifference of SP and the AT&SF railroad superintendents to the racialized and national appeals of their own commissary companies. Although W. H. Sharp probably did not like Roman Gonzalez or Robert Zarate, he kept both men in business despite the efforts of his own official labor agency to create an Anglo-run choke hold over the migration of Mexican track workers.[70]

The failure of Anglo-led commissary companies to stamp out their Mexican competition reflected not so much a contradiction in corporate hiring policy, then, as the commissaries' inability to meet the labor needs of the railroad companies during moments of peak labor demand. During one such labor shortage in the summer of 1907, AT&SF general superintendent J. L. Hibbard requested eight hundred track workers from his official commissary provider, the Holmes Supply Company, but stated in his letter's conclusion that "I doubt very much if you have come within that number of filling our requisitions for a long time." Representatives of the Holmes Supply Company made no effort to deny this fact, but rather stated to one U.S. congressman in 1910 that "at no time within the past five years

[69] Testimony of Roman Gonzalez, April 28, 1910, Exhibit 9, ibid., 6; ibid., 20.
[70] Ibid.

have we been able to supply the railroad with the number of men desired."[71] Although the commissary companies employed Mexican runners in Mexico, they did not possess the numerous personal connections to families and communities that many Mexican labor agents did. Gonzalez and Zarate exploited that advantage during flush times by maintaining extensive ties to families and friends in the countryside of Mexico that could help them mobilize workers in moments of labor scarcity in the United States.

The closest that Roman Gonzalez came to establishing a secure position within a U.S. corporation occurred in 1923, when he supplied three thousand Mexican track workers to the AT&SF along his old territory. Gonzalez also landed contracts with the Great Western Sugar Company and the American Beet Sugar Company in 1924, two of the nation's largest sugar beet concerns. But Gonzalez had not become indispensable to any of these companies. To the contrary, he continued to supply laborers to corporations only above and beyond what their own hiring agents could procure. The number of North American corporations sending their official labor agents directly to El Paso in the early 1920s had never been greater, particularly after immigration restriction closed traditional European sources of unskilled labor. Company agents from as far away as Ontario, Canada, now competed alongside Roman Gonzalez and his traditional competitors. As the demand for Mexican labor slackened during the 1920s, Gonzalez once again faced financial crisis. By 1927, just one year before Paul Taylor interviewed all of El Paso's labor agents, the Gonzalez Labor Agency went officially and irrevocably "defunct."[72]

One of Gonzalez's newest competitors in the 1920s provides insight into some of the enduring features of the relationship between corporations and padrones in El Paso. Like the L. H. Manning Company, the S.W.& A. Labor Agency was affiliated in 1928 with a large corporation, the American Beet Sugar Company.[73] Founded in 1902 in Fort Worth, Texas, the S.W.& A. Labor Agency had, by the 1920s, perfected as sophisticated and profitable a system of job fees as ever existed among Mexican laborers in the Southwest. According to Mr. Benedict, an attorney for the American Beet Sugar Company whom Paul Taylor interviewed in 1928, the S.W.& A. Labor Agency charged all railroad workers "two and a half or three dollars per head" to get a job, while sugar beet workers paid three dollars a head and five dollars for a family. The profits from this fee system were shared among labor agency officials with a man named Heckman, labor superintendent for the American Beet Sugar Company, who found jobs for "about eight to ten

---

[71] J. L. Hibbard to Holmes Supply Company, September 26, 1907, Exhibit 24, ibid., 2; Holmes Supply Company to J. W. Jencks, September 27, 1907, Exhibit 25, ibid.

[72] J. R. Silva interview by Paul Taylor, 1928, doc. no. 106-110, BANC-MSS-74/187c, Paul S. Taylor Papers.

[73] The founder of the S. W. & A. Labor Agency, one "Mr. Kennedy," started his business, like Gonzalez, by rounding up the city's "vagrants" with the help of the Fort Worth police department. See Mr. Kennedy interview by Paul Taylor, 1928, doc. no. 26-31, BANC-MSS-74/187c, Paul S. Taylor Papers.

thousand laborers a year." Like Skliris, Heckman kept his fee system hidden from public view, though it escaped the attention of few Mexican workers. As Mr. Benedict recalled, "Heckman doesn't deal with the offices of the railroad, but with some of the division superintendents around Kansas City. He gives something to three or four who know about the arrangement."[74] Here indeed was a figure who had streamlined his power to hire and fire workers and who deserved, perhaps better than any labor agent for Mexican workers in 1928, the name "padrone."

Conclusion

In 1919 labor economist Sumner Schlicter of the University of Wisconsin published a study titled *The Turnover of Factory Labor*, which outlined his suggestions for how corporations should hire and fire their unskilled employees. Applying the principles of scientific management to corporate hiring practices, Schlicter advocated the creation of "central employment departments" and personnel managers in every major corporation in the land. The traditional manner of hiring unskilled workers, Schlicter asserted, vested far too much power in the hands of the foreman. "Hiring by foremen," Schlicter wrote, "results in a lack of coordination. One department may be dropping help while another is hiring the same kind of help." In addition to being inefficient, hiring through foremen diluted the moral character and quality of the work force: "There is no assurance that the foreman is a good judge of men. Selection should be left to the specialist." The specialist that Schlicter had in mind was an employment manager, a man who, in addition to understanding the particular employment needs of a given company, possessed "keen insight into human nature and an exceptional ability to handle men." Schlicter grounded many of his arguments on an article by sociologist Richard Feiss, entitled "Personal Relationship as a Basis of Scientific Management," a piece that underscored Schlicter's faith in the efficiency of personalized, even familylike, relations between employees and their employment manager.[75]

Several corporations had already taken some of Schlicter's insights to heart during the recent world war, as personnel managers, employment managers, and labor superintendents proliferated in corporate bureaucracies across the country. Foremen never again would exercise the kind of unchallenged authority over the hiring of unskilled workers as they had formerly enjoyed before World War I.[76] Many of the crucial bases of padrone power vanished with this erosion of the foreman's authority. Likewise, many of the services that padrones on occasion

---

74 Mr. Benedict interview with Paul Taylor, 1928, doc. no. 140-340, Paul S. Taylor Papers.

75 Sumner Schlicter, *The Turnover of Factory Labor* (New York, 1919), 281–284, 309. See Richard A. Feiss, "Personal Relationship as a Basis for Scientific Management," *Bulletin of the Society to Promote the Science of Management* 1 (1914): 6.

76 For a discussion of all three corporate positions, see Montgomery, *Fall of the House of Labor*, 236–244. For a less historical overview of the personnel manager's function in the corporation, see Tony J. Watson, *The Personnel Managers: A Study in the Sociology of Work and Employment* (Boston, 1977); Jacoby, *Employing Bureaucracy*, 47–49.

provided immigrant workers – job security, legal counsel, even "fatherly" protection – had become bureaucratized within corporate employment departments.

But Schlicter's enthusiasm for the "modern" employment manager's noble and moral attributes obscured many of the continuities in corporate hiring practices between 1900 and 1930. In the 1920s, corporations experienced much less pressure to institute Schlicter's reforms, in part because labor turnover dropped considerably and steadily during the decade.[77] Moreover, even corporations that did create new positions to manage employment issues did not see any reduction in the degree of padronelike "abuses" within their companies. Labor superintendent Heckman's fee system represented only the most egregious example of a method of labor recruitment and hiring that, as Paul Taylor's interviews suggest, was still commonplace in American corporations during the late 1920s.[78]

Perhaps more important, Schlicter's progressive sentiments obscured the role of the padrone himself in shaping the evolution of corporate hiring practices. Although Antonio Cordasco's aspiration to become "king of the laborers" seemed at first to be antithetical to Schlicter's modern system of labor management, his migration system was the most efficient and best organized method for acquiring and managing unskilled labor that the CPR had yet adopted. Skliris's job fee and commissary system in Bingham Canyon likewise represented a significant departure for the Utah Copper Company. Both men's innovations and vast organization helped transform the nature of labor recruitment and labor management at both the CPR and the Kennecott Corporation well after Cordasco and Skliris had resigned. For both corporations, Cordasco and Skliris marked an important moment in the centralization and transformation of each corporation's hiring practices. What they accomplished as padrones was almost precisely what Schlicter himself called for in the creation of a centralized corporate labor department that also personalized social relations between employees and the company.

Indeed, what the careers of Cordasco, Skliris, and Gonzalez underscore more directly is how fundamentally modern padrones were. Each of their careers was, in sharply different ways, bound up with the cultural and economic modernization of the corporation in North America. Several factors distinguished each padrone's relationship to the corporation: his formal or informal status within the corporation's hiring bureaucracy, the role of foremen within the company and each padrone's migration system, and the degree of entrepreneurial independence that each padrone possessed within the corporation. Corporate hiring policies, or lack

---

[77] Jacoby, *Employing Bureaucracy*, 173–174.

[78] Locating the precise difference between Anglo labor agents and padrones in Paul Taylor's interviews is a difficult task. The manager of the Gunn Supply Company of Ogden, Utah, for example, stated that the purpose of his business, founded in 1911, had been "to end the gang or padrone system of labor" among Utah's Greek and Japanese laborers. But the same manager neglected to explain what distinguished his labor-contracting business, which assessed workers two dollars to get a job, from the older padrone system. See Manager of the Gunn Supply Company interview by Paul Taylor, 1928, doc. no. 51-851, BANC-MSS-74/187c, Paul S. Taylor Papers.

thereof, were crucial in determining the parameters of each padrone's migration business. If George Burns was instrumental in organizing Cordasco's success by granting him commissary responsibilities and helping him acquire steamship agencies, managers of the Southern Pacific were equally instrumental in minimizing opportunities for Gonzalez by organizing their own labor agency and weakening the need for immigrant middlemen.

But corporate labor policy did not create padronism, for padrones directly and indirectly manipulated the opportunities that existed within the corporation. Skliris was perhaps the most entrepreneurial and effective in commodifying his control over the hiring and firing of unskilled workers and in directly reshaping corporate hiring practices at the Utah Copper Company. Although excluded from official corporate channels, Gonzalez likewise reshaped the evolution of corporate hiring practices in El Paso by maintaining an entrepreneurial business for three decades, one that placed at least partial limits on any commissary company's control over El Paso's labor-contracting business. The competition offered by Gonzalez and the Zarate-Avina Labor Agency in both prosperous and lean times placed restrictions on the fees that corporations could exact from their employees. Job fees in El Paso – at roughly one dollar per man – remained much lower than in either Montreal or Utah throughout the early twentieth century. Equally important, Gonzalez and Zarate-Avina pioneered new techniques for recruiting labor and using local legal devices to their advantage, lessons that the Anglo commissaries studied closely (see Chapter 3). The relationships between Gonzalez, Cordasco, Skliris, and their respective corporations were not so much hostile or antithetical as symbiotic; as both entrepreneurs and corporate employees, padrones shaped the corporation's evolution even as they were profoundly affected by particular corporate hiring practices.

If tourists to Bingham Canyon in 1912 had properly understood the modernity of the padrone system that had brought immigrant men with strong arms and backs to the open pit, they might also have understood why the North American West, site of allegedly primitive frontier values, could also host some of the most modern corporations on the planet. What made corporations in the North American West at least potentially so modern were not the steam shovels tearing down whole mountains or the numbers or kinds of new railroad lines they built, but their remarkable dexterity in mobilizing men thousands of miles across space for particular corporate purposes. Transatlantic steamship companies in the nineteenth century had long been quickening the time it took for passengers to cross the ocean, contributing to that era's "annihilation of space." But it was corporations in the North American West and the padrones who did their bidding that best learned to organize immigrant labor markets at sites of labor demand, creating truly disposable work forces that could be mobilized from remote corners of the earth to equally remote industrial islands at the drop of a hat, whether to lay railroad ties, harvest beets, break a strike, or load low-grade copper ore onto trains. The nature of that modernity scared many observers, some of whom chose not to see it or instead vilified the men called padrones. The challenge for companies who relied on padrones was to persuade those watching that their modernity was also truly progressive. In that campaign, more about the rhetoric of free labor and the legal system than about geographies of labor and space, they possessed no more sophisticated partner than the padrone himself, who not only helped invent truly transnational labor markets but also garbed himself in the language of law, free labor, and progress – the subject of the next chapter.

CHAPTER THREE

Defenders of Contract

On October 7, 1902, James Hughes, inspector for the U.S. Bureau of Immigration, embarked on an undercover mission to document violations of the nation's contract labor law at the hands of an immigrant padrone from Croatia named Joseph Pajnic. Hughes's investigation took him from Philadelphia to Memphis, Tennessee, then on to the swamp forests of Belzomi, Mississippi. Initially, his work seemed promising, for in Memphis he discovered many more contract laborers than anticipated, fully "600 Croatians, most of whom are stave and railroad tie cutters, in the St. Nicholas Hotel and five or six boarding houses in Poplar Street." But when Hughes followed a band of thirteen Croatians from Memphis to Mississippi, his investigation began to stumble. Hoping to find the ringleader of the Croatian migration system in Belzomi, Hughes instead discovered that Pajnic had "left the morning of our arrival," having been tipped off by a compatriot in Memphis. His cover blown, Hughes subsequently found that "it was impossible to get any sworn statements" from Croatian workers, most of whom were reluctant to talk to him. Hughes soon concluded that no legal proceedings could be brought against the Croatian labor agent and returned to Philadelphia, dispirited, but determined to catch the very next padrone who attempted to import contract laborers through the port of Philadelphia.[1]

At first glance, the encounter between Hughes and the Croatian workers appears to be a gigantic and tragic miscommunication. If only Hughes had explained himself and his noble purpose to the stave cutters more patiently – and perhaps in Croatian – then perhaps they would have given him more of their time and understood he was trying to help them. And if only the stave cutters had not been so afraid of Pajnic, they might have seen this interaction for what it was: a chance to liberate themselves from the immoral and un-American clutches of their padrone in the swamp forests of Mississippi. The problem with this romantic reading of events, one that typified middle-class reaction to a range of encounters

---

[1] James Hughes to the Honorable John Rodgers, October 16, 1902, "Thirteen Croatians" file, Records of the Office of the Commissioner of Immigration, Port of Philadelphia, RG 85, National Archives, Philadelphia.

between reformers and immigrants during the Progressive Era, is that it distorts the reasons why these transient men probably refused Hughes's offer of help. Freedom in this case came with a stiff price tag: immediate deportation from the country as contract laborers or, at best, work at rock-bottom wages in a factory near Philadelphia, far from family or friends in Mississippi.[2] Like Christian women who sought to "rescue" immigrant prostitutes in the late nineteenth and early twentieth centuries, special agent Hughes overlooked the coercive and culturally specific starting points of the emancipation he proffered – accepting his authority and being sundered from one's community, however poor and overworked it may have been.[3]

A tragic reading of the interaction between Hughes and Croatian stave cutters likewise obscures the complex ways in which both immigration officials and immigrant padrones benefited from their furtive interactions with one another. For U.S. immigration officials, padrones clarified the often murky distinctions between free and unfree labor, valorizing the heroic work of men like Hughes as well as the Bureau of Immigration's requests for more congressional aid. Although Hughes failed to catch Pajnic, he succeeded in defending the principles of free labor and voluntary contract so crucial to the nation's political and legal systems.[4] But padrones also gained something from the chase: prestige among both their compatriots and company managers for having eluded the immigration agent and the long reach of the U.S. legal system.

The symbiotic interactions between padrones and border agents extended beyond the interior of the United States and its geographic frontiers in North America. While special agent Hughes carried his mandates into the swamp forests of Mississippi, other U.S. border agents carried them to Canada, Mexico, and much of Europe as well. Likewise, padrones eluded the reach of U.S. border officials not simply in the murky backwaters of the U.S. South, a region whose productive relations had long confounded easy distinctions between free and unfree labor, but wherever U.S. border agents traveled abroad. The meanings of free labor and voluntary contract, cornerstones of an allegedly exceptional American political system, were frequently defended and forged beyond the nation's immediate boundaries. Moreover, the U.S. contract labor law was only part of a larger international effort among nation-states in Europe, the Americas, and Asia to regulate the movement of migrants under contract after 1900. Padrones in North America, who gained power from this international geography, were only one of several entrepreneurs who stimulated the creation of national boundaries by

---

[2] Immigrants without family in the United States and with less than ten dollars were typically detained by U.S. immigration authorities, and either deported as paupers likely to become a public charge or "offered" work in the port city. See Records of the Special Board of Inquiry, 1894–1907, Port of Philadelphia, reels 1–16, RG 85 National Archives, Washington, D.C.

[3] See Peggy Pascoe, *Relations of Rescue: The Search for Female Moral Authority in the American West, 1874–1939* (New York, 1990).

[4] On the importance of notions of voluntary contract, see Tomlins, *Law, Labor, and Ideology*, 289–290.

remaining beyond the law's reach. Neither padrones nor the heroic efforts of men like special agent Hughes were exceptional to the United States.[5]

Contracts and Coercion

Although many residents of North America considered the United States a nation of unparalleled civil and legal freedoms, a history of its legislative attempts to control padronism suggests how unstable notions of voluntary contract and free labor remained after 1865. Between 1874 and 1925 the U.S. Congress expended considerable effort to eliminate the padrone system from North America. In 1874 Congress passed a resolution designed to "prevent the practice of enslaving, buying, selling, or using Italian children." Known informally as the padrone statute, the law responded to lurid revelations in the penny press and in the fiction of Horatio Alger that numerous Fagin-like padrones were flourishing in New York and Philadelphia. The law stipulated that anyone who held "any other person in involuntary confinement or to any involuntary service" should be "deemed guilty of a felony and pay a fine not exceeding $5,000.00." The padrone statute naturalized differences between free and unfree labor relations by suggesting that all Italian boys were being held against their will.[6] The padrone had corrupted the freedom of Italian boys not with a coercive contract but by preventing them, under threat of beatings and torture, from quitting.

But the law had little impact on actual padrones, as few Italian "boys" proved willing to turn in their guardians. Consequently, the law's failure only encouraged additional legislation. In 1885 Congress passed the Foran Act, designed to "prohibit the importation and migration of foreigners and aliens under contract or agreement to perform labor in the United States."[7] Although the Foran Act sought

5   Most examinations of U.S. immigration policy consider the political debates surrounding the passage of particular laws rather than how those laws were enforced on different U.S. borders. See Mink, *Old Labor and New Immigrants*; Saxton, *The Indispenable Enemy*; Kitty Calavita, *U.S. Immigration Law and the Control of Labor, 1820–1924* (London, 1984). For exceptions, see Lucy Sayler, *Laws Harsh as Tigers: Chinese Immigrants and the Shaping of Modern Immigration Law* (Chapel Hill, 1995), xiii–xv.

6   U.S. Congress, House, *Congressional Record*, 43rd Congress, 1st session, June 1, 1874, 4443.

7   The Foran Act formally overturned the nation's first contract labor law, passed in 1864, which sought to stimulate the importation of skilled workers. The paternalistic purpose of the original contract labor law was manifest in its creation of the United States Emigration Office, an organization whose primary duty was "to make contracts with the different railroads and transportation companies, to be furnished to such immigrants ... and to protect such immigrants from imposition and fraud." That such contracts could themselves become an "imposition" upon free laborers seems not to have bothered framers of the law. On the original contract labor law, see U.S. Congress, House, *Congressional Record*, 38th Congress, 1st session, Chapter 246, July 4, 1864; on the Foran Act, see U.S. Congress, Senate, *Congressional Record*, 48th Congress, 2nd session, Chapter 164, February 26, 1885; on the Foran Act's passage, see Charlotte Erickson, *American Industry and the European Immigrant, 1860–1885* (Cambridge, Mass., 1957), 19–20; Mink, *Old Labor and New Immigrants*, 98; and Catherine Collomp, "Unions, Civics, and National Identity: Organized Labor's Reaction to Immigration, 1881–1897," in Marianne Debouzy, ed., *In the Shadow of the Statue of Liberty: Immigrants, Workers, and Citizens in the American Republic, 1880–1920* (Urbana, 1992), 232–233.

to protect American workers rather than Italian boys by deporting them from the country, both laws sought to penalize the importer of immigrant workers. Like the padrone law, the Foran Act specified fines of up to a thousand dollars on individuals or companies caught importing laborers under contract. By deporting all workers who had been brought to the nation under contract, the Foran Act sought to combat padronism at its root and address the larger problem of coerced migration.

But if the Foran Act and the 1874 padrone law shared certain goals, the Foran Act nonetheless made no clear distinction between voluntary and involuntary service. Instead, it repudiated an entire class of contracts as violations of the free labor system. Passed with the full support of Terence Powderly and thousands of Knights of Labor (KOL) assemblies across the country, the Foran Act represented one of the KOL's few major legislative successes at the national level. At the heart of the Foran Act was a direct challenge to the notion that all contracts were voluntary and free. The Foran Act not only made the importation of immigrant workers under contract illegal but declared that "all contracts" made between parties to import alien workers for "labor and service" were "utterly void and of no effect" in the United States. Here indeed was language that seemed consistent with the KOL's anticontract republicanism, an ideology that deemed contracts to be inimical to republican freedoms. The Knights of Labor were, as William Forbath has demonstrated, some of the most articulate and vehement critics of the legal doctrine of liberty of contract, declaring it no more than a smokescreen to the harsh reality of "wage slavery."[8]

An examination of how the Foran Act was interpreted after 1885, however, demonstrates that federal judges made every attempt to reconcile its anticontract dimensions with the liberty of contract doctrine.[9] This was accomplished in large measure by reviving distinctions between voluntary and coerced migrations. In 1886, for example, a federal circuit court of appeals judge in Michigan argued that the contract labor law was meant to exclude only "an ignorant and servile class of foreign laborers," but "does not purport to inhibit or discourage the immigration of foreign laborers in general." In making such a distinction, the Michigan judge exonerated voluntary contracts and made servility a function of

---

[8] Forbath, "Ambiguities of Free Labor," 806; U.S. Congress, Senate, *Congressional Record*, 48th Congress, 2nd session, Chapter 164, February 26, 1885, Section 2, 332–333. On the racialized meanings of "wage slavery," see Roediger, *The Wages of Whiteness*. Why Forbath ignored the Foran Act in his study of organized labor is puzzling, but perhaps reflects the pervasive racism that surrounded its debate and passage, sentiments that hardly squared with his celebration of working-class republicanism. See Forbath, *Law and the Shaping of the American Labor Movement*.

[9] The "liberty of contract" doctrine was the liberal constitutional heir of an older notion of republican liberty which guaranteed the free laborer the "right to pursue his own calling," whatever that might be. By the 1880s, however, the courts equated the liberty of contract doctrine more narrowly with the right to alienate one's labor for wages. See Forbath, "The Ambiguities of Free Labor," 769–770; Tomlins, *Labor, Law, and Ideology*, 290. For a good overview of the liberty of contract doctrine in its changing social context of the 1880s, see Eric Foner, *The Story of American Freedom* (New York, 1998), 125–130.

the immigrant's race and class. Contracts were no longer the cause of workers' oppression. Rather, coercion reflected the "ignorant and servile" character of certain immigrants, whose alleged gullibility made them easy prey for padrones and other swindlers.[10]

Subsequent Supreme Court rulings on the Foran Act further codified the racialized and skill-based criteria by which the law was to be administered. In 1895 Justice Peckham of the Sixth Circuit Court of Appeals in Louisiana argued that A. Seeliger, a sugar plantation chemist imported under contract from Germany, should not be deported because the Foran Act was designed primarily to "stay the influx of cheap and unskilled labor." The contract that Seeliger signed was "neither forced, unnatural, or unusual," according to Justice Peckham, but rather a voluntary one in perfect keeping with the nation's legal and political system. Peckham did not elaborate precisely on what made Seeliger's contract voluntary and the contracts of Hungarian laborers involuntary and "unnatural." But Peckham's skill-based distinction became encoded into the immigration legislation of 1903, which stated that "skilled labor may be imported, if labor of like kind . . . can not be found in this country."[11]

These exemptions to the Foran Act proved very difficult for port officials to enact when examining thousands of immigrants daily. What, after all, separated the supposedly "ignorant and servile" contract laborer from the rest of the steerage-class immigrants arriving each day? To Terence Powderly, former KOL leader and U.S. commissioner of immigration between 1898 and 1902, all Hungarian and Slavic immigrants were "servile" contract laborers.[12] Most immigration inspectors possessed less simplistic criteria and attempted to determine whether arriving immigrants possessed a contract for work, "express or implied," in the United States. If the immigrant acknowledged that he or she had procured work before arriving in Philadelphia, they were detained for further questioning by a "special board of inquiry." Evidence for debarment typically depended on an immigrant's admission to having an explicit promise of employment, something few were careless enough to make given the consequences.[13]

For immigrant workers traveling to the United States, the contract labor law presented the first and perhaps most confusing encounter with an American legal system ostensibly devoted to the ideals of free labor and voluntary contract. The immigrants were required to satisfy two contradictory demands. First, they had to

[10] *United States vs. Craig*, Records of the U.S. Supreme Court, 1886, in *Federal Reporter* (Washington, D.C., 1886), 798. The court exonerated even the illegal contract, stating "a careful perusal of the section will demonstrate that the penalty is not attached to the making of the illegal contract, but to assisting, encouraging, or soliciting the migration of the alien to perform labor or service here." See ibid., 799.

[11] *United States vs. Laws*, 163 U.S. 258, 16 Sup. Ct. 998, Records of the U.S. Supreme Court, 1895, in *Federal Reporter* (Washington, D.C., 1895), 263; U.S. Congress, House, *Congressional Record*, 57th Congress, 2nd session, March 3, 1903, Chapter 1012, 1214.

[12] Terence Powderly, *Thirty Years of Labor* (Columbus, Ohio, 1890), 429.

[13] Records of the Special Board of Inquiry, 1894–1896, Port of Philadelphia, reels 1–3, RG 85, National Archives, Washington, D.C.

convince immigration inspectors they would not become a "public charge," a result of immigration laws enacted by Congress in 1875 and 1882 that among others excluded criminals and paupers.[14] Immigrants who appeared indigent and had little "show money" were either returned to their home country at steamship company expense or compelled to accept wage work in the immediate vicinity, usually as day laborers in municipal construction projects. Yet immigrants also had to persuade the same officials that no job was waiting for them when they reached their final destination in the United States. One government investigator summarized this "curious contradiction" in 1901: "If the immigrant cannot support himself he is sent back as liable to become a public charge. If he has provided beforehand for self-support he is sent back as liable to displace American workmen."[15]

One of the frustrating consequences for U.S. immigration officials of this "curious contradiction" was that the Foran Act excluded primarily those immigrants it was designed to protect, namely individuals whose families had managed to secure work for them in America. Those debarred hardly seemed to fit the racialized criteria of being an "ignorant and servile class" of workers. On the contrary, it was those most trusting of immigration inspectors and their presumed passion for freedom who revealed their true arrangements for work in the United States. For most immigrants, the vast majority of whom had some kind of job awaiting them, the first lesson they learned in accommodating the American legal system was deception. For some, this lesson came not a moment too soon. When Russian immigrant Nikifor Stasewicz was questioned by the special board of inquiry of Philadelphia in 1907, he initially stated that his brother had promised him a job, having "spoken to the boss" in advance of his arrival. But after immigration inspectors voted to debar him, Stasewicz spoke with some compatriots who informed him of the contract labor law's "requirements." Stasewicz immediately demanded an appeal and changed his testimony, stating, correctly this time, "that he had no work in sight, and had not been promised work."[16] Stasewicz was subsequently admitted with the rest of his Russian compatriots who proceeded to their destination in Philadelphia and soon began work.

The U.S. Bureau of Immigration sought to redress the Foran Act's manifold

---

[14] For the language of the 1882 Immigration Act, see Edith Abbott, ed., *Immigration: Select Documents and Case Records* (Chicago, 1924), 186. See also Sayler, *Laws as Harsh as Tigers*, 5–15.

[15] U.S. Congress, House, *Reports of the U.S. Industrial Commission*, 56th Congress, 1901, vol. 15, 647–648.

[16] On job arrangements among new arrivals, see Bodnar, *The Transplanted*, 57–61; Records of the Special Board of Inquiry, February 20, 1907, Port of Philadelphia, reel 14, RG 85, National Archives, Washington, D.C. In 1909, U.S. immigration inspector John Gruenberg described similar situations throughout the nation in which "large numbers of aliens" who had been detained by special boards of inquiry, changed their testimony "when they realized their testimony would lead to their deportation." John Gruenberg to Daniel Keefe, May 21, 1909, 2, file 52066/3, box 79, Records of the Bureau of Immigration, Immigration Subject Correspondence, RG 85.

failings by strengthening its ability to deport any immigrant suspected of being a contract laborer.[17] But restricting the rights of immigrant aliens did not clarify the meaning of "voluntary" immigration, nor did it secure the moral purpose of the Foran Act. For U.S. immigration officials, this work was accomplished by their discovery of the immigrant padrone, a figure whose moral depravity justified their attempts to police the boundaries of the nation's free labor legal system. The growing importance of the padrone to immigration officials was manifest in government investigations of the Foran Act and the nation's larger immigration "problem." In 1888 the Ford Committee discovered a host of violations of the Foran Act. Steamship agents, for example, rarely screened their passengers for contract laborers, and labor agents routinely imported hundreds of workers at a time into North American cities. Padrones, however, were scarcely mentioned in the seven-hundred page committee report. When the word did appear, it produced confusion between the commissioners and their witnesses. After describing how his compatriots were systematically swindled by Italian labor contractors, A. Monaco, Italian vice-consul in New York City, was asked by chairman Ford whether such men were sometimes "in your language called padroni?" Monaco replied "No, sir," and asserted the padrone no longer existed in New York.[18]

By 1894, however, the padrone had become the U.S. Bureau of Immigration's most important lever for calling upon Congress to increase appropriations for enforcing the Foran Act. In a letter to the U.S. Senate, immigration commissioner Herman Stump warned that "a large portion of the Italian immigration into the United States have been and are at the present time imported under conditions of servitude." Stump boldly claimed that "the padrone system and similar traffic in human beings is . . . spreading to immigrants from Japan, Syria, Arabia, and other countries, and in order to eradicate the evil active measures should be taken at once."[19] Such measures included the creation of an "immigrant fund" or a head tax on all incoming immigrants, which would finance the immigration service's attempts to catch padrones and protect American workmen from their machinations.

Stump's assertions simplified many of the ambiguities surrounding the contract labor law's problems of enforcement. Although he admitted that "the records of this Bureau do not show to what extent the padrone system prevails in the United States," his call to contain the moral evil helped quiet any congressional opposition to expanding his agency's budget.[20] More important, his portrait of the

---

[17] In *Nishimura Ekiu vs. United States*, the U.S. Supreme Court affirmed the authority of immigration inspectors to exclude immigrant aliens, even if their "rights" to fair legal representation had been violated by the same inspectors. See *Nishimura Ekiu vs. United States*, 142 U.S. 652, Records of the U.S. Supreme Court, 1891, in *Supreme Court Reporter* (Washington, D.C., 1891), 651–664. For a discussion of the Nishimura Ekiu case, see Sayler, *Laws Harsh as Tigers*, 51–55, 97.

[18] Testimony of A. Monaco, *The Ford Committee on Contract Labor Violations*, U.S. Congress, House, 50th Congress, 2nd session, 1888, 60; Testimony of Robert Marzo, ibid., 79.

[19] U.S. Congress, Senate, *Congressional Record*, 53rd Congress, 2nd Session, June 20, 1894, Ex. Doc 114, 2.

[20] Ibid., 2–3.

padrone's intrigues against Italian "children" clarified the Foran Act's moral purpose. In so doing, Stump helped transform the Foran Act from a critique of the doctrine of voluntary contract to an instrument of its ideological defense.

If fear of padrones helped sharpen the moral focus of U.S. immigration agents, padrone activities also remained sufficiently clandestine for border officials to claim progress in their campaign against them. In 1894 Stump asserted that the padrone's power was increasing but also that the government had the upper hand in the struggle. Wrote Stump, "after the investigation of the Ford Committee, the padrone changed his manner of doing business. He became ostensibly an Italian banker, and now conducts his affairs secretly through agents or bosses." Once agents had succeeded in driving the padrone underground, the next step was to hire more immigrant inspectors and more rigorous "boards of special inquiry" in every major port in the country. The subsequent failure of such efforts was chronicled three years later by government muckraker John Koren in his bulletin to the labor department, *The Padrone System and Padrone Banks*. By 1897 the padrone system had indeed spread to Syrian immigrants and other groups in America's greatest cities, as Stump had warned. Stated Koren, "So far all efforts made in New York to exterminate the padrone system have failed, so firmly is it rooted." Yet, like Stump, Koren lauded the progress that government officials were making in combating the padrone, asserting in his introduction that "The padrone has become practically extinct through the more stringent enforcement of the contract labor law."[21]

The padrone's cancerlike growth and imminent demise at the hands of U.S. immigration officials persisted as central themes in government studies of immigration well into the twentieth century. Although the Dillingham Commission's investigation into "contract and induced immigration" found that the padrone system had "diminished rapidly" among Italians in 1911 because of strict enforcement of the Foran Act, it also discovered that the system had continued to spread among "new" immigrant groups, flourishing especially among Greeks, Turks, Mexicans, and Bulgarians. By 1912, even that small progress had been reversed as the New York State Bureau of Industries and Immigration discovered that among Italian laborers in upstate New York, a region where it remained "impossible to bring the licensed padrone or the employment agent to task," the padrone was "all powerful."[22]

The padrone's familiar narrative role – his clandestine and phoenixlike power that was continually sundered by U.S. border bureaucrats – suggests one reason the padrone remained a persistent, albeit elusive figure between 1874 and 1925. The padrone summarized a complex mix of middle-class anxieties about a

---

[21] Ibid., 2; Koren, *The Padrone System*, 115, 121. On similar dynamics within bureaucracies, see Murray Edelman, *The Symbolic Uses of Politics* (Urbana, 1964); and Edelman, *Constructing the Political Spectacle* (Chicago, 1988).

[22] U.S. Congress, Senate, *The Dillingham Commission: Immigrants in Industries*, 61st Congress, 2nd session, 1911, vol. 1, 392; New York State, *Second Annual Report of the New York State Bureau of Industries and Immigration* (New York, 1912), 19.

growing immigrant working class, one whose perceived cultural "traditions" seemed both exotic and threatening.[23] These anxieties did not disappear with the progressive march of industrial growth but, on the contrary, grew and flourished with rapid urban and industrial change. By summarizing such displaced concerns, the padrone did not clarify the actual difference between free and unfree labor. Rather, he helped make emerging cultural and economic contradictions within industrial capitalism more compatible to its advocates by reaffirming the perceived cultural distance between allegedly "free" American workers and racially stigmatized "unfree" immigrants. The padrone's continual discovery and demise at the hands of U.S. immigration officials thus redeemed the ambiguities of both the Foran Act and free labor ideology, while legitimating the U.S. legal system's expanding power over both immigrants and native-born citizens.

But what impact, if any, did padrones have on the evolution of immigration bureaucracies and laws outside the geographical borders of the United States? Were the padrone's significance and role unique to the United States, as exceptional still as Turner's frontier? A brief look at Canada's immigration laws suggests that padrones there also played the part of symbiotic villains to heroic and ambitious immigration bureaucrats. In 1897 Canada passed the Alien Labor Act, which, like the Foran Act, made it unlawful for any "person, company, partnership or corporation, in any manner to pre-pay the transportation of, or ... assist or solicit the importation or immigration of any alien or foreigner into Canada under contract or agreement ... to perform labour or service of any kind in Canada."[24] Padrones did not figure prominently in the initial debate and passage of the Alien Labor Act, but became quite conspicuous in its revision and strengthening in 1905, which imposed penalties on labor agents who "misrepresented" the work that immigrants would complete within Canada. The key villain in the debate to strengthen Canada's contract labor law was none other than Antonio Cordasco, whose exploits had been exposed by the Royal Commission's investigation the previous summer.

Cordasco's activities redeemed the tarnished reputation of Canadian government ministers, whose previous Royal Commission in 1902 had given its blessing to the CPR's recruitment of Chinese workers and been extremely unpopular among Canadians, especially residents in the West. In their investigation of Cordasco and other "fraudulent" figures, by contrast, members of the Royal Commission in 1904 condemned the activities of the CPR and its practice of importing immigrant workers, highlighting the deleterious impacts on both the exploited immigrants and Canadian workers whose wages were depressed by "cheap" labor. In so doing, Canadian commissioners met some of the demands of organized labor and partially reclaimed their authority as ostensibly impartial defenders of the

---

[23] On middle-class fears of an urban working class during the Progressive Era, see Paul Boyer, *Urban Masses and Moral Order in America, 1820–1920* (Cambridge, Mass., 1978), and Robert Wiebe, *The Search for Order, 1877–1920* (New York, 1967).

[24] Canadian Parliament, *Revised Statutes of Canada* (Ottawa, 1897), vols. 60–61, chap. 11, 1, cited in Avery, *Reluctant Host*, 35.

public interest, despite the fact that many Canadians continued to believe the CPR rather than the Royal Commission created Canada's immigration policies.[25]

Mexico, by contrast, possessed no laws regulating emigration or immigration until 1929 when it excluded Chinese immigrants, belatedly following in the footsteps of its North American neighbors.[26] Mexico never outlawed the importation of immigrants under contract or attempted to regulate the activity of padrones or passenger agents. The comparative weakness of the Mexican border service reflected the weakness of the Mexican state itself before and during the Mexican Revolution. Municipalities in the provinces of Guanajuato and Jalisco passed local laws attempting to restrict the activity of labor agents in 1908, but such laws could not address what were problems national and transnational in scope. The ideological imperatives around which a border service in Mexico might have crystallized were further complicated by the fact that Mexico was both a host and a sending country for migration. Although Mexican border officials possessed many potential targets to identify as national villains, they had little clarity over whether entrepreneurs of migration were polluting the nation or helping construct it.

Lawmakers in European countries experiencing heavy out-migration, by contrast, justified expanding their bureaucratic authority by fastening upon the most visible entrepreneur of migration in their midst, the steamship company agent. These men posed a different threat from padrones to nationalist fictions, conjuring up images of parasitism rather than internal cancers. Yet, like padrones, they functioned to clarify the cultural boundaries of citizenship and national identity. Perhaps the most notorious steamship agent in Europe in the early twentieth century was Frank Missler, a man who single-handedly inspired the nation of Bulgaria to pass an emigration law that created a border bureaucracy and a legal mechanism for regulating the movement of citizens across its new borders.[27]

Similar emigration laws had already been passed in Italy, which faced a dramatic exodus of its population in the 1890s. In 1897, Italian lawmakers forbade the emigration of its subjects under contract, penalizing the villainous passenger agent with civil and criminal penalties for abetting this, and creating a growing bureaucracy of immigration officials stationed throughout Italy's major ports. Greek lawmakers, in turn, passed laws to restrict the activities of passenger agents and described them in moralistic terms as a "national scourge." A proposed emigration bill in 1913 not only outlawed the emigration of Greek subjects under contract but sought to make passenger agents patriots, stipulating that every licensed

[25] Avery, *Reluctant Host*, 37.
[26] Evelyn Hu-DeHart, "Racism and Anti-Chinese Persecution in Sonora, Mexico, 1876–1932," *Amerasia* 9:2 (1982): 1–27; José Jorge Gomez-Izquierdo, *El movimiento antichino en Mexico, 1871–1934: Problemas del racismo y del nacionalismo durante la Revolucion Mexicana* (Mexico City, 1991); and Leo M. Jacques, "The Anti-Chinese Legislative and Press Campaign in Sonora, Mexico, 1916–1921," *Immigrants and Minorities* 5:2 (July 1986): 167–180.
[27] "The Emigration Law of Bulgaria," 13th National Assembly of Bulgaria, 5th Session, January 6, 1908, Exhibit 23, in John Gruenberg to Honorable Daniel J. Keefe, Commissioner General of Immigration, December 22, 1908, file 52066A, box 79, Records of the Bureau of Immigration, Immigration Subject Correspondence, RG 85.

agent donate annually seventy transatlantic tickets to the Greek Ministry of the Interior for "the repatriation of needy Greek citizens."[28] These expansions in the state's regulatory powers shared a common purpose and a single enemy: preserving the nation's perceived vitality against the activities of corrupt foreign-born passenger agents.

As in the United States, European legal efforts did not put passenger agents out of business but instead increased the agents' expertise in evading legal barriers, thereby inviting further expansions of state power in regulating emigration. Just how far those expansions might go was manifest in central Europe, where, according to U.S. immigration inspector Marcus Braun in 1905, "the Hungarian government created a monopoly for emigration." Sent to Europe to "inquire into the matter of importing contract labor to the United States to work on the railroads, in the mines, and upon large public works," Braun discovered no padrones but an efficient state-run employment bureau. Rather than legislating the foreign passenger agent out of business, Hungarian government agents had instead taken over the business of prominent steamship agents like Frank Missler. The contours of their monopoly were indeed vast and impressive. According to Braun, hundreds of sub-agents, many of them poorly compensated civil-service workers, scoured the countryside of Hungary "with a drum from street to street" spreading fabulous tales of wealth in the United States and Canada. For every emigrant that subagents secured for travel on the state-owned Cunard steamship line, they received a small commission. The Hungarian state used all of the powers at its disposal to make money from the commerce of migration. Citizens applying for a passport were immediately visited by representatives of the state-run "central ticket office," while "every railroad conductor," according to Braun, was "under the instruction to maintain a careful watch that no person should get beyond the Hungarian border without first securing tickets from the 'monopoly.'"[29]

Such state-run monopolies created a number of ironic transformations in which the moralistic roles of heroic border agent and the villainous foreign-born passenger agent were reversed. According to Braun, about a third of all emigrants from Hungary escaped the central ticket office by relying on the clever instructions of "agents from Germany," principally men working for Frank Missler. The parasitic "blood-suckers" and "usurers" that Hungarian emigrants condemned were not Missler and his men, but subagents for Hungary's central ticket office and the state-run monopoly.

Had Braun contemplated these ironic reversals, he might have been better

---

28 Robin Foerster, *The Italian Emigration of our Times* (Cambridge, Mass., 1919). Jonathan Schulman to the Secretary of State, June 7, 1913, American Legation, Athens, Records of the U.S. Department of State, Central Files, file 868.561 1/8, RG 59, National Archives, Washington, D.C.; "Law on Emigration and Travel," translated from Greek, Law 2475, Article 17, July 24, 1920, ibid.

29 Braun to Sargent, June 3, 1905, file 52011/B, box 78, folder 1, Records of the Bureau of Immigration, Immigration Subject Correspondence, RG 85; Braun to Sargent, June 13, 1905, 13, ibid.

prepared for the scandal that subsequently erupted around him and his European discoveries. No sooner had Braun begun to send his reports to the U.S. commissioner general of immigration, Frank Sargent, in 1905, than Hungarian government officials launched a concerted campaign to blacken Braun's reputation. Claiming that Braun, who was himself a Jewish emigrant from Hungary, had fled an "arrest order for swindling" his compatriots in 1891, Hungarian officials also asserted that Braun had been bribed by the North Atlantic Steamship Company, a competitor of the Cunard Line, and was seeking to exploit Hungarian emigrants. Braun replied that all claims against him were "malicious libels and falsehoods," but the effort to defend himself put him in "ill health as a result of the ordeal." Both sides in this rhetorical battle sought to paint their adversaries as immoral men who had sold out their compatriots. Braun's struggles to maintain the moral high ground were bolstered when he caught Hungarian officials in the act of opening his correspondence to U.S. commissioner Frank Sargent. The incident probably saved Braun his job, as did his documentation of Hungary's monopolistic control over emigration.[30]

The "Marcus Braun affair," as it became known, did not make U.S. border agents rethink their relationship to padrones in North America. But his discoveries did highlight the international context that shaped the implementation of contract labor law and the varied relations that sprang up between border officials and border entrepreneurs. Those relations ranged from symbiotic to competitive, as was evident in the efforts of Hungarian and Italian border agents to outlaw or outcompete passenger agents. Those variations could also exist within a single nation's borders. Although the requirements of the Foran Act did not, in theory, vary according to which geographic border or port of entry one entered, in practice its "curious contradictions" created a wide disparity of arrangements on U.S. borders, with padrone power waxing or waning as a result.

Padrones and Contract Labor Law

At the peak of its power, Antonio Cordasco's migration business successfully circumvented contract labor laws in not one but three countries. Cordasco's most important contact in Europe, former steamship agent Frank Ludwig, initially rose to prominence in 1901 after being indicted and fined for violating Italy's contract labor law. Rather than comply with such rulings, Ludwig instead fled the country and reopened his agency in Chiasso, Switzerland, a town just across the Italian border, which he transformed into the major staging ground for the illegal emigration of Italian workers to both North and South America. There, Ludwig and his agents imparted their wisdom on how to evade immigration laws in the countries of final destination. Well prepared and drilled for the questions that would follow at each border they crossed, Ludwig's workers sailed past U.S. border authorities in New York, where they were met by Cordasco's agent Anthony

---

[30] Braun to Sargent, June 14, 1905, 4, 14, ibid.

Aiello who coached them on how to evade Canada's laws while escorting them to Montreal.[31]

U.S. immigration officers became aware of Ludwig's business operations at the peak of Cordasco's power in 1903 when Marcus Braun first traveled to Europe to document violations of the Foran Act. His investigations took him into many a rough, industrial neighborhood in Europe's major cities, but he was unprepared for what he encountered in Chiasso, Switzerland. "I have the honor," Braun wrote to the Justice Department in 1903, "to report that whatever I saw prior to my arrival at Chiasso was nothing in comparison to what I saw and learned while travelling in Italy and the south of France." Here in Chiasso Braun discovered the belly of the beast he had been pursuing, and in Frank Ludwig he came face-to-face with its personification. At once fascinated and repelled by Ludwig, Braun described him as typical of a special class of men who "laugh at the measures adopted against the transportation of their people." To Braun, Ludwig was morally depraved, not merely because he was himself a fugitive from the law, but because he was skilled at teaching deception, having "laborers instructed so well as not to entertain any fear of deportation."[32]

One reason U.S. immigration officials were concerned about Cordasco and Ludwig was that they had long been suspicious of a "Canadian back door" through which immigrants circumvented U.S. laws. In 1888 New York State Immigration Commissioner Charles Tinkor stated to the Ford Committee that numerous immigrants "rejected at Castle Garden, New York had been landed in Halifax," and subsequently shown up again at Castle Garden to meet incoming relatives. To cut off such evasions, the U.S. Treasury Department reached an agreement with Canada's major transportation companies in 1893 to police jointly the U.S.-Canadian border and enforce U.S. immigration laws. The Canadian Agreement, as it became known, established that U.S. immigration officers would be allowed to board Canadian railroad and steamship vessels and inspect all U.S.-bound passengers. The Canadian transportation companies agreed to supply U.S. officials with manifest lists and to wait to sell railroad tickets to U.S.-bound passengers until after they had been inspected. Canadian companies in turn received important right-of-way clearances across pieces of U.S. territory in both northern New England and parts of North Dakota and Minnesota. The cooperation between U.S. officials and Canadian companies was thought to be vital to securing "some sort of control" over the Canadian border, as one U.S. agent put it, a border that remained

---

[31] *The Braun Report*, Records of the Bureau of Immigration, Immigration Subject Correspondence, RG 85, National Archives, Washington, D.C.; Testimony of Rodolphe Candori, *Royal Commission*, 11; Harney, "Montreal's King of Italian Labour," 64; Knoepfelmacher to Braun, May 31, 1903, *The Braun Report*. Most Italian immigrants traveled with established steamship companies, but occasionally Ludwig chartered his own steamship, known as a "tramp steamer," and thereby reaped a much larger profit from the sale of tickets. See testimony of Antonio Sicari, *Royal Commission*, 36. On "tramp steamers," see also *Ford Committee on Contract Labor Violations*, 13.

[32] Knoepfelmacher to Braun, May 31, 1903, *The Braun Report*; also cited in Harney, "Montreal's King of Italian Labour," 63.

largely open, unguarded, and quite permeable in 1893. The Canadian Agreement was revised and strengthened in 1901 and again in 1903, in each case expanding the cooperation between U.S. officials and Canadian transportation companies.[33] Along the U.S.-Canadian border, the Foran Act was enforced not solely by U.S. immigration officials but also by Canadian transportation companies, including the Canadian Pacific Railway (CPR).

But why would the CPR sign the Canadian Agreement of 1901, pledging to strengthen its enforcement of the U.S. Foran Act, and simultaneously hire Cordasco, who routinely violated contract labor laws in several countries? One reason may have been that Cordasco helped the CPR evade Canada's Alien Labor Act. But unlike many U.S. companies using the padrone's services, the CPR did not really need Cordasco to circumvent Canada's contract labor law, something it did with relative impunity throughout the early twentieth century. Although the CPR was occasionally censured and fined by the Canadian government for having broken the law, the company continued to import workers under contract to break strikes throughout the Canadian West. Despite the passage of laws against contract labor in 1897 and the signing of several "Canadian Agreements," Canadian borders remained largely open and unregulated, preempting the need for the padrone's services among many Canadian corporations.

To understand why the CPR made Cordasco the sole Italian labor agent at the same moment it agreed to enforce the Foran Act, one must consider the international context of U.S. immigration laws and their uneven enforcement. The CPR signed the 1901 Canadian Agreement in response to two legal developments. First, U.S. officials threatened to close completely the U.S.-Canadian border if the CPR did not stop the growing number of Chinese immigrants who came to Canada on CPR steamships and promptly snuck across the border to the United States. A closed border would have disastrous consequences for the CPR, which not only recruited unskilled labor through U.S. ports and American farmers to the Canadian prairies, but possessed track lines cutting across U.S. territory. Second, Canadian lawmakers in 1901 also sought to curtail Chinese immigration to Canada by increasing the head tax on all incoming Chinese men. Consequently, by "voluntarily" restricting the number of Chinese immigrants it imported in the summer of 1901, the CPR secured the favor of both Canadian and U.S. immigration officials simultaneously.

By signing the Canadian Agreements of 1901, the CPR in fact conceded very little to U.S. border authorities, but instead increased its quasi-judicial power as an

---

[33] U.S. Congress, House, *Ford Committee on Contract Labor Violations*, 262; U.S. Congress, House, *Reports of the U.S. Industrial Commission*, 56th Congress, 1901, vol. 15, 446–448; Memorandum regarding the Establishment in Canada of Immigrants by Officials of the United States Immigration Department, February 1, 1905, 2–4, Department of the Interior, Canada, in file 51564/4-4, box 38, Records of the Bureau of Immigration, Immigration Subject Correspondence, RG 85; U.S. Commissioner General of Immigration to Certain Transportation Lines of the Dominion of Canada, November 1, 1901, ibid.; Updated Canadian Agreement, July 15, 1903, file 51564/4-3, ibid.

enforcer of U.S. immigration laws.[34] That expanded role created an ideal opening
for Cordasco for both pragmatic and ideological reasons. By eliminating one of
the CPR's traditional sources of cheap labor, the Canadian Agreement of 1901
expanded the company's need for inexpensive workers. Signing the Canadian
Agreement thus ironically increased the CPR's need for a middleman who could
import workers directly to Canada without jeopardizing the company's relationship with the U.S. Bureau of Immigration. Hiring Cordasco kept CPR lines running during the key summer months with an abundant supply of inexpensive
workers, while simultaneously letting Cordasco assume the risks of any confrontation with U.S. authorities should the new back door be discovered. When
U.S. immigration officials indeed learned of Cordasco's tactics in 1903, they
blamed the archaic padrone system more than CPR officials and corporations for
violating the Canadian Agreements and the Foran Act. Cordasco not only secured
the CPR strikebreakers and inexpensive workers during the summer but also
preserved its cordial relationship with the U.S. Bureau of Immigration and its self-
serving role as an enforcer of U.S. immigration laws.

Leon Skliris faced a strikingly different challenge in evading detection by U.S.
immigration officials and gaining power from the U.S. border. Because Utah-
bound Greeks could indeed be deported as contract laborers, Skliris had to obscure
his ties to immigrant workers in a far more systematic and clandestine manner.
Skliris's agents instructed Greeks coming to Ellis Island to state they had not
prearranged a particular job. In addition, they were to give fictitious addresses
to immigration authorities. Skliris's labor agency was located on the block
between 531 and 539 West Second Street South in the Greek quarter of Salt Lake
City, but his imported workers listed 531, 533, 535, 537, and 539 West Second
Street South as their final destinations. They also gave a variety of responses to the
question of which family relation or acquaintance was living at their final destination in Salt Lake City. Their responses in March 1912 indicated that twenty-three
different cousins and sixteen brothers, all from separate families, lived between
531 and 539 West Second Street South. Many of these imported men may indeed
have had family relations waiting for them in Utah, but none of them lived at
Skliris's labor agency.[35]

Throughout Skliris's rise to power, U.S. immigration inspectors were aware
of this form of evading the contract labor law. In 1904 New York's commissioner
of immigration at Ellis Island, William Williams, tracked down the addresses of
105 New York–bound immigrants on the steamship *Pannonia* and discovered that
forty-six men "gave faulty addresses, some of them relating to places which were
empty lots." Williams suggested that immigration inspectors impose a ten-dollar
fine on anyone giving such "a faulty manifestation." But little came of his idea, nor

34 Frank Sargent, "Digest of and Comment on Report of Immigrant Inspector Marcus Braun,"
    September 20, 1907, 32, file 51630/44F, box 44, ibid.
35 Steamship Manifest Lists, March 1912, Records of the Department of Immigration and Natu-
    ralization, RG 85.

did inspectors catch on to Skliris's system over the ensuing decade. The reasons for this were largely logistical; the time required to track down faulty addresses was daunting, especially when immigrants had to wait at government expense at Ellis Island during the investigation. The problem became especially difficult to research when the final destinations immigrants listed were not in New York but ranged across the continent. The U.S. Bureau of Immigration continued to study the problem of fictitious addresses and commissioned Marcus Braun to investigate the situation in the summer of 1909. But Braun's efforts only highlighted the extent of the problem. Like Williams, he proffered no solution for detecting fictitious addresses in a feasible and thorough manner.[36]

The U.S. Bureau of Immigration nonetheless made heroic attempts to track down the most blatant examples of fictitious addresses among Greek immigrants, focusing the bulk of their energy at the port of New York where most entered the continent. Their best investigator in this task was a naturalized Greek immigrant from Turkey named Andre Seraphic, whose research between 1903 and 1910 produced a fifteen-page report for the Dillingham Commission of 1911 entitled "The Greek Padrone System in the United States." In contrast to John Koren's study of the padrone system among adult Italian laborers on the railroad, Seraphic's report focused on the exploitation of Greek boys in shoe-shining establishments. Greek parents were crucial agents in this virtual "slave trade," according to Seraphic, initiating the first link in the "coerced migration" of the boys to America. Seraphic also chronicled the practice of "pseudofathering," whereby Greek boys changed their last name to match their padrone's in order not to be deported or questioned as a suspected contract laborer. As Seraphic demonstrated with several wrenching anecdotes, little in these contracts protected Greek boys from exploitation by their "pseudofathers" in the United States, who made their bootblack "sons" work in unsanitary and oppressive conditions.[37]

By defining the problem of padronism as one involving boys rather than adult men, Seraphic appealed to the sympathies of white middle-class reformers. Just sixteen of the eighty-one Greek bootblacks Seraphic interviewed in New York City in 1907, however, were below the age of eighteen. Indeed, a majority of the "boys" Seraphic interviewed were at least twenty years old, while some were married fathers in their mid-thirties. Such disparities between Seraphic's unpublished research notes and his published report highlight the ideological demands placed on many immigration inspectors. By defining padronism as a child labor problem, Seraphic not only resurrected an older and morally reliable notion of who and what the padrone was, but he highlighted the progress he and others were having in controlling the Greek padrone system. According to Seraphic, fully one-third of all Greek "boys" had been returned to Greece. His efforts had made the law

[36] William Williams to Commissioner General of Immigration, November 17, 1904, file 52600/16, box 127, Records of the Bureau of Immigration, Immigration Subject Correspondence, RG 85; William Williams to Commissioner General of Immigration, September 16, 1909, ibid.

[37] U.S. Congress, Senate, *The Dillingham Commission*, 396, 401.

"instrumental in indicting and convicting quite a number of padrones ... and these convictions were purposely given wide publicity in the Greek press."[38]

But a closer look at Seraphic's unpublished research files once again suggests a far more complicated relationship between Greek padrones and the American legal system. Seraphic never mentioned in his published report the resistance Greek "boys" offered to being liberated by his efforts. In a letter to the commissioner general of immigration, Seraphic candidly described the difficulties he experienced in securing affidavits against Greek padrone William Nicholson in 1903:

Finding it impossible to obtain any truthful statement from the boys in Nicholson's presence, I took a few of them, concerning whom I had positive information that they came to the United States in violation of the Alien Contract Labor Law, with me, to a place where, by close questioning, I was enabled to secure the three enclosed affidavits.[39]

Like inspector James Hughes, Seraphic overlooked the coercive features of his emancipatory "help" – the "close questioning," the isolation away from peers and compatriots – and of the contract labor law itself. For these Greek immigrants, cooperation with Seraphic meant probable deportation and additional punishments from the padrone for having given damaging information to immigration authorities. Convinced of his own and the law's virtue, Seraphic blamed the padrone for the boys' reluctance to cooperate with him, asserting in his published report that "padrones, through intentional misrepresentations to these boys, succeed in convincing them that justice is seldom administered in this country, and that it is purchasable."[40]

But perhaps the greatest testament to the Greek padrone's ability, as Seraphic put it, "to leave no traces that might possibly involve them in any trouble" was the absence in this seven-year investigation of any reference to Leon Skliris. Seraphic briefly mentioned the existence of padronism among "Greek railroad workers in the West," but in contrast to the rest of his study, he provided little detailed information on the western railroad sector. Seraphic certainly possessed numerous opportunities and information leads that might have pointed him toward Skliris's migration empire. In 1904 Frank Sargent, commissioner general of the U.S. Bureau of Immigration, received several unsolicited letters from A. W. Charter, a resident of Salt Lake City, outlining how "one Leonidas Skliris has been encouraging the migration of Greek workers into the state" by "a most inglorious system of padronage."[41] But no follow-up occurred. In the summer of 1912 Greek

[38] A. Seraphic, "List of Shine Establishments Run by Greeks," Spring 1907, file 51520/34D, box 32, Records of the Bureau of Immigration, Immigration Subject Correspondence, RG 85; U.S Congress, Senate, *The Dillingham Commission*, 400.

[39] Seraphic to Sargent, April 29, 1903, "Greek Boys" file, Contract Labor Violations, Port of Philadelphia, RG 85, National Archives, Philadelphia.

[40] U.S. Congress, Senate, *The Dillingham Commission*, 403.

[41] A. W. Charter to F. P. Sargent, November 29, 1904, file 52011/A, box 78, Records of the Bureau of Immigration, Immigration Subject Correspondence, RG 85.

immigrant George Julius, a foreman for the Denver and Rio Grande Railroad, wrote a series of letters to the attorney general of the United States exposing the fact that "a certain Greek has a contract with the Rio Grande and Western Pacific Railroad companies to deduct a dollar a month out of each Greek laborer that obtains a job." Julius's letters were forwarded to U.S. immigration inspector Voler Viles of Salt Lake City in the fall of 1912, but nothing further came of the investigation. Although some U.S. immigration officials had heard of Skliris by 1912, none forwarded his information to Seraphic or made Skliris the subject of a systematic investigation.

Seraphic's failure to discover Skliris is even more striking when one considers how keenly aware he was of regional variations in the Greek padrone system. As Seraphic remarked, "padrones know well that the nearer to a port of entry the destination of a young alien ... the more likely he is to be detained by immigration authorities."[42] Unfortunately, Seraphic also believed the commonly held assumption that padronism was primarily an urban phenomenon concentrated in the largest of America's cities. Consequently, he never traveled farther west than Nebraska in his search for Greek padrones. Equally important, he was most passionately moved by the seeming moral clarity of the exploitation of Greek "boys." Even if they were no younger in fact than western track workers and miners, bootblacks in shoe-shining establishments simply possessed more resonance to Seraphic and his peers in the Bureau of Immigration. If racialized distinctions between servile and honorable immigrants did not clarify the meaning of voluntary contracts and free labor, surely narratives of childhood exploitation did.

Seraphic's ideological predispositions about the locations and cast of Greek padrones may have blinded him to Skliris's padrone system, but the laws he sought to enforce nonetheless played an important role in the evolution of Skliris's migration business. Seraphic's efforts to expose the Greek padrone system discouraged many corporations from directly recruiting Greeks to North America, while simultaneously increasing the demand for someone like Skliris. The local and national publicity about the Greek padrone system in 1911 and 1912 did not so much jeopardize Skliris's career as momentarily legitimate it in the eyes of Utah's corporate managers. Skliris's legal skills in evading immigration authorities were crucial, not incidental, to his success. Here indeed was a man who could seemingly dispense with legal borders and the punishments for violating them at will.

Like Cordasco and Skliris, Roman Gonzalez possessed a talent for circumventing immigration laws. In spite of amendments to the Foran Act in 1907 that explicitly forbade soliciting immigrants with the promise of work "express or implied," Gonzalez routinely sent letters to Mexicans informing them of employment. In one such letter, Gonzalez stated to a Mexican railroad foreman that he should "wait until about the middle of the present month, at which time I will have frequent requests for shipments.... it gives me great pleasure to receive again your

---

[42] U.S. Congress, Senate, *The Dillingham Commission*, 401.

order and that of your friends." Gonzalez also relied on Mexican agents to evade local laws in Mexico designed to prevent Mexicans from leaving their haciendas. In the 1890s local Mexican landowners in Jalisco and Guanajuato banded together to pass municipal laws designed to prevent workers from leaving the region. Such laws had little impact on migration until 1910, when the mayor of the city of Guanajuato, himself a farm owner, took the unusual step of "having peons who had been contracted for work in the U.S. taken off the trains after they had purchased tickets," according to one U.S. immigration inspector. When these efforts failed, the mayor appealed to the governor of the province, who assigned policemen to all railroad stations "to prevent men being taken away by these labor agents to work in the United States."[43] Such contracts were deemed coercive by local Mexican officials, who ironically used them to justify increasing their own power to coerce Mexican migrants and keep them "on the farm."

Yet Gonzalez's agents foiled these efforts by making arrangements with prospective immigrants away from train stations and without formal written contracts that could, as one U.S. immigration inspector put it, "be controlled by the mayor's office." The result, according to U.S. immigration agent Frank Stone, was "that the taking of these men off the trains (in Guanajuato) did not prevent their leaving as they later bought tickets to the nearest station ... and on arriving there purchased through tickets to Juarez." Gonzalez's agents even raided industrial work forces in central Mexico in 1908, recruiting two hundred Mexican workers from "a lumber tract in the vicinity of Zamorra, Michoacan," according to Charles Williams, the American businessman who owned the land.[44]

If Mexico's municipal laws proved no lasting detriment to Gonzalez's migration business, they could in fact be turned to his advantage in evading U.S. immigration laws. In Ciudad Juarez, Gonzalez possessed close ties to a municipal official named Jurado who ran the "Seccion de Emigration" for the city, an office created by the mayor of Juarez where all incoming emigrants registered. According to agent Stone, Jurado took kickbacks from Gonzalez in return for services rendered: instructions to each emigrant on what to tell U.S. immigration authorities and directions to Gonzalez's labor agency once across the bridge in El Paso. Although Stone never produced definitive proof of this relationship, he noted that emigrants crossing El Paso's bridge in the afternoon were more likely to choose Gonzalez's labor agency, a reflection of Jurado's success in "coaching" emigrants on how to cross the border. By contrast, those arriving in the early morning by train "usually came without coaching," according to Stone, and proceeded to a variety of labor agencies in El Paso, highlighting Jurado's power to throw business to Gonzalez. Although Gonzalez denied such a connection, he admitted paying money to municipal officials in Juarez to get twenty of his recruited men out of jail. Such casual admissions suggest that, at the very least, Gonzalez frequently interacted

[43] R. G. Gonzalez to Lino Rodriguez, March 1, 1910, Exhibit 13, *Stone Report*; ibid., 7; George Pulford to Charles Berkshire, July 27, 1912, 2, file 52546/31E, box 126, Records of the Bureau of Immigration, Immigration Subject Correspondence, RG 85.

[44] *Stone Report*, 6, 7, 12.

with Juarez officials to move and recruit men across the border and into his labor agency.[45] The power that both Gonzalez and these Mexican municipal officials possessed grew in direct relation to the enforcement of the U.S. contract labor law.

Gonzalez's ability to enlist the "help" of Mexican officials in circumventing the Foran Act earned him a reputation as being "the most pernicious of any of the violators of our law," according to Stone. Yet much of Gonzalez's early success as a labor agent in El Paso grew out of his expertise as an enforcer of municipal vagrancy laws and his connections to municipal authorities on both sides of the Rio Grande. Anglo-run commissaries had long sought to acquire the expertise of someone like Gonzalez by hiring Mexican runners or *renganchistas* who scoured the Mexican countryside and gave workers instructions on how to cross the border. But other labor agencies were unable to benefit from Gonzalez's connections to municipal officials in Juarez. William Henry of the Holmes Supply Company acknowledged the power these municipal connections imparted to Gonzalez in 1909 when he stated to Stone "the Mexican employment agencies are taking an unfair advantage by not obeying the immigration laws." Henry's comment was self-serving, to be sure, as he sought to discredit his competitors and avoid acknowledging how his own company had long recruited workers directly from Mexico in direct violation of the Foran Act. But like other Anglo-run labor agencies in El Paso, Henry was playing catch-up to Gonzalez, trying to copy his example of using local laws and local officials to violate national immigration laws.[46]

Perhaps the best example of Gonzalez's "unfair advantage" occurred in the spring of 1910 when, in a rare moment, his men, unable to cross the border, were deported back to Juarez as contract laborers. Instead of losing power over these men, however, Gonzalez and his Mexican rivals, Robert Zarate and Isaac Avina, managed to find them industrial and railroad jobs in Mexico. As inspector Stone stated in 1910, "R. G. Gonzalez and Zarate & Avina . . . are lately shipping those Mexicans who come to Juarez and are turned back out to interior points in Mexico. Within the past two weeks as many as 700 were shipped from Juarez."[47] By using legal mechanisms on both sides of the border to exploit workers on both sides of the border, Gonzalez seemed to possess the basis for establishing a convincing choke hold over the migration of his compatriots, both north and south, through El Paso. Like few other padrones in North America, Gonzalez worked both sides of the Foran Act in Mexico and the United States, potentially eliminating any risk should his Mexican clients in fact be deported.

To understand why Gonzalez's legal expertise failed to grant him any kind of monopoly, we need to examine more carefully how U.S immigration officials policed the Mexican border between 1885 and 1930. Although Gonzalez gained power by evading U.S. immigration laws, the Foran Act was never well enforced

[45] Ibid., 35, 37; Statement of Roman G. Gonzalez, April 28, 1910, El Paso, Texas, 15, Exhibit 9, ibid.
[46] Statement of William M. Henry, May 14, 1910, El Paso, Texas, Exhibit 6, ibid.
[47] Ibid., 19.

in El Paso. U.S. border officials certainly tried to do their jobs: fully 52 out of the 175 cases initiated by the federal government under the Foran Act between 1886 and 1890 originated in El Paso. The problem was not in securing convictions, but in keeping the excluded immigrants out of the country once convicted. When immigrants were deported under the Foran Act in New York, they were sent back to Europe at the steamship company's expense. In El Paso, deported workers merely waited a few hours in Ciudad Juarez before crossing over to El Paso under cover of night. Sometimes they even crossed during the day. U.S. inspector Charles Babcock recalled in 1908 that "sometime ago fifteen Mexicans were refused admission on account of being contract laborers." Later in the day, inspector Bryan observed ten of the fifteen "aliens" in downtown El Paso. Immigration inspector Marcus Braun summarized how such evasions occurred in 1909 when he stated Mexican contract laborers reach the United States "by simply wandering or being carried a few miles off our examining station and crossing the border by foot." The root problem was the geography of policing a two-thousand-mile boundary that "is largely imaginary" and enforcing legislation that "has had in mind sea ports." The consequence, according to Marcus Braun, was that their efforts at El Paso were "a joke, a hollow mockery" of efforts elsewhere.[48]

Faced with a demoralizing situation on the U.S.-Mexican border, U.S. immigration officials appointed a new commissioner to El Paso in 1908, Frank Berkshire, a man praised as being "preeminently fitted ... to accomplish a brilliant success of the Herculean task set before him in the complete rehabilitation of the service on the Mexican border." For one year Berkshire studied the nature of the "problem," evaluating the investigations of previous immigration inspectors in El Paso. One of the most credible was compiled by Marcus Braun, who concluded in 1907 that "the greatest help in making the laws effective on the Mexican border would be the procurement of an agreement with the Mexican government." In 1908 immigration inspector Charles Babcock likewise called for "a reciprocal agreement with the adjoining Republic." Had the U.S. Bureau of Immigration taken Babcock's and Braun's advice, the flagrant violations of the Foran Act might have been curtailed and Gonzalez's power to exploit loopholes increased.[49]

[48] Marcus Braun to the Commissioner General of Immigration, February 12, 1907, 14, file 52320/1, box 95, Records of the Bureau of Immigration, Immigration Subject Correspondence, RG 85; Frank Berkshire to the Commissioner General of Immigration, June 30, 1910, *Stone Report*, 4; Marcus Braun to Commissioner General of Immigration, February 12, 1907, 11, file 52320/1, box 95, Records of the Bureau of Immigration, Immigration Subject Correspondence, RG 85; Charles Babcock to the Honorable F. P. Sargent, January 10, 1908, 5, file 51748/11A, box 78, ibid. Just one-third of the U.S. government's cases against alleged contract laborers produced a conviction between 1886 and 1890, while over half were dismissed on account of "insufficient evidence" or because "alleged facts could not be proven." But in El Paso, 40 percent of all cases led to convictions. See U.S. Congress, House, *Congressional Record*, 51st Congress, 1st Session, February 14, 1890, House Ex. Doc. 206.

[49] Charles Babcock to F. P. Sargent, January 11, 1908, 20, file 51748/11B, box 54, Records of the Bureau of Immigration, Immigration Subject Correspondence, RG 85; F. P. Sargent, "Digest and Comment upon Report of Immigrant Inspector Marcus Braun," September 20, 1907, 11, file 51630/44F, box 44, ibid.

Unfortunately for Gonzalez, the Mexican Agreements that Berkshire enacted in 1910, far from strengthening the Foran Act, annulled it. The first provision stated that "the employment and shipping of alien laborers to designated points upon definite orders shall be bona fide." In addition to allowing workers to be imported under contract, the Mexican Agreements sought to eliminate "abuses" within El Paso's labor-contracting business. In practice, this meant severely limiting the power of any independent or Mexican labor agencies. Those agents not an "official" or sole representative of a given railroad company would henceforth be refused permission to recruit workers at the bridge in El Paso. Renganchistas were particularly hard hit by Berkshire's Mexican Agreements. Rather than earning money on a commission basis, which had been their greatest source of revenue, they now had to be paid a salary as an employee of one of the Anglo-run commissary companies. Furthermore, companies could no longer choose their own renganchistas. "Renganchistas ... shall not be employed unless acceptable to immigration authorities.... Such employees are to be promptly dismissed upon receiving notice from the Immigration Service that they are objectionable and they shall not thereafter be employed." The purpose of these rules, according to Berkshire, was to eliminate Mexican entrepreneurs, like Gonzalez, who flourished on the boundaries of the "official" corporate labor agencies in El Paso. Stated Berkshire, "by a rigid adherence to these principles ..., this Service can compel the corporations interested to assume responsibility for the acts of their own agents and employees."[50]

Berkshire's diagnosis of the "problem" on the Mexican border was not merely that immigrants were being imported under contract but that corporations had not streamlined their hiring practices. It was here, in the competition between labor agents – some of them sanctioned by corporations and others not – that abuses developed. According to Berkshire in 1910, "the present arrangement of having four distinct labor agents representing the Santa Fe system has been and is still unsatisfactory to this Service, creating, as it does, a spirit of active competition with its consequent abuses. The elimination of the labor agent as he is known today is imperative."[51] Although Berkshire claimed to desire the complete elimination of all labor agencies, the Mexican Agreements in practice strengthened the power of the Anglo-run commissaries in El Paso at the direct expense of men like Roman Gonzalez. Berkshire would no doubt have been impressed by the monopolistic arrangement between Antonio Cordasco and the CPR. But Gonzalez was not the kind of modern man Berkshire had in mind for becoming the sole representative of any of El Paso's railroads. Indeed, Gonzalez was explicitly excluded from the meetings between Berkshire and "official" labor agencies in El Paso – Holmes Supply, Hanlin Supply, and the L. H. Manning Company – that created and adopted the Mexican Agreements.

---

[50] Charles Berkshire, "Rules to Govern Labor Agents engaged in the employment of Alien Labourers at El Paso, Texas, destined to Railway and Railway Construction Work," file 52546/31D, box 126, ibid.; Charles Berkshire to the Commissioner General of Immigration, November 25, 1911, 2, ibid.

[51] Ibid., 3.

The impact of the Mexican Agreements on Gonzalez's labor contracting business was dramatic and severe. Between July 1909 and July 1910, Gonzalez had been a major factor in the local labor market, exporting about 15 percent of all Mexicans out of El Paso, despite having no official sanction by the railroads. Between July 1910 and July 1911, however, he exported just five hundred workers, less than one-tenth of his previous annual total during a year when migration through El Paso increased. What the Holmes Supply Company and its cohorts had accomplished in El Paso by 1911 was quite similar to what Cordasco had achieved vis-à-vis the Canadian Agreements: the power to regulate, as sole representatives for their railroads, migration over the border. Both the Canadian and Mexican Agreements served to enhance the prestige, power, and control of particular labor agents at the expense of others, creating monopolistic choke holds where previously none had emerged. But the agreements accomplished these transformations in opposite fashions. While the Mexican Agreements flagrantly violated the Foran Act's letter and spirit, the Canadian Agreements nominally strengthened its enforcement.

The consequence of these differences between the Mexican and Canadian Agreements proved devastating to Gonzalez. Had the U.S.-Mexican border been governed by an agreement that sought to slow or restrain the exodus of Mexican workers under contract, Gonzalez might indeed have become "king" of Mexican workers. Instead, he became a kind of competitor to the U.S. Bureau of Immigration itself, which allied itself with his Anglo-American competitors in El Paso. The relationship between padrones and U.S. immigration officials remained symbiotic, then, as long as border officials felt compelled to enforce the Foran Act. When they were unable to do so, or actively competed with padrones to organize the migration of workers, padrone power suffered.

Yet padrones did not gain power only as outlaws – by circumventing the law's requirements – but also as practitioners and even enforcers of immigration law. Had Gonzalez been a party to the Mexican Agreements, his business might indeed have benefited despite their annulling the Foran Act. Gonzalez's failure reflected not only the lack of an effective border in El Paso, but his own lack of control over U.S. border authorities. Gonzalez's connections to the mayor's office in Ciudad Juarez and the Seccion de Emigration were simply not as powerful as those wielded by the Anglo-American commissaries through the U.S. Bureau of Immigration. The Anglo-American commissaries had studied well Gonzalez's technique of using local legal opportunities and turned that insight to their decisive advantage through Frank Berkshire and the U.S. Bureau of Immigration.

The double-edged impact of the U.S. Bureau of Immigration on Gonzalez's career highlights the dilemma padrones confronted in trying to acquire control over the international migrations of their compatriots. They could, as Gonzalez, Cordasco, and Skliris each did, hone techniques for evading the immigration laws of several nations and thereby gain a competitive niche in the international labor market. Or they could more directly attempt to buy or gain influence within border bureaucracies as "legitimate" importers of workers. The opportunities for such legitimacy in North America varied not so much by legal precedence – both Canada and the United States maintained laws that explicitly forbade importing workers under contract – but by how regional borders were enforced and who policed them. Antonio Cordasco and Roman Gonzalez both operated along borders that were difficult for U.S. immigration officials to police. The Canadian Agreements secured Cordasco's position within the CPR, however, while the Mexican Agreements eliminated Gonzalez's control over most Kansas– and Oklahoma–bound Mexican track workers. The meanings and impact of immigration laws were indeterminate, reflecting varied political, cultural, and geographic pressures. The key difference between the two borders was not the law itself, but who enforced it. In Canada a company – the CPR – with particular hiring needs made immigration policy, whereas in El Paso the Foran Act remained controlled by an immigration bureaucrat with a dim view of his southern neighbors.

The uneven nature of North American political borders was apparent not only on land but at its seaports, where a variety of opportunities and liabilities developed for padrones and passenger agents. Frank Missler assiduously studied all of the port cities of the United States for loopholes in the Foran Act's enforcement. One of Missler's fliers, distributed throughout eastern Europe in 1907, stated that "F. Missler has such intimate relations with the officials at the American ports of landing, that each emigrant by this line is sure and guaranteed to land without any difficulties." When U.S. immigration inspector John Gruenberg was sent to Baltimore and Galveston to investigate these claims, he concluded that "the rumor that Missler enjoyed special privileges at those ports ... is based upon the envy of his competitors." Nonetheless, much of his evidence suggested just how skillfully Missler exploited the perception of his power over U.S. immigration authorities. One letter from seven prospective emigrants in Bulgaria asked Missler "Is it true that we would be admitted without hindrance via Baltimore? ... We are afraid to pass via New York, lest we be returned."[52]

Missler gained power not simply by evading immigration authorities but by directly negotiating with them. Although he never enjoyed the explicit approval of the U.S. Bureau of Immigration, he won the official sanction of the Louisiana State Board of Immigration in 1907, a statewide organization created to import immigrants directly to Louisiana's sugar plantations and lumber camps. Missler agreed through his agent Marco Kosulitch in July 1907 to send one thousand Bulgarian immigrants to the port of New Orleans, where they met Charles Schuler, of the state immigration board. Schuler gave Missler his assurances that all the men "would have no trouble at their landing in New Orleans," and further agreed to split a commission with Missler of two dollars per man, a fee charged to immigrants by Louisiana's immigration authorities. Missler never realized large

[52] Michael Dumbalakoff, affidavit, November 7, 1908, Thessaloniki, Greece, 2, Exhibit 16, in John Gruenberg to Daniel Keefe, May 21, 1909, file 52066/3, box 79, ibid.; John Gruenberg to Daniel Keefe, December 22, 1908, 2, file 52066/A, box 79, ibid.; Todor Kostoff to Mr. Jakich Missler, Mr. Director, undated, Exhibit 20, in John Gruenberg to the Honorable Daniel J. Keefe, file 52066/3, box 79, ibid.

profits from his association with the state of Louisiana, largely because word soon spread among immigrants that working conditions there were atrocious. Indeed, the conditions of work among these emigrants in the U.S. South helped fuel the campaign for an emigration law in Bulgaria. Missler's arrangements and the international controversies they ignited highlight the extent to which labor market entrepreneurs gained power not only as outlaws but as agents of the state itself.[53]

For U.S. and Canadian immigration authorities, these "legitimate" aspects of padrone power – the ways padrones allied themselves with municipal, state, and even federal officials and actively used the legal system – were the most difficult to combat and the most threatening. Padrones' remaining beyond the reach of zealous border agents was one thing; padrones' becoming border agents quite another. Law-abiding padrones challenged the most basic premises under which both Canadian and U.S. immigration officials labored: that they were defending exceptionally free legal systems, and that the exotic padrone and his racialized compatriots were incapable of independence and self-government. If padrones could be competitors or even allies in administering the law, what indeed were Canadian and U.S. immigration authorities defending in the forests of Mississippi and British Columbia, the ports of New York and Montreal, or along "imaginary" borders throughout the North American West?

Apostles of Liberty of Contract

For the Canadian investigators of Cordasco's labor-contracting business in the summer of 1904, perhaps the most maddening revelations were not the details of his tribute system, but his self-righteous claims to being a modern and law-abiding entrepreneur. During his direct examination by government authorities, Cordasco boasted that all of his men signed contracts upon arriving in Montreal. Reading a letter to his Italian agent Antonio Paretti, he stated "each man gets a contract in Italian, containing the clear conditions under which they will have to work, in which is specified the length of time, salary, etc. In one word there will be no tricks or schemes." Like a true apostle of the liberty of contract doctrine, Cordasco portrayed his contracts as self-evident proof of the progressive nature of his social relations with immigrant workers. When Canadian government investigators questioned Cordasco about his job fees, he claimed simply "I took what was right" and insisted that immigrant workers came to Montreal only "by their own free will." When government lawyers pressed him on the "donations" that immigrant workers made to him before and after his coronation, Cordasco replied without irony "they forced me to take their money."[54]

---

[53] If the U.S. South was indeed exceptional, it was in relation to eastern European labor markets and emigration bureaucracies, not only the "free" labor arrangements in the U.S. North. See Michael Dumbalakoff, Affidavit, 9, 31, file 52066/3, box 79, ibid.

[54] Antonio Cordasco to Antonio Paretti, March 1, 1904, *Royal Commission*, 80; Testimony of Antonio Cordasco, ibid., 76; Antonio Cordasco to Angelo de Santis, Buffalo, N.Y., February 19, 1904, ibid., 130; Testimony of Antonio Cordasco, ibid., 120.

Cordasco's manipulation of free labor ideology infuriated Judge John Winchester, the chief Canadian commissioner, who attempted to characterize him as an ignorant and primitive man. But such vilifications proved difficult to make. If Cordasco was indeed primitive and ignorant, why was he also sole Italian labor agent for the most modern railroad corporation in Canada? What distinguished his social relations to immigrant workers from any other Canadian employer? By insisting that his tribute system – much of it created with the endorsement and capital of the CPR – was voluntary, Cordasco threatened, perhaps unwittingly, to expose the coercion inherent in many waged social relations. Unable to avoid such unhappy and unsettling contradictions, Judge Winchester was compelled to condemn both Cordasco and the CPR in his final report to Canada's minister of labor.[55]

Although Skliris successfully avoided the public scrutiny that crippled Cordasco's migration business, he likewise used labor contracts to sanction his tribute system. All Greek workers in Utah signed a contract that explicitly "authorized" Skliris to deduct one dollar a month from their pay. Skliris also used the courts to establish his power among Greek labor contractors in the Intermountain West. A series of civil court cases between 1905 and 1911 involving Leon Skliris, Nicholas Stathakos, William Caravelis, and Leon's brother, Stavros, not only sorted out some of the complicated debts between these Greek labor contractors but also clarified the nature and boundaries of their business relations. In *Walker Brothers vs. William Caravelis et al.*, Caravelis made it clear that although he and Skliris disagreed over who controlled the shared profits of their labor contracting business, they were no longer in a state of antagonism. Stated Caravelis, "I have known Leon Skliris all my life. I knew him in the old country.... I am a labor contractor; Mr. Skliris is a labor contractor. Our business does not now interfere." Sensing Skliris's superior legal expertise perhaps, Caravelis glossed over continuing antagonisms between the two men. In the coming months, however, both men sued each other and Skliris emerged with the upper hand over his former mentor, solidifying his power as the preeminent Greek padrone in the region.[56]

If Skliris's success in the U.S. courthouse gave him legitimacy in the eyes of corporate managers, it also fed his reputation as a ruthless autocrat among many of his compatriots. Nicknamed the "czar of the Greeks," Skliris was to many Greek workers a law unto himself.[57] His track record using the U.S. legal system

---

[55] Statement of the Honorable Ino Winchester, ibid., xxxviii–xxxix.

[56] Testimony of William Caravelis, *Walker Brothers vs. William Caravelis*, April 18, 1908, Case 1938, Records of the Supreme Court of Utah; *William Caravelis vs. Leonidas G. Skliris*, June 12, 1906, Case 8715, Records of the 3rd District Civil Court, Salt Lake County; *William Caravelis vs. Leon G. Skliris*, June 30, 1908, Case 10394, Records of the 3rd District Civil Court, Salt Lake County; see also *Steve G. Skliris vs. Leon G. Skliris*, August 11, 1906, Case 8637, Records of the 3rd District Civil Court, Salt Lake County.

[57] Theodore Saloutos captured the authoritarian nature of padrone power when he wrote that "the decision of the padrone often was law among the immigrants." See Theodore Saloutos, *The Greeks in the United States* (Cambridge, Mass., 1964), 48.

was indeed stunning. Skliris never lost a court case between 1904 and 1914 and frequently used the courts to reverse any financial setbacks that came his way. His most ingenious triumph occurred in 1908 when he sued the Giles American Mercantile Agency for having wrongfully garnished $198.36 out of his salary as a labor agent for the United States Mining Company in Bingham Canyon. According to his complaint, the Giles American Mercantile Company had confused him with a man named Louis Skliris, whom Leonidas claimed he had never seen or met. He conceded that his imposter, Louis, had indeed purchased $198.36 worth of services at St. Marks Hospital in 1905 in the interest of six injured Greek workers, who needed "certain medical attention, nursing, board, care and keeping." But Leonidas asserted that "his name is not Louis Skliris and that he is not and never has been known by said name." Circuit judge C. W. Morse was persuaded by Leonidas's case and concluded that "said Louis Skliris is not the same person as Leonidas G. Skliris," rewarding Leonidas his full judgment plus costs.[58]

In point of fact, Louis and Leonidas were the same person. To his closest friends he was Louis, but to a larger American public, he was Leonidas G. Skliris. To certain of his business associates, by contrast, Skliris went by the first name of Gust, the name he also put down on his petition to become a naturalized American citizen in 1905.[59] In the court case of *Walker Brothers vs. Caravelis & Company* in 1906, Caravelis explained why Skliris used his father's name instead of his own in the partnership they had briefly formed: "Mr. Skliris asked me – told me – he says: 'On account of having some outstanding obligations, I do not like to put my name in the articles of incorporation.' He asked me to let him use some other name, his father's name. I told him it was alright with me; I would have no objection."[60] Caravelis offered a rare but revealing look into the way Skliris manipulated both the legal system and his compatriots by creating fictional selves that could represent him when expedient and likewise disappear when necessary. If Skliris exploited the indeterminacy of the Foran Act and its notions of free labor and voluntary contract to his advantage, he also quite literally made himself an indeterminate legal subject, capable of transforming himself at the drop of a hat from Louis to Leon to Gust.

Like Skliris, Roman Gonzalez excelled in using the U.S. legal system as an expedient tool for his business interests. As a policeman, Gonzalez not only used his discretionary power over vagrancy laws to set up his labor agency, but also to enforce credit relations among those who failed to pay their debts or rent. Yet these "legal" machinations posed little ideological challenge to the authority of border officials or municipal leaders in El Paso. To the contrary, these same local immigration and municipal officials sanctioned such practices for controlling

[58] See *Leonidas G. Skliris vs. Giles American Mercantile Agency, a Corporation, C. Frank Emery, Sheriff of Salt Lake County,* April 5, 1909, Case 8080, Records of the 3rd District Civil Court, Salt Lake County.

[59] Records of Gust Skliris, August 11, 1905, Naturalization Files, Salt Lake County, Utah State Archives, Salt Lake City, Utah.

[60] Testimony of William Caravelis, *Walker Brothers vs. William Caravelis*, Records of the 3rd District Civil Court, Salt Lake County.

migrant Mexicans. Indeed, vagrancy laws were an important part of progressive reform in El Paso, and few municipal reformers objected to Gonzalez's use of them before 1909.

But Gonzalez's connections to municipal officials in Ciudad Juarez were another matter, one that raised troubling questions about the progressive nature of the U.S. legal system. What, after all, distinguished Gonzalez's legal coercions in El Paso from those in Ciudad Juarez? The comparison between the U.S. and Mexican legal systems was itself unsettling to many municipal officials and immigration inspectors in El Paso. Gonzalez's connections to the Seccion de Emigration represented a logical extension of his work as a policeman enforcing the vagrancy law in Chihuahuita. In both instances, he used the backing of municipal officials in Mexico and the United States to organize his labor contracting business. Yet such similarities flew in the face of received wisdom about the emancipated nature of the U.S. legal system and the correspondingly coercive and degraded status of Mexican jurisprudence. If U.S. lawmakers deemed unskilled Mexican immigrants incapable of self-government, so too were Mexican lawmakers. Consequently, U.S. immigration officials sought to vilify all of Gonzalez's business activities, after learning of his links to the Seccion de Emigration.

Both Stone and Berkshire were nonetheless unprepared for the full political and ideological challenge Gonzalez would make to their authority and legitimacy. In January 1912, one year after implementing the Mexican Agreements, Gonzalez charged in a direct appeal to the U.S. commissioner-general of immigration, that Frank Berkshire had systematically violated the spirit and letter of U.S. immigration law by encouraging American commissaries to export workers while hindering all other labor agents from so doing. As evidence, Gonzalez recounted two incidents. The first occurred in July 1911 and involved fifty track workers whom Gonzalez attempted to send to Kansas, filling an order for the Atchison, Topeka and the Santa Fe Railway. Berkshire, however, intervened and would not allow the men to be sent under Gonzalez's authority, claiming that "he had not been officially designated as the 'exclusive representative' of the said Railway Company." The fifty men were detained at the border and Gonzalez lost the contract. The second incident involved interventions at the border, whereby inspectors placed immigrants before a board of special inquiry if they indicated they were headed to Gonzalez's office.[61]

Gonzalez's appeal, prepared with the help of the respected law firm of Caldwell and Sweeney in El Paso, used these incidents to claim Berkshire was using the Mexican Agreements to "drive every labor agency out of business except those three in whose interests he seems to administer his office." In particular, Gonzalez objected to the requirement within the Mexican Agreements that only official labor agencies – those who "have regular contracts of permanent employment with the railroad" – could supply the companies with laborers. According to Gonzalez's

---

[61] Affidavit of R. G. Gonzalez, January 11, 1912, in Frank Berkshire to Commissioner General of Immigration, file 52546/31E, box 125, Records of the Bureau of Immigration, Immigration Subject Correspondence, RG 85; Affidavit of Juan Muniz, January 16, 1912, 4, file 52546/31F, box 126, ibid.

lawyers, "This rule . . . is un-American, arbitrary and scandalous" because it made contracts compulsory rather than voluntary aspects of the commerce of migration through El Paso. In addition, Gonzalez objected to a rule that forbade labor agents from using their names in soliciting men in Ciudad Juarez or any other place within Mexico for work in the United States. "It prevents the alien from choosing a man of his own nationality, if he so desires," stated the appeal, and thus undermined the possibility of free and open competition among Anglo and Mexican labor agencies. Equally important, Gonzalez asserted that Berkshire only selectively enforced the Mexican Agreements, unfair as they already were, thus allowing the Anglo commissaries to corral hundreds of Mexican laborers for several days at a stretch while waiting for future work orders, an explicit violation of article 2 of the Mexican Agreements.[62] In each claim, the padrone's traditional vices – forging coercive rather than voluntary contracts and squelching "free" competition and choice – were turned upside down and leveled against Frank Berkshire and the U.S. Bureau of Immigration.

Nowhere was Gonzalez's skillful use of free labor rhetoric and even the language of American populism more apparent than in his affidavit, which charged Berkshire with having only "partly succeeded in crushing out the small man without influence or money in favor of the large ones."[63] Gonzalez remade himself here into a Horatio Alger–like hero fighting against monopolies and corruption in the U.S. legal system. This refrain appeared throughout his longer appeal and was most conspicuous in the castigation of Berkshire as a kind of padronelike villain by the attorney I. W. Caldwell, whose own affidavit stated that Berkshire "is a dull man, not destitute of the cunning often connected with obtuseness of mind. His business has brought him into contact with the poor, the ignorant, the friendless and the foreigner, over whom he has practically limitless power. . . . Mr. Berkshire is a petty tyrant whenever he dares to be . . . [he] is acting in the interest, not of the government, but of others."[64] Caldwell's critique completely reversed the traditional image of the immoral padrone and the virtuous U.S. immigration inspector. Berkshire was not simply corrupt but a stunning replica of the padrone stereotype, a man who lived off "the poor, the ignorant, the friendless." As evidence for these claims, Gonzalez's appeal contained an affidavit by Juan Muniz, a former renganchista for the Holmes Supply Company, who stated Berkshire had gone on "frequent hunting trips" with the presidents of the Anglo commissaries and had even accepted a fifteen thousand dollar bribe from them to secure his continued cooperation.[65]

Gonzalez's appeal prompted an immediate investigation into "the immigration problem" at El Paso by Commerce Department lawyer Charles Earl in February

[62] Caldwell and Sweeny to Commissioner General of Immigration, January 11, 1912, 4, 7, 10, file 52546/31F, box 126, ibid.

[63] Affidavit of R. G. Gonzalez, January 11, 1912, 2, file 52546/31E, ibid.

[64] Affidavit of W. M. Caldwell, January 11, 1912, 3, file 52546/31F, ibid.

[65] Affidavit of Juan Muniz, January 16, 1912, 6, ibid. For a brief discussion of inspector Berkshire's activities in El Paso, see Sanchez, *Becoming Mexican American*, 51–54.

1912, who candidly acknowledged that "this subject is many-sided and complex and difficult to understand from mere documents." Earl's confusion was understandable given how neatly Gonzalez's appeal paralleled Berkshire's own moralistic judgments against Mexican labor agents in El Paso. Earl's initial report reached no conclusion as to who the real padrone was in El Paso but rather ended with a question. As long as strong labor demand exists in El Paso, Earl commented, "the Government can not prevent its being known, nor can it prevent offers of employment being made to admitted aliens. But whether it should actively sanction such a demand and facilitate such offers of employment ... in a Government establishment, is a serious question."[66]

Earl's questioning of the basic premise behind the Mexican Agreements prompted Berkshire to send a ten-page statement to the commissioner-general of immigration one month later, defending both the agreements and his reputation. Berkshire argued that the Mexican Agreements were ultimately designed to lead to "the complete elimination of the labor agents" in El Paso. Once this had been accomplished, "rules governing them will no longer be necessary" and questions about the government's role in facilitating such migrations would become irrelevant. But Berkshire did not clarify what distinguished a labor agent from an official corporate representative or why the contracts of Mexican labor agents were coercive and those of the L. H. Manning Company were voluntary. Nor did Berkshire answer Gonzalez's claim that he had discriminated against him by excluding him from the meeting that produced the Mexican Agreements. Berkshire was perhaps more effective in dismissing the charges of corruption against himself. To Caldwell's accusation of being a tyrant, Berkshire replied merely "no comment." But to Juan Muniz's claim that he had accepted bribes, Berkshire stated "I emphatically denounce ... the dastardly and malicious perjurer" and claimed he "does not speak English" and "his understanding of English is very imperfect."[67] By claiming racial and cultural affinity with his superiors in the Bureau of Immigration, Berkshire hoped to discredit all of Gonzalez's claims against him.

Berkshire's rebuttal was ultimately unpersuasive to his superiors in the U.S. Bureau of Immigration, not because immigration authorities were sympathetic to Mexican culture or Mexicans but because Gonzalez's arguments and the evidence amassed against Berkshire were simply irrefutable. In July 1912 a special investigator for the bureau, Richard Taylor, concluded that Berkshire "has simply become a party to an agreement whereby those interested are permitted to secure, with his approval, a class of laborers against the admission of which the law is directly aimed." Taylor recommended that despite the "curious contradictions" at the heart of the Foran Act and the peculiar difficulty of enforcing it at El Paso, Berkshire should nonetheless try to enforce the law. "If he is not in a position to make debarments effective, he should at least make an attempt to do so."[68] Why?

---

[66] Frank Berkshire to Commissioner General of Immigration, May 24, 1912, *Stone Report*, 2.
[67] *Stone Report*, 9.
[68] Richard H. Taylor to Commissioner General of Immigration, July 9, 1912, ibid., 2, 4.

Because to do otherwise undermined the heroic purpose and perceived integrity of the U.S. Bureau of Immigration at every port of entry in the nation. Berkshire's "solution" in El Paso exploded many of the same fictions that honorable, law-abiding padrones did: that U.S. immigration officials were heroically defending the nation's cultural and political ideals against racially degraded and unfree immigrants like the padrone.

The immediate consequence of Taylor's censure of Berkshire was the suspension of the Mexican Agreements in El Paso and increased efforts by Berkshire to enforce the letter of the Foran Act. Berkshire launched his new campaign to uphold the law not against the Anglo-run commissaries or the major railroad lines in El Paso – the most obvious targets – but instead investigated the Medina Dam and Irrigation Company in Laredo, Texas, which had recently imported hundreds of workers from Mexico.[69] In so doing, Berkshire probably saved his job, diverting attention from his contentious relations with the labor-contracting community of El Paso. Never again, however, would he possess the free rein he had momentarily wielded in administering the U.S.-Mexican border. Gonzalez's appeal had thus been remarkably successful, not only in tarnishing Berkshire's reputation but in upending the legal fictions under which most border officials operated. If Gonzalez could become the American populist, a defender of free labor and U.S. immigration laws, and Berkshire the villain who violated them, what precisely was the difference between them? While Berkshire retained his position as chief immigration officer at El Paso for another decade, this question continued to plague him and limit his power. Gonzalez continued to exploit his place on the margins of El Paso's labor market, using the legal system as best he could, coercing "vagrant" residents of Chihuahuita into taking jobs while also defending the principles of free labor and fair competition when politically expedient.

Conclusion

Although padrones may have seemed antithetical to everything that an exceptional American identity represented, they ironically confirmed one of Frederick Jackson Turner's central insights about the formation of U.S. national identity. When Turner argued that American character was forged on its western borders, he highlighted how, in less nationalistic terms, the periphery of the United States defined its core, how the nation-state organized itself at its borders. If the alleged savagery of native peoples helped define and redeem Turner's American civilization, so too did padrones help solidify the modernity and heroism of U.S. border agents and the political system they policed. The "frontiers" that padrones and border agents traversed existed not in the western United States as a single line of settlement but on all sides of the U.S. nation-state in 1900: at its port cities, from New York and San Francisco to Galveston, Texas, and along the entire Canadian-U.S. and Mexican-U.S. borders.

[69] Frank Berkshire to the Honorable Charles A. Boynton, September 6, 1912, ibid.

Cordasco, Skliris, and Gonzalez each used immigration laws and notions of free labor to acquire cultural power over their compatriots and legitimacy in the eyes of company officials throughout the North American West. But the impact of the legal systems and immigration laws they evaded was not symmetrical. For Gonzalez, lax enforcement of the Foran Act and its subsequent annulment under the Mexican Agreements dramatically weakened his ability to control sites of either labor supply or labor demand. Although Gonzalez successfully used the U.S. legal system to challenge and overturn the Mexican Agreements, he remained unable to gain any enduring control over the larger, more lucrative commerce of migration through El Paso because there existed no effective political boundary between the two nations. For Skliris, however, the U.S. Bureau of Immigration's more rigorous attempts to enforce the Foran Act at the port of New York helped create the legal niches that he exploited in Utah and the Intermountain West. Cordasco, in turn, gained power from the contract labor laws of three countries. Of these, Canada's Alien Labor Act was routinely violated by Canadian companies and was perhaps the least beneficial to Cordasco. The Canadian back door to the Foran Act and the Canadian Agreements designed to counter it, by contrast, served for a time to strengthen his monopolistic control over the transnational migration of Italians to Canada. The impact of the Foran Act was not confined to the United States but shaped the organization of labor migration on both sides of its national frontiers. The legal spaces that padrones exploited were transnational political phenomena, not literal geographies of land. They varied by how well contract labor laws were enforced, what kinds of agents sought to enforce them, and how effectively border officials policed padrones or competed with them.

Just as padrones exploited the uneven spaces that U.S. and Canadian immigration officials created, so did immigration officials thrive on how padrones took advantage of their legal opportunities. On the one hand, padrones helped reconcile ambiguities intrinsic to the Foran Act and Canada's Alien Labor Act, securing, at least momentarily, their progressive meaning to immigration officials of both countries.[70] The boundaries between free and unfree labor, voluntary and involuntary migration, coercive and consensual contracts, so crucial to the alleged progressive purpose of the Foran Act and the Alien Labor Act, were in practice profoundly ambiguous and difficult to discern. Padrones clarified, however temporarily, these conceptual ambiguities to immigration officials by embodying everything unfree, racially degraded, or unpatriotic that the law was supposed to control. Perhaps more important, immigration officials took advantage of the same legal indeterminacies that padrones did by using the ideological challenges of men like Cordasco, Skliris, and Gonzalez to justify expanding the state's control over the migrations of its foreign-born workers, citizen and alien alike.

---

[70] On the indeterminate meanings and effects of law, see Christopher L. Tomlins and Andrew J. King, "Labor, Law, and History," in Christopher L. Tomlins and Andrew J. King, eds., *Labor Law in America: Historical and Critical Essays* (Baltimore, 1992), 15.

Although Gonzalez may have gotten the better of Frank Berkshire in 1912, Berkshire's attempt to regulate migration through El Paso became an important precedent for the work of the U.S. Employment Service in El Paso and elsewhere between 1917 and 1919.[71]

The geography of padrone power and the legislative expansions it inspired, moreover, were not confined to the United States or North America, but were truly international in character, shaping the careers of labor market entrepreneurs and border bureaucrats in Europe as well. Frank Missler's brief success in evading the Foran Act in the sugarcane fields of Louisiana did not bring him exceptional wealth, nor did Marcus Braun's discoveries of contract labor violations in Hungary and Chiasso, Switzerland, give him much enduring security as an undercover inspector for the U.S. Bureau of Immigration. But both men helped spark expansions in the power and claims of border bureaucracies: Braun's European discoveries helped lay the basis for the U.S. Immigration Act of 1907, which further expanded the racialized criteria of the Foran Act and the discretionary power of U.S. border agents, while Missler's misadventures with the Louisiana State Board of Immigration inspired Bulgarian lawmakers to create an emigration bureaucracy.

But if the symbiotic interactions between padrones, passenger agents, and immigration officials defined much of the history of these immigration and emigration laws, neither lawmakers nor labor market entrepreneurs owned the law and interpretations of free labor and voluntary contract. Immigrant workers in El Paso, Montreal, and Salt Lake City would in time adapt notions of free labor to their own ends and challenge the views of both immigration officials and immigrant padrones in North America. Immigrant workers grounded their ideas of free labor and contractual obligation not so much in interpretations of contract labor law or formal legal precedents, but in the potentially explosive forms of familial obligation and manly identity that also went into the making and unmaking of padrone authority, the subject of the next chapter.

---

[71] On the history of public employment agencies, see Shelby M. Harrison, *Public Employment Offices: Their Purpose, Structure, and Methods* (New York, 1924). On the origins of the Bracero Program among Mexican workers, see Henry P. Anderson, *The Bracero Program in California* (New York, 1976); Kitty Calavita, *Inside the State: The Bracero Program, Immigration, and the I.N.S.* (New York, 1992).

PART TWO

Reinventing Free Labor

CHAPTER FOUR

Manhood Mobilized

For Italian railroad worker Cesidio Simboli and his co-workers in Indiana in 1902, obligations to family members often seemed as onerous as the exactions they paid their padrone, an Italian named Fulvio. Indeed, for one of Cesidio's co-workers the burdens of being a father and the oppressions of the padrone system blurred under the daily stress of "pick and shovel" work. When he dropped a steel rail and injured his foot one day, his long simmering anger exploded: "Are we slaves, beasts, or men, sir?" he demanded of Fulvio, who calmly responded that he was free to quit whenever he chose. Cesidio's partner hesitated, then muttered to himself "God, if I did not have wife and children in Italy!" and began tending to his wounds before returning to work with "the resignation of a slave."[1]

For this track worker, free labor was meaningless outside the constraints of familial obligations. The freedom proffered to him by his padrone – that of quitting – was an option seemingly unavailable to him and thousands of Italian fathers like him working in Indiana, Canada, and elsewhere. To do so would have been to strand his dependents in Italy without a monthly remittance, a sign to them that he had failed to fulfill his manly duties as father and provider. And yet to accept quietly the burdens of industrial work and padrone exactions without a fight also seemed unmanly. By his own estimation, Cesidio's partner was more of a slave or a beast than a man, as he decided to submit to Fulvio's authority without a fight. Better to accept emasculation in North America, perhaps, than to become unmanly in one's home village, where all hoped to return after the work season ended.

Not all Italian fathers resolved this dilemma in the same fashion. Indeed, transnational migration transformed how men defined family duties and their manhood. For many sojourners, this process of redefinition was closely tied to questions posed by mobility. Where, put simply, was male authority located while men were on the move? How would patriarchal power function when men, of necessity, performed "women"'s work on the move and when fathers were largely

---

[1] Cesidio Simboli, "When the Boss Went Too Far," *World Outlook* (October 1917), in Wayne Moquin and Charles Van Doren, eds., *A Documentary History of Italian Americans* (New York, 1973), 147–148.

absent?[2] As we shall see, immigrant men located manhood in distinct places: some, like Cesidio's partner, accepted emasculation in North America to preserve manhood in their home villages where they purchased land or secured dowries for their sisters. Others relocated their families to North America, sending for their wives and children, thus reconstituting their manhood and independence by importing their own dependents. Still others reclaimed their manhood not in fatherhood, real or imagined, but in fraternal fashion, forging brotherly bonds with co-workers. Many of these men claimed their manhood in mobility, quitting jobs at the drop of a hat in North America, even if it temporarily threatened their dependents in home villages. In each case, the freedoms, burdens, and expectations of wage work – the very meaning of free labor itself – were directly linked to manly privileges in Italy, Greece, Mexico, and the North American West.[3]

At the same time, padrones sought to profit from the diverse ways immigrants transformed manhood and immigrant family ties. Some, like the Italian padrones Fulvio and Cordasco, profited primarily from the mobility of married men and their paternal commitments to wives and dependents overseas. Skliris and Gonzalez, by contrast, sought riches from the transience of single men and their diverse domestic commitments in North America. If padrones exploited distinct family relations, they also sought power by embodying and representing the distinct forms of manhood that sojourning men crafted on the move. Cordasco presented himself to immigrant workers as a prototype of honorable fatherhood, whereas Skliris strove to embody fraternal virtues as a single man's man. Their successes and failures reflected not merely their respective talents as manly performers in North America but also the particular meanings and location of male authority in the villages that Greek, Italian, and Mexican men left behind.

Family Ties at Home

Examining how emigrants from Greece, Italy, and Mexico defined manhood at the beginning of the twentieth century is a daunting task for several reasons. First,

---

[2] On the importance of "where gender can be located," see Ava Baron, "Gender and Labor History," in Ava Baron, ed., *Work Engendered: Toward a New History of American Labor* (Ithaca, 1991), 36; Susan Lee Johnson, "'A Memory Sweet to Soldiers': The Significance of Gender in the History of the American West," *Western Historical Quarterly* 24:4 (November 1993): 499. On the importance of unpaid housework to notions of class at varied points of production, see Jeanne Boydston, "To Earn Her Daily Bread: Housework and Antebellum Working-Class Subsistence," *Radical History Review* 35 (April 1986), 7–25. See also Boydston, *Home and Work*; Eileen Boris and Cynthia Daniels, *Homework: Historical and Contemporary Perspectives on Paid Labor at Home* (Urbana, 1989); Judith Coffin, *The Politics of Women's Work: The Paris Garment Trades, 1750–1915* (Princeton, 1996).

[3] On the practice of Italian fathers sending for their wives and families, see Yans-McLaughlin, *Family and Community*, 96–97; Donna Gabaccia, *From Sicily to Elizabeth Street: Housing and Social Change among Italian Immigrants, 1880–1930* (Albany, 1984), 58–60; On different forms of working-class manhood among single and married men, see Mary Blewett, *Men, Women, and Work: Class, Gender, and Protest in the New England Shoe Industry* (Urbana, 1988); Patricia Cooper, "The 'Travelling Fraternity': Union Cigar Makers and Geographic

the topic has been approached in widely disparate ways by anthropologists, demographers, and historians of the family. Anthropologists have long grappled with the complexities of manhood in Mediterranean cultures, producing a remarkably rich ethnographic literature. But their monographs rarely consider the historical dimensions of manhood or family bonds.[4] Demographers and family historians, by contrast, have paid close attention to historical change and continuity in their studies of Greek, Italian, and Mexican families in the nineteenth and twentieth centuries. But rather than discuss concepts like manhood, they have focused primarily on demographic evidence, considering the average ages for men and women at marriage in a given locale, whether new couples lived on their own, and whether families were nuclear or extended.[5] One result of these strikingly different approaches is that manhood and patriarchy remain oddly transhistorical concepts, connoting, as historian Linda Gordon recently put it, "continuity at the expense of change and variation." Although she has defined them as a "particular ... system of father domination," little attention has been paid to specific differences between patriarchy's literal and symbolic forms or the varieties of familial language, fraternal and paternal, that have constituted male power.[6]

Mobility, 1900–1919," in Eric H. Monkkonen, ed., *Walking to Work: Tramps in America, 1790–1935* (Lincoln, 1984), 118–140.

[4] On Greek ethnographies, see Campbell, *Honour, Family, and Patronage*; Juliet Du Boulay, *Portrait of a Greek Mountain Village* (Oxford, 1974); Michael Herzfeld, *The Poetics of Manhood: Contest and Identity in a Cretan Mountain Village* (Princeton, 1985). On Italian ethnographies, see A. L. Maraspini, *The Study of an Italian Village* (Paris, 1968); John A. Davis, *Land and Family in Pisticci* (London, 1973). For exceptions that use history, see Rudolph Bell, *Fate and Honor*.

[5] On Greek family history, see Sant Cassia, *The Making of the Modern Greek Family*; Peter Loizos and Evthymios Papataxiarchis, "Introduction," in Peter Loizos and Evthymios Papataxiarchis, eds., *Contested Identities: Gender and Kinship in Modern Greece* (Princeton, 1991), 3–9; Roxanne Cafantzoglou, "The Household Formation Pattern of a Vlach Mountain Community of Greece: Syrako, 1898–1929," *Journal of Family History* 19:1 (1994): 79–98; and Violetta Hionidou, "Nuptiality Patterns and Household Structure on the Greek Island of Mykonos, 1849–1959," *Journal of Family History* 20:1 (1995): 67–102. On Italian family history, see Kertzer and Hogan, *Family, Political Economy, and Demographic Change*, 7, 117, 139; Marzio Barbagli and David Kertzer, "An Introduction to the History of Italian Family Life," *Journal of Family History* 15:4 (1990): 369–383; and Pier Paolo Viazzo and Dionigi Albera, "The Peasant Family in Northern Italy, 1750–1930: A Reassessment," *Journal of Family History* 15:4 (1990): 461–482.

[6] Linda Gordon and Allen Hunter, "Not All Male Dominance is Patriarchal," *Radical History Review* 71 (1998): 72; See also Teresa Meade and Pamela Haag, "Persistent Patriarchy?: Ghost or Reality?" ibid., 92–93. I use patriarchy more narrowly in this chapter to describe the economic and cultural power fathers wielded within families of origin. I describe the symbolic meanings of fatherhood, which flourished outside familial contexts, as paternalism. Likewise, I use fraternalism to describe ideologies of brotherhood rather than the specific power brothers wielded in families of origin. For an excellent discussion of the ahistoricity of patriarchy as a concept, see Carole Pateman, *The Sexual Contract* (Stanford, 1988), 19–38. On distinctions between patriarchy and paternalism, see Bowman, *Masters and Lords*, 162; Gerald Noiriel, "Du 'patronage' au 'paternalisme': La restructuration des formes de domination de la main-d'oeuvrière dans l'industrie metalurgique français," *Le Mouvement Social* 144 (1988): 17–36.

Complicating our task further is a sea change in how both anthropologists and demographers have conceptualized manhood and family history in Greece, Italy, and Mexico. Until 1980, these scholars spoke with some confidence about the existence of a "Mediterranean family" and a unified cultural system of meaning that supported it, a complex of "Mediterranean shame and honor" that extended even to Latin America.[7] Recent scholarship has questioned these paradigms from a number of vantage points. Some anthropologists have criticized the ways other anthropologists have imposed Eurocentric values on a romanticized and exoticized Mediterranean region. Feminist anthropologists have additionally challenged the static and two-dimensional portrayal of women in Mediterranean societies. Demographers and family historians, in turn, have discovered a much greater variety of households and marriage patterns in the region than previously thought. The diversity of these family forms has led some demographers and anthropologists to question the existence of a single "national culture" or family form in any Mediterranean country.[8]

Given these complexities, generalizing about the meanings of manhood among diverse Greek, Italian, and Mexican families could lead to oversimplification and distortion. The task gains some clarity, however, when one considers the specific geographical origins of the men that Cordasco, Skliris, and Gonzalez imported. Ship manifest lists collected at the port of New York City shed light on the origins and family structures of nearly two thousand Canada-bound Italians and Utah-bound Greeks. At the peak of Cordasco's power in 1904, Italians from the northern

For histories of patriarchy, see Gerda Lerner, *The Creation of Patriarchy* (New York, 1986); Julie Hardwick, *The Practice of Patriarchy: Gender and the Politics of Household Authority in Early Modern France* (University Station, PA, 1998); Susan K. Beese, *Restructuring Patriarchy: The Modernization of Gender Inequality in Brazil, 1914–1940* (Chapel Hill, 1996).

[7] On the Mediterranean family pattern, see Peter Laslett, "Family and Household as Work Group and Kin Group: Areas of Traditional Europe Compared," in Richard Wall, Jean Robin, and Peter Laslett, eds., *Family Forms in Historic Europe* (Cambridge, 1983), 513–563; and J. G. Peristiany, ed., *Mediterranean Family Structures* (Cambridge, 1976). On the Mediterranean system of shame and honor, see Jean Peristiany, *Honour and Shame: The Values of Mediterranean Society* (Chicago, 1966); Julian Pitt-Rivers, *The People of the Sierra* (Chicago, 1961); John A. Davis, *People of the Mediterranean* (London, 1977); and David Gilmore, "Introduction: The Shame of Dishonor," in David Gilmore, ed., *Honor and Shame and the Unity of the Mediterranean* (Washington, D.C., 1987), 2–21.

[8] Michael Herzfeld, "Social Tensions and Inheritance by Lot in Three Greek Villages," *Anthropological Quarterly* 53:2 (1980): 92; Michael Herzfeld, "'As in Your Own House': Hospitality, Ethnography, and the Stereotype of Mediterranean Society," in Gilmore, *Honor and Shame and the Unity of the Mediterranean*, 75–89; Jill Dubisch, "Gender, Kinship, and Religion: Reconstructing the Anthropology of Greece," in Loizos and Papataxiarchis, *Contested Identities*, 29–46; Kertzer and Hogan, *Family, Political Economy, and Demographic Change*, 7, 117, 139; and Barbagli and Kertzer, "An Introduction to the History of Italian Family Life," 380. Despite these critiques and the problems of ahistoricity inherent in using anthropology to study the past, some historians continue to rely on older anthropological models. See Ramon Gutierrez, *When Jesus Came, the Corn Mothers Went Away: Marriage, Sexuality, and Power in New Mexico, 1500–1846* (Stanford, 1991); and Steven J. Stern, *The Secret History of Gender: Men, Women, and Power in Late Colonial Mexico* (Chapel Hill, 1995), 45–69.

province of Veneto composed 40 percent of the total Canada-bound migration, with the remaining 60 percent coming from several provinces in south-central Italy (see Maps 4.1A, 4.1B). Greeks traveling to Utah between 1907 and 1912, the peak years of Skliris's power, came mostly from the Peloponnese and the island of Crete (see Maps 4.2A, 4.2B). The origins of Mexican emigrants, in turn, have been difficult to locate given the paucity of information collected by U.S. border officials. Remittances sent to Mexico in the 1920s, however, suggest that nearly two-thirds of the Mexicans passing through El Paso left from provinces just west of Mexico City: Michoacan, Guanajuato, and Jalisco (see Map 4.3).[9]

A comparison of these locales suggests telling demographic and cultural similarities. First, marriages in central Italy, the Peloponnese, and central Mexico featured grooms much older than their wives and patrilocal residence practices whereby a bride moved in with the groom's family after marriage. In central and northeastern Italy, such multiple family households were relatively common within nearly all social classes, but especially among Italian sharecroppers, the group most likely to emigrate to North America and Canada. The same pattern held true in the Greek Peloponnese and in Crete, where a wife joined the household of her husband's family at marriage. Detailed demographic studies of Mexican household structure in the nineteenth century are lacking, but historians of the Mexican family have likewise suggested that a powerful multiple-family household flourished in Mexico, one that subordinated both women and sons to an elder father's power.[10]

In all three regions, manhood was defined primarily in patriarchal terms in 1900, though the power wielded by fathers was by no means static. Rather, patriarchal power was in varying degrees of historical transition between two arenas of male authority: the extended family household, in which numerous nuclear families, servants, and other nonkin household members lived under the rule of a single patriarch; and the nuclear family, in which a father ruled, at least in theory, his wife and children.[11] Marriage remained a cornerstone of male power in both contexts,

[9] Manuel Gamio, *Mexican Immigration to the United States: A Study of Human Migration and Adjustment* (Chicago, 1930), 18–19.

[10] On patrilocal family structures within central Italy, see David I. Kertzer, *Family Life in Central Italy, 1880–1910: Sharecropping, Wage Labor, and Coresidence* (New Brunswick, 1984). On Italy more generally, see Barbagli and Kertzer, "An Introduction to the History of Italian Family Life," 374–376. On patrilocality within Greek family structures, see Loizos and Papataxiarchis, "Introduction," in *Contested Identities*, 5–9. On extended Mexican family structures in the colonial period, see Steven J. Stern, *The Secret History of Gender*; and Patricia Seed, *To Love, Honor, and Obey in Colonial Mexico: Conflicts over Marriage Choice, 1574–1821* (Stanford, 1988). On extended families in the twentieth century, see Larissa Lomnitz and Marisol Prez-Lizaur, "Dynastic Growth and Survival Strategies: The Solidarity of Mexican Grand-Families," in Elizabeth Jelin, ed., *Family, Household and Gender Relations in Latin America* (London, 1991), 123–132; and Lorissa Lomnitz and Marisol Prez-Lizaur, *A Mexican Elite Family, 1820–1980: Kinship, Class, and Culture* (Princeton, 1987).

[11] Carole Pateman has suggested that the transition from classical to modern patriarchy in Europe was accomplished by 1800. But the timing and degree of that transition varied throughout Europe and Latin America. See Pateman, *The Sexual Contract*, 24–25; Mary Murray, *The*

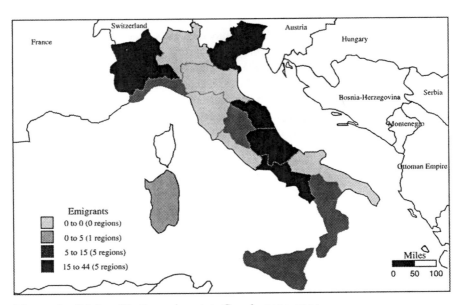

Map 4.1A. Origins of Italian emigrants to Canada, 1904–1914

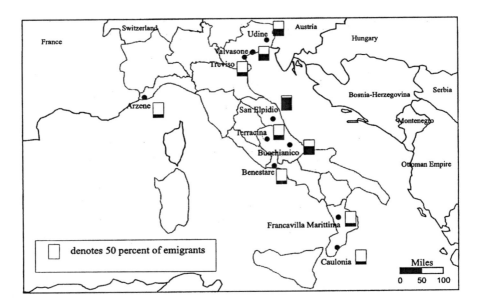

Map 4.1B. Origins of Italian emigrants to Canada: Top ten villages, 1901–1904

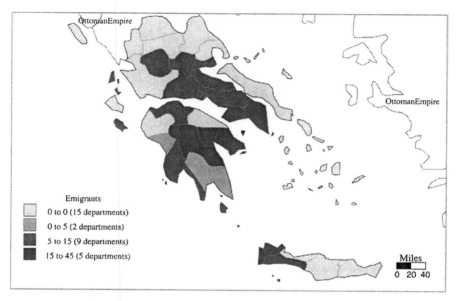

Map 4.2A. Origins of Greek emigrants to Utah: 1907–1912

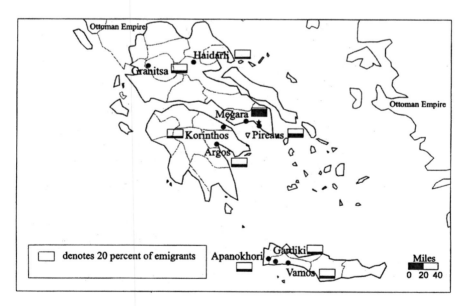

Map 4.2B. Origins of Greek emigrants to Utah: Top ten villages, 1907–1912

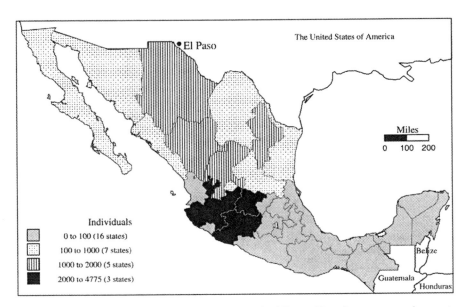

Map 4.3. Origins of Mexican emigrants to the United States: Based on money orders sent home, July–August 1926

granting husbands property rights over a new wife's dowry possessions, securing paternal inheritances, and giving them legal control over the labor of their wives. These advantages were not confined to patrilocal communities, but in these arenas "men dominated," according to Peter Loizos, with "property, names, and reputations . . . basically under male control, transferred from father to sons."[12]

The marriage laws of Italy, Greece, and Mexico in 1900 did not sanction an inviolate patriarchal power but themselves reflected changes in the location of male authority. In Mexico the adoption of the Napoleonic Code after 1821 reversed many of the Bourbon reforms of the late eighteenth century, which had expanded the power of patriarchs to choose their adult children's marriage partners. By adopting the Napoleonic Code, Mexicans abolished patria potestas, or the father's rule, beyond childhood, and celebrated marriage as a "pact between individuals and not among families." In Italy, the Savoy Code, established when the Kingdom of Italy was created in 1861, limited patria potestas over adult children and granted daughters and sons equal inheritance rights. Greek marriage laws in the nineteenth century likewise weakened the power of patriarchs to control family resources.[13]

But if these laws limited traditional patriarchal power, they also expanded the

---

Law of the Father?: Patriarchy in the Transition from Feudalism to Capitalism (London, 1995); and Juliet Flower, *The Regime of the Brother: After the Patriarchy* (London, 1991).

[12] Loizos and Papataxiarchis, "Introduction," in *Contested Identities*, 9.

[13] Gutierrez, *When Jesus Came, the Corn Mothers Went Away*, 315; Chiara Saraceno, "Women, Family, and the Law, 1750–1942," *Journal of Family History* 15:4 (1990): 430–432, 434; Sant Cassia, *The Making of the Modern Greek Family*, 21–22.

authority of husbands in marriage. The Napoleonic Code in Mexico reduced a wife's freedom to make economic transactions or protect her property as long as the husband lived, while the Savoy Code in Italy authorized a husband to administer his wife's property, his daughter's dowry, and "whatever common property was acquired after marriage." The Savoy Code made explicit its goal of centralizing the husband's power. "The independence of the wife," stated its second section, "in addition to offending the rights of the family, would be contrary to ... the deference which the wife owes her husband, who is head of the household and best suited by nature to protect her interests." In Greece, a husband's power increased with the invigoration of the dowry system. Rather than being vehicles to women's equal inheritance, dowries instead functioned as vehicles for Greek men to secure their property claims in a new nation struggling to invent a new system of property transmission. For most Greek women, marriage and free labor were incongruous concepts regardless of a woman's social position. Here in the civil contracts of marriage and the dowry were foundations of a reconfigured patriarchal authority.[14]

Yet true "father rule" remained an ideal rather than a historical reality in both extended households and nuclear families of Greece, Italy, and Mexico in 1900. Not only did wives, sons, and daughters find ways to escape the abuses of husbands and fathers, but they frequently used kinship and community networks to compel them to live up to their masculine responsibilities and obligations in the family. Men did not negotiate their manhood only within their families, moreover, but also in homosocial contexts, whether drinking in taverns or coffeehouses, playing cards, or occasionally fighting each other in a variety of competitive arenas. Such activities frequently existed in tension with the domestic commitments that married men enjoyed as husbands and family members. Homosocial entertainments and fulfilling one's domestic responsibilities did not necessarily conflict, but many Greek, Italian, and Mexican men struggled to be manly in both contexts simultaneously.

Tensions between patriarchal and fraternal arenas of male authority and loyalty were apparent among the single and married men who decided to leave their villages and emigrate to North America. At the moment of his departure to the United States, Greek immigrant Haralambos Kambouris struggled to decide where he would spend his final hours in Greece: with his sisters and brother-in-law or with a group of male friends throwing a party for him and his cohorts who were leaving. Kambouris ultimately chose his family and the domestic duties they

[14] Sant Cassia, *The Making of the Modern Greek Family*, 21–22. On "the impossibility of a marriage contract which decrees that a bride once wed shall never labor," see Margaret Alexiou, "Sons, Wives, and Mothers: Reality and Fantasy in Some Modern Greek Ballads," *Journal of Modern Greek Studies* 1:1 (1983): 87. On Greek dowries more generally, see Juliet du Boulay, "The Meaning of Dowry: Changing Values in Rural Greece," *Journal of Modern Greek Studies* 1:1 (1984): 248. On Italian dowries, see Luigi Villari, *Italian Life in Town and Country* (New York, 1903), 121. On a similar evolution of marriage law in the United States, see Stanley, "Conjugal Bonds and Wage Labor," 471–490; and Amy Dru Stanky, *From Bondage to Contract: Wage Labor, Marriage, and the Market in the Age of Slave Emancipation* (Cambridge, 1998), 138–174.

represented, but he nonetheless expressed keen longing to join his fraternal friends later in the evening. "It made me sad to have to miss such a party," he recalled in his diary, "but I had no choice for I knew how much love my brother-in-law had for me and if I didn't go, it would cost him a lot of money."[15] In claiming he had "no choice," Kambouris highlighted the primacy of familial duties over fraternal ties. His honor and identity as a man were best expressed by dining with sisters and kin in Piraeus and acquiring dowry monies for them in North America rather than partying with fraternal "kin" in either location.

But what was historically distinct about the dilemmas that Greek, Italian, and Mexican men experienced in 1900? Kambouris's struggle to reconcile fraternal and familial ties was widely shared by potential emigrants, but not all possessed the same domestic commitments, nor did they honor them in the same fashion.[16] By 1900 two groups of men were likely to emigrate from these nations, corresponding to distinct moments of conflict within patriarchal families: first, single men between the ages of seventeen and twenty-four whose manhood was not yet vested in marriage and its conflicts, and second, husbands between the ages of twenty-five and thirty-five, whose power over children and wives was attenuated by both economic pressures and the men's subordinate position in multiple-family households. These overlapping groups were evident in the emigrant streams from Italy to Canada and from Greece to Utah in the early twentieth century. The mean age of Italian men traveling to Canada in 1901 and 1904 was twenty-eight, and roughly 60 percent of the total were married. Greeks bound to Utah between 1907 and 1912, by contrast, were predominantly single men between the ages of eighteen and twenty-four (see Figure 4.1). Less than 30 percent of Greek men were married upon arriving in the United States, and most listed their fathers as the closest relative in Greece.[17]

Although both Greek and Italian emigrants left villages that were patrilocal, they were adapting to different moments of familial tension. In the sharecropping families of central Italy, two problems loomed large in the early twentieth century: generating enough household income and maintaining a stable family structure under one household head. The emigration of young husbands killed two birds with one stone: it brought much needed cash into multiple-family households and diffused tensions between young husbands and their fathers. Emigration acted as a particularly effective safety valve for family tensions among Italian sharecroppers, whose patrilocal structure remained remarkably constant between 1860 and

[15] Haralambos Kambouris, "Sojourn in America," 5, August 28, 1912, Greek Archives, Marriott Library. Translated from Greek by Helen Papanikolas.

[16] On traditions of Italian and Greek men's migration before 1885, see Kertzer and Hogan, *Family, Political Economy, and Demographic Change*, 10–13; Susan Buck Sutton, "What Is a Village in a Nation of Migrants?" *Journal of Modern Greek Studies* 6 (1988): 187–188. On the role of Mexican and Italian men's migration in strengthening communities in one place, see Deutsch, *No Separate Refuge*, 49; and Bell, *Fate and Honor*, 196–197.

[17] Steamship Manifest Lists, Port of New York, March 1901, March 1904, March 1907, March 1910, March 1912, March 1914, Records of the U.S. Department of Immigration and Naturalization, RG 85. See Table 4.1 in Appendix A.

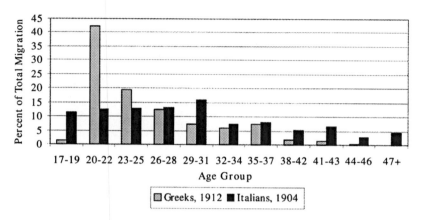

Figure 4.1. Age profile of Greek and Italian immigrants at peak of padrone power

1920, despite massive economic and political upheavals in the Italian countryside. Throughout this period, sons brought their brides into the parental household so that children grew up "surrounded by their paternal grandparents, paternal uncles, and their patrilateral cousins."[18] That stability was maintained through the continuous migration of young fathers (see Figure 4.2).

In Greece, by contrast, sharecropping was rare, and two distinct forms of agricultural production coexisted and overlapped: animal husbandry, primarily of sheep and goats among mountain-dwelling shepherds, and intensive agricultural production of olives, figs, and currants. Most farmers owned their own land, though because of Greek inheritance customs a family's possessions were often scattered throughout a village. As in Italy, household structure – deciding when and whether a son would become his own household head – posed one problem to the reproduction of patriarchal power. But inheritance loomed as an even larger problem given the necessity of providing dowries for daughters and dividing simple landholdings or flocks of sheep into ever smaller groups for sons. Consequently, it was the emigration of younger sons rather than new husbands that better alleviated the twin difficulties of securing dowries for sisters and keeping patrimonial estates intact (see Figure 4.3).[19]

Not all Italian emigrants were married, however, nor were all Greeks bound to Utah single. The existence of substantial minorities of single Italians and married Greeks in each migration suggests that economic and generational tensions affecting a family's decision to send single or married sons abroad were inextricably bound up with each other. The strain on patriarchal authority was a financial crisis

[18] Bell, *Fate and Honor*, 198; Kertzer, *Family Life in Central Italy*, 111–130; Kertzer and Hogan, *Family, Political Economy, and Demographic Change*, 177.
[19] Campbell, *Honour, Family, and Patronage*, 82; Du Boulay, "The Meaning of Dowry," 250; Herzfeld, "Social Tension and Inheritance by Lot," 96–97; Hionidou, "Nuptiality Patterns," 86.

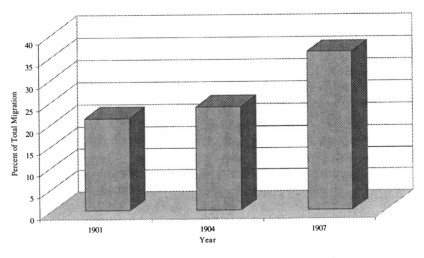

Figure 4.2. Italian single men, aged 18–23, among the Canada-bound, 1901–1907

as much as a generational problem.[20] But if common economic factors could prompt the emigration of both single and married men, these groups nonetheless possessed very different familial burdens and masculine responsibilities in their home villages. Single Greek and Italian emigrants were obliged to help secure dowry money for their sisters, whereas married emigrants typically sought to supplement the income of their father's household. Both burdens possessed clear rewards for the honorable emigrant who would discharge his duties faithfully: the cultural and financial advantages of marriage, the preservation of the larger patrimonial estate, and the hope of becoming its head.

Although most emigrants understood and accepted their familial duties, many migrated to escape patriarchal authority. "My father was very strict," recalled Jesus Garza to anthropologist Manuel Gamio in the early 1920s. "He would hardly let us go out on the street.... I waited one day until my father went out and then I took money out of the strong box, gold coins especially." Garza's escape after robbing his father mirrored Asuncio Flores's experience in Michoacan in the mid-1920s. "I ran away from home," Flores recalled, "on account of a beating my father gave me because I quarreled with another boy. He beat me on a street corner; then I went home and robbed him of some money and took a train ... to Ciudad

---

[20] A closer look at variations within each migration suggests that proximity to railroads also influenced a family's decision to send a son or a husband abroad. In the north-central Peloponnese, where intensive cultivation of currants had boomed after the Athens-Nemea Railroad was completed, a higher percentage of Greek emigrants were married fathers. Emigrants from remote villages in the mountainous regions of western Crete, by contrast, were almost all single. See Table 4.2 in Appendix A. On the impact of the Athens-Nemea Railroad, see Sutton, "What Is a Village," 198–199.

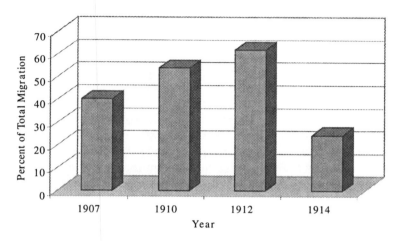

Figure 4.3. Greek single men, aged 18–23, among the Utah-bound, 1907–1914

Juarez."[21] The beating itself was bad enough; his public humiliation and loss of honor, however, demanded drastic action.

The emigration of sons and young fathers exemplified both creative solutions to patriarchal tensions and the potential breakdown of patriarchal power. Just what kind of male authority migrant men would create for themselves remained uncertain. But for both married and single emigrants, manhood in the villages they left was tied to patriarchal privileges and obligations. For single men, manhood existed largely as a promise of two as yet unfulfilled rewards: one's paternal inheritance and a marriage partner who would secure honor, offspring, prestige, and domestic labor to the husband's new household. For married sojourners manhood was closely associated with the household's economic security and their eventual control over it. Although tensions existed between fraternal and familial forms of manhood, most sojourners linked manhood to the privileges of fatherhood.

Manhood on the Move

Precisely where masculine authority was located in the North American West was anything but self-evident. To newly arrived Greek immigrant Harry Mantos, the region looked less like a particular place than a process of constant movement. Between 1907 and 1909, Mantos rapidly moved from job to job. He began 1907 laying railroad track near Salt Lake City, then took a water-main construction job in Twin Falls, Idaho, and later a position loading mail for the Union Pacific

[21] Manuel Gamio, *The Mexican Immigrant, His Life Story: Autobiographical Documents* (Chicago, 1931), 15, 112. On struggles by wives and children to limit patriarchal power, see Stern, *The Secret History of Gender*, 19; Griswold del Castillo, *La Familia*, 27–32; Deutsch, *No Separate Refuge*, 48; Bell, *Fate and Honor*, 92–93; Dubisch, "Gender, Kinship, and Religion," 29–46.

Railroad in Green River, Wyoming, before securing a position as a copper mucker in Bingham, Utah. The next year brought more movement. In the spring, Mantos left Utah for a bootblack job in Omaha, Nebraska, returned to Green River to work as a track laborer, and eventually traveled to Deadwood, South Dakota, to make cans. He returned to Bingham in the winter of 1908 and remained there until the summer of 1909, when he and three hundred Greek co-workers went on strike for a pay increase. Two months later, he moved to Seattle, Washington, to make boats. In virtually every job except the last, Mantos paid tribute to padrones to get his position, however onerous, temporary, and poorly paid.[22]

To many American-born observers, the constant mobility of men like Harry Mantos was evidence of a peculiar affliction, one that summarized everything unmanly about the culture of immigrant workers. Nativist intellectuals attributed their relentless mobility to individual cultural and moral weakness, whereas liberal commentators looked to economic and environmental causes.[23] But both groups depicted migrant men as culturally impoverished figures. Devoid of the domestic attachments that in crucial respects defined middle-class manhood and respectability, these "birds of passage" were seen as beyond the redemption of familial or paternal care.

Men like Mantos were hardly the first group of male wage earners to be perceived as unmanly. Middle-class reformer Samuel Eliot echoed the opinion of many wage workers and union leaders in 1871 when he argued that "to put a man upon wages is to put him in the position of dependent." The longer he works for wages "the less of a man he becomes." By 1900 trade unions in North America had transformed their critique of wage earning into a demand for a "living wage," as Lawrence Glickman has demonstrated, one quite compatible with patriarchal assumptions about a husband's power at the workplace and at home. But if the fear of wages was subsiding within an American-born working class, the manly status of unskilled immigrant workers remained uncertain. Indeed, for transient Greeks, Italians, and Mexicans, whose familial duties seemed nonexistent to nativist onlookers, the labor movement's campaign for a "living wage" only intensified their emasculation in North America. In 1902 the American Federation of Labor (AFL) president Samuel Gompers condemned not wage labor but unskilled

---

[22] John Harry Mantos interview by Louis Cononelos, Salt Lake City, December 9, 1974, American West Center, University of Utah. Mantos returned to Greece in 1922 as an American citizen, but fifteen years later was again working in Bingham's open pit at the age of fifty-nine.

[23] On racialized explanations of mobility, see sociologist Edward Alsworth Ross's *The Old World in the New: The Significance of Past and Present Immigration to the American People* (New York: 1914), 95–119; Carleton Parker, *The Casual Laborer, and Other Essays* (New York, 1920); Alice Solenberger, *One Thousand Homeless Men: A Study of Original Records* (New York, 1911). For liberal analyses of the "problem" of mobility, see William Leiserson's *Adjusting Immigrant and Industry* (New York, 1924), 28–48; Schlicter, *The Turnover of Factory Labor*; Nels Anderson, *The Hobo: The Sociology of the Homeless Man* (Chicago, 1923); Nels Anderson, *Men on the Move* (Chicago, 1940). For dissenting views that deemed mobility to be manly, see Jack London, *The Road* (London, 1907), 24–26, 59–60.

immigrant workers, whose low wages made them "a degraded, a debased, and demoralized manhood."[24]

Harry Mantos and his Italian and Mexican co-workers, of course, were not the orphaned or emasculated men of middle-class and working-class perception. Quite unseen to contemporary observers and subsequent historians were the family ties that enabled men like Harry Mantos to "bounce" between four jobs each work season.[25] The power of those family ties was apparent in the migration streams to Utah and Montreal. Ties to wives, children, siblings, and parents varied significantly between Italian and Greek men, but family connections in North America were prominent for both groups. Almost half of all Montreal-bound Italians in 1904 listed some family member as already present in Montreal. Among Utah-bound Greeks in 1912, the percentage was even higher: fully four out of five possessed kin who were waiting for them in Utah.[26] Among Mexicans passing through El Paso, literary sources likewise suggest kin relations facilitated migration throughout North America, even for those fleeing patriarchal power. Jesus Garza, having robbed and abandoned his father, traveled to Dallas to find his cousin.

Yet mobility challenged where and how immigrant men defined family ties, honor, and manhood. If protecting and controlling the labor of children and wives had been a central feature of honorable manhood in their home villages, how would such honor be maintained in North America when families were absent and men performed most "domestic" work on the move? Manhood in Greece, Italy, and Mexico had never been simply contingent on controlling women's labor, but everywhere sojourners traveled in the West, they confronted obstacles to recreating the patriarchal forms of manhood they had left behind. Sojourners were not devoid of family ties, as Samuel Gompers suggested, but their family relations were dramatically transformed by mobility and the rigorous demands of industrial life in North America.

For Italian track workers in Canada, domestic life revolved around the boxcars in which they were temporarily housed. Poorly ventilated, unheated, and unlit,

---

[24] Michael Kimmel, *Manhood in America: A Cultural History* (New York, 1996), 84; Lawrence Glickman, *A Living Wage: American Workers and the Making of Consumer Society* (Ithaca, 1997), 42. For a general discussion of the crisis of manliness among middle-class American men, see Anthony Rotundo, *American Manhood: Transformations in Masculinity from the Revolution to the Modern Era* (New York, 1993); Clyde Griffen and Mark Carnes, eds., *Meanings for Manhood: Constructions of Masculinity in Victorian America* (Chicago, 1990). For England, see Michael Roper and John Tosh, eds., *Manful Assertions: Masculinities in Britain since 1800* (London, 1992).

[25] Several historians have emphasized the culturally impoverishing impact of mobility. See David T. Courtwright, *Violent Land: Single Men and Social Disorder from the Frontier to the Inner City* (Cambridge, 1996), 170–182; Way, *Common Labour*, 167–170; Melvyn Dubofsky, *We Shall Be All: A History of the Industrial Workers of the World* (Chicago, 1969), 5.

[26] Steamship Manifest Lists, Port of New York, March 1901, March 1904, March 1907, March 1910, March 1912, March 1914, Records of the Department of Immigration and Naturalization, RG 85. See Table 4.1 in Appendix A.

such facilities provided Italian track workers minimal shelter from the rain, cold, and occasional snow during a summer in the Canadian Rockies. At the same time, boxcars served as breeding grounds for viruses, infections, and mosquitoes. Italian laborer Giuseppe Zolaire testified that when "out on work" he was "bitten by black flies," but in his boxcar he was constantly "bitten by mosquitoes." Italian foreman Thomas Cozzolino was compelled to take his entire track gang to Ottawa in 1901 because the road they were building was "through the woods and the mosquitoes were terrible."[27]

Italian sojourners enjoyed few of the domestic amenities they were accustomed to in their home villages or that Cordasco or Skliris enjoyed as wealthy padrones in Montreal or in Utah's fine hotels. Domestic life was created out of necessity and with whatever supplies could be gathered after an excruciating twelve-hour day with a pick and shovel. One of the most revealing firsthand accounts of the domestic life of Italian track workers was offered by Dominic Ciolli, a twenty-one-year-old medical student, who worked on a railroad in Indiana in 1914:

I tramped out to a large string of dilapidated boxcars, the home of the track gang.... On both sides of the cars, on the ground, were rusty perforated tin boxes, propped up by stones. These were stoves. Heaps of rubbish covered the ground, and the general appearance of the immediate surroundings, combined with the undefinable stench, gave me an idea of the interior of these commodious dwellings.

Ciolli's disdain partially reflected his middle-class upbringing, but few Italian track workers in fact experienced much attachment to these "homes." If these Italian kitchens were makeshift affairs, they produced meals memorable only for their bad qualities. "They cooked their meals in blackened kettles," recalled Ciolli, "devouring more soot than food." Italian track worker Cesidio Simboli echoed Ciolli's observations in 1917 when he told a reporter that "the food was not even fit for dogs. The bread oftentimes had mould on it, and the beans, sardines, salami, bolognas, and macaroni were of the cheapest sort."[28]

Immigrant miners lived in equally unappealing circumstances. Greeks miners in Utah resided in ramshackle boardinghouses or even worse, as Steve Kalaides recalled: "We found we had no place to stay in Bingham and so we did something that was very common in Greece. We found a bank of dirt and against it we dug out and formed a half cave and enclosed it with wood.... And four of us lived in there." Both radical and conservative commentators saw nothing but squalor in such dwellings. New York's Socialist daily, The Call, described Bingham's residences

---

27 Testimony of Giuseppe Zolaire, *Royal Commission*, 35; Thomas Cozzolino, Diary, "Tramping and Contracting: An Italian Gang Boss of 1901," in Irving Abella and David Millar, eds., *The Canadian Worker in the Twentieth Century* (Toronto, 1981), 7.
28 Dominic Ciolli, "The 'Wop' in the Track Gang," *Immigrants in America Review* (July 1916), in Moquin and Van Doren, *A Documentary History of Italian Americans*, 141–142; Simboli, "When the Boss Went Too Far," 148.

in 1912 as "ill smelling places ... not fit to house a dog, let alone so many human beings," while the probusiness *Engineering and Mining Journal* of Salt Lake City described Bingham as "a sewer four miles long."[29]

Dislocation and alienation were indeed powerful elements of immigrant workers' lives throughout the North American West.[30] Greek immigrant Haralambos Kambouris traveled extensively during his first three years in America, working unskilled jobs for a few months at a time in between periods of unemployment. Having used up his last dollar in Oregon, he wrote a poem entitled "Peripeteias," or "Wanderings," which expressed his disillusionment with mobility:

Like a crazy man I wander.
From town to town I walk.
Where I go I do not know.

Upon a hill I sit
and cry my troubles,
my bitterness and groans,
and my despair.

With weeping eyes,
bitter songs I sing.
I write them down on paper
and tears sprinkle them.[31]

His tears did not, by his own estimation, make him any less of a man. But his constant mobility did, compromising his sense of control, independence, and autonomy.

Kambouris's alienation would have resonated with many Mexicans on the move. "I have left the best of my life and my strength here," recalled Guanajuato-born sugar beet worker Juan Berzunol in 1926, "sprinkling with the sweat of my brow the fields and factories of these gringos." Another Mexican recalled going "from place to place, wherever there was work.... Those early days were days of very, very hard work, of ideals and hopes dashed to pieces, of bitter disappointments." Such collective frustrations were captured in the lyrics of a popular Mexican folk song at the time, "Los Enganchados" (The hooked ones): "Some unloaded rails, and others unloaded ties, And others threw out thousands of curses." These lyrics did not call into question the manhood of the singers, but like Kambouris's poetry, longed for domestic comforts while cursing the arbitrary aspects of industrial life. One of the most powerful such curses appeared in the

---

[29] Steve Kalaides interview by Helen Papanikolas, Salt Lake City, March 22, 1973, Greek Archives; *New York Call*, October 6, 1912, 3; *Salt Lake Mining and Engineering Journal*, October 13, 1912, 1.

[30] On similar themes in the experience of Irish canal workers, see Peter Way, "Evil Humors and Ardent Spirits: The Rough Culture of Canal Construction Laborers," *Journal of American History* 79:4 (March 1997): 1408.

[31] Kambouris, "Sojourn in America," 52, December 28, 1914, Greek Archives.

editorial page of the Greek newspaper *Ergatis* after two cousins were killed unloading copper ore. "May thunder and fire rain down upon the smelter, which has poured poison into the glasses of many parents."[32]

If industrial work and its perils made men nostalgic for families back home, family ties in North America were sources of only mixed comfort to sojourners. After months of wandering the land with no work in 1914, Kambouris contemplated suicide but stopped short. "Only one idea kept me from this drastic action ... my mother and five orphaned sisters who had no one to protect them but me." Kambouris's devotion to his patriarchal duties literally saved his life. Yet those same responsibilities depressed him: "Indebted, penniless, family burdens came all at once into my mind and made me insane." Kambouris's family ties in North America likewise proved both helpful and harmful. Uncle Nakos, who lived in Seattle, promised Kambouris work in the spring of 1914 during his nephew's worst bout of unemployment but, instead, left him stranded in a remote lumber camp. "Our only food was coffee in the morning, sardines at noon, and beans in the evening.... All this we endured because of my Uncle Nakos." Kambouris's other relative, Uncle Isidore of Bingham, proved more welcoming but also wound up suing his nephew for "disturbing the peace" after Kambouris failed to check with him before seeking a Greek woman's hand in marriage. Conflicts between Greek uncles and nephews were hardly unique to North America, but Isidore's decision to pursue his patriarchal claims in a U.S. court highlights the failure of Greek male elders to organize the life choices of their sons and nephews in North America.[33]

Nowhere were the limits to patriarchal power more apparent than among fathers who emigrated to the United States together with their sons. Mexican immigrant Wenceslao Iglesias recalled his horror and humiliation as a track worker when confronted with an example of a father's disempowerment: "All three (two sons and a father) were working and the old man began to rest. The foreman came to insult him and struck him. The sons instead of going to defend him fled and the old man did the same.... That angered me."[34] Iglesias condemned all three men as cowardly and dishonorable. The failed masculinity he perceived was not imposed by nativist Americans but rather reflected the geographic limits of patriarchal authority within Mexican families in North America. Mobility and industrial work transformed, from Iglesias's perspective, a father and his sons into three equally dependent and unmanly wage workers.

The limits to patriarchal authority in North America were brilliantly sketched in the short biography of Greek immigrant George Kyranakos, published in a directory of Utah's Greek businesses in 1912. A series of comic vignettes rather than a progressive tale of success in America, the biography portrays Kyranakos bouncing between sporadic wage work and failed business endeavors throughout

[32] Gamio, *The Mexican Immigrant*, 147; Taylor, *Mexican Labor in the United States*, vol. 2, 268; Gamio, *Mexican Immigration to the United States*, 85–86; *Ergatis*, October 10, 1908, 2.

[33] Kambouris, "Sojourn in America," 61–62, May 10, 1915, Greek Archives; ibid., 43–45, March 20, 1914.

[34] Gamio, *The Mexican Immigrant*, 177.

the West. An almost complete inversion of the heroes in Horatio Alger's fiction, Kyranakos never prospered but managed to escape disasters by luck rather than individual merit. He happened to skip work, for example, the day a mine explosion killed forty men at the Colorado and Iron Fuel Company in Delagona, Colorado. A month later he left San Francisco the day before the 1906 earthquake. Promised a foreman's job on the Western Pacific Railroad, he soon discovered the company had instead given him work "throwing muck with a wheelbarrow." When he quit and tried returning to Reno, the train went "off the track and into the creek." When he finally secured some money as a photographer and became engaged to a "good girl," the union fell apart when his best man at the wedding ceremony "started to change the wreathes on the heads and my wreath caught on my toupe, it dropping down." Horrified, his would-be bride "called a taxi and went away."[35] Through each of these farcical calamities, George persevered by recalling the advice his father dispensed when he left home – "be honest and don't get excited." George's fanciful experiences hardly exemplified the wisdom of his father's authority. Rather, his mantralike repetition of that comic advice suggested the irrelevancy of most paternal admonitions. The power of fathers remained elusive for Kyranakos and thousands of Greeks like him in North America.

Where, then, did immigrant sojourners, married and single, find their moorings as men in North America? The locations that individuals chose varied, but most found solace and affirmation in a fraternal culture built from bonds of fictive kinship.[36] By transforming male friends into "family," sojourners created bonds among male "family" members that were egalitarian rather than patriarchal or hierarchical. In so doing, sojourners did not necessarily reject all of the varied assumptions and privileges of patriarchal manhood. Indeed, ties to family members of origin in both North America and home villages remained strong. But fraternal culture dramatically expanded the boundaries of kinship, transforming not only which family bonds mattered to sojourning men, but also how they understood the rights and duties of honorable manhood.[37]

For many emigrants, the need for kin immediately presented itself in North

[35] George P. Kyranakos, *Biography of George P. Kyranakos from K. Stania Vion, Greece* (Salt Lake City, 1912), Greek Archives.

[36] By "fictive kin," I refer to the men and women whom immigrants chose as adults to be family members, rather than the family members they were related to by birth. By describing such family members as "fictive," I do not mean to suggest they were less powerful or real than family members of origin, but simply distinct from them. On the fictive element within all kinship ties, see Kath Weston, *Families We Choose: Lesbians, Gays, Kinship* (New York, 1991).

[37] On fraternalism within native-born and middle-class contexts in the United States in 1900, see Mark C. Carnes, *Secret Ritual and Manhood in Victorian America* (New Haven, 1989); Mary Ann Clawson, *Constructing Brotherhood: Class, Gender, and Fraternalism* (Princeton, 1989); Lynn Dumenil, *Freemasonry and American Culture, 1880–1939* (Princeton, 1984). On fraternalism within western working-class contexts, see Elizabeth Jameson, *All that Glitters: Class, Conflict, and Community in Cripple Creek* (Urbana, 1998), 87–113; Gunther Peck, "Manly Gambles: The Politics of Risk on the Comstock Lode," *Journal Of Social History* 26:4 (Summer 1993): 701–723.

America. Greek emigrant George Lamb recalled being stuck at the U.S. border without any family sponsors until an older friend from his village offered to "take George as my son." Having thus been adopted, Lamb subsequently acquired a job through his new father's cousin who worked as a foreman on the Denver and Rio Grande (D&RG). Fictive kin were vital to survival for Jesus Garza as well. While looking for his cousin in Dallas, Jesus discovered kin among his fellow track workers, who showed him how to survive on the move. "My best pal was a Mexican and we cared for each other more than brothers. When one didn't have money the other did and we helped each other in everything."[38]

These fraternal bonds were grounded in the everyday risks that wage earners shared on the job. When Haralambos Kambouris learned that three workers would have to be fired from his railroad work gang, his compatriots took turns working a few days each "until payday so they could get paid and look for work." Similar kinds of mutualism were apparent among Mexican track workers. When Bonifacio Ortega dislocated his arm on the job, his "fellow countrymen" visited him in the hospital everyday and brought him food and "presents." After recovering and returning to work, Bonifacio led the effort to help another compatriot whose wife had died, "getting enough money together to buy a coffin and enough so that he could go and take the body to Jalisco."[39] Thus, fraternal culture did not necessarily exist in opposition to traditional family ties; here it worked to support Mexican men's connections to their families of origin in Jalisco.

Fraternal culture was also rooted in the mutualistic ways men shared tasks of unpaid work in their new domestic contexts. Although Italian track workers in Indiana complained bitterly about the "soot" they cooked, a Mexican track worker in Indiana boasted of his cooking prowess: "I did not know how to cook when I came here, but I have learned so that now I can cook better than a woman. We six men all buy our groceries and keep them in a separate box. We all use the same kitchen and the same bedrooms." If pride in one's domestic skills was something quite new for this Mexican man, the meanings of domestic work were slower to change. The central purpose of Mexican men cooking rather than buying prepared food or paying someone to cook for them was to provide financial support for their families in Mexico. The very mobility that redefined patterns of domestic labor also put constraints on what this new work meant. When this same Mexican track worker attempted to formalize his new domestic arrangements, he met considerable resistance from his domestic partners. "I would like to buy the food wholesale," he explained, "but the other men do not agree. They are irregular in buying and do not want a large supply because they want to be free to leave at a moment's notice." The domestic life these track workers created remained a necessity, not a preference.[40]

The reluctance of many immigrants to systematize their domestic arrangements suggests that new domestic work routines challenged immigrant men's

---

[38] Gamio, *The Mexican Immigrant*, 18.
[39] Kambouris, "Sojourn in America," 25, March 1, 1914; Gamio, *The Mexican Immigrant*, 67.
[40] Taylor, *Mexican Labor in the United States*, vol. 2, 184.

assumptions about the appropriate competencies of men and women. Some immigrants did indeed adopt highly formalized domestic work routines. Coal miner Angelo Georgedes recalled that "Greek fellows working in the mine ... would take regular turns, some to clean the house and some to cook.... One day one would fix the breakfast, (or) fix lunches the night before." But most Greek sojourners preferred not to see these new domestic routines as well organized, even if they carefully rotated all household work. Typical was the perspective of Greek miner Steve Kalaides who remembered cooking but downplayed its significance. "We'd sort of take turns cooking," he admitted, "but it was a very haphazard arrangement."[41]

Although immigrants adopted mutualistic strategies for coping with the demands of paid and unpaid work, many remained ambivalent about the merits and meaning of the fraternal culture they created on the move. That ambivalence was particularly apparent in their diverse reactions to the many homosocial entertainments that flourished among men of numerous origins in the West. Although drinking, dancing, gambling, and prostitution were familiar to many sojourners before emigrating, the importance of homosocial amusements was dramatically amplified in the West, as were the commonalities and tensions they created among sojourning men. For Mexican immigrant Jesus Garza, the opportunities to see "American prostitutes" did not induce shame but rather solidified bonds between his co-workers, a practice not unlike treating his drinking partners at a saloon. Beer and sex were hardly equivalent commodities, particularly to the women who worked as prostitutes and sought to limit the risks and abuses of their work as best they could. But for sojourners like Garza, paying women for sex was an important element of fraternal manhood's egalitarian rights and privileges. For Haralambos Kambouris, by contrast, visiting a prostitute was unthinkable precisely because it would have dishonored his manhood and ties to family members in Greece. Tensions between behaviors deemed moral and immoral pervaded the varied world of fraternal entertainments among immigrant sojourners.[42]

For some, conflicts over where male honor was located fueled nostalgia for the patriarchal contexts that immigrants had left. Consider, for example, the lyrics to the 1920s Mexican ballad "El rancho donde yo naci" (The farm where I was born), popular among Mexican immigrants in Texas:

I don't care to dance
in the halls that you have here,
what I want is an earth floor
like on the farm where I was born.

[41] Angelo Georgedes, *Reminiscences of Life and Moving to America* (Madison, 1973), 4–5; Steve Kalaides interview by Helen Papanikolas, June 30, 1972, Greek Archives.

[42] Gamio, *The Mexican Immigrant*, 21. On prostitution in the West, see Anne Butler, *Daughters of Joy, Sisters of Mercy: Prostitution in the American West, 1865–1890* (Urbana, 1985); Marion S. Goldman, *Gold Diggers and Silver Miners: Prostitution and Social Life on the Comstock Lode* (Ann Arbor, 1981); and Paula Petrik, *No Step Backward: Women and Family on the Rocky Mountain Frontier, Helena, Montana, 1865–1900* (Helena, Montana, 1987).

I don't care for your
automatic pistols that you have here,
what I want is a black rifle
like on the farm where I was born.

I don't care for your
silk shirts that you have here,
what I want is a suit of blue jumpers
like on the farm where I was born.[43]

No mention is made of fathers in this song, but the images of agrarian Mexican life, replete with earth floors, black rifles, and blue jumpers, evoked the patrilocal arenas in which Mexican manhood was performed and defined. In contrast to Jesus Garza, who thoroughly enjoyed the advantages of fraternal culture, these Mexican songwriters lamented the new venues of manly performance in the West – the dance halls, automatic pistols, and silk shirts. In these faster-paced arenas, the location of family boundaries, the meaning of kinship and Mexican manhood, seemed unstable and insecure.

But sojourners' nostalgia for a more secure manhood did not prevent many from also experiencing relief at having escaped patriarchal expectations and restraints in their home villages. Fictive kinship may in fact have been compatible with ties to one's family of origin on the move, but in the patrilocal villages that Greek, Italian, and Mexican men left, friendships between nonkin were comparatively rare and often deemed hostile to family interests.[44] Fictive kinship and friendship among men in North America, by contrast, were not only far more conspicuous but rightly understood among sojourners as vital to survival.

Among fictive kin, some sojourning men found not only friendships but sexual gratification, having fewer restraints on their behavior than in home villages. Yet little explicit evidence of a gay subculture survives in the fragmented documentary records of Italian, Greek, and Mexican sojourners in the West, despite remarkable similarities between their fraternal culture and the bachelor culture studied by historian George Chauncey in New York City during the same period.[45] One reason for the apparent invisibility of gay men in rural contexts was the same mobility that helped create a visible gay subculture in cities like New York and San Francisco. When working in the rural West during the summer work season, there were few places where gay men would be censured, policed, or identified, consequently leaving few if any documentary traces of their presence.[46] During the off-season,

---

[43] Gamio, *Mexican Immigration to the United States*, 88.

[44] Campbell, *Honour, Family, and Patronage*, 205; Sydel F. Silverman, "Agricultural Organization, Social Structure, and Values in Italy: Amoral Familism Reconsidered," *American Anthropologist* 70:1 (February 1968): 1–20.

[45] On New York City's bachelor culture, see George Chauncey, *Gay New York: Gender, Urban Culture, and the Making of the Gay Male World, 1890–1940* (New York, 1994), 79–81.

[46] Such freedom was not entirely beneficial, however, for mobility also meant gay men were isolated from each other on the move.

by contrast, the same sojourners who had evaded public scrutiny swelled the urban boardinghouses and working-class neighborhoods where gay subcultures flourished.

If fraternal culture created new opportunities for a variety of male friendships and relationships, it also expanded the importance of the performative arenas in which men sought to define themselves. For Greek immigrants in Utah, dancing was perhaps the most popular activity. Like miners in the California Gold Rush, most of this dancing occurred between men. Homosocial dancing was not new for Greek men or an adaptation to necessity, as some of the most virile dances in Greece involved chains of men following a leader who pivoted, lept, and spun while male onlookers evaluated his athleticism. These dances exemplified the performative nature of Greek manhood, one that Michael Herzfeld aptly described as focusing less on "being a good man" than on "being good at being a man."[47]

Such performances could indeed be memorable. Greek immigrant Peter Demiris of Salt Lake City recalled sixty years after the fact that "in the streets of Greektown they would get out and dance their various dances from some of the provinces from which they came. They came from so many different parts of Greece and the islands. The Cretans came wearing their pantaloons." Like a Scottish kilt, Cretan pantaloons resembled a woman's dress, but were symbols of Cretan manhood, displayed only on holidays and national celebrations (see Plate 13). Jack Tallas recalled the enthusiasm he and his compatriots felt about dancing in coffeehouses. "They had Greek musicians and dance every night. They danced on Sunday and every day, every day. I would say about the same thing in Bingham. That's all they had then."[48] Greek patrons danced not only when Cretan miners put on their pantaloons, but every time a musician arrived and men, in work clothes, cleared the tables.

Although dancing was not new to Greek sojourners or exclusive to the fraternal culture they created in North America, its cultural meaning changed dramatically in the West. Traditionally, Greeks celebrated their name days rather than birthdays, the day in the religious calendar when their patron saint was annually commemorated. In Utah, however, Greeks celebrated not only the name days of their blood relatives, but the name days of fictive kin throughout the larger fraternal community. Steve Kalaides recalled the frequent preparations for such activities: "We men did the cooking because there were so many of us. And we had ... lamb and goat cheese and goats which we roasted on our name days. We had a name day almost every day there were so many of us." The boundaries of this fraternal "family" were much larger than any kinship network in Greece. Indeed, the 1908 observance of

---

[47] Susan Johnson, "Of Fiddles and Fandangos," in " 'The Gold She Gathered': Difference, Domination, and California's Southern Mines, 1848–1853" (Ph.D. diss., Yale University, 1993). On the centrality of dancing to notions of Greek manhood, see Herzfeld, *The Poetics of Manhood*, 16; David G. Gilmore, *Manhood in the Making: Cultural Concepts of Masculinity* (New Haven, 1990), 30–55.

[48] Peter Demiris interview by Helen Papanikolas, Salt Lake City, June 30, 1972, 6, Greek Archives; Jack Tallas interview by Theodore Paulos, Salt Lake City, January 18, 1971, ibid.

Greek Orthodox Christmas in Bingham became an occasion of working-class fraternity. As the newspaper *Ergatis* recounted, "the thing which aroused the excitement of the Italians, Americans, and Austrians was the fact that a man wearing Cretan clothes started dancing. All were soon drunk and all began dancing with the Greeks together. ... The celebration gave the Greeks the reputations of being 'good fellows.'"[49] Although middle-class observers pathologized such dancing as frivolous, no such perceptions existed among the workers of Bingham who saw in their festivities hallmarks of fraternal manhood and working-class solidarity.

Greek dancing in Bingham might transform strangers into working-class kin or "good fellows," but such displays as often led to friction between men. Because manhood was something performed, it was also highly unstable. According to Peter Demiris, many Greek dances produced confrontations with American bystanders. "The Cretans ... stood in the streets and gazed after the American women and this caused a great deal of consternation among the American people." What began as an athletic performance for compatriots, ended as a sexualized boast to American onlookers. Such efforts to claim sexual power in North America frequently ended in violence. Greek immigrant George Chares, for example, was shot and killed by George Cushman, an American cook in Bingham, after Chares "was supposedly caught peeking into Cushman's bedroom window." No mention was made in the newspaper report whether Cushman was alone in his bed or with a sexual partner, but Chares' modest provocation justified drastic action. Cushman's bullets highlight how insecure one man's virility could be in this fraternal world where, as George Chauncey put it, "virility was confirmed by other men." Manhood was fragile, lost or gained with a single untimely peep through a window.[50]

One photograph that captures the symbolic and performative dimensions of fraternal manhood among Greek immigrants depicts twelve residents of Bingham Canyon in 1911, all from Crete, holding bottles of cognac in their left hands and pistols or revolvers in their right (see Plate 15). All of the men sport handlebar mustaches and their best American clothes and look directly into the camera with expressions ranging from pride to stoic indifference. The photograph is striking not only as a candid portrayal of the symbols of Greek manhood – mustaches, alcohol, and pistols – but also as an affirmation of their new American identities. No nostalgia for earth floors or Cretan pantaloons appears in this photo: only black shoes, ties, and suits, symbols of their success and new manhood in North America.[51]

---

[49] Steve Kalaides interview by Helen Papanikolas, Salt Lake City, March 22, 1973, ibid.; *Ergatis*, January 18, 1908, 5.

[50] Peter Demiris interview by Helen Papanikolas, June 30, 1972, Greek Archives; *Deseret Evening News*, August 19, 1908, 3; Chauncey, *Gay New York*, 80. On the performative nature of gender identity more generally, see Judith Butler, *Gender Trouble: Feminism and the Subversion of Identity* (New York, 1990).

[51] The photograph, located at the Utah State Historical Society, Salt Lake City, was chosen to be part of the Ellis Island museum in 1990, but was subsequently removed after several Greek Americans protested its presence, claiming it confirmed a stereotypical view of Greeks as members of the mafia (personal correspondence, 1994, Helen Papanikolas, Salt Lake City, Utah).

Although the photograph has recently stirred controversy among Greek Americans for evoking a stereotyped image of their ethnic group, guns were indeed prevalent among the first generation. According to Greek miner Angelo Georgedes, "the first thing that they [Greeks] do, the first dollar they earn, they would go buy themselves a gun."[52]

Greeks were hardly alone in their enthusiasm for firearms, a penchant manifest in the folk songs that Mexican solos sang on the move during the 1910s and 1920s. In the tragedy of Gregorio Cortez, popular initially along the Texas-Mexican border but subsequently throughout the U.S. Southwest, the hero defends himself and his brother against a racist American sheriff by killing him with a pistol. Cortez is eventually taken down by a band of three hundred Americans in San Antonio, but he dies – like the Greeks pictured in Utah, with "his pistol in his hand." In the ballad of Jesus Cadena, who carries a thirty-eight caliber revolver and is accompanied by twelve well-armed disciples, Cadena is confronted by an adversary who picks a fight. But this Jesus refuses to turn the other cheek and replies "I will not put away my pistol. Now I will make you do as I please, or I shall send you away from this world." As the confrontation between the groups of men intensifies "daggers and pistols could be seen everywhere. But they did nothing, because they recognized one another."[53] Cadena's power as a man comes not simply from owning a powerful gun but in revealing it openly. Here, in a fraternity of highly visible weaponry, Cadena makes his escape and claims an elusive manhood.

Stories of pistol-wielding Mexicans represented a male fantasy for most solos who sang and heard such songs, but they also highlight connections between violence and fraternity. On the one hand, violence between men involving cards, debts, knives, and pistols could indeed sunder fraternal and familial bonds. It was not uncommon, for example, for blood brothers to fight over games of chance, even to the point of injury and fatality. But such contests also created a medium of risk taking and danger necessary for the performance of manhood and creation of fraternal bonds among sojourners. Most immigrants fought and gambled by the same rules, taking the same risks in games of chance, working on similar jobs, and sharing domestic chores. By playing, working, cooking, and competing together, even to the point of violence, immigrants became men and brothers simultaneously.[54]

Yet the violence depicted and implied in these sources raises thorny questions about the fraternal culture that emerged among Greek, Mexican, and Italian

---

[52] Georgedes, *Reminiscences of Life and Moving to America*, 5.

[53] Gamio, *Mexican Immigration to the United States*, 98–100.

[54] On the mutualistic nature of gambling and physical contests among working-class men, see Eliot Gorn, *The Manly Art: Bare-Knuckle Prize Fighting in America* (Ithaca, 1986), 129–147; Ann Fabian, *Card Sharps, Dream Books, and Bucket Shops: Gambling in Nineteenth-Century America* (Ithaca, 1990); Peck, "Manly Gambles," 705–710. For less romantic assessments of working-class men's violence and its impact on women, see Pamela Haag, "'The Ill-Use of a Wife': Working-Class Violence in Domestic and Public New York City, 1860–1880," *Journal of Social History* 25:3 (Spring 1992): 447–478; and Way, "Evil Humors and Ardent Spirits," 1397–1410.

sojourners in the West. To what degree if any were the patterns of violence among immigrant sojourners western in origin or character? As historian Carlos Schwantes has suggested, Greek, Italian, and Mexican immigrant men composed only one portion of a much larger group of wage-earning men in the West, who worked in the region's extractive industries and lived primarily in the company of other men well into the 1930s. The forms of violence that surrounded immigrant sojourners' fraternal recreations – drinking, gambling, dancing, and paying prostitutes for sex – were hardly exclusive to immigrant sojourners but had long been associated in popular venues with a boisterous frontier culture dominated by single men.[55]

But viewing violence among immigrant sojourners in the West as an outgrowth of frontier culture neglects the transnational and working-class contexts from which both violence and immigrant manhood emerged. Immigrants, after all, were no strangers to pistols and their manly symbolism. In Crete and parts of the Peloponnese, infant boys were named "pistoli" until baptized. Greeks and Mexicans both purchased firearms in North America not to become westerners but rather to protect themselves against nativists, many of whom fancied themselves cowboys. Angelo Georgedes explained his compatriots' desire for guns in one word: "protection." In the ballad of Gregorio Cortez, the hero shoots an American sheriff because he is a racist trying to kill his brother. Moreover, much of the violence among immigrant sojourners involved industrial conflicts not based in a primitive frontier but, as Melvyn Dubofsky succinctly put it, "in a citadel of American industrialism and capitalism."[56]

Rooting the violence of fraternal culture in a frontier of skewed sex ratios also obscures the complexity of fraternal culture in the West and the central tensions that characterized its expression and development. Fraternalism was the dominant language and institution of manhood among a great variety of men in the West at the turn of the twentieth century. In Cripple Creek, Colorado, fraternalism was defined and institutionalized by married men and their working-class families, whose members condemned the activities of mobile and unmarried workers. For

[55] Carlos Schwantes, "The Concept of the Wageworkers' Frontier: A Framework for Future Research," *Western Historical Quarterly* 18 (January 1987): 39–55. The most recent link between violence and the frontier is Courtwright, *Violent Land*. For critiques of the connection between violence and frontier culture, see Roger D. McGrath, *Gunfighters, Highwaymen, and Vigilantes: Violence on the Frontier* (Berkeley, 1984), 247–260; Robert Dykstra, *The Cattle Towns* (New York, 1968), 112–148; Dykstra, "Field Notes: Overdosing on Dodge City," *Western Historical Quarterly* 27 (Winter 1996): 505–514.

[56] Patrick Leigh Fermor, *Mani: Travels in the Southern Peloponnese* (London, 1958), 86. On the industrial origins of western violence, see Melvyn Dubofsky, *We Shall Be All*, 56. On connections between industrialization and myths of the frontier, see Richard Slotkin, *The Fatal Environment: The Myth of the Frontier in the Age of Industrialization, 1800–1890* (New York, 1985). On the radical political potential of western outlawry and frontier ideologies, see Richard White, "Outlaw Gangs of the Middle Border: American Social Bandits," *Western Historical Quarterly* 12 (October 1981): 387–408; Peck, "Manly Gambles," 720–725; and Schwantes, "The Concept of the Wageworkers' Frontier," 51–55.

persistent workers in mining towns like Butte, Montana, mobility likewise represented a threat to fraternalism and its principles. Transient Greek, Italian, and Mexican sojourners were thought to be violent and uncivilized men, unworthy of fraternal solidarity or support. For Greek, Italian, and Mexican sojourners, by contrast, fraternalism flourished precisely because of workers' mobility, not in spite of it. In communities such as Bingham Canyon, Greeks were in fact less likely than American-born residents to break the law or disturb the peace, despite the fact that most American men were married and lived with their families, while Greeks were single and lived in boardinghouses.[56] Indeed, the only crime for which Greeks were overrepresented was carrying a concealed weapon, suggesting the symbolic importance guns possessed for them (see Table 4.5 in Appendix A). For Greeks, the shadow of the gun, it would seem, was more important than actually using it.

These varied manifestations of fraternalism in the West highlight the importance of conflicts over mobility and the boundaries of kinship in fraternalism's development. Differences between the fraternalism of the Butte Miners' Union and of Greek dancers in coffeehouses involved not merely questions of manly style and performative skill but varying boundaries and definitions of kinship. Greeks in Bingham built fraternity out of kinship with both single and married sojourners whose families of origin were thousands of miles distant. Married Irish miners, in turn, built fraternity around the privileges of owning homes and having wives who labored within them. Those differences reflected not simply tensions between single and married men or between transient and persistent men, but also conflicts between families of choice and families of origin.

These conflicts over the boundaries of kinship not only divided single Greeks from married Irishmen in mining towns like Bingham and Butte but also left many individual men ambivalent and confused about where to define kinship and manhood. For Haralambos Kambouris, fictive kinship and loyalties to family members of origin initially pulled at right angles to each other. During his first year in the West, Kambouris devoted himself to fulfilling duties to his sisters and his mother. Just before leaving Greece Kambouris had fallen in love with a young woman named Vangelio, but then broke off the relationship because "my situation did not allow me to have erotic feelings." As he became overcome with loneliness in North America, however, he began a secret correspondence with her to arrange their marriage. She agreed to marry him, and he sent her a bracelet. But when Kambouris's mother discovered the plans, she became furious and gave her son an ultimatum: "either break your relations with her or you will refrain from being called my child." With great regret, Kambouris ended the relationship with Vangelio a second time, honoring duties to his parents and sisters.[58]

But the breakup had taken its toll on Kambouris. Shortly after urging Vangelio

---

[57] Schwantes, "The Concept of the Wageworkers' Frontier," 39–42; Jameson, *All that Glitters*, 87–113; Emmons, *The Butte Irish*, 94–132.

[58] Kambouris, "Sojourn in America," 20, October 8, 1912; ibid., 44, March 20, 1914.

never to write him again, he penned this angry poem to his mother: "You say that I have ignored mothers and sisters, and that I have loved a cheap woman who is full of shame.... All this you did so that I would cease to love this maiden whom I loved faithfully and sincerely.... And now mother, you have made me brainless and insane." Kambouris never sent the poem, but proceeded to begin another clandestine courtship through the mail, this one with a Greek woman he had never met and to whom he referred in his diary as "the unknown one." When Demetra Villiotis replied that she needed permission from her brother before she could marry him, Kambouris quickly wrote him asking for his consent, which the brother gave "with pleasure." News of the engagement infuriated his family in Utah and Greece, leading his Uncle Nakos to take him to court after an angry exchange. Kambouris found solace from such conflicts among his many new brothers. After losing his court case, Kambouris, still a bachelor, left the court-house with friends and "all in a group went to a beer parlor and there drinking beer passed the rest of the day."[59]

The halting and conflicted relocation of Kambouris's family loyalties from his mother and sisters to fraternal brothers in North America and "the unknown one" also transformed his perception of wage work and the risks it entailed. When earn-ing money for his sister's dowries, wage work and the constant threat of unem-ployment were extraordinarily onerous to Kambouris. His commitments to five sisters may have kept him from suicide, but the wage work itself "was unbearable." Upon securing his own marriage partner, however, his perception of wage work and unemployment improved dramatically. "I felt happier," Kambouris wrote, "with the idea that the unknown one would share my principles and from then on my unemployment did not scare me." Kambouris now confidently asserted that "I was very satisfied with my work and always cheerful about my fiance."[60]

But if Kambouris discovered freedom in wage labor because of his decision to bring a wife to North America, others remained ambivalent about marriage. Some, such as Mexican immigrant Nivardo del Rio, regretted bringing their families to the United States: "I sacrifice more now that I am married and have children," a complaint that colored his perception of wage work as well. "I have made a fortune three times and three times I have lost it, so that it seems I shall never be indepen-dent.... That is what I hate most, having to be a slave." A young single Mexican likewise saw his freedoms in opposition to family duties, though for him wage work was liberatory. "In Mexico mi padre is boss; here I am boss. If I go back to Mexico, then mi padre will be boss again." Other Mexicans remained uncertain about where to locate their manly rights. Carlos Ibanez refused to be married in the United States because "in this country, a man who opposes his wife loses her and even his wages if he isn't careful." To Ibanez, marriage in the United States meant emasculation: "He who lets himself be bossed by a woman isn't a man." By contrast, Anastacio Cortes decided to bring his wife to the United States because

[59] Ibid., 50–51, August 27, 1914; ibid., 69, April 3, 1915; ibid., 79, April 9, 1915.
[60] Ibid., 60, January 20, 1915; ibid., 75, April 2, 1915.

he missed his children's "caresses" after being forced to sleep "with some other companions as poor as he was in a room full of bedbugs." Fraternal culture horrified Cortes and he longed for the day when his wife "cooked and washed the dishes and clothes for him."[61] These men divided over the emancipatory potential of fraternalism and whether it was compatible with ties to families of origin. Were commitments to fraternalism and fatherhood compatible? Where should manly freedoms be located?

Immigrant workers forged answers to these questions not in a vacuum, but in dialogue with the padrone, a man who combined, in theory, the roles of father, brother, and employer. The transnational relocation of family ties and the reconfiguration of manhood were closely tied to the ways padrones mobilized men, both literally and culturally. For padrones, the task was daunting because no single kind of mobility and manhood characterized the fraternal culture that immigrant men had created. If padrones succeeded by exploiting distinct kinds of worker mobility, so too did they seek profits from distinct kinds of immigrant kin connections. The challenge for padrones was twofold: first, how would they gain power from the varied forms of men's geographic mobility? Second, how would they control and represent immigrant family ties? Would padrones seek authority within patriarchal or fraternal forms of manhood, within ties to blood relatives or to fictive kin? How, in short, would padrones mobilize both men and manhood?

Mobilizing Manhood

Demographic evidence culled from passenger manifest lists highlights the double-edged relationship between immigrant family ties and padrone authority. Although Skliris and Cordasco imported thousands of immigrant workers directly to the North American West at the peaks of their power, they did not initially gain power by prompting new chain migrations, whereby a pioneering immigrant generates a self-sustaining flow of immigrants by sending passage money to his or her relatives. Rather they gained power by reorganizing and intensifying ongoing chain migrations to North America. Yet the evidence also suggests that chain migration had a destabilizing impact on padrone power over time. By 1907, Italian families no longer needed Cordasco's aid to arrange transatlantic passages. Their growing control over Italian migration was manifest in the increasing percentages of immigrants who already possessed family members in North America upon arriving in New York (see Figure 4.4). When Italian foreman Rafaele di Zazza sent for his wife and children in the fall of 1903, he eliminated any need for his boss, Cordasco, to send remittances to his wife. A similar pattern became evident among Utah-bound Greeks by 1914.[62] Haralambos Kambouris preempted the

---

[61] Gamio, *The Mexican Immigrant*, 154–155; Taylor, *Mexican Labor in the United States*, vol. 2, 200; Gamio, *The Mexican Immigrant*, 47, 205.

[62] Steamship Manifest Lists, Port of New York, March 1901, March 1904, March 1907, March 1910, March 1912, March 1914, Records of the Department of Immigration and Naturalization, RG 85. See Table 4.4 in Appendix A.

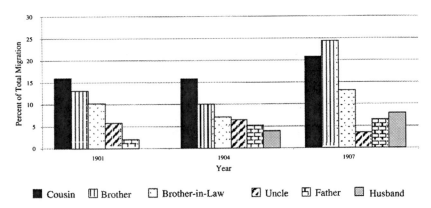

Figure 4.4. Closest family relation in Canada among Canada-bound Italians, 1901–1907

need for any middlemen to facilitate migration when the unknown one finally arrived in 1916.

The presence of women in Greek, Italian, and Mexican migration pools and the growing power of nuclear families in North America did not by themselves destabilize padrone authority. Skliris, Gonzalez, and Cordasco each lost power well before nuclear families predominated. Although the initial migration of a few Italian and Greek women paralleled crises in padrone authority, other padrones flourished by directly exploiting the labor of women and children. Indeed, Italian padrones in the berry fields of New Jersey employed women and children, as Cindy Hahamovitch has demonstrated. Likewise, the presence of Mexican women could facilitate rather than weaken a padrone's power. In the Mexican ballad "La de la 'nagua azul" (She of the blue skirt), the male singer returns to the United States with his wife and has these words for his padrone: "What do you say, my contractor? Didn't I tell you I'd be back? Send me wherever you will, because now I bring someone with me." If the presence of Rafaele Di Zazza's family emboldened him to challenge Cordasco, precisely the opposite pattern was evident here as this husband's newfound male privileges expanded his tolerance of the padrone. To understand the full instability of the padrone's power, we need to look beyond the crosscutting roles of actual family relations and consider how padrones represented manhood to their compatriots.[63]

When Antonio Cordasco first came to power as the sole Italian labor agent for the CPR, he made little effort to portray himself as a familial figure to Italian workers. His advertisements stated merely that "work is available." On February 27, 1904, by contrast, the newly coronated king published a letter in the Italian newspaper *Corriere del Canada*, advertising his business in explicitly paternal

---

[63] Cindy Hahamovitch, *The Fruits of their Labor: Atlantic Coast Farmworkers and the Making of Migrant Poverty, 1870–1945* (Chapel Hill, 1997), 42–46; Gamio, *Mexican Immigration to the United States*, 90–91.

terms: "The Italian laborers ... find in Cordasco a father, a friend, who not only helps and protects them, but puts them in a position to provide for their families and their aged parents." Cordasco crafted this paternal image not only in newspaper advertisements but also in his public life-style. During his coronation he celebrated the recent birth of his seventh child, a son, proclaiming to all his honorable and manly status as a married father with a large family.[64] His apparent success as a prolific progenitor sanctioned his public claims to being the metaphoric father of Italian communities in Montreal and elsewhere in Canada. Here indeed was a patriarchal leader whom Italian fathers could emulate as their own manly representative.

Cordasco's conscious decision to portray himself as a model father made good sense because most of his men were married fathers and presumably aspired to the same values and privileges. By reminding Italian sojourners of their fatherly duties, Cordasco affirmed the family ties that kept Italian men on track and paying him tributes. The irony of Cordasco's coronation, however, is that it accelerated an erosion of his authority. Cordasco had crafted the parade not as a truly confident father or king, but in reaction to a growing challenge to his power. That challenge came from several sources: CPR managers uncertain of Cordasco's loyalty and utility to the company, rival Italian labor contractors who wanted to break up his monopoly supplying labor, and newly congregated immigrant workers and foremen tired of paying him tributes. When he heard of the resentment his coronation was generating among workers, Cordasco decided to provide beer to all who had marched in his honor. Rather than drink the beer their tributes had purchased, however, the drink-loving men dumped it in the streets, even while foremen delivered speeches praising the virtues of their paternal boss.

Italian workers' defiance did not go unnoticed by Cordasco or his foremen, some of whom shared their workers' disgruntlement. Cordasco responded by writing a letter to his foremen, one week after the coronation, urging them to remain manly and loyal. "Italian bosses and under-bosses," the letter began, "do not show a double face, but only one. Have a soldier's courage and apply to the elegant and solid bank of Antonio Cordasco if you do not want to weep over your misfortunes in the spring."[65] By calling for a single public face of familial loyalty, Cordasco's letter ironically highlighted his growing social distance from Italian workers. Indeed, his letter encoded a mixed message regarding the manhood of Italian foremen that was itself "double-faced." On the one hand, Cordasco praised the soldierlike qualities of his subordinates, suggesting their manhood would be solidified by maintaining one face of public loyalty. Yet he also questioned their manhood by suggesting they would weep and be lesser men should they not obey him.

---

[64] *Corriere del Canada*, February 27, 1904, 1, in *Royal Commission*, 102; Testimony of Antonio Cordasco, ibid., 116.

[65] Antonio Cordasco to the Army of Pick and Shovel, in *Corriere del Canada*, February 20, 1904, 2, in *Royal Commission*, 106.

The defensive nature of Cordasco's paternal warnings were even more clearly manifest in a letter he addressed to "the army of pick and shovel," also posted one week after his coronation.

Those who will not have their names entered in our books will tear their hair out in despair and call Mr. Cordasco, Lordship, Don Antonio, "Let me go to work!" "No! Never!" will be answered to them. "Go to those through whom you sent your money away." A forewarned man is a forearmed man. By order.

Cordasco's warning represented a fantasy of how he wished to relate to Italian workers: as an all-powerful patriarch dispensing mercy to loyal and deferential subjects. The fatherhood that Cordasco sought to embody in his stagecraft was a traditional one indeed, in which the power of the father was supreme over all subjects, child and adult alike. Whether acting as protector or punisher, both aspects of Cordasco's behavior affirmed patria potestas, the father's right to control the experience of all adult children in Canada.[66]

Notions of father rule were undoubtedly familiar to Italians, but the concept clashed with their more egalitarian expectations of fraternal manhood. As temperatures began to rise among hungry workers and foremen waiting for work in June 1904, several of them confronted Cordasco directly as equals rather than as paternal subjects. Typical was the experience of foreman Michelle Cilla, who requested a full refund of job fees for his forty-member work gang. Cordasco responded not with the language of traditional patriarchy or patria potestas, but in a language respected within fraternal culture: he brandished his gun. Placing a loaded revolver to Cilla's forehead, Cordasco threatened "to pull forty drops of blood" from him before refunding his forty dollars. Cordasco's aggressiveness worked for the time being, as Cilla left speechless and empty-handed.

Yet Cordasco's attempts to represent himself as an embodiment of both Italian fatherhood and fraternal manhood were proving self-destructive. No sooner had his foremen placed the paternal crown on his head than hitherto invisible minions began to shake the stage, hoping to topple his crown or, as Cordasco perceived matters, turn it into a crown of thorns. When the chief commissioner for the Canadian government sarcastically suggested in July that "there seems to be a great want of Christianity" in workers' treatment of their king, Cordasco promptly compared himself to Christ: "Like our Lord, the Jews took him and said we want to kill him."[67] Having elevated his job as a labor agent to a divine calling, Cordasco

---

[66] Ibid. Several historians have noted the combination of benevolence and coercion within paternal social relations, be they "precapitalist" or "capitalist." See Eugene Genovese, *Roll, Jordan, Roll: The World the Slaves Made* (New York, 1973), 4; Bowman, *Masters and Lords*, 182; Stanley Buder, *Pullman: An Experiment in Industrial Order and Community Planning, 1880–1930* (New York, 1967); Hall, *Like a Family*; Dolores Janiewski, "Southern Honor, Southern Dishonor: Managerial Ideology and the Construction of Gender, Race, and Class in Southern Industry," in Baron, *Work Engendered*, 70–91.

[67] Testimonies of John Winchester and Antonio Cordasco, June 22, 1904, *Royal Commission*, 87.

had a hard time disentangling his spiritual and commercial roles. That Cordasco may have sincerely believed in his varied manly virtues highlights not so much his capacity for self-delusion, as the complexities of fraternal culture and the unstable nature of the ideologies he articulated. Rather than quieting Italian workers, his manly performances spurred them to claim these same manly rights in North America. The presence of Rafaele di Zazza's family in Montreal and his new status as a father emboldened him to sue Cordasco for damages and unpaid job fees in the summer of 1904. Likewise, Michelle Cilla responded to Cordasco's revolver by taking him to court for having defrauded him of his men's job fees and rights. Cordasco's manly performances had proved unstable ground for maintaining power as a padrone.

Like Cordasco, Leon Skliris articulated a familial public image at precisely the moment his social relations with Greek workers became impersonalized. When Skliris became a labor agent for the D&RG railroad in 1904, he traveled with his foremen and workers, supervising their work and eating with them daily. By 1907, however, Skliris had acquired several contracts supplying Greek workers to mining and railroad interests throughout Utah and Colorado and had removed himself from daily circulation to the top floor of the Hotel Utah. Instead of face-to-face encounters, he relied on his friend Panayiotis Siouris, editor of Salt Lake City's Greek newspaper *Ergatis*, to project his newly minted benevolent image. In the winter of 1907, Siouris published a letter from Skliris to the "Workers of Utah," in which he stated his altruistic motives as a labor agent: "I came here to organize jobs for those who don't have them during the cold winter. And I am delighted to announce I have found jobs for many, many of my dear compatriots."[68]

Perhaps the most convincing aspect of Skliris's benevolence was a letter that eight miners wrote in the winter of 1908: "We consider it our duty to express in public our deepest thanks to our great protector, Leonidas Skliris, the only person who is unfailingly energetic in defending the worker in his every care and need." This letter paled in comparison to editor Siouris's rhetorical flourishes. When Skliris finished a two-month business trip to California in the winter of 1908, his return to the Hotel Utah was heralded by Siouris in terms that would have made Cordasco jealous: "All the laboring world felt relieved about the arrival of Mr. Skliris today, for whom they have long awaited like a Messiah. There is the widespread belief that all unemployed Greeks here will soon have jobs."[69] Siouris's hyperbole aside, many Greek workers hoped Skliris would indeed be their patron in 1908 and provide them steady work.

Yet several important differences distinguished the imagery and ideology of Skliris's benevolence from Cordasco's paternalism. Rather than present himself as

[68] Leon Skliris, "Workers of Utah," *Ergatis*, October 13, 1907, 5.

[69] Dimitrios Voulgaris, Apostolis Karayiannopoulos, Fotis Prousalis, Alex Dimitriou, Dimitris Papadopoulos, Miltos Lambrou, Gabriel Andreas, and Ahileus Zaras to the editor, *Ergatis*, July 27, 1908, 3; "Skliris in Our City," *Ergatis*, May 30, 1908, 1.

a patriarch, an embodiment of fatherly virtues, the unmarried Skliris depicted himself in 1908 as a brother to Greek workers, a "compatriot" rather than a ruler. Skliris sought to embody in his private life the fraternal virtues that he articulated in more formal contexts. If Cordasco portrayed himself as a picture of perfect fatherhood, Skliris was forever traveling to California and Colorado "on business," glamorizing the same mobility that so many Greeks experienced every day. When in Utah, Skliris frequently threw lavish parties at the luxurious Hotel Utah for his chosen guests. Although there is no evidence that Skliris ever frequented the brothels of his working-class compatriots, his freewheeling life-style perpetuated the notion he was similar to the men he exploited. Indeed, he rose to prominence on the shoulders of single Greeks between the ages of eighteen and twenty-three, whose growing presence within the Utah-bound Greek migration paralleled Skliris's growing power as a padrone (see Figure 4.2).[70]

But Skliris's apparent success in 1908 in portraying himself as a single man's man should not obscure the divisive political context from which his fraternal benevolence emerged. Just a few months before Siouris published Skliris's letter to his "dear compatriots," he had called upon every Greek worker "who has been unjustly treated by his boss to write us every detail." Siouris published several of the ensuing avalanche of letters, but only those that condemned Skliris's former partner and rival, William Caravelis of Pocatello, Idaho. Rather than a "messiah," Caravelis was described as a "creature not Greek, not even human," a "tramp who sucks your sweat," in both cases because he charged workers exorbitant job fees.[71] Such letters differed over who was and was not honorable and manly, but they concurred in distinguishing between good and bad padrones, thus legitimating Skliris's authority in 1907.

But Siouris unwittingly had stimulated a discourse about what constituted manhood and honor in North America that proved increasingly troublesome to Skliris. Throughout the controversy over Caravelis, Siouris sought to inspire Greek immigrants' sense of manhood, urging them to expose their exploiters in America. "Remember that our fathers did not think about their families, their property, or their lives in crushing the Turks. Rather they sacrificed everything for the sake of freedom, which they gave us as an inheritance." Taking risks for one's political freedom, rather than fulfilling one's domestic duties to family, was the marker of manhood to Siouris. Yet Siouris also chastised Greek workers for taking too many manly risks when Americans were watching. When three Greeks beat their American supervisor with sticks after he fired a friend, Siouris exhorted workers to "be smart, be reasonable. Realize that only with discipline can you have a stable job. Don't be brave young men because here it is not powerful and doesn't work." Taking risks for political freedom was, apparently, not manly in every situation: it depended on who was watching. Perhaps most distressing to Siouris was that such behavior undermined Skliris's credibility as their fraternal protector:

---

[70] See Table 4.2 in Appendix A.
[71] *Ergatis*, February 29, 1908, 3, 7; March 8, 1908, 1.

"How do you expect Mr. Skliris to give you jobs when you don't conform to general expectations?"[72]

The "general expectations" of appropriate male conduct had been changed dramatically by transnational mobility and industrial work, however. Everywhere Skliris and Siouris looked in 1908, violence against the "great protector" was growing. In the spring of 1908 a number of Greek workers loyal to Skliris in Bingham fought those critical of him "with guns, knives, sticks, and picks." Later that summer, one of Skliris's interpreters, George Demetrakopoulos, was shot and killed by another Greek, Steve Flemetis, after Flemetis had been dismissed for not paying his job fees. Skliris responded to these growing challenges to his authority by seeking greater control over the newspaper *Ergatis*. Although editor Siouris had never published a single critical word about him, Skliris shut the newspaper down in late 1908, gaining possession of the printing equipment by Christmas.[73] Better to have no voice for himself or loyal workers, perhaps, than have the paper fall into hostile hands. Even loyal speech, moreover, had not increased Skliris's popularity, with every proclamation of his fraternal benevolence followed by acts of violence and rebellion against him.

Skliris's projections of manhood did not signal his immediate demise as a padrone as they had for Cordasco. One reason, perhaps, was that before 1911 Skliris was largely unsuccessful in profiting from the domestic lives or consumption patterns of his mobile compatriots. In 1904 Skliris opened his own coffeehouse in Salt Lake City in partnership with Nicholas Stathakos and Will Caravelis. But the coffeehouse consistently lost money and had to be bailed out with profits from his labor-contracting business. In 1907 Skliris sold his remaining interest and cut his ties to Caravelis as competition for clientele was stiff among coffeehouses. The profits from gambling and prostitution in turn – two conspicuous aspects of Greek fraternal culture – likewise remained decentralized. The biggest "redlight house" in Bingham, according to Greek miner Jack Tallas, was run by an American "head lady ... [who] didn't work, but tell her girls what to do, when to go to the doctor." In Pocatello, Idaho, the biggest brothel, the Sisters Hotel, was likewise run by a woman in 1912, this one a Greek named Stella Poulos, who supervised an international work force of French and American women.[74] The profits from prostitution remained beyond Skliris's grasp because of the intense competition these female entrepreneurs created.

When Skliris acquired control over the Panhellenic Grocery Store in 1911,

---

[72] Panayiotis Siouris, "O Ergatis for the Worker," *Ergatis*, March 25, 1908, 1; "The Brave Men," *Ergatis*, July 4, 1908, 3.

[73] *Western Newspaper Union vs. Joseph P. Sharp*, March 2, 1909, Case 11090, Records of the 3rd District Civil Court, Salt Lake County.

[74] *Walker Brothers vs. Caravelis and Company*, 67–68, Records of the 3rd District Civil Court, Salt Lake County; *L. G. Skliris vs. W. J. Caravelis*, Case 8189, May 18, 1906, ibid; Jack Tallas interview by Theodore Paulos, Salt Lake City, January 18, 1971, Greek Archives; *State of Idaho vs. Stella Poulos, Mary Shaw, Mark MacIntyre, Gust Poulos, et al.* Case 4123, December 1, 1919, Records of Idaho District Court, Bannock County Courthouse, Pocatello, Idaho.

however, he acquired the same monopolistic power that Cordasco exercised over the consumption habits of his compatriots. Such expansions of Skliris's power also produced the greatest crisis in his career. When Greek workers went on strike against the Utah Copper Company in the fall of 1912, Skliris confronted directly the full performative power and violence of the fraternal culture he had sought to represent. Greek workers not only denounced him as a dishonorable tyrant but demonstrated their command over the manly arts of war by stockpiling guns, ammunition, and dynamite. Each collective action was accompanied by tremendous displays of firepower. The decision to strike was announced by "shooting off firearms," while the subsequent walkout turned Bingham Canyon into a war zone. "With eight hundred foreign strikers armed with rifles and revolvers," reported a terrified journalist for the *Deseret Evening News*, "raking the mine workings with a hail of lead at every attempt of railroad employees or deputy sheriffs to enter the grounds, the strike situation has reached its initial crisis." The impressive firepower succeeded in intimidating the union's opponents, though no one was injured in all of the shooting. When not firing their revolvers over the heads of deputy sheriffs, striking Greeks passed much of their time building bonfires on the hills above the open pit and dancing. Unlike their gunplay, these performances were generally misunderstood by onlookers, even sympathetic ones, who described the men as "shouting and howling among themselves . . . like the cries of coyotes."[75] But for the immigrant men who danced and watched, these occasions built fraternal bonds across ethnic lines and demonstrated the superior manhood of the men on strike.

The militancy of immigrant strikers succeeded in pressuring the management of the Utah Copper Company to fire Skliris as its labor agent. Even more affirming to Greek workers' sense of manhood, however, was Skliris's ignominious departure from Salt Lake City a few days after his dismissal. Fearing for his life, Skliris fled the Hotel Utah, legend has it, dressed as a woman in what must have been the gendered performance of his lifetime. That legend, recalled by Greek immigrants sixty years after the strike, suggests just how powerful notions of male honor remained to immigrant workers. The biggest revenge for these strikers was not simply making Skliris resign, but stripping him of his celebrated single manhood in subsequent tellings and retellings of the event.[76]

Skliris had one risky opportunity to redeem his manhood three years later after he had returned to Utah in a bid to rebuild his labor-contracting business. When Cretan immigrant George Pologeorgi by chance met Skliris on the street in front of the Hotel Utah, a brief argument ensued in which Skliris called Pologeorgi a "traitor and a coward." Pologeorgi responded by pulling out a pistol and shooting Skliris in the stomach. Undeterred, Skliris grabbed Pologeorgi and "succeeded in wresting the gun from his hands," while holding him on the sidewalk until a

[75] *Ogden Standard*, September 19, 1912, 5.
[76] George Lamb interview by Helen Papanikolas, Salt Lake City, September 3, 1972, Greek Archives.

policeman came to his aid. The manly performance continued, however, as both parties subsequently defended their actions to reporters. Skliris described Pologeorgi as a "homicidal maniac" while highlighting his own virility:

I was walking north toward the Hotel Utah, reading a sports extra about the Willard Johnson fight, and continued to read while Pologeorgi walked with me. Suddenly Pologeorgi, who is a powerful man, gripped me and fired a shot. It was the first shot which struck me, not the second, as has been stated. I could scarcely realize that I was shot, but instantly grabbed the revolver and seized it.

Pologeorgi, by contrast, claimed Skliris was dishonorable because he swindled money from workers and, perhaps worst of all, had insulted Pologeorgi's manhood. "I am a Cretan," stated Pologeorgi through an interpreter, "and all my brothers and men relatives have died fighting the Turks, and I will not let any man call me a traitor and a coward."[77] Fraternal manhood had come back to hound Skliris with a vengeance. Though his performance impressed the American reporters, it did not make him labor agent for the Utah Copper Company again.

For Roman Gonzalez, calculations over how best to mobilize notions of manhood were largely irrelevant in his struggles as a labor agent. Unlike Cordasco or Skliris, Gonzalez never attempted to project a paternal or fraternal image to his compatriots. As a brothel owner, he was an unlikely candidate to become a metaphoric and honorable father to Mexican sojourners, but he also failed to become a representative bachelor for Mexican workers. Gonzalez rarely traveled on business as Skliris did, and the mobility that Skliris popularized only hampered Gonzalez's profits as a labor agent. Gonzalez's reticence in manipulating symbols of manhood, whether fraternal or paternal, did not reflect any humility on his part. Rather, such ideological fictions were unnecessary in his everyday social interactions with Mexican workers, with whom he bargained face-to-face throughout his career. Gonzalez would no doubt like to have risen above his social circumstances, but his inability to control the mobility of his countrymen meant there was less social distance between him and his clients. Consequently, he experienced little necessity to articulate a brotherly or paternalistic persona.

Rather than devote energy to representing Mexican manhood, Gonzalez struggled, like many entrepreneurs, to squeeze a profit from the domestic lives of transient Mexican men. When he opened the Sultana Athletic Club in 1906, the former policeman catered explicitly to the social activities of Mexican solos passing through El Paso each spring and fall. Here Gonzalez not only reaped profits from the labor of Mexican women who worked as dancers and prostitutes at the club, he also recruited men for work on the railroad. His club provided him with a small degree of economic stability as a labor agent, before municipal authorities sued

---

[77] "Skliris Describes Recent Shooting," *Salt Lake Tribune*, April 15, 1915, 12; "Leon Skliris is Shot Down in Street," ibid., April 6, 1915, 1.

him in 1916 for operating a "disorderly house" and selling "spirituous, vinous, and malt liqueurs ... on said premises."[78] From 1909 to 1910, Gonzalez also ran a boardinghouse in Ciudad Juarez for his transient customers, run by a retired Mexican prostitute and her two sons. These women were crucial to Gonzalez's business endeavors. His profits as a pimp never enabled him to become a metaphoric father or brother to Mexican solos, but they helped keep him in the labor-contracting business during lean seasons when competition squeezed out all but the most tenacious.

Yet if the hard work of Mexican prostitutes gave Gonzalez a small measure of economic security, the fraternal activities of Mexican solos – drinking, gambling, buying sex, and fighting – dramatically cut into the profits that he and other boardinghouse owners made. Jose Stefa ran a boardinghouse in Gary, Indiana, and received $1.15 a day directly from a nearby steel company for each man he boarded, but as he remarked, "I have to buy my own mattresses and linoleum and everything.... There is no profit in this business." Anglo commissary agents also complained in 1927 that "Mexicans don't like boarding camps. They want to cook for themselves. They like their own cooking and we carry a full line of Mexican food for the Mexicans." Independent labor agent B. J. Kerley echoed these observations in 1929. "The Mexicans are getting more ashamed of doing their own cooking, but most of them still don't want to board.... The Mexican has to get up at 4:30 or 5:00 A.M. in order to get his own food." Kerley expressed hope that Mexican track workers would eventually abandon their "primitive" attachment to cooking, but in so doing he underscored how successfully they had resisted the efforts of all parties to manipulate their domestic habits over the past three decades.[79]

Because of that success, Mexican workers were freer to create their own forms of fictive kinship and familial protectors. The Mexican immigrants of Moline, Iowa, possessed no padrone but needed intermediaries all the same. The solution they reached was to enter a grocery store owned by an American woman named Mrs. W. E. Duffy in 1923 and adopt her as their patron.[80] Duffy recalled the incident to George Edson in 1927:

Some years ago some Mexicans came into my shop and the ringleader informed me that they wished me to learn Spanish, explaining that their heads were hard and that English was out of the question for the majority of them; that they desired to buy their provisions at my store, and that they would gladly help me learn the language.

---

[78] *The State of Texas vs. R. G. Gonzalez and the Sultana Athletic Club, a Corporation*, Case 13458, April 10, 1916, Records of the 65th District Civil Court, El Paso County Courthouse.

[79] José Stefa to George Edson, September 26, 1926, "Interviews with Labor Contractors" file, BANC-MSS-74/187c, Paul S. Taylor Papers; William Clark interview, El Paso, 1928, ibid.

[80] In making distinctions between patronage and paternalism, I am indebted to the work of Gerald Noiriel, although I do not imbed the difference, as he does, within the peculiar teleologies of French industrial development in the nineteenth century. See Noiriel, "Du 'patronage' au 'paternalisme,'" 17–20.

Nicknamed "Benita," Mrs. Duffy soon learned Spanish and began building her persona as a fictive godmother to these Mexican workers, mediating the diverse cultural and economic spaces that separated them from American culture. According
to investigator George Edson, the Mexican workers came to her "for everything – to
call the doctor, priest or undertaker, to arrange for births, marriages, and funerals,
to talk to lawyers, bankers, and policemen." Others brought her their paychecks to
cash, while "never questioning her reliability." Unlike the "king of the Italian laborers," Benita was the creation of Mexican workers, a woman whose complex role as
a surrogate godmother eased their alienation from U.S. political and legal culture.[81]

Perhaps because Duffy was a fictive kin of workers' own making and choosing,
she experienced a remarkable level of intimacy with her clients. Duffy heard all
kinds of gossip in her store and claimed to know "all their secrets," including
the real names of numerous men fleeing the law and their domestic responsibilities. The information they trusted to Duffy more often than not involved sensitive
negotiations with American authorities. "Mexicans have come to her in the middle
of the night, confessing with bloody hands that they have just killed Tio Pablo or
Pedro," stated Edson, "and she tells them to go home. . . . These things are a heavy
responsibility for Mrs. Duffy, but if she once betrayed the trust they repose in her,
her influence over them would fade away."[82] Edson's comment highlights
how fragile and circumspect workers' loyalty to Benita in fact was, despite her
intimate relationship to them. Duffy's role was not prescriptive – to remind them
of their familial or manly duties or embody one form of manhood – but rather to
help these Mexican men articulate tensions over where male honor was located
within fraternal culture. Should they settle their differences with male compatriots
with violence or provide for their families in Mexico? Mexicans did not seek
answers to such questions from Benita, only a safe place to articulate their dilemmas. Their sanction of Benita's power, freely given though it had been, was
contingent on her not judging or condemning their actions. If Mexican manhood
on the move was unstable and changing, so too was Benita's job, a position that
could easily be lost or taken away.

Indeed, in spite of Duffy's best efforts to keep the trust of her male clients, she
ultimately lost power to another fictive family member, a Mexican businessman
named Jesus Reynosa. With the lumber company's blessing and sanction, Reynosa
built a housing development next to the Mexican community above the flood plain
of the nearby river and opened a grocery store that directly usurped Benita's business. Although she protested to all her customers that Reynosa was "crooked,"
Duffy was unable to hold onto her clientele, and the company town was built under
Jesus's supervision. Fictive kinship remained a useful tool in the hands of Mexican
workers after Benita's downfall, but they confronted a far more sophisticated
adversary in Jesus and lumber company managers, who had studied the merits of
familylike personnel managers in creating their company town.

[81] George L. Edson, February 28, 1927, "Interviews with Labor Contractors," BANC-MSS-
74/187c, Paul S. Taylor Papers; George L. Edson, "Mexicans at Fort Madison, Iowa," March
8, 1927, ibid.
[82] Ibid.

Conclusion

Toward the end of his diary, Haralambos Kambouris tried to wrap up his story with a happy ending by suggesting his engagement to Demetra Villiotis had transformed his perceptions of wage work. In order to make his narrative exemplify those sentiments, Kambouris separated the story of his engagement from his chronicle of work and unemployment, ending the diary with his betrothal to the beautiful "unknown one." Yet a close look at the dates of his previous entries suggests how difficult it was for him to make these narratives of work and romance concurrent and truly compatible. One of his most despairing poems – "Fate," which begins "O! My bad fate that abandoned me here in these foreign places and has destroyed me" – was composed shortly after the unknown one agreed to marry him. In spite of his earnest desires to make his betrothal an event that liberated him, wage work remained profoundly oppressive and his economic prospects gloomy. Where, after all, would he and Demetra live? How would he possibly support her without steady work? What kind of a man was he becoming? Although Kambouris did not explicitly voice such doubts, he ended his last entry with the lament "I wish I had the strength to narrate," acknowledging the great effort it had taken to make his story about becoming a man, or "his own boss," in marriage and work, one narrative.

Kambouris's struggle to unite his stories of love and work highlights how closely intertwined wage labor relations and family ties, notions of free labor and manhood, were among thousands of Greek, Italian, and Mexican men in the North American West. For Kambouris and his fellow sojourners, free labor was as much a narrative of family relations as a specific set of legal and contractual obligations. Becoming one's own boss – the essential narrative fiction of free labor ideology – was to thousands of immigrants also a story of families creating men. Sojourners included very different people within their families, however, and their kin members created distinct kinds of men and manhood. Becoming one's own boss resonated especially well among those who sought to be household heads, patriarchs, or fathers in their home villages or within a nuclear family in North America. Such men held fast to literal notions of family ties and devoted themselves to preserving and strengthening male privileges in their home villages. But many others embraced egalitarian understandings of male family roles that envisioned brotherhood as a model of manhood and located family within fictive kin in North America. Free labor for these men was less about becoming one's own individual boss than finding forms of collective emancipation and independence. The transition from paternal to fraternal culture among male sojourners was not linear or seamless, but rather full of painful dilemmas as they struggled to reconcile what were competing notions and locations of manhood and familial obligation.

For padrones, the reconfiguration of immigrant manhood created numerous opportunities, as they made it their business to profit from the varieties of mobility and manhood practiced by their sojourning compatriots. Cordasco and Skliris grew rich by exploiting distinct forms of mobility among married and single men respectively. Their varied attempts to embody the manly virtues of Italian fatherhood and Greek bachelorhood, by contrast, proved far less successful and enduring. One reason was that the connections between families of origin and the meanings of fictive kinship, between fathers and fatherhood, brothers and brotherhood, were never precise or linear. Although tensions between fraternal and paternal forms of manhood complicated the life of immigrants like Haralambos Kambouris, others used whatever manly practices best suited them in a given situation. Thus Cordasco could seek to embody the idealized virtues of patriarchal fatherhood one moment, and all the performative violence of fraternal brotherhood the next. More than most, Cordasco and Skliris understood that manhood was something performed, whether paternally or fraternally. Like any good performers, they possessed more than one costume.

But it was not the performative nature of fraternal or paternal manhood that foiled Skliris's and Cordasco's bids for power. Rather, both men appropriated ideologies of manhood in response to the ongoing mobilizations of immigrant workers. Fictive kinship was indeed a powerful tool in the hands of padrones, but its utility and power were controlled primarily by those who needed it most: immigrant men on the move. Intended to offset the growing social distance between themselves and their compatriots, Cordasco's paternalism and Skliris's fraternalism ironically stimulated resistance to their power. Cordasco's coronation heralded not so much the triumph of his patriarchal rule as the beginning of a rebellion among Italian fathers who wished to claim their own paternal rights as free laborers in North America. Skliris likewise learned to his chagrin in 1908, 1912, and again in 1915 that attempts to embody the virtues of fraternal manhood could be both dangerous and costly. Immigrant workers' mobilizations were rooted not only in intertwined ideas of manhood and free labor, however, but in the meaning and location of immigrant community, the subject of the next chapter.

CHAPTER FIVE

Mobilizing Community

At the peak of his despair, Haralambos Kambouris seemed bereft of any community in North America. Stuck in Oregon without money, work, or hope, he expressed complete alienation from his environment. "Here in the town of Roseburg, I find myself afflicted with the ocean's turbulence, dead but not buried," he wrote in one poem, entitled "All Is Black to Me." The only community Kambouris could see in Roseburg was an imagined one that he had left in Greece. "It would be a great happiness to all of us, if we could once more see our beloved country," he lamented in another poem entitled "In a Foreign Land," which concluded with a warning to imagined compatriots: "Countrymen, friends, relatives, if you want to be joyful, Don't leave our sweet country."[1]

Kambouris's anguish confirmed what a host of middle-class reformers and many subsequent historians have argued were the debilitating and corrosive effects of mobility.[2] Yet to freeze the picture at the moment of Kambouris's greatest despair obscures the most remarkable aspect of his life story. Within just two years of writing these anguished poems, he had become a booster for the Greek community of Utah, writing tragedies and comedies for church functions and traveling minstrel shows. Moreover, Kambouris ultimately chose to leave "his sweet country" and make Utah his permanent home after briefly returning to Greece with his wife Demetra in the 1920s. To understand his dramatic relocation, one must consider the power of both local and imagined communities in organizing his experience in North America. Even in his most depressed moments, Kambouris affirmed an intimate connection to transient compatriots and expressed a vision of community that proved vital to his new duties as the playwright for Utah's Greek community. His diary, while not written for a public theater, was itself an experiment in imagining community as he wrote to an audience sympathetic to his desperate struggles. That audience was located not in Greece but within the fraternal community that he and other transient men were creating in the North American West.

[1] Haralambos Kambouris, "Sojourn in America," 55, February 2, 1915, Greek Archives; ibid., 53, January 18, 1915.

[2] On the corrosive impact of mobility on community formation, see Courtwright, *Violent Land*, 171; Way, *Common Labour*, 168; Piore, *Birds of Passage*, 70–71.

Not all Greeks were transients in Utah, however, nor did all seek to appreciate or understand the experience of mobility. Far more conspicuous than Kambouris's poetry and plays were the community-building efforts of immigrant businessmen who created the institutional foundations of community in Utah, chartering an official organization entitled "The Greek Community of Utah." But while they founded and named community institutions, they did not literally constitute the Greek community. Rather, community was forged from the efforts and struggles of different groups of immigrants – padrones, businessmen, transient track workers and miners – who possessed distinct views of where to locate the ethnic community, who belonged to it, and who could represent it. Conflicts between persistent and transient immigrants did not hinder the formation of community, but rather stimulated its institutional growth. The same pathways between city and countryside that padrones profited from also shaped the ways immigrants constructed their communities, ethnic, racial, and national.[3]

Historians have long recognized that community, both as an idea and a set of experienced social relations, has been bitterly contested. Fewer historians have explored the importance of spatial dynamics in shaping the cultural processes of community formation. To many, "community" has been synonymous with persistence and the presence of women and families who put down roots in a given location. Ethnicity has been formulated as an identity tied to fixed places – to the neighborhoods, business districts, and urban contexts that many immigrants inhabited.[4] But local community possessed no self-evident boundaries for Mexican, Greek, and Italian immigrants in the West. Where, after all, would immigrants locate community when they occupied not one but several disparate locales simultaneously? Which organizations would express community solidarities when local experience varied so dramatically for "stable" businessmen and "floating" track workers?

Establishing who belonged to the community at the local level of lived experience was only one dimension of the problem. Integrating people's experiences and expectations of community into larger imagined visions of community was another. Greek, Italian, and Mexican immigrants understood and defined the boundaries of local community, however dispersed, in close connection to the

---

[3] On the important role of immigrant elites in shaping the organization of ethnic cultures, see Timothy Smith, "New Approaches to the History of Immigration in Twentieth-Century America," *American Historical Review* 71 (July 1966): 1265–1279; and Kerby Miller, "Class, Culture, and Immigrant Group Identity in the United States: The Case of Irish-American Identity," in Virginia Yans-McLaughlin, ed., *Immigration Reconsidered: History, Sociology, and Politics* (New York, 1990), 96–129. On the role of rural-urban connections in shaping culture in isolated contexts, see William Cronon, "Kennecott Journey: The Paths out of Town," in William Cronon, George Miles, and Jay Gitlin, eds., *Under an Open Sky: Rethinking America's Western Past* (New York, 1992), 28–51.

[4] See Way, *Common Labour*, 167. Among numerous fine case studies that focus on the persistent, see Josef F. Barton, *Peasants and Strangers: Italians, Rumanians, and Slovaks in an American City, 1890–1950* (Cambridge, 1975); Bodnar, Simon, and Weber, *Lives of Their Own*; Emmons, *The Butte Irish*; and Jameson, *All that Glitters*.

imagined communities of race and nation. Just as tensions between stable and transient immigrants shaped the institutional evolution of ethnic community, so did they shape how immigrants embraced or eschewed the elusive privileges of citizenship and whiteness in North America. Padrones sought power by commodifying their compatriots' movement not only through geographic space and between jobs but also across overlapping community boundaries: the ethnic group, the race, and the nation-state. Their success and failure in controlling their compatriots' passages across cultural and national boundaries reflected the diverse contours of local community that persistent and transient immigrants crafted in the North American West.[5]

Transient Communities

Haralambos Kambouris's discovery of community in North America paralleled his finding a Greek bride and creating a family with her in Utah. But his personal transformation should not obscure the complex ways sojourning men forged communities in North America well before women arrived.[6] Greeks created community on the move not only in networks of fictive kinship but in village societies, fraternal groups that provided members insurance and a modicum of financial security. These organizations helped channel information between fellow villagers in Utah and Greece, while raising money for community improvements in both locations. A few weeks before Greek Orthodox Christmas in 1907, for example, the *Ergatis* published a list of thirty-two men who had donated a total of $256 for "the building of a new church in Stomi, Parnassus."[7] Village associations were strongest among immigrants well connected by chain migrations. Residents of Megara and Stomi, Greece, began sending their compatriots to Utah as early as 1904 and by 1907 had sent several hundred fellow villagers to Utah.

Village societies functioned like an extended family to encourage and occasionally enforce ties of mutual obligation among their members. When Megara-born Petros Georgakis was caught embezzling eighty-seven dollars from the village society's coffers in 1907, his compatriots publicly declared in *Ergatis* "he was no longer considered a compatriot."[8] Georgakis subsequently fled Utah

---

[5] On community as an imagined construct, see Benedict Anderson, *Imagined Communities: Reflections on the Origin and Spread of Nationalism* (London, 1983); Iain Chambers, *Migrancy, Culture, Identity* (London, 1994); and Jacobson, *Special Sorrows*, 2–10. On return migration's impact on community formation in both sending and receiving nations, see Frank Thistlewaite, "Migration from Europe Overseas in the Nineteenth and Twentieth Centuries," *XIe Congres International des Sciences Historiques* (Stockholm, 1960), 32–60; and Cinel, *The National Integration of Italian Return Migration.*

[6] For many community historians, women and children are the sine qua non of community history. See, for example, John Mack Faragher's otherwise exemplary article, "Americans, Mexicans, Metis: A Community Approach to the Comparative Study of North American Frontiers," in Cronon, Miles, and Gitlin, *Under an Open Sky*, 95.

[7] *Ergatis*, December 21, 1907, 5.

[8] Ibid., October 12, 1907, 3.

for Chicago, but two of his fellow villagers found him there and beat him for dishonoring them. For these "Megariotes," as they called themselves, community and ethnic identity were governed by the same codes of honor that defined immigrant family relations. When Georgakis was expelled from his village association, he lost his manhood and his status as a compatriot.

Historians of immigration have emphasized the continuities of local tradition in shaping the village-bound lives of transplanted urban wage earners. Much of this scholarship has focused on the successful transplantation of village traditions such as *campanilismo*, an Italian notion in which community was defined by the sound of the village church bell.[9] Those outside earshot of the bell were thought to be beyond the community's borders. For the majority of Greek immigrants in Utah, however, village societies created communities on the move, increasing immigrant workers' security wherever they traveled. Village organizations were not transplanted to a particular urban neighborhood, but rather stimulated the mobility of Greek workers throughout the continent. This geographic expansion was manifest in the wide dispersion of Megariotes in North America. Eighteen of the twenty-eight Megariotes arriving in New York on the transatlantic steamer, *La Gascagne* on March 22, 1907, for example, were bound for Utah, but the others were destined for Chicago, New York, Cleveland, Ohio, and St. Louis.[10] Village societies may have preserved loyalties to one place, but they also transformed the Old World village community, building bonds across space far greater and more varied than that established by a single church bell's toll.

For many Greek sojourners in Utah, then, local community was an idea associated with both their home villages and their transient lives throughout the West. The census of 1910 provides a picture of the geographic dispersion of Utah's temporary Greek settlements. Salt Lake City's Greektown, with its seven hundred full-time residents in 1910, was the most conspicuous Hellenic community in Utah, but Bingham Canyon possessed the largest number of Greeks with over twelve hundred. In the nearby towns of Garfield, Midvale, and Magna, groups of between five and six hundred worked in the smelters, while between one hundred and three hundred Greeks worked in the coal towns of Castle Gate, Sunnyside, and Helper in eastern Utah. Even smaller groups could be found in the coal

---

[9] Herbert Gans, *The Urban Villagers: Group and Class in the Life of Italian Americans* (New York, 1962). See also Franc Sturino's claim that "migration, in both its sojourn and settler forms, can be seen as an attempt to maintain community with village patterns, rather than as an abrogation of them." Franc Sturino, *Forging the Chain: A Case Study of Italian Migration to North America, 1880–1930* (Toronto, 1990), 195–196. On Italian localism, see Humbert Nelli, *Italians in Chicago, 1880–1930: A Study in Ethnic Mobility* (New York, 1970). On the strength of Mexican village ties, see Camarillo, *Chicanos in a Changing Society*; and Ricardo Romo, *East Los Angeles: History of a Barrio* (Austin, 1983). On Greek village identities, see Helen Papanikolas, "Toil and Rage." On the overstated importance of campanilismo in North American cities, see John Briggs, *An Italian Passage: Immigrants to Three American Cities, 1890–1930* (New Haven, 1979).

[10] Steamship Manifest Lists, Port of New York, March 22, 1907, Records of the U.S. Department of Immigration and Naturalization, RG 85.

camps of Hiawatha, Clear Creek, and Kenilworth. Most of these immigrants were not permanent residents but were caught in motion by census counters.

At the center of each Greek settlement was the coffeehouse, an institution that catered both to year-round residents and scores of transient immigrants. Coffeehouses brought persistent and mobile immigrants together: all six coffeehouses of Salt Lake City, for example, were located within a block of the Denver and Rio Grande Railway station. According to Greek immigrant Paul Borovilos, "one could hardly find anybody at the coffeehouses" on a summer day "because all was out on the railroads, or in the city digging the ditches for the sewers and the water lines."[11] But at night, Salt Lake City's coffeehouses filled up with single Greek men who "have to get their supper" and who had "time to kill." The Paradise Coffeehouse in Salt Lake City was one of the most ornate, carefully designed to evoke memories of home and family while simultaneously creating space for new community identities. Patrons were invited to "sip their wonderful coffee, suck their water pipes, or taste the excellent ice cream," while watching puppet shows that "make everyone laugh."[12] Ice cream was something new to the coffeehouse, as was the sparkling fountain, but such amenities ironically helped sustain the nostalgia experienced by men like Kambouris, an element vital to any coffeehouse's economic success.

As a meeting ground between persistent and transient Greeks, the coffeehouse expressed both traditional and new aspects of the communities that mobile Greek workers were creating. On the one hand, it functioned to maintain ties to families of origin with letters from family members sent to the local coffeehouse. Much of the entertainment there likewise affirmed cultural ties to Greece. Frequently performed, for example, was the karaghiozi, or puppet show, in which the "slyly stupid Greek always got the better of the supposedly crafty Turk." In Helper, Utah, the coffeehouse doubled as the local church, serving as the site for religious ceremonies and national holidays. According to immigrant Jack Tallas, the proprietor kept a priest's religious vestments behind the bar.[13]

But the coffeehouse was not merely a place that "drew minds away from America and back toward nostalgic memories of the old country," as one immigration historian put it. Greek workers also discussed job conditions and grievances in coffeehouses, much as American miners did in local union halls. The coffeehouse brought Greek immigrants in Utah into frequent contact with compatriots beyond the confines of their particular village. Megariotes, despite their large numbers and well-organized presence in Utah, never created their own coffeehouse. "Compatriots" comprised not merely fellow villagers, but any friend or coworker who could play the familiar games of backgammon and tabli, no matter what their accent or particular origin in the Greek diaspora. As historian Helen Papanikolas has suggested, coffeehouses functioned as ethnic "melting pots,"

---

[11] Paul Borovilos interview by Helen Papanikolas, Salt Lake City, April 1, 1970, American West Center.

[12] *Ergatis*, October 12, 1907, 4.

[13] Papanikolas, "Toil and Rage," 118–119; Jack Tallas interview by Theodore Paulos, Salt Lake City, January 18, 1971, Greek Archives.

Plate 1. "The Padrone." This famous illustration of the dapper Italian villain from *Frank Leslie's Illustrated Newspaper* was accompanied by an article describing the activities of his working-class compatriots. "They are hired to railway, road, and sewer builders, where cheap hewers of wood or diggers of earth are required, in droves, all under the beck and bid of the smart and wicked padrone." *Frank Leslie's Illustrated Newspaper*, Staff Artist, August 11, 1888. Courtesy of the Perry-Castaneda Library, the University of Texas at Austin.

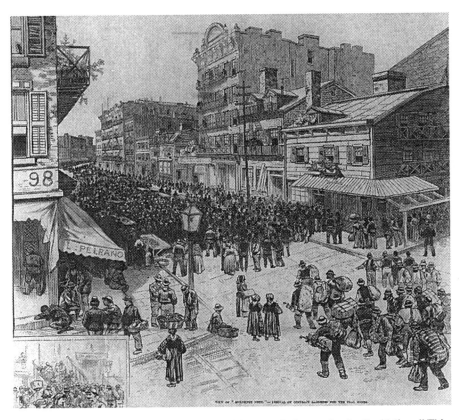

Plate 2. "View of 'Mulberry End' – Arrival of Contract Laborers for the Coal Mines." This illustration exemplifies the faceless and victimized status most Italian immigrants possessed in native-born American eyes. *Frank Leslie's Illustrated Newspaper*, Staff Artist, August 11, 1888. Courtesy of the Perry-Castaneda Library, the University of Texas at Austin.

Plate 3. Antonio Cordasco, his crown, flowers, and two wreaths, presented to him on the occasion of his coronation as "King of the Laborers," Montreal, February 1904. Royal Commissions Collection, PA no. 122612, Courtesy of the National Archives of Canada, Ottawa.

Plate 4. Photographic tribute to Antonio Cordasco by his foremen on the Canadian Pacific Railway. All of Cordasco's foremen donated money to pay for his coronation; he had threatened to have their photos published upside down if they did not contribute their time and money. *Corriere del Canada*, January 23, 1904, RG 33/99, Volume 1, Microfilm T-3473, Courtesy of the National Archives of Canada, Ottawa.

Plate 5. Names of over one thousand Italian workers who donated money to pay for Cordasco's coronation. Note the emblems of wealth and manly status in Cordasco's picture – the open box of cigars, a bottle of liquor, and his obedient dog under the table. *Corriere del Canada*, January 23, 1904, RG 33/99, Volume 1, Microfilm T-3473, Courtesy of the National Archives of Canada, Ottawa.

Antonio Cordasco

Ufficio di Collocamento al Lavoro

MONTREAL, _____ 190_

No. progressivo

Il signor.......... ....
....
paternità.......... ....
abitante in.......... ....
ha pagato $.......... per essere collocato al lavoro in qualità di.......... ....presso qualsiasi Compagnia Ferroviaria—o costruttrice —o con contrattori—od in altri lavori durante la.......... ....stagione estiva alle condizioni e norme spiegate e rilasciate nel foglio da questo staccato.

La quota di registrazione non sarà restituita per nessun motivo.

Il turno pel collocamento al lavoro incomincia, col primo uomo registrato dalla data del.......... ....

Registrato coll'interprete.......... ....

Firma del Registrato al collocamento al Lavoro
....

Telefono MAIN 1359   Ufficio di Collocamento al Lavoro   Telegram: A. CORDASCO

ANTONIO CORDASCO

Italian Labor Agent.   375 St. James St., MONTREAL, Canada.

MONTREAL, _____ 190_

Numero progressivo

Il Signor.......... ....ha pagato $.......... per essere collocato al lavoro in qualità di.......... ....presso qualsiasi Compagnia ferroviaria—o costruttori—o con contrattori—od in fattorie —od in altri lavori, durante la.......... ....stagione estiva, osservando le seguenti condizioni e norme:

1° Il collocamento al lavoro verrà eseguito per turno incominciando dal primo uomo registrato dalla data del.......... ....

2° Il principio del lavoro si intende che avrà luogo nell'epoca della richiesta a quest'ufficio per parte delle diverse Compagnie, o Contrattori, o Fattorie, etc.

3° Coloro che si registrano nella nota di un Interprete, dovranno attendere il collocamento al lavoro in ordine del turno progressivo cui è registrato l'Interprete che loro stessi si sono scelti.

4° La quota pagata per registrazione non verrà restituita per nessun motivo.

5° Coloro che sono registrati, avranno diritto—in modo equo—senza alcuna spesa, alle buste da lettere, carta da lettere, nonché l'identificazione nei cecks, Money order, etc, che avessero da incassare presso, l'Ufficio Postale, Banche od Express in Montreal, Ca.

6° Per qualsiasi schiarimento sui lavori, o per le partenze per i lavori, tutti coloro che si sono segnati nella nota di un interprete dovranno a questi rivolgersi; e chi non si sarà scelto un interprete potrà rivolgersi a quest'ufficio dalle ore 9½ alle 11 a.m. o dalle 3 alle 4½ p.m. di ciacun giorno non festivo.

7° Tutti i giorni —eccettuati i festivi—saranno distribuite le lettere giacenti in quest'ufficio dalle ore 9½ alle 10 a.m.; dalle ore 1½ alle 2 e dalle 4½ alle 5 p.m.

8° Gli interpreti dovranno attenersi a quanto è sopra esposto e ne dovranno dare spiegazione ai loro uomini.

9° Le condizioni in genere pel lavoro e salario saranno fissate al momento del collocamento al lavoro.

A. CORDASCO.

Registrato coll'interprete.

Plate 6. Labor contract of Antonio Cordasco specifying the job fees, wage rate, duration of employment, and variety of services that he supplied to workers, including mail delivery and the means of remitting money to Italy. Omitted were the additional fees for traveling to obscure work sites. Note the royal crest of Italy to the left of Cordasco's name and the Canadian beaver to the right. RG 33/99, Volume I, Microfilm T-3473. Courtesy of the National Archives of Canada, Ottawa.

Plate 7. Italian immigrants laying track for the Canadian Pacific Railway in Saskatchewan, early twentieth century. Frontier College Collection, PA no. 011723, Courtesy of the National Archives of Canada, Ottawa.

Plate 8. Railway construction on the Canadian Pacific Railway in British Columbia, early twentieth century. Note the two foremen, wearing suits and vests with stop watches, standing apart from the men. Frontier College Collection, PA no. 046151, Courtesy of the National Archives of Canada, Ottawa.

Plate 9. Italian laborers working in a rock cut in British Columbia, circa 1910. Two men took turns pounding, while one held and pivoted the drill to help it cut more quickly. Frontier College Collection, PA no. 046155, Courtesy of the National Archives of Canada, Ottawa.

Plate 10. Interior of bunkhouse for Canadian Pacific Railway section gang workers in the Canadian Rockies, circa 1900. Although bunkhouses were as crowded as the boxcars that Italian extra-gang workers occupied during the summer work season, bunkhouses did at least possess stoves, a necessity, given their longer work season. Frontier College Collection, PA no. 038620, Courtesy of the National Archives of Canada, Ottawa.

Plate 11. Canadian Pacific Railway Cantilever Bridge crossing over the Fraser River at Cisco, British Columbia, circa 1910, site of a major strike against the railroad company in 1912. Note the foreman standing to the front of the first push car. Frontier College Collection, PA no. 025036, Courtesy of the National Archives of Canada, Ottawa.

Plate 12. Leonidas Skliris, at the age of twenty-eight, as he appeared in the *Ergatis* on April 7, 1908. Greek photo archives, 921, no. 13539, Courtesy of the Utah State Historical Society.

Plate 13. Greek immigrant Jim Gavrilis of Rhoumeli Greece wearing traditional male dress, the Foustanella, and Greek immigrant Steve Grillos of Crete wearing pantaloons and vrakes, an amulet of earth from his home village, in 1916. Note the revolver at Gavrilis's waist and the knife next to Grillos's amulet. Greek photo archives, C-239, no. 18, Courtesy of the Utah State Historical Society.

Plate 14. Greek immigrants George Zaros, Chris Heleotes (sitting) and Angelo Heleotes posing for a photograph in their best American clothes, 1908. Greek photo archives, C-239, no. 59, Courtesy of the Utah State Historical Society.

Plate 15. Greek immigrants from Crete posing for photograph with bottles of cognac and revolvers as signs of manhood and affluence and sprigs of basil as symbols of friendship and fraternity, circa 1912, Bingham Canyon, Utah. Greek photo archives, Courtesy of the Utah State Historical Society.

Plate 16. Interior of a Greek coffeehouse, Ogden, Utah, in the early 1900s. Note the religious articles behind the bar. Greek photo archives, Courtesy of the Utah State Historical Society.

Plate 17. Greek boardinghouses in upper Bingham Canyon, Utah, circa 1910. Greek photo archives, C-239, no. 45. Courtesy of the Utah State Historical Society.

Plate 18. Greek muckers working in the coal mines of Carbon County, Utah, circa 1910.
Greek photo archives, C-239, no. 19, Courtesy of the Utah State Historical Society.

Plate 19. View of the Utah Copper Company's open-pit mine in 1909, just two years after opening. Note the steam shovels at work dumping ore onto a nearby train car and immigrant workers laying new railroad ties for the next load. Utah Copper Collection, C-275, no. 8912, Courtesy of the Utah State Historical Society.

Plate 20. Roman Gonzalez in 1910 at the age of forty-three. Records of the Department of Immigration and Naturalization, RG 85, File 52546/31B, Folder 2, Box 125. Courtesy of the National Archives, Washington, D.C.

Plate 21. Roman Gonzalez's office stationery, 1910. Although he possessed no official standing with the Atchison, Topeka and the Santa Fe Railroad Company, he used its name on his stationery to improve his credibility with the Mexican clients to whom he wrote during the off-season. Note as well the image of Mexican laborers at work laying track on a flat landscape. Records of the Department of Immigration and Naturalization, RG 85, file 52546/31B, folder 2, box 125. Courtesy of the National Archives, Washington, D.C.

Plate 22. Roman Gonzalez's business card, 1910, with the logo of the Atchison, Topeka, and the Santa Fe Railroad Company as well as its touristic promotional to visit the Grand Canyon. Records of the Department of Immigration and Naturalization, RG 85, file 52546/31B, folder 2, box 125. Courtesy of the National Archives, Washington, D.C.

Plate 23. Mexican "solos" under contract to the Colorado Iron and Fuel Company leaving their families near Guadalajara, Mexico, 1907. Records of the Department of Immigration and Naturalization, RG 85, file 52320/1, box 95. Courtesy of the National Archives, Washington, D.C.

Plate 24. Portrait of a Mexican railroad worker in Texas, circa 1910. The Runyon Photo Collection, CN no. 06346, the Center for American History, the University of Texas at Austin.

Plate 25. Mexican boardinghouse, end of track, West Texas, circa 1900. Prints and Photographs Collection, Railroad, the Center for American History, the University of Texas at Austin.

places where localistic frames of reference became building blocks for more geo-graphically expansive notions of ethnic community in North America.[14] It was in the coffeehouse that villagers from Megara and Stomi first became compatriots, first imagined a larger Greek ethnic identity in North America.

Italian track workers in western Canada, like Greeks in Utah, stayed closely in touch with their fellow villagers. Italian laborer Antonio Sicari stated to Royal Commission investigators that he had come to Canada in the spring of 1904 with "twenty of my fellow villagers," all of whom registered with Cordasco in the same work gang. Village loyalties were as crucial as family connections in constructing work gangs. Most foremen not only knew their laborers personally but had often grown up with them and recruited them as a group to come to North America. Some track gangs occasionally contained men from both northern and central Italy, but more often their composition mirrored local village ties that were crucial to sur-vival in North America. Foreman Pompei Bianco, for example, allowed only fellow villagers from Somite Cheta into his 104-member work gang in 1903. Like their Greek counterparts, however, Italian track workers did not create communities merely by preserving village loyalties. Rather, they forged new ones during the work season and after when they wintered in "little Italies" throughout North America. Although many track workers returned to Italy in the off-season, increas-ing numbers spent the winter in Montreal, working at odd jobs in the burgeoning city. Year-round Italian communities were also beginning to form in the Canadian Northwest, as immigrants decided to winter in British Columbia, Manitoba, and Saskatchewan. In the spring of 1904 the Canadian Pacific Railway hired nearly a quarter of its total Italian work force in Winnipeg locally, up from zero in 1901 when all were hired out of Montreal through Cordasco.[15]

The formation of these Italian communities in small towns like Michel, British Columbia, Medicine Hat, Saskatchewan, and Copper Cliff, Ontario, did not signal the end of sojourning among Italian immigrants, but rather its expansion through-out Canada. Indeed, only when sojourning slowed after 1911 did transient Italian settlements in northern and western Canada begin to decline as immigrants returned to Italy or moved to Montreal and Toronto. These patterns highlight what was between 1901 and 1911 an almost continuous movement of men between isolated work sites during the summer work season and larger urban neighbor-hoods during the winter months. In the saloons and boardinghouses of these larger "little Italies," Italian sojourners not only caught up with friends, family members, and fellow villagers but, like Greek workers in coffeehouses, developed geo-graphically expansive notions of immigrant community on both sides of the U.S.-Canadian border and throughout the Americas.[16]

[14] Charles C. Moskos, "Georgakas on Greek Americans: A Response," *Journal of Hellenic Dias-pora* 14:1–2 (Spring 1987): 59; Papanikolas, "Toil and Rage," 118.

[15] Testimony of Antonio Sicari, *Royal Commission*, 36; Testimony of Pompei Bianco, ibid., 29; Testimony of John Skinner, ibid., 23.

[16] On transnational approaches to Italian migration, see Robert Harney, "The Commerce of Migration," *Canadian Ethnic Studies* 9:1 (1977): 42–53; Samuel Baily and Frank Ramella, *One Family, Two Worlds: An Italian Family's Correspondence across the Atlantic, 1901–1922*

The transnational character of transient workers' communities was abundantly manifest in the comments of Mexican workers to sociologist Paul Taylor in the 1920s. While many lamented the hardships of life on the move, others expressed a kind of confidence and power in their ability to go almost anywhere work was available. Stated one track worker to Taylor in 1928, "If things are good here in the United States, we come here to work. If they are better in Panama, or Colombia, or Peru, tomorrow or the next day we will go down there. We are only here for a short time." The seeming nonchalance of this track worker toward international travel reflected his confidence in the skills that he and other Mexicans possessed as transients. Those skills created a sense of community manifested in the plural voice they used to describe their lives on the move: "We the laborers live here like birds of the air," stated another track worker in 1928. "When the work closes down, we are away to any place we hear of steady work."

If steady work was the goal for nearly all Mexican workers, so too was returning to their home villages in the off-season. As Sarah Deutsch has shown in her study of Mexican Americans in Colorado and New Mexico, men obtaining railroad work and other forms of wage employment effectively maintained the Hispanic village's viability during a period of growing economic dislocation. These migration strategies helped create what Deutsch has called a "regional community," one whose boundaries remained linked to particular towns, but which flourished across vast spaces in the Southwest. Deutsch's insights into the flexible and dynamic aspects of Mexican village life were equally true of Greek and Italian villages.[17] Like Greek and Italian sojourners, the regional community of the Mexican immigrant was defined not simply by his village loyalties but by the transient communities he created while sojourning.

Communities of Mexican men typically congregated near sites of industrial work. The geography of their temporary settlement was documented in 1927 by Labor Department investigator George Edson, who spent two years touring the midwestern United States. Many Mexican communities were sequestered on the edge of small towns or in railroad stockyards near "hobo" camps, invisible to local American residents. In the small town of Manly, Iowa, for example, Edson found just fifty Mexicans, all of them male track workers living in boxcars, while

(New Brunswick, 1988); Gabaccia, *Militants and Migrants*; and Bruno Ramirez, *On the Move: French-Canadian and Italian Migrants in the North Atlantic Economy, 1860–1914* (Toronto, 1991). On transitions in Montreal's Italian community, see Bruno Ramirez, "The Italians of Montreal: From Sojourning to Settlement, 1900–1921," in Robert Harney and J. Vincenza Scarpaci, eds., *Little Italies in North America* (Toronto, 1981), 76. Greek settlements in Utah underwent a similar geographic transition during the 1910s, with isolated Greektowns in places like Price growing in size and number during the first decade of migration to Utah but declining rapidly after 1913.

[17] Deutsch, *No Separate Refuge*, 35, 40—41. According to Susan Buck Sutton, Greek villages likewise "grew and declined" with great frequency in the late nineteenth century. Mobility did not weaken a community but helped it move to new locations, stimulating an explosion of new villages in the Greek countryside. See Sutton, "What Is a Village," 187–188.

in the sugar beet town of Albert Lea, Minnesota, he found eighty-seven "idle beet workers" living in shacks on the edge of town. Most of these men had not decided to settle permanently in the North, but only to pass the winter, in contrast to the majority of their compatriots who had returned to Mexico. These wintering communities were largest near manufacturing centers, where Mexicans found year-round employment. Pontiac, Michigan, for example, possessed a Mexican community of approximately five hundred individuals in 1927, while twelve hundred Mexicans worked in Omaha, Nebraska, in the packinghouses.[18]

Within each of these transient communities, Mexican workers formed mutual aid organizations which helped local residents and those passing through town. As Emilio Zamora and Zaragosa Vargas have shown in Texas and Detroit respectively, *mutualista* organizations helped Mexican workers improve their material circumstances with health benefits and insurance and defend their political interests in the United States and Mexico. Although local chapters of the "Benito Juarez" society in Laredo, Texas, and Indiana Harbor, Indiana, comprised many long-term residents of these Mexican communities, they were adapted to the needs of their transient working-class compatriots. Membership dues were quite low and transient members were encouraged to transfer their standing to another local chapter or to a "sister" organization when they moved on to a new sojourning community. Like the Greek coffeehouse, Mexican mutual aid societies sprang up in even the smallest and most temporary of Mexican settlements. One Mexican researcher, Luis Recinos, commented in 1926 that "It is rare to find a city with fifty of more Mexicans that does not have a Mexican society."[19]

Mexican mutual aid societies, Italian and Greek village societies, coffeehouses and ethnic saloons, informal fraternal networks among all three groups – each of these provided transient workers a sense of community while sojourning. As communities, they were distinguished in part by the varied proximities of women, but they did not become communities because of women's presence or absence. Rather, the work of cultural reproduction – crucial to the process of community formation – was undertaken by sojourning men as well. There were several dimensions to this cultural work: adapting notions of kinship and village community to the vagaries of life on the move, passing on their skills and knowledge as transients to future "generations" of sojourning men, and joining village societies and mutual aid organizations wherever sojourners meandered in the West.

[18] George L. Edson, November 1, 1926, "Interviews with Labor Contractors" file, BANC-MSS-74/187c, Paul S. Taylor Papers; ibid., September 27, 1927.

[19] Zaragosa Vargas, *Proletarians of the North: A History of Mexican Industrial Workers in Detroit and the Midwest, 1917–1933* (California, 1993), 149–155; Emilio Zamora, *The World of the Mexican Worker in Texas* (College Station, 1993), 72, 86–109; Jeffrey Marcos Garcilazo, "'Traqueros': Mexican Railroad Workers in the United States, 1870–1930" (Ph.D. diss., University of California at Santa Barbara, 1995); George L. Edson, November 10, 1926, "Interviews with Labor Contractors" file, BANC-MSS-74/187c, Paul S. Taylor Papers; Report by Luis Recinos, Manuel Gamio Papers, cited in Zamora, *The World of the Mexican Worker*, 93.

But who, if anyone, did transient communities exclude? What were the boundaries of transient community, and how were they created by factors outside the control of sojourners? Answering these questions requires briefly considering the role of racial and national ideologies in shaping the experience of mobile workers. Transience did not preclude membership in the white race in the minds of most middle-class North Americans, but it vastly complicated the processes by which some sought to claim white status. Whiteness was not, as Neil Foley and others have demonstrated, an immutable or monolithic racial category, but one filled with variation and hierarchy at the turn of the century. Consider the distinctions made by a track foreman in Texas to Paul Taylor about the workers he had employed over the years: "My gang of Mexicans is as good as any gang I ever had, and I have worked white men, Greeks, Chinese, and Negroes." Neither Greeks nor Mexicans were "white" by this foreman's estimation, though his praise of Mexicans suggests differences among nonwhites. Rather than fitting into a single black-white dichotomy, Mexicans, Greeks, and Italians in the West occupied places within a varied hierarchy containing several gradations of both whiteness and nonwhiteness.[20]

Precisely where transient Greeks, Italians, or Mexicans landed in that hierarchy varied by context and locale. Whiteness was contingent upon what occupations immigrant workers assumed, where they lived, where their families – however defined – were located, what other immigrant or nonwhite groups were present, whether they were citizens and could vote, and whether they were persistent or transient. Being a member of a residentially persistent community did not guarantee one whiteness; indeed, some of the greatest racial violence against Greeks, Chinese, Mexicans, and Italians in the North American West was directed at those who claimed permanent community status. In 1908 the established Greek residents of Omaha, Nebraska, for example, were driven out of town and watched their shops and homes burn. Transience, by contrast, was almost always a marker of nonwhiteness in the West in 1900. The best illustration of that was the ambiguous racial status of "hoboes," transient men known in any other context as white, Anglo-Saxon Protestants.[21]

For transient Greeks in Utah, several local factors shaped their racialization as

[20] Taylor, *Mexican Labor in the United States*, vol. 1, 356. On the history of whiteness among "new" immigrants, see Foley, *The White Scourge*; and Matthew Jacobson, *Whiteness of a Different Color: European Immigrants and the Alchemy of Race* (Cambridge, Mass., 1998). On the history of racial hierarchies in the U.S. West, see Ronald Takaki, *Iron Cages: Race and Culture in 19th-Century America* (New York, 1979); Alexander Saxton, *The Rise and Fall of the White Republic: Class Politics and Mass Culture in Nineteenth-Century America* (London, 1990), 269–291; Tomas Almaguer, *Racial Fault Lines: The Historical Origins of White Supremacy in California* (Berkeley, 1994).

[21] On the removal of Chinese immigrants from Anglo communities, see Saxton, *The Indispensable Enemy*; on the forced departure of Greeks from Omaha, Nebraska, see Lawrence H. Larson and Barbara J. Cottrell, *The Gate City: A History of Omaha* (Boulder, 1982), 164–166; on the racial status of hoboes, see Todd Allen DePastino, "From Hobohemia to Skid Row: Homelessness and American Culture, 1870–1950" (Ph.D. diss., Yale University, 1996).

nonwhite elements in the population. In 1900 Bingham was a community comprised primarily of skilled underground silver miners from Sweden, Finland, England, and the United States. In 1910, by contrast, the majority of occupation holders were unskilled copper miners from Japan, Italy, Serbia, and Greece working above ground in the Utah Copper Company's open pit.[22] Differences in skill were as much ideological and cultural designations as objective and technological criteria in this rapidly changing community. In 1910 Greeks primarily worked as "muckers" and track workers, loading and unloading copper ore and laying and relaying track for the gigantic steam shovels that were literally devouring a mountain of copper ore. The worst jobs were held by the Japanese who earned $1.50 a day for rappelling off ledges in the open pit to set dynamite strikes.[23]

Tensions between "skilled" and "unskilled" workers fueled racial antagonisms, but they did not create or constitute them. Indeed, much of the racialization of Greek workers occurred off the job as they struggled to create communities on the go. In Utah, Greeks were thought to be lawless, dirty, lewd, and lazy, images that paralleled then current racial stereotypes of African Americans in the South. Indeed, when the Ku Klux Klan organized chapters in Utah during the late 1910s and 1920s, it was a Greek man who was nearly lynched for allegedly raping a white woman. He was saved only when a large crowd of well-armed Greek men arrived on the scene. Such racialized fears had been prominent in Utah for some time, fueled in part by the performative rituals of fraternal culture. A belief that Greek men were "stealing" white American women led Salt Lake City officials to prosecute several Greek businessmen as "white slavers" in 1908 and to pass a municipal ordinance forbidding any Greek men from employing American women.[24]

In El Paso, Mexican workers likewise entered a labor market segmented by racial fault lines that confined most Mexicans to pick and shovel work. On the railroads and in sugar beet fields, however, no skill differences separated Mexican and Irish track workers or native-born "white" American workers. A racialized skill hierarchy nonetheless developed between them, primarily along lines of persistence and transience within the railroad work force: Mexicans in the Southwest

[22] See Table 5.1 in Appendix A. U.S. Bureau of the Census, *Thirteenth Census of the United States, 1910. Population Schedules*, Salt Lake County, Utah, 1910.

[23] On deskilling, see Harry Braverman, *Labor and Monopoly Capital: The Degradation of Work in the Twentieth Century* (New York, 1974); on the selective gains made by skilled, native-born workers, see Gavin Wright, "Labor History and Labor Economics," in Gavin Wright, ed., *The Future of Economic History* (Boston, 1987), 332. On the creation of a racially "segmented and divided" work force between 1890 and 1920, see Richard Edwards, David Gordon, and Michael Reich, *Segmented Work, Divided Workers: The Historical Transformation of Labor in the United States* (Cambridge, 1982).

[24] On descriptions of Greeks as "dagoes," see *Ergatis*, November 16, 1907, 1. On the Ku Klux Klan in Utah, see Papanikolas, "Toil and Rage," 130–135. On the passage of laws restricting Greek employment of white women, see *Ergatis*, January 18, 1908, 1. On white slavery during the Progressive Era, see Edward J. Bristow, *Prostitution and Prejudice: The Jewish Fight against White Slavery, 1870–1939* (Oxford, 1982); Frederick K. Grittner, *White Slavery: Myth, Ideology, and American Law* (New York, 1990); Timothy J. Gilfoyle, *City of Eros: New York City, Prostitution, and the Commercialization of Sex, 1820–1920* (New York, 1992), 256.

formed "extra" gangs, assembled for seasonal work, whereas Irishmen and Americans formed section gangs, which tended to work all year.[25]

For Mexicans, whiteness varied by class differences, but was not a literal expression of social and economic status. Even the best-educated Mexican residents in Texas experienced difficulties being considered white. According to Benito Rodriguez, consul general to Mexico in the 1920s, "about five or ten percent of the Mexicans" in Texas "call themselves 'blancos.' Most of them say 'Americanos.' The people here refer to whites, Greeks, Italians, and Mexicans." Even though Rodriguez deemed most Greek, Italian, and Mexican nationals to be nonwhite, he considered himself to be a "blanco." When in San Antonio, however, he tried to rent a room, but was told "all our tenants are white" by the landlady, who continued "if you will say you are Spanish I will rent to you." Here was how a small number of well-educated Mexicans might claim "whiteness," changing if need be their country of origin. But Rodriguez refused the offer to become Spanish and instead tried to reverse the ethnoracial hierarchy depriving him of a room. "I replied that I would rather be a dog than a Spaniard, a German, or a Jew. I think the landlady was a German Jew." Comparing the Jewish landlady to a dog might have won him points with anti-Semites in Texas, but it did not give him a "white" room. The difficulties that Rodriguez, a well-regarded Mexican professional, experienced suggest how hard it was for any Mexican to climb the ethnoracial ladder of whiteness in Texas.[26]

Yet geographic mobility provided at least some hope. Although few Mexican workers were considered white in Chicago during the 1920s, some Mexicans found more racial "wiggle room" in multiethnic cities. An employment manager of a steel company in South Chicago, Dave Medalie, praised his Mexican employees in 1926, elevating them above several other "new" immigrants. "I prefer the Mexicans to the others, Italians, Croats, Serbs, etc. The Mexicans are cleaner in person about their work." In Texas, by contrast, even sympathetic whites typically saw Mexicans as unequal to European immigrants. Frank Hoepner, a Texas cotton grower of "distinguished southern ancestry," summarized the mutable but enduring racial distinctions between Mexicans and European immigrants in 1927: "The Mexican makes a fair to middling good citizen and does not try to assimilate. The Bohunks want to intermarry with whites. Yes, they're white, but they're not our kind of white.... There never will be any race question with the Mexicans." From Hoepner's perspective, Mexican cotton workers were preferable to Hungarian "bohunks" or Italians and Greeks precisely because Mexicans left

---

[25] On racial tensions among railroad workers in North America, see Shelton Stromquist, *A Generation of Boomers: The Pattern of Railroad Labor Conflict in Nineteenth Century America* (Urbana, 1987); Eric Arnesen, "'Like Banquo's Ghost, It Will Not Down': The Race Question and the American Railroad Brotherhoods," *American Historical Review* 99 (December 1994): 1601–1634.

[26] Benito Rodriguez interview by Paul Taylor, El Paso, Texas, 1928, doc. no. 18-23, BANC-MSS-74/187c, Paul S. Taylor Papers; on hierarchies of whiteness in Mexico, see Foley, *The White Scourge*, 60–61.

racial hierarchies secure, unquestioned, and natural.[27] In Texas at least, they would never become white and certainly not "our kind of white." These regional differences suggest not only that whiteness was highly mutable but also insecure. Whiteness could be attained, but it could also be lost.

The instability of white racial identity was dramatically apparent among Italian immigrants working in western Canada. One railroad contractor in British Columbia divided all of his CPR employees into two fluid categories: "white men" comprising immigrants from Scandinavia, Britain, and French Canada, and "wops" or "bohunks," including immigrants from eastern and southern Europe. "We distinguish white men. Austrians and Italians we don't call them white men. I don't know that it's hardly fair but it's customary." Although the contractor made just two distinctions – between white and nonwhite – he also acknowledged variety within each category, in part by his candid misgivings about the racial distinctions he was making. Italians, however, were located near the bottom of that racial pyramid, just above Chinese immigrants, deemed by most to be the antithesis of "white" labor.[28] One small indication of this was that Cordasco was given the responsibility in his commissary for supplying both Italian and Chinese workers, a pairing that suggested how interchangeable they were to CPR managers.

"Bohunks" and Italians may have been deemed one kind of white in Texas, but in western Canada they were explicitly "not white men." One key difference between these locales was their distinct ethnic and racial makeup. In Texas, the presence of thousands of Mexicans helped make Italians white; in Canada, the absence of Mexicans or a newer immigrant group with an equally liminal racial identity helped keep Italians nonwhite. But transience also possessed distinct racial meanings. Because nearly four out of five residents were new arrivals to British Columbia in 1900, residential persistence and land ownership became unusually important barometers of whiteness, in contrast to many areas in Texas where large numbers of poor landed whites complicated the relationship between landownership and white racial identity. In western Canada, Italians were particularly unlikely candidates to become white, not simply because they lacked

---

[27] Dave Medalie interview by Paul Taylor, 1928, "Calumet Region, Employers" file, BANC-MSS-74/187c, Paul S. Taylor Papers; Frank Hoepner interview by George Edson, 1927, Z-4 R, box 1, ibid. The whitest Mexican in El Paso in 1910 was businessman Felix Martinez, who owned a newspaper and financial interests in several railroad and construction companies. His prominence led to an appointment by President Woodrow Wilson in 1915 to be chairman of the U.S. Commission to the Panama Pacific International Exposition in San Francisco. See Garcia, *Desert Immigrants*, 82–83.

[28] Andrew Ross McCormack, "Wobblies and Blanketstiffs: The Constituency of the IWW in Western Canada," in W. J. C. Cherwinski and Gregory S. Kealey, eds., *Lectures in Canadian Labour and Working-Class History* (St. John's, Newfoundland, 1985), 104. On the Chinese in Canada and racist practices against them, see Con, *From China to Canada*; and Avery, *Reluctant Host*, 43–59. For histories of white racial ideology and politics in western Canada, see Peter Ward, *White Canada Forever: Popular Attitudes and Public Policy towards Orientals in British Columbia* (Montreal, 1978); and Patricia E. Roy, *A White Man's Province: British Columbia Politicians and Chinese and Japanese Immigrants, 1858–1914* (Vancouver, 1989).

Canadian citizenship, but because they were the most mobile and least "landed" of any immigrant group in the region. The features of Italian workers that made them attractive to CPR managers – being unlikely to jump their jobs or settle their own land – also made them least likely to be deemed white by residents of British Columbia.

Notions of whiteness thus reflected local and regional configurations of economic power throughout North America. But for residents of North America, whiteness was also an integral part of U.S. and Canadian national identities. As many scholars have demonstrated, whiteness in the United States was closely connected to the rights and practices of U.S. citizenship.[29] Irishmen who "became white" during the nineteenth century, for example, did so within strongly partisan, electoral contexts. Yet whiteness was not peculiar to the Democratic and Republican parties in the United States or to partisan struggles in western Canada. Whiteness may have been learned in North American political struggles, but race and nationalism were closely linked concepts to most immigrants well before they emigrated. For Greeks in their homeland, racial identity was inseparable from Greek nationalism and the centuries-old struggle against the Ottoman Empire. Italian nationalists in the late nineteenth century also linked notions of race and nation, not so much to create a hierarchy among diverse citizens, but to buttress a myth of national purity in opposition to other nations. Race likewise played an important role in defining Mexican nationalism, though as a racially mixed *mestizo* people. Unlike their Italian and Greek counterparts, Mexican nationalists held notions of whiteness and racial purity in contempt, in part because of their historic opposition to the United States, whose ideologies of white nationhood and Manifest Destiny had been used to rationalize the conquest of Mexico.[30]

---

[29] On the political context for the creation of whiteness in the United States, see Roediger, *The Wages of Whiteness*; and Saxton, *The Rise and Fall of the White Republic*, 142–153. On the expanding power of municipal, state, and federal governments to regulate communities of migrant workers on the East Coast, see Hahamovitch, *The Fruits of Their Labor*, 55–112. In the western United States, see Mark Reisler, *By the Sweat of Their Brow: Mexican Immigrant Labor in the United States, 1900–1940* (London, 1976); Calavita, *Inside the State*; Guerin-Gonzalez, *Mexican Workers and American Dreams*. In Canada, see Avery, *Reluctant Host*; Roy, *A White Man's Province*; and Ward, *White Canada Forever*.

[30] Of many fine studies linking race and nationalism in the United States, see Jacobson, *Whiteness of a Different Color*; and Gail Bederman, *Manliness and Civilization: A Cultural History of Gender and Race in the United States, 1880–1917* (Chicago, 1995). Although the historical connections between ideas of race and Italian and Greek nationalism are abundant, the role of whiteness in those nationalistic discourses remains largely unstudied. On histories of Greek nationalism that touch on race, see Alexander Kosmas Kyrou, "Greek Nationalism and Diasporic Politics in America, 1900–1949: Background and Analysis of Ethnic Responses to Wartime Crisis" (Ph.D. diss., Indiana University, 1993); Theodore George Tatsios, *The Megali Idea and the Greek-Turkish War of 1897: The Impact of the Cretan Problem on Greek Irredentism, 1866–1897* (Boulder, 1984), 41–65; and Demetrius John Cassavetti, *Hellas and the Balkan Wars* (New York, 1914), 350–359. On race and Italian nationalism in Italy, see Ronald S. Consulo, *Italian Nationalism: From Its Origins to World War II* (Malabar, Fla., 1990); Aliza S. Wong, "Green, White, Red – and Yellow: The Imaging of China in the Construction of the

But if these varied links between race and nation were familiar to Greek, Italian, and Mexican sojourners, few initially found much appeal in white racial identity in North America. Not only were all three groups viewed as nonwhite by native-born North Americans, but whiteness was closely associated with U.S. and Canadian nationalisms. The skepticism many Greek, Italian, or Mexican immigrants possessed toward both whiteness and U.S. or Canadian citizenship was reflected in their dim view of North America's legal systems. Juan Castillo, a Mexican immigrant picking cotton in Texas, summarized the sentiments of many of his compatriots in 1927 when he stated, "There is a law for the Americans but none for the Mexicans." According to another Mexican worker in Chicago in 1928, "The Mexicans get little protection in the courts. The Mexicans are learning that you must buy justice." Many Greeks were similarly disillusioned by the hollow promises of the U.S. legal system. When local police officers unjustly jailed a Greek coal miner in 1914 for allegedly provoking his nativist attackers, Angelo Georgedes turned the language of civilization and racial nationalism in North America on its head: "Well, I thought America was a different country. I thought Turks were barbarians, but looks like here they are just as bad and worse."[31]

For many transient workers and their communities, citizenship itself, whether in the United States, Canada, or their country of origin, seemed a dubious building block for community. Indeed, many sojourners became mobile in conscious opposition to the requirements of national citizenship. A large number of both Mexican and Greek immigrants came to the United States fleeing their governments' military service requirements. Others such as Haralambos Kambouris expressed tacit opposition to the obligations of citizenship. Kambouris recalled that when the Balkan War broke out just as they arrived in New York, "the captain of the ship came on deck and announced that Greece had declared war on Turkey" and that they would return anyone wanting to fight free of charge. "All the crew shouted for the King and for the Greek army," Kambouris recollected, but "no one ... asked to return and in a few moments we disembarked." A few days later, tensions between those fulfilling and those fleeing their citizenship duties were sharply juxtaposed when Kambouris passed a trainload of his compatriots in Kansas City who were returning to fight. "When the train came to a stop, the boys came to the windows holding small Greek flags and all together, with one voice,

Italian Nation" (M.A. thesis, University of Colorado, 1997). On race and nationalism among Italian immigrants, see Philip Bean, "Fatherland and Adopted Land: Irish, German, and Italian-American Nationalism" (Ph.D. diss., University of Rochester, 1994); and Patricia Wood, "Nationalism from the Margins: The Development of National and Ethnic Identities among Italian Immigrants in Alberta and British Columbia, 1880–1980" (Ph.D. diss., Duke University, 1995). On intersections between Mexican nationalism and race, see Mauricio Tenorio-Trillo, *Mexico at the World's Fairs: Crafting a Modern Nation* (Berkeley, 1996), 87–93.

[31] Juan Castillo interview by Paul Taylor, Catarina, Texas, 1928, doc. no. 284-454, BANC-MSS-74/187c, Paul S. Taylor Papers; Taylor, *Mexican Labor in the United States*, vol. 2, 151; Angelo Georgedes, *Reminiscences of Life and Moving to America* (Madison, 1973). On the hostility of many Mexican immigrants to U.S. citizenship, see Gutierrez, *Walls and Mirrors*, 88–95.

shouted 'Long live Greece! Long live the King of Greece! Long live the Greek army and navy!' And from us came another shout, 'Live long!!'"[32]

Such pragmatic reactions to the romantic call of nationalism did not reflect the prepolitical outlook of Greek peasants as some historians and anthropologists have contended.[33] Kambouris and his fellow sojourners were quite conscious of the political meanings and risks associated with their decisions not to fight. Moreover, there were obvious political explanations for such resistance: the imposed and largely unpopular nature of the Greek monarchy, despite the increasing popularity of the "great idea," a nationalist dream of resurrecting all of ancient Greece. Similar ambivalence characterized Mexican sojourners' relationship to the Mexican state, particularly before the collapse of the regime of Porfirio Diaz in 1911. Italian immigrants, whose nation had only recently been realized in 1861, were likewise uncertain patriots in 1900 and remained deeply divided between northern and southern regions.[34]

Yet if transience could express opposition to the power of the state and the requirements of national citizenship, transience also paradoxically stimulated deeply patriotic sentiments among many immigrants. Indeed, the idea of imagined national community grew rather than faded in importance for men on the move. This was manifest in Kambouris's encounter with returning Greek sojourners, whose love of Greece had grown dramatically while sojourning. Kambouris would himself become much more patriotic after several months of mobility in the West, composing poems to his homeland and imagining audiences of fraternal "compatriots" rather than family and kin alone. As Matthew Jacobson and others have demonstrated, immigrant diasporas played a vital role in the creation of ethnic nationalisms, precisely because the experience of sojourning stimulated yearnings for a homeland and the imaginative creation of a national culture.[35] Transient immigrants did not reimagine nationhood and citizenship in a vacuum,

[32] Kambouris "Sojourn in America," 13, October 1, 1912, Greek Archives.

[33] According to anthropologist Edward Banfield, "amoral familism" or the desire to "maximize the material, short-run advantage of the nuclear family" over and beyond any communal and political obligations characterized the world views of most Mediterranean peasants. See Edward Banfield, *The Moral Basis of a Backward Society* (Glencoe, 1958), 85. For an adaptation of that argument, see Silverman, "Agricultural Organization, Social Structure, and Values in Italy," 1.

[34] Theodore J. Anton interview by Theodore Paulos, Salt Lake City, January 28, 1972, Greek Archives. On the weakness of the Greek monarchy between 1860 and 1914, see Richard Clogg, *A Concise History of Greece* (Cambridge, 1992), 77–97; John S. Koliopoulos, *Brigands with a Cause: Brigandage and Irredentism in Modern Greece, 1821–1912* (Oxford, 1987); and Tatsios, *The Megali Idea*. On obstacles to Italian national unity during the same period, see Cinel, *The National Integration of Italian Return Migration*, 45–55. On limits to Mexican nationalism before the revolution, see Friedrich Katz, *The Secret War in Mexico: Europe, the United States, and the Mexican Revolution* (Chicago, 1981).

[35] Jacobson, *Special Sorrows*, 15–22; Victor R. Greene, *For God and Country: The Rise of Polish and Lithuanian Ethnic Consciousness in America, 1860–1910* (Madison, 1975), 3–4; Pasquale Verdicchio, *Bound by Distance: Rethinking Nationalism through the Italian Diaspora* (Madison, 1997).

however, but in dialogue with persistent immigrants who built many of the institutional foundations of immigrant community in the West.

Persistent Communities

Although the vast majority of Greek immigrants in Utah remained members of a transient working class in 1910, a small middle class had nonetheless emerged in nearly every Greek settlement in Utah. Comprising coffeehouse owners, saloon owners, bankers, boardinghouse keepers, grocers, the occasional newspaper editor, lawyer, and doctor, these immigrants thrived on the commerce generated by sojourning. Salt Lake City's Greektown quickly became the center for the most successful immigrants in the Intermountain West. A comparison of the occupational makeup of the two largest Greek communities in Utah – Salt Lake City and Bingham Canyon – in 1910 reveals that Salt Lake maintained double the percentage of skilled professionals and businessmen. Perhaps more significant, Salt Lake's Greeks, whether working-class or middle-class residents, were far more likely to speak English.[36]

But middle-class Greeks in Utah were not all stable and persistent family men within their local communities. Most of Utah's Greek coffeehouse owners, liquor dealers, and grocers had only recently left the ranks of wage earners and remained closely tied to their transient compatriots. In mining towns like Bingham, businesses frequently went belly up after a few months and their owners returned to wage work. Greek merchants possessed an interest in remaining in Bingham as long as possible to build up their reputations and a loyal clientele, but their high rates of failure suggest just how difficult this could be. Bingham's municipal license records between 1908 and 1913 reveal that 40 percent of all new Greek businesses closed after just three months and fully three-fourths went out of business after just one year.[37] Such failure rates made George Kyranakos the perfect representative for aspiring Greek businessmen in Utah. His first business enterprise ended in disaster when the oranges he hoped to sell began to rot and were later thrown at him by a gang of ruffians. But Kyranakos was also resilient and after returning to wage work eventually became a success as a photographer. His frequent trips between the ranks of worker and small businessman highlight what were gray occupational boundaries among Greek immigrants.

Perhaps the biggest social and economic cleavage was not between workers and businessmen but within Utah's diverse Greek middle class. In both Bingham and Salt Lake City, an elite group of businessmen quickly emerged that possessed far more financial security than the average grocer who bounced from job to job. Andrew Pappas, first president of the Greek community of Utah in 1905, owned saloons, hotels, and coffeehouses in both Salt Lake City and Bingham and never once changed his residence between 1905 and 1915. Nicholas Stathakos,

[36] See Table 5.2 in Appendix A.
[37] See Table 5.3 in Appendix A.

vice-president of the Greek community, owned the National Bank of the Republic and amassed a small stock fortune in local mining companies. While the total assets controlled by Pappas and Stathakos did not make them extraordinarily wealthy by American standards, they were far more successful than most struggling Greek proprietors. One measure of Stathakos's wealth was that he sent for his wife and children to join him in 1908 and bought them a house, replete with fine furnishings and a piano. The only Greek wealthier than Stathakos in Utah was Leon Skliris, who chose to remain on the margins of Utah's Greek middle class, living apart in the Hotel Utah and traveling much of the year on business.

The social distance separating men like Pappas, Stathakos, and Skliris from Utah's more transient Greek middle class was highlighted by the contentious business relations between them. In the spring of 1910 a lawsuit brought against Pappas by a onetime business partner alleged that Pappas had relied upon his partner's "ignorance of the English language" to gain control of his business, the Hermes Hotel.[38] Stathakos similarly profited from his compatriots' lack of familiarity with English and American banking practices. Between 1905 and 1915 dozens of small businessmen and workers trusted him to remit their earnings to relatives in Greece. In addition to charging them fees for remittances, Stathakos paid his Greek depositors no interest on their savings and reinvested them in interest-bearing accounts with American banks, a practice that was exposed in 1916 amid considerable controversy.[39]

The emergence of a small and highly stratified middle class within Montreal's little Italy closely paralleled patterns among Greeks in Utah. As the transportation hub of Canada, Montreal soon became a center of Italian entrepreneurial activity. Though transience remained high among Montreal's Italian boardinghouse owners, grocers, barbers, bakers, butchers, and bankers, a growing number of them had begun settling more permanently in the city by 1904. Montreal's persistent Italian community remained small, but it was beginning to transcend its earlier dependence on provisioning sojourners. By 1904 increasing numbers of Italians had found year-round employment in Montreal's burgeoning manufacturing sector.[40]

Alberto Dini, Cordasco's chief rival in the labor-contracting business, exemplified the developing interests of Montreal's persistent middle-class Italian community. Like Cordasco, Dini possessed an important stake in the commerce of migration, but his financial interests were closely tied to Montreal's persistent Italian and Canadian communities. Unlike Cordasco, Dini possessed no single

---

[38] Pappas allegedly forged his partner's signature to a bill of sale. See *Konstantinos Hatziskos vs. Andrew Pappas*, March 2, 1911, Case 13625, Records of the 3rd District Civil Court, Salt Lake County.

[39] A public audit of Stathakos's banking practices found that for years "no distinction was made as between personal and company business. Company funds have been used for all purposes." See *T. Koliopoulos vs. N. P. Stathakos*, February 18, 1916, Case 21002, 12, ibid.

[40] Ramirez, "From Sojourning to Settlement," 63.

corporate sponsor, but relied on a great number of contacts with local construction and small railroad firms in eastern Canada. In addition to operating a labor agency, Dini owned a bank and a grocery business that imported Mediterranean foodstuffs for local residents. His businesses served two intermingled groups of immigrants: sojourners wintering in Montreal and more permanent wage-earning residents.[41]

In El Paso, opportunities for Mexican businessmen were similarly located in providing services to a burgeoning population of both persistent and sojourning Mexicans. Most Mexican businesses were confined to the barrio of Chihuahuita, where a variety flourished. They included Mexican "restaurants, general stores, tailors, photographers, bakeries, labor contractors, laundries, clothing stores, bookstores, meat markets, interpreters, and translators, real estate salesmen, watchmakers, furniture stores, drugstores, saloons, and moneylenders." Two different groups were prominent in El Paso in the early twentieth century: those providing services to year-round barrio residents such as bakers and laundries and those providing services to transient sojourners such as labor contractors, interpreters, and moneylenders. Although most Mexican businessmen aimed to attract both groups, success in the long term depended on the barrio's year-round residents.[42]

The status of immigrant businessmen varied within the residential communities of Montreal's little Italy, Salt Lake City's Greektown, and El Paso's barrio. The wealthiest among them comprised an elite, while the poorest shopkeepers struggled to stay out of the ranks of wage labor. Most of the persistent immigrant businessmen in El Paso, Salt Lake City, and Montreal made money by supplying services to both persistent and transient compatriots. Yet not all middle-class immigrants themselves remained in one location, just as all workers were not transient. Building community around the interests and visions of persistent immigrants was thus no easy task.[43] How would padrones and middle-class immigrants reach out to transient workers in building ideas of "common ground"? And how would workers respond to those diverse efforts?

[41] The largest sources of year-round employment in Montreal were the CPR's giant Angus works, which in 1904 began building and servicing all of the company's machinery. See Ramirez, "Brief Encounters: Italian Immigrant Workers and the CPR, 1900–1930," *Labour/Le Travail* 17 (Spring 1986): 9–27; Ramirez, *Les premier Italiens de Montreal: L'origine de la petite Italie du Quebec* (Montreal, 1984).

[42] Garcia, *Desert Immigrants*, 79, 80. The transition from sojourning to settlement was bumpier for El Paso's Mexicans because the Mexican Revolution produced a large influx of refugees. See Michele Gomilla, "Los Refugiados y los Comerciantes: Mexican Refugees and Businessmen in Downtown El Paso, 1910–1920" (M.A. thesis, University of Texas at El Paso, 1990).

[43] Ethnicity and nationalism should not be conflated, a distinction frequently obscured in much U.S. immigration history. On the role of nationalisms in defining ethnic culture, see Jacobson, *Special Sorrows*, 3; David Montgomery, "Nationalism, American Patriotism, and Class Consciousness among Immigrant Workers in the United States in the Epoch of World War One," in Dirk Hoerder, ed., *"Struggle a Hard Battle": Essays on Working-Class Immigrants* (Dekalb, 1987), 327–352; and Eric Hobsbawm, *Nations and Nationalism since 1780: Programme, Myth, Reality* (Cambridge, 1990): 63–67.

Citizens All!

In Utah, middle-class Greek leaders sought to build a permanent foundation for ethnic community by creating an American corporation entitled "The Greek Community of Utah," whose stated mission was to construct the Holy Trinity Greek Orthodox Church in Salt Lake City. Led by Andrew Pappas and Nicholas Stathakos, the organization successfully raised enough money to purchase land and construct a church in downtown Salt Lake by 1907. Stathakos and Pappas also sought to define the format of community governance by establishing bylaws that spelled out how community leaders would make decisions and how the community would choose its leaders. All members were entitled to vote in annual elections for a ten-member board of trustees, which "supervised the good conduct of the church" and managed "all of the property and affairs of the community." If "ten or more members of the community have reasons to doubt the faithful management of the funds of the community," one board member and two petitioners could audit the community's books.[44]

But if the bylaws of the organization suggested a democratic format for community governance, they nonetheless excluded most itinerant, working-class Greeks. At fifty cents a month, dues for membership were relatively modest, but the requirement that all members make "a written application stating the acceptance of all the articles of the bylaws" excluded many sojourners, half of whom were illiterate. Maintaining membership was also difficult. If members missed paying their dues three months in a row, they were automatically kicked out, a restriction that excluded most seasonal track and mine workers. Finally, voting privileges – key to influencing the choice of trustees – were limited to members who had been in good standing for at least one year. Membership and its powers were quite explicitly reserved for persistent Greeks.[45]

Yet not all Greek businessmen imagined ethnic community between the walls of the new church. Leon Skliris shared many of Stathakos's and Pappas's goals in establishing a "respectable" Greek community, but he was also ambivalent about grounding it exclusively in one Salt Lake neighborhood. Skliris initially favored creating a nationalist organization with local chapters throughout the West that would raise money for the Greek Royal Navy. "We wanted to raise money to build a Greek battleship," Skliris later recalled, "and a meeting was called to secure subscriptions." Meeting at the Odd Fellows Hall in Salt Lake, however, the group changed direction under Stathakos's initiative and decided instead to construct a church in Salt Lake City. Skliris did not publicly oppose the endeavor, but he rarely attended church functions and had little interest in becoming a pillar of this local community.[46]

---

[44] *By-laws of the Greek Community of Utah* (Salt Lake City, 1905), Articles 1, 12, 19, 25, Public Records Collection, Bingham Canyon, Utah State Archives, Salt Lake City, Utah.

[45] Ibid., Articles 3, 4.

[46] See *Walker Brothers vs. Caravelis*, 75, Records of the Utah Supreme Court, 1908, Utah State Archives. While Leon Skliris kept his distance from the church, his brother, Evangelos, maintained closer ties to it, serving as a member of the board of trustees. See Minutes of the Holy

Instead of becoming a regular church member, Skliris poured his energy into building the Kanaris Society in 1907, an organization devoted to liberating all Greek lands from the Ottoman Empire with battleships. Kanaris sought to avoid any of the contentious debates then dividing Utah's Greek immigrants. As Skliris explained, "our association is a patriotic union and its only target is to contribute to the raising of money for the national Navy. Consequently, it doesn't claim to represent the public opinion of Greeks in Utah." Instead, the organization sponsored several fund-raising events at coffeehouses throughout the region. A party held at the Olympia Coffeehouse in Salt Lake City on the anniversary of Greek independence featured bazoukia music, karaghiozi shows, beer, commemorative buttons, "electric lights," and lamb. Lent apparently did not deter meat consumption when battleships were at stake. Similar parties were held at a Bingham coffeehouse, with Skliris giving speeches at both events.[47]

Skliris's success as a nationalist fund raiser reflected his skill in exacting tributes from mobile Greeks.[48] Yet, the Kanaris Society was not merely a device for making money but rather a vehicle for creating a community impervious to class and social conflict. By making coffeehouses rather than the Holy Trinity Church the basis of Kanaris operations, Skliris succeeded in bridging some of the gaps between persistent and transient Greeks. The Kanaris Society, like Skliris himself, had no single base of power, but operated in scattered pockets throughout the West, connecting settled and mobile immigrants to a powerful and geographically flexible notion of national community. All Greek immigrants, no matter how lonely or isolated, could join this nationalistic mobilization.

Skliris's attempts to mobilize Greek workers around nationalist themes in the spring of 1908 also represented an alternative to the pressing questions about working-class exploitation dividing Greek workers at that moment. Skliris's highly public campaign stood in sharp contrast to the diffident actions of Pappas and Stathakos, who exhibited little interest in organizing their working-class compatriots. In 1910 only one out of twenty Greeks in the state was in fact a member of the official ethnic community. Although more men occasionally attended funeral services, the Holy Trinity Church possessed only tenuous links with the majority of migrant workers. During the severe recession of 1908, the church briefly established a "common table" to provide food to indigent Greeks in Salt Lake City. But the effort was disbanded just three months after its creation.[49]

Trinity Greek Orthodox Church, Minute Book 1, September 1910–September 1912, Holy Trinity Greek Orthodox Church, Salt Lake City.

[47] *Ergatis*, September 28, 1907, 1; ibid., October 26, 1907, 1.

[48] Accusations of fraud did occasionally damage Kanaris fund-raising efforts. In 1910, future Greek newspaper editor Peter Fifles posted signs in Midvale, Bingham, and Salt Lake City denouncing Gust Karigianes for having embezzled all of the money raised for the Greek navy from a karaghiozi show entitled "Golfa." Karigianes, a clerk in Stathakos's bank, denied the charge and sued Fifles. See *Gust Karigianes vs. Peter Fifles*, October 16, 1910, Case 13419, Records of the 3rd District Court, Salt Lake County.

[49] Minutes of the Holy Trinity Greek Orthodox Church, Minute Book 1, September 1910, Holy Trinity Greek Orthodox Church; *Ergatis*, March, 14, 1908, 1.

The limits of the official community's influence were dramatically manifest during Greek religious and national holidays. Within Salt Lake City's Greektown, Christmas was an occasion for demonstrating the civility of English-speaking Greeks. In 1908 *Ergatis* reported that Christmas culminated at the Orthodox church, which was "decorated properly with flags and candles." Most noteworthy was the fact that "many distinguished Americans," including lawyers, judges, and journalists, attended the service. According to editor Siouris, "all were greatly impressed." Three years later, Orthodox Christmas in Salt Lake once again served as a moment of cultural presentation to a professional American audience. The *Deseret Evening News* reported that "candles ... were seen everywhere," and added that "the wee tots of Greekdom are happy again" since St. Nicholas had finally returned. There were, in fact, very few Greek "tots" in Salt Lake City except in the family of Nicholas Stathakos, who in all likelihood contacted the paper himself and presented the festivities in their most Americanized light.[50]

Among transient Greek workers, by contrast, no such civility was observed on Greek holidays. Haralambos Kambouris and five fellow track workers celebrated their first Greek Easter in an Oregon desert in 1913 as best they could. After working on Holy Saturday, a custom unheard of in Greece, they made preparations for a feast on Sunday. George Tournavitis "slaughtered the lamb and barbecued it.... Others had got the wood for the fire. I went to town and bought dye for the eggs." Although Kambouris lamented the fact that "there was no Greek church," his fraternal cohort remedied that circumstance with two things dear to their hearts: alcohol and singing. "We had bought two barrels of beer, one six gallons and the other, eight," Kambouris recalled, giving each celebrant roughly two and half gallons. Sunday was truly joyous. "When the lamb was done, we ate it around noon, chanting 'Christ is arisen' many times and whatever Resurrection psalms we knew. We sang other songs as well, drank beer, and became dizzy and finished the celebration because we could remain no longer." Although their festivity impressed some American track workers who according to Kambouris "admired the way we roasted the lamb," and perhaps how they consumed fourteen gallons of beer between them, the celebration remained limited to the Greek work gang that had prepared the food.[51]

Such was not the case in Bingham where Greek holidays became moments of working-class celebration. Greek Christmas in Bingham in 1911 "struck terror into the hearts of the peaceful citizens of Bingham," according to the *Salt Lake Tribune,* and began with an explosion of "a dozen sticks of giant powder" in Bingham. After much gunfire, the immigrants migrated to the coffeehouses, where the festivities continued in earnest with drinking, fireworks, and more revolver shots. Joining the party were hundreds of "Austrians," many of them ethnic Serbians, and even a few Japanese miners, as the crowd migrated from the Parthenon Coffeehouse to the Balkan Bar and finally to the American-owned Bingham Bar.[52]

[50] *Ergatis,* January 11, 1908, 4; *Deseret Evening News,* January 6, 1911, 1.
[51] Haralambos Kambouris, "Sojourn in America," 29–30, April 26, 1914, Greek Archives.
[52] *Salt Lake Tribune,* January 10, 1911, 3.

Like middle-class Greeks in Salt Lake City, these celebrants possessed an audience beyond the boundaries of the ethnic enclave. But rather than finding common ground with white American lawyers and journalists, these Greeks recast their religious traditions within the culturally heterodox world of Utah's immigrant and nonwhite working class.

Their behavior provoked consternation among leaders of the official Greek community. When Bingham residents celebrated Greek independence day in 1908 with gunshots and drinking, editor Siouris stated that "all Greeks should try to realize the true meaning of March 25th, rather than merely celebrating it as if it were their own name day." In the same issue Siouris criticized how Bingham's Greeks conducted themselves on and off the job. "Greeks have often proved to be rebellious.... The Greeks have to be more careful, consider their faults, and conform to our advice." When five Greek workers from Garfield beat up their American supervisor two months later, Siouris condemned them for failing to heed his warnings. "All our previous advice, all the advice of outstanding Greeks to the laborers have proved to be useless. Greek workers seem to be by nature rebellious."[53]

Although Siouris claimed to be publishing a paper "for the worker," his criticisms increasingly reflected the sensibilities of middle-class Greeks in Utah. In one editorial, he chastised those workers who had skipped town after payday without repaying their debts to local businessmen:

What would happen to laborers if people in the Greek community were not so generous with their credit?... And now, where are you? Now that you have money, you have vanished. Shame on you. The community doesn't demand but expects that you give what you can back. All the men who gave you credit in the meantime want their money back.

The "community," in Siouris's view, was constituted primarily by its honorable middle-class leaders and businessmen in opposition to "shameful" transient Greeks. That such workers might have left town as part of some other community – one comprising transient wage earners – seems not to have occurred to Siouris or been worthy of the label of "community." Siouris sought to curb what he considered the financial opportunism of transient workers by encouraging the formation of a merchants' association that would "protect each member from bad creditors." By policing the behavior of both transient workers and rapacious labor agents, Siouris aspired to fashion a moral conscience within the Greek community of Utah. But in so doing he closely supported the attempts of Salt Lake City's businessmen to create an immigrant community that was persistent, respectable, and middle class in its outlook.[54]

The most powerful vehicle that Siouris championed for accomplishing this

[53] *Ergatis*, April 18, 1908, 1, 2; ibid., July 4, 1908, 3.
[54] *Ergatis*, "For the Workers," April 18, 1908, 5; ibid., December 28, 1907, 1; Ernest K. Pappas, President, Parthenon Mercantile Company, to the Editor, December 28, 1907, 5. As subscriptions to *Ergatis* plummeted in the summer of 1908, Siouris sought to remind workers that "Ergatis from its beginning had as its program the protection of Greek workers, something which they truly need.... Ergatis has a great task to perform ... to teach and guide and lead all

objective was for all Greeks to become English-speaking American citizens. "We believe," Siouris asserted in the winter of 1908, "that the Greeks who come here should conform to the ethics and customs of this country. They should seem assimilated to Americans, while keeping their patriotic flame alive hidden in their breast." Although few Greeks had successfully walked this tightrope between national communities, Siouris was confident even illiterate workers would gain a measure of power and social acceptance by switching allegiances. "American citizenship won't transform the real Greek," Siouris asserted in another editorial, but instead will "bring himself closer to the American people" and help "erase the horrible insult that we receive via the words 'Dago, Dago.'"[55] U.S. citizenship, it was hoped, would redeem the rebellious behavior of working-class Greeks and thereby whiten their "race."

Siouris's citizenship campaign received a huge boost when Leon Skliris became its chief spokesman during the winter of 1907. On December 10, 1907, Skliris boasted to an American reporter that "within a few weeks, about six hundred Greeks will apply for citizenship." Only fifty did so in the ensuing two weeks, nearly all of them businessmen, but Skliris continued to champion U.S. citizenship. "I always try to persuade Greeks to realize that it is for their own good to become American citizens," stated Skliris in *Ergatis*. "This is the most progressive country in the world and every smart Greek can help the progress of this country. Those who are not of this disposition, we don't want here."[56]

In promoting U.S. citizenship, Skliris recognized an opportunity to expand his authority on several fronts. Within the Greek community, the citizenship drive provided him another occasion to create "common ground" between persistent and transient Greeks and preserve his authority among all social classes. Equally important, U.S. citizenship burnished Skliris's reputation among corporate sponsors as an ethnic leader who could keep Greek workers law-abiding. Not coincidentally, the citizenship drive also created a new political channel Skliris could control. In the fall of 1908, he attempted to deliver the Greek vote, small as it was, urging Greeks to vote for the Republican ticket. Stated Skliris: "The fate of all Greeks in this country rides upon Mr. Taft's victory.... They should vote exclusively for him and in this way serve their hospitable country, while simultaneously protecting their own interests."[57]

Given his role as the leader of a nonpartisan Greek nationalism, Skliris's advocacy of U.S. citizenship and the Republican Party were indeed remarkable.

---

those who need it and on the other hand to improve today's situation concerning the laborers and their jobs," ibid., August 5, 1908, 1.

[55] Panayiotis Siouris, "The Greeks in America," *Ergatis*, February 1, 1908, 1; Siouris, "American Citizens All," ibid., November 16, 1907, 1. Much of the racism that Greeks experienced was quite specific to Greek culture. Consider, for example, the letter by a worker to *Ergatis* in which he begged Siouris to tell him "who this Aristotle was because every American comes daily and shouts it at me." See Letter to the Editor, ibid., November 16, 1907, 1.

[56] *Salt Lake Evening Telegram*, December 10, 1907, 1. For the Greek translation of the English original, see "The Greeks Are Faithful to Uncle Sam," *Ergatis*, December 14, 1907, 3.

[57] *Ergatis*, October 17, 1908, 1.

Whether or not Skliris truly believed that Greek and U.S. nationalisms were compatible, he acted out of pragmatic necessities in both campaigns. The Kanaris Society was one answer to rising working-class anger against the padrone system in 1908. Moreover, Skliris's U.S. citizenship drive began a few days after local newspapers suggested U.S. immigration officials might deport Greeks from Utah as contract laborers under the Foran Act. Becoming a citizen of the United States seemed the best way to defend oneself against the U.S. state. Skliris did not openly reveal such calculations but, instead, sought to link Greek and American national identities around common notions of progress and democracy. Stated Skliris, "We love this democratic country next best to our own dear Greece; we never forget . . . those terrible times when Greece was struggling for her independence. That is why we want our countrymen to enjoy the benefits and privileges of citizenship." As U.S. citizens, Greek workers would acquire the same democratic rights that nonwhite Ottomans had suppressed for three centuries. Between August 10 and September 1, 1905, most Greek businessmen in Salt Lake City agreed with Skliris and declared to an American justice of the peace in Salt Lake their "bona fide intention to become citizens of the United States" and, equally significant, "to renounce all allegiance and fidelity . . . to the King of Greece."[58]

Greek workers, by contrast, demonstrated little enthusiasm for Skliris's dualistic nationalism. Indeed, just thirty laboring men answered his call to become naturalized in 1907, nearly all of them year-round residents of Salt Lake City. These thirty men represented a tiny fraction of the total population of Greek workers in the region. U.S. citizenship possessed an even weaker appeal among Greek workers living outside of Salt Lake City. In Bingham, just two workers petitioned for naturalization during the entire year of 1908. Despite editor Siouris's claims that "the word division was not in the Greek community of Utah's dictionary," Greeks remained deeply divided over the location of ethnic and national community and the merits of whiteness and citizenship.[59] Those divisions reflected not only class tensions between transient and persistent Greeks, but also regional identities in Greece: most naturalized Greeks came from the Peloponnese with comparatively few immigrants from Crete (see Maps 5.1A, 5.1B).

Royal Dreams

When Antonio Cordasco was crowned "king of the laborers" by his foremen in February 1904, he sought to persuade doubting CPR officials that he still

[58] *Salt Lake Evening Telegram*, December 10, 1907, 1; "The Naturalization of Greeks," *Ergatis*, December 14, 1907, 1; Naturalization Files, August 9, 1905–September 1, 1905, Salt Lake County, Utah State Archives.

[59] Naturalization files, 1905–1915, Salt Lake County, Utah State Archives; "Long Live Unification," *Ergatis*, May 17, 1908, 1. The percentage of Greeks petitioning for U.S. citizenship in Salt Lake County who were working-class decreased between 1907 and 1914 from 69 to 33 percent. The thirty Greek workers who decided to become U.S. citizens in December 1907 represented a high-water mark in the popularity of working-class U.S. citizenship and of Skliris as a leader of Greek workers.

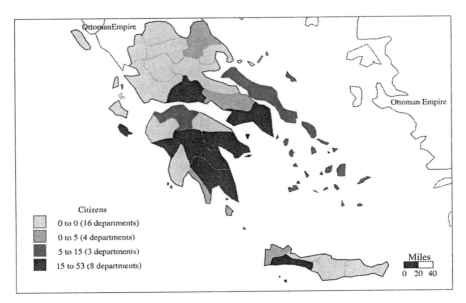

Map 5.1A. Origins of naturalized Greeks in Utah, 1902–1912

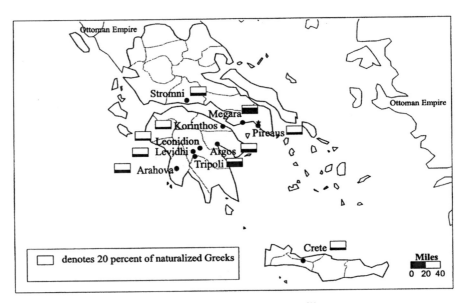

Map 5.1B. Origins of naturalized Greeks in Utah: Top ten villages, 1907–1912

controlled Italian workers with an iron fist. But he also sought to transform how his compatriots located and defined community in North America. Here, for the first time, was their own king, a man who embodied not only the virtues of Italian fatherhood but also of the Italian monarchy.[60] In so doing, Cordasco hitched his career to a notion of imagined community not bound by any local place or neighborhood. Wherever Italian workers traveled in North America, Cordasco would remain their king, their point of connection to a royal community in both North America and Italy. As patriarch and king, Cordasco sought to reinforce loyalties to communities in Italy.

But just as Cordasco's patriarchal ambitions stimulated fathers to challenge his authority, so did his royalist pretensions fuel a crisis over how Italians would represent themselves in Canada. The organization most horrified by Cordasco's coronation was the Italian Immigration Aid Society, founded in the fall of 1902. Like the official Greek Community of Utah, the society was an exclusive organization, comprising just twenty-five men, all of them wealthy, literate businessmen "interested in the welfare of Italian immigrants." Funded directly by the Italian government, the principal aim of the society was to "assist and encourage Italian emigrants" by limiting transience and the racialized stigmas attached to it by "colonizing" sojourners on lands provided by Canadian provincial governments. The vast tracts of public land still available at the turn of the century convinced board members that "Canada is the Eldorado of the present day." In order to take advantage of these "free lands," the society proposed having local governments hire Italian agents who would not only help the immigrant find good land and purchase tools, but also select those immigrants "who are competent and able to become agriculturalists in Canada."[61] In theory, this new and progressive Italian yeomanry would be whiter and more prosperous than transient wage earners.

While the aid society's dream of an Italian yeomanry in North America was shared by many Italian government officials, it also mirrored the efforts of middle-class reformers throughout North America to "redeem" immigrants from the pathologies of the city by making them agriculturalists. Here, surely, was a path to free labor for these racially degraded immigrants – free soil – as old or older than the Republican Party.[62] One of the most explicitly racist of such middle-class

---

[60] For those who missed the coronation, Cordasco displayed his crown in a glass case in his labor agency. Those who could not come to his office, such as Canada's deputy minister of labor Mackenzie King, received pictures of the crown with "royal" insignias in June 1904. See Harney, "Montreal's King of Italian Labour," 58.

[61] *Constitution of the Immigration Aid Society for Canada in Montreal* (Montreal, 1902), Articles 15, 16, and 42, Records of the Royal Commission's Investigation, RG 33/99, Microfiche 3473, Canadian National Archives, Ottawa; *First Annual Report of the Italian Immigration Aid Society for Canada* (Montreal, 1904), 3, ibid.

[62] On the agrarian origins of free labor ideology, see Foner, *Free Soil, Free Labor, Free Men,* 124–125; and Reeve Huston, "Land and Freedom: The New York Anti-Rent Wars and the Construction of Free Labor in the Antebellum North," in Eric Arnesen, Julie Greene, and Bruce Laurie, eds., *Labor Histories: Class, Politics, and the Working-Class Experience* (Urbana, 1998), 19–44.

reform efforts was the Industrial Removal Organization (IRO), founded in New York City in 1900. Dedicated to cleaning up North American cities by literally exporting its immigrant "problems" to the countryside, the IRO's actions recalled the historic efforts of municipal reformers to send their "worthy" poor to home-steads west of the Mississippi. In Montreal, the aid society's affinity for such solutions was manifest in its track record of "protecting the Italian immigrant." In its first annual report of 1903, the society listed four cases of "protection." In three of them, the immigrants were removed from Montreal.[63]

If colonizing Italian sojourners was the society's long-term goal, breaking Cordasco's monopolistic control over the CPR's hiring of unskilled labor was their immediate objective. To that end, the society established a labor agency for Italian immigrants in 1903 that they claimed would be administered "honestly" and according to the principles of free labor and freedom of contract. Rather than charging workers fees of one to three dollars for a job, the society solicited a fifty-cent "tax" for its work in finding compatriots jobs with Canadian employers. The revenues thus generated were not to profit the twenty-five members of the corpo-ration but to make both workers and employers honor their contracts, "paying law costs in law suits ... when brought to compel the fulfillment of contracts of employment." In addition, the society used its funds to "lend money to those Ital-ians who would be desirable immigrants to Canada," stimulating the migration of compatriots much as Cordasco had done but without his undesired influence.[64]

The society's goal of defending contracts and cleaning up the "speculators and cheaters" of Italian migration was a tricky task, however. Drawing distinc-tions between desirable and undesirable Italian immigrants ironically legitimated nativist rhetoric about the unwashed and undesirable Italian "dago." The rhetoric of colonization affirmed the connection between landownership and whiteness that kept so many Italian sojourners nonwhite in Canada. Much of the society's credi-bility was also compromised by the fact that Alberto Dini was its vice-president between 1903 and 1905. Perhaps because of his prominence and the competition he created for the society's labor agency, only a handful of Italians sought employment through the society in 1903 and 1904. In the summer of 1903, society president Charles Catelli attempted to change this situation by writing a series of letters to corporate officials, offering them the services of the Italian Immigration Aid Society. But Catelli's efforts produced only a polite response from George Burns, who expressed his "entire satisfaction" with Cordasco.[65]

[63] Testimony of Francesco Mazza, *Royal Commission*, 110; *Annual Reports of the Industrial Removal Office* (New York, 1900–1910); Iver Bernstein, *The New York City Draft Riots: Their Significance for American Society and Politics in the Age of the Civil War* (New York, 1990), 183; *Bollettino della Societa di Patronato Dell' Immigrazione Italiana in Canada, Montreal* (Montreal 1903), 13, Records of the Royal Commission's Investigation, RG 33/99.
[64] Typically, the society sought to oblige Italian workers to finish the terms of their seasonal work contracts. See *Constitution of the Immigration Aid Society for Canada in Montreal*, chap. 2, Articles 3, 4, 8, 9, 13.
[65] C. Mariotti to D. McNicoll, General Manager, CPR, March 5, 1903, *Royal Commission*, 13; Letter from George Burns, Special Agent, to C. Mariotti, March 16, 1903, ibid.

Although Catelli failed to turn nonwhite Italian sojourners into free laboring colonists or to break Cordasco's monopoly on CPR employment, he succeeded in angering Cordasco, who blasted the society's benevolence just days after being crowned king:

A poor man has no money for food and the great alms you gave to him are 20 cents. Do you believe a man can live a month on 20 cents? But the 20,000 liras that the Italian government pays every year are they kept in the bank to get interest on them? Give to eat to whom is in need instead to interfere in somebody else's business.

Cordasco himself offered unemployed compatriots nothing, but he threatened to expose the society's misuse of Italian government funds to officials in Italy. Warned Cordasco, "in a short time all will come to the knowledge of the Italian government."[66] Cordasco's conflict with the aid society suggests his coronation was also intended to silence opposition to his claim of being the nationalist representative of Italians in Canada.

But while Cordasco was busy wrapping himself in the symbolic garments of Italian royalty, the aid society was successfully manipulating government officials in both Canada and Italy. As historian Bruno Ramirez has demonstrated, the aid society was instrumental in sparking the Canadian government's investigation into the "fraudulent activities of labor agencies" during the summer of 1904. Although Dini and other members of the society were questioned by the Royal Commission, they received lenient treatment. Commissioners quickly accepted Dini's claim that he had not placed advertisements calling for ten thousand men, while Cordasco was grilled for over two hours.[67] In the report's conclusions, Dini was not even mentioned, while Cordasco and the CPR were given responsibility for having corrupted Montreal's labor market.

Dini's success in collaborating with leaders of the aid society to discredit his chief rival did not solve the problem of representation within the Italian community, however. Like middle-class Greek leaders in Utah, leaders of the Italian Immigration Aid Society were committed to a dualistic national identity. On the one hand, the aid society fervently promoted Italian nationalism, waging its campaign for racial and cultural legitimacy in Canada with royal symbols and insignias of its own. No member of the aid society was ever coronated, but it did order royal-looking uniforms for its members and prominently displayed them just two months before Cordasco's coronation. The Italian government paid for their uniforms itself under the leadership of Count Mazza, an Italian nobleman given the title of "honorary president" of the society. At the same time, however, the aid society strongly pushed Canadianization through colonization. The aid society expressed this dualism in its legal origins. As if to underscore the compatibility of Italian nationalism and Canadian colonization by a whitened

[66] Antonio Cordasco to R. Candori, February 19, 1904, Records of the Royal Commission's Investigation, RG 33/99.
[67] Ramirez, "The Italians of Montreal," 70; Testimony of Alberto Dini, *Royal Commission*, 2.

Italian yeomanry, the aid society took its origin from the Canadian legal system, specifically from an "Act respecting Immigration Aid Societies" culled from the *Revised Statutes of Canada*.[68] The importance of the Canadian legal system to the society's genesis and structure was emblematized by the seal on the cover of its English-language constitution – a Canadian maple leaf.

Tensions between Canadian and Italian forms of national authority erupted dramatically just six months after Cordasco was dismissed from the CPR. On January 2, 1905, Dini was elected "by a majority of voices" to become the new president of the society, upsetting the current president Charles Catelli. Outraged by Dini's success, Catelli persuaded Count Mazza, the Italian consul, to maintain him as the president and strip Dini of the office, using an obscure statute in the constitution that gave the "Ministry of Foreign Affairs in Rome" the ultimate power of certifying the results of an election. The action provoked a dramatic confrontation within Montreal's Italian community between Dini's supporters and the Italian consul. A mass meeting organized by Dini brought out nearly two thousand Italians, according to the *Montreal Star*, ostensibly to protest Count Mazza's actions. When little came of Dini's petition and mass meeting, he took Catelli to court, claiming the authority of the Canadian legal system since he had been elected to the presidency of a Canadian corporation. Dini ironically lost the case, however, when the Canadian judge, impressed by Count Mazza's royal credentials, ruled that Dini "has no serious ground of complaint" and dismissed his petition "without costs."[69]

Dini's legal battles dramatized enduring tensions within Montreal's Italian community over how it would represent itself. Would it be a community that governed itself by decree of the Italian monarchy or a white "colony" that possessed a separate identity, one governed by Canadian laws and political leaders? Perhaps more important, how would the leadership of any Italian community legitimate itself in the eyes of sojourning workers? No clear answers emerged from the bitter disputes between Cordasco, Catelli, and Dini between July 1904 and January 1905, but the society was transformed by the conflict. Although Catelli remained the society's president, he abandoned his plans for colonizing Italian workers in the Canadian plains. Henceforth, the society began seeking ways to build a "respectable" Italian community in Montreal that not only united elite factions, but brought together persistent and transient, middle-class and working-class Italians. This would be a difficult task, as most Italians remained sojourners, mobilizing themselves and their families for decades to come.

[68] *Constitution of the Immigration Aid Society for Canada in Montreal*, cover and chap. 4, Article 51, 19; *Revised Statutes of Canada* (Ottawa, 1886) chap. 66, 35 Victoria, c. 29.

[69] *Constitution of the Immigration Aid Society for Canada in Montreal*, chap. 5, Article 66, 23; "Faction Fight in Italian Colony," *Montreal Star*, February 15, 1905, 3; see *Alberto Dini vs. Carlo O. Catelli*, February 20, 1905, Case 2707, Records of the Superior Court, District of Montreal.

Racial Pedigrees

As the principal administrator of vagrancy laws in El Paso between 1901 and 1905, Roman Gonzalez literally determined the boundaries of its persistent Mexican American community. In so doing, he not only kept the streets "clean" for U.S. police officials but confirmed a common racial stereotype about the character of local Mexicans. As Italian labor agent Michael Buonocore of Pittsburgh put it, all Mexicans were "vagrant, dirty, and lazy." Gonzalez saw himself as an exception to the rule, but his work as a policeman and a labor contractor consistently drew strength from the racial hierarchy that effectively segregated most Mexicans from civic life. "There is work in plenty for the Mexican laborers on the railroads to the North," Gonzalez told the *El Paso Times* in 1905, "but the Mexicans can not stand the cold.... They are weak and it devolves upon the railroad company to send them back to El Paso." Gonzalez criticized his compatriots in terms that evoked the most pervasive racial generalizations of the day, echoing the sentiments of one American sugar beet grower in Texas in 1926: "The Mexican is the best damn dog any white man ever had.... He can take the heat but he can't take the cold."[70]

Even as Gonzalez sought power over his compatriots by articulating common misperceptions, he nonetheless sought to whiten himself in the eyes of both Americans and his barrio compatriots. His most deliberate attempt occurred in 1900 when he became an American citizen. Although born in Mexico, Gonzalez renounced his loyalty not to Porfirio Diaz but to the king of Spain, thereby strengthening his claim to being a white leader with "pure" European blood in contrast to Mexican "Indians."[71] Becoming a U.S. citizen would not make Gonzalez white overnight, but it would help him straddle the boundaries of both national and racial identities and thereby gain power over his compatriots.

That was, at least, Gonzalez's hope. If perceptions of racial difference helped create the cultural space padrones mediated, they did not empower all padrones equally. One reason Gonzalez's citizenship switch did not produce cultural authority was that citizenship rights and whiteness were not in fact synonymous. As a policeman in the United States, whiteness did indeed seem to be within his grasp. But upon leaving the force, Gonzalez quickly learned that he no longer mattered to El Paso's political leaders. Those boundaries were manifest in Gonzalez's attempts to gain authority as a civic leader in El Paso. In the spring of 1906, just months after formally leaving El Paso's police force, Gonzalez

---

[70] Michael Buonocore interview by George Edson, Pittsburgh, September 10, 1926, "Interviews with Labor Contractors" file, BANC-MSS-74/187c, Paul S. Taylor Papers; "Can't Stand the Cold," *El Paso Times*, February 6, 1907, 5; Sugar Beet Grower interview by Paul Taylor, Julesberg, Colorado, 1928, doc. no. 72-872, BANC-MSS-74/187c, Paul S. Taylor Papers.

[71] El Paso County, Naturalization Files, March 5, 1900, file 3488, microfilm 48, El Paso County Courthouse, El Paso, Texas. For similar attempts to manipulate national and racial status among Polish and Jewish leaders, see Jacobson, *Special Sorrows*, 182–200.

petitioned the El Paso City Council to hire the twenty-five-member Diaz music band, "under the leadership of one of the best band masters of the Republic of Mexico," for two civic concerts.[72] As a citizen of the United States and a Mexican American, Gonzalez seemed a perfect candidate to promote such events and to mediate the social gulf between El Paso's City Council and its Mexican American citizens. But Gonzalez's petition was quickly turned down. He had been hired to police the barrio, not to represent it or give it legitimate status within El Paso.

Gonzalez's failure to become an effective political broker also underscored the drawbacks he confronted in advocating U.S. citizenship. For Skliris, becoming an American citizen seemed one vehicle to respectability and power. For Gonzalez, by contrast, such hybridized national identities were far more perilous, given political realities in both El Paso and Mexico between 1900 and 1920. For all sides in the Mexican Revolution, hostility to the United States was a basic tenet of emergent Mexican nationalism.[73] Advocating American citizenship to acquire power over Mexican communities turned out to be a contradiction in terms. Moreover, many transient Mexicans recognized that race was more powerful than citizenship in shaping the boundaries of their experience. A Mexican farm worker in California explained his reluctance to become a U.S. citizen in 1940 after decades of work in the United States. "I'm not interested in being a citizen because first of all it would mean nothing to anyone – I would be a citizen in name only – with no privileges or considerations. I would still be a 'dirty Mexican.'" One measure of that sentiment in the early 1920s was the contempt many Mexicans expressed for the pretensions of men like Gonzalez. "Many Mexicans don't speak the language their mothers taught them," went the lyrics of one popular folk song, "and go about saying they are Spanish and denying their country's flag.... Some are darker than chapote [black tar] but they pretend to be Saxon; They go about powdered to the back of the neck and wear skirts for trousers." The cultural authority Gonzalez sought as a white American cop proved elusive. Indeed, to many Mexicans, attempts to whiten oneself with "Spanish" blood only emasculated the would-be Mexican leader, as whiteness was equated with feminine powders on the "back of the neck."[74]

[72] On the marginality of El Paso's Mexican middle class between 1880 and 1920, see Garcia, *Desert Immigrants*, 82. On tensions between Mexicans and Mexican Americans around questions of nationalism, see Sanchez, *Becoming Mexican American*, 87–128; See R. G. Gonzalez to the El Paso City Council, June 14, 1906, Minutes of the City Council of El Paso, vol. 1, 512, Southwest Collection, El Paso Public Library, El Paso, Texas.

[73] On the importance of anti-Americanism to Mexican nationalists during the revolution, see John M. Hart, *Revolutionary Mexico: The Coming and Process of the Mexican Revolution* (Berkeley, 1987). See also Alan Knight, *The Mexican Revolution*, vols. 1 and 2 (Cambridge, 1986).

[74] Special Survey of the Mexican colony at Hick's Camp, California, conducted by the California Division of Immigration and Housing, box 27, "Mexican-Housing," Carey McWilliams Collection, Special Collections, University Research Library, University of California, Los Angeles. Cited in Gutierrez, *Walls and Mirrors*, 89; Juan Castillo interview by Taylor, doc. no. 284-454, BANC-MSS-74/187c, Paul S. Taylor Papers; Taylor, *Mexican Labor in the United States*, vol. 2, vii.

Perhaps recognizing such hostility, Gonzalez attempted to rectify the damage his citizenship switch had caused by changing his original naturalization papers in 1915, declaring to an American judge that his identification with Spain had been the result of "error and inadvertence of the clerk of said court" and that he had been "at all time prior to his admission to citizenship of the United States ... a citizen of Mexico."[75] At the peak of the Mexican Revolution, Gonzalez deemed whiteness and U.S. citizenship less important than a patriotic Mexican heritage to establishing power among his compatriots. Although he amended the public record, the revolution was too advanced and his career too checkered for him to become a representative of either the national or racial community to transient Mexicans.

Conclusion

The creation and institutionalization of community – always a contested process – was particularly contentious among immigrant workers and immigrant businessmen in the North American West during the early twentieth century. Struggles between them over the boundaries of ethnic, racial, and national community were hardly unique to immigrants in the region. Like their counterparts in the immigrant neighborhoods of New York, Boston, and Philadelphia, middle-class immigrant leaders in Montreal, El Paso, and Salt Lake City attempted to muffle an emerging working-class culture among their compatriots, using the imposed but malleable ideologies of race and nationalism to their specific ends. But the remarkable transience of immigrant workers vastly complicated the process by which ethnic elites gained and maintained power. Because traditional institutions and sites of power – the church, the polling place, the neighborhood itself – rarely reached transient men like Harry Mantos or Jesus Garza, immigrant leaders struggled to find ways to locate and represent immigrant community among sojourners.

Middle-class immigrants were also deeply divided over the merits of transience and its connection to immigrant community. Should ethnicity be built around institutions that brought transient and persistent immigrants together or that excluded "less desirable" elements? If some businessmen wanted to create more representative ethnic institutions that could indeed mobilize larger constituencies when necessary, others sought to distance themselves from their nonwhite brethren. Officers of the Greek Community of Utah and the Italian Immigration Aid Society, for example, excluded transient members from their ranks and sought to eliminate transience by restricting immigrant community to fixed places: the Holy Trinity Church and the Canadian plains. Padrones, by contrast, profited directly from workers' mobility and from the perception among corporate executives that they were disposable. Consequently, they attempted to invent forms of imagined national community that would transcend any fixed locales and

---

[75] *Ex parte vs. R. G. Gonzalez*, September 22, 1915, Case 3488, Records of the 65th District Civil Court, El Paso County Courthouse.

neighborhoods. Rather than advocate colonization, Cordasco deployed nationalist symbols in an effort to unite sojourning Italians. Skliris likewise eschewed community-building efforts in Salt Lake City's Greektown in favor of more expansive forms of community: Greek nationalism and U.S. citizenship. Gonzalez, in turn, attempted to create a patriotic and whitened Mexican American identity, using his varied statuses as a onetime citizen of Mexico, Spain, and the United States to claim statuses as a racial and national leader of Mexican sojourners.

Yet the imagined communities of race and nation remained ambiguous and troubling sources of authority for padrones. Because Gonzalez, Skliris, and Cordasco gained power by manipulating the boundaries between persistent and transient immigrants, citizen and alien, white and nonwhite immigrants, their own membership within these different local, national, and racial communities remained of necessity ambiguous. Padrones were at their most powerful when they could remain both inside and outside any particular place or imagined space. By becoming "king of the laborers," Antonio Cordasco cast his lot with sojourning Italian workers and consequently left himself vulnerable to the attack of Montreal's Italian middle-class community. Roman Gonzalez, by contrast, was too closely tied to the persistent Mexican community of Chihuahuita and was unable to transcend its narrow boundaries. Leon Skliris was most successful in remaining both within and without several immigrant communities, becoming a representative for Greek nationalism and American citizenship.

Immigrant workers were also internally divided by questions that transience and community location posed, having been exploited, taxed, coerced, and expelled from various locales all in the name of community. And yet transient workers succeeded in creating remarkably vibrant ethnic and working-class communities on the move. They were built, out of necessity, across local, regional, and national boundaries. In their boxcars, coffeehouses, and boardinghouses, immigrant workers constructed fraternal ties and communal bonds quite distinct from the institutions founded by middle-class immigrants, and they consistently subverted elite immigrants' quest for "respectability" and power. If padrones' paternal and fraternal manhood were defensive articulations, so too were their nationalist and racialized visions of community. The power of transient communities was manifest not in enduring working-class institutions but in the complex ways they limited the varied efforts of middle-class businessmen to define community and determine what it should represent. In that struggle, audiences outside the immigrant group played a key role. While padrones and businessmen embraced aspects of North American political culture – U.S. citizenship, Canadian maple leaves, colonization schemes, and the rhetoric of whiteness – to burnish their reputations, so did many immigrant workers embrace aspects of American political culture while sojourning, the subject of the next chapter.

CHAPTER SIX

The Spaces of Freedom

The July day in 1902 when Cesidio Simbali and twelve Italian track workers in Indiana reclaimed their freedom began like many others that summer: hot and oppressive. Their padrone, Fulvio, was driving them hard when one of them injured himself and asked, "are we slaves, beasts or men, sir?" His question, full of indignation and anger, bore striking parallels to the anguished queries other immigrant sojourners were to raise in North America over the ensuing decade. In 1911, after being fed nothing but "crackers and sardines" for two days in a speeding train, whose windows had been boarded shut to keep workers from jumping, a Mexican immigrant named José asked angrily, "Is this the land of liberty?" Greek workers in Utah put the matter more bluntly the same year when they asked the governor of Utah, William Spry, "Where are we? In the free country of Amerika or in a country ruled by a despotic form of government?"[1]

For Italian, Mexican, and Greek workers, asking such questions initially produced few tangible changes or gains. No one heard José's question, and Greek workers would wait two months for Governor Spry's disappointing reply. For Cesidio's partner, questioning the padrone actually seemed to make matters worse as he returned to work moments later "with the resignation of a slave." But questions can be powerful catalysts of social change. The Italian track worker's defiant question laid the basis for an even more dramatic confrontation with Fulvio that afternoon. It began when an itinerant Italian organ grinder approached along isolated railway tracks and induced Cesidio's entire gang to drop their picks and shovels and listen to their compatriot play and sing. Rather than allow his tired men a brief respite, Fulvio demanded that the organ grinder stop playing. When the organ grinder refused, Fulvio punched him in the face. Under any circumstance, Fulvio's action would have provoked the anger of Italian workers, but even Cesidio was unprepared for what ensued. "The outraged gang surged forward like a solid, fearful phalanx," he recalled, and began pummeling Fulvio and his

---

[1] "The Future of Mexican Immigration: A Story on the Outside Looking In," José of Old Mexico, 1928, box 1, Z-R-4, Paul S. Taylor Papers; "Fifty Greek and Crete Men to Utah Government," petition, February 2, 1911, file "G," box 10, William S. Spry Papers.

henchmen, who were soon begging for mercy after being "dragged left and right."[2] Fulvio managed to flee the enraged workers, who later resumed their work without padrone interference. In a matter of a few minutes, Cesidio's once emasculated and "enslaved" partner had reclaimed his manhood and freedom in North America, if only for a moment.

While the actions of Cesidio's work gang were decisive, their meaning was more ambiguous. Punching Fulvio in the face may have vindicated one aspect of Cesidio's and his partner's manhood, but at the expense of connections to family members in Italy. Getting rid of Fulvio also did not solve the question of who would replace him. Although Cesidio's narrative ends in progressive fashion with the workers' victory over Fulvio, the new foreman quite likely continued to charge workers job fees and high prices for food.

But judging immigrant workers as failures because their next foreman also exploited his power to hire and fire unskilled workers distorts their accomplishment and the character of their resistance. A few immigrant workers did indeed reach the collective realization that free labor was nothing but a smokescreen for their oppression: that the rights to quit and to make contracts were fictions, that the varied forms of manliness performed by padrones were mere ideologies used to exploit them, that whiteness and citizenship were tragic distractions keeping them divided and unable to grasp their true interests. Yet such compelling critiques of power relations rarely emerged among Greek, Italian, and Mexican sojourners. Rather than reject notions of free labor and contractual obligation, most immigrant workers in time demanded what they saw as their inheritance in North America: the right to quit their jobs without penalty, the right to sue their padrones, and the right to strike or mount collective protests when necessary. What pushed them to resistance was not their abandonment of free labor ideology, but rather its reinvention, one propelled by the realization that padrones had broken their promises and that they had a right to demand something better in "the free country of Amerika."[3]

The process by which immigrant workers claimed and transformed free labor was filled with setbacks and contradictions. Immigrant workers experienced little

---

[2] Simboli, "When the Boss Went Too Far," 149.

[3] On the political uses of free labor ideology among working-class immigrants, see Gary Gerstle, *Working-Class Americanism: The Politics of Labor in a Textile City, 1914–1960* (Cambridge, 1989), 5–15; and Rudolph Vecoli, "'Free Country': The American Republic Viewed by the American Left," in Marianne Debouzy, ed., *In the Shadow of the Statue of Liberty: Immigrants, Workers, and Citizens in the American Republic, 1880–1920* (Urbana, 1992), 23–44; and Leon Fink, "The New Labor History and the Powers of Historical Pessimism: Consensus, Hegemony, and the Case of the Knights of Labor," *Journal of American History* 75 (June 1988): 115–136. On studies that explore how the law and free labor ideology furthered working-class interests during the 1930s, see Lizabeth Cohen, *Making a New Deal: Industrial Workers in Chicago, 1919–1939* (Cambridge, 1990); and Melvyn Dubofsky, *The State and Labor in Modern America* (Chapel Hill, 1994). For dissenting narratives, see Christopher Tomlins, *The State and the Unions: Labor Relations, Law, and the Organized Labor Movement in America, 1880–1960* (Cambridge, 1985).

agreement about what free labor meant or where that freedom was located. Greek workers' question, "Is this the land of liberty?" led them to a series of dilemmas. Could freedom be secured through formal legal institutions, such as the courts and the governor's office, or in actions outside the law? In citizenship or in working-class internationalism? In the privileges of fatherhood or in bonds of fraternity? In the status of a white worker or in the solidarity of nonwhite immigrants? In persistent or transient communities? This chapter examines the complex story of how immigrant workers claimed the crosscutting elements of free labor ideology in North America, exploring the consequences for both padrones and working-class organizations.

Fleeing the Padrone

If transnational mobility fueled the growth of padrone power, mobility in the West nonetheless possessed liberatory meanings to many immigrants. Most left their home villages with very high hopes of life in the West. "I came here very happy," recalled Mexican Isidro Osorio of Guanajuato in 1927, "because I was about to learn about a new country which had been made known to us by the boys of the town. . . . I came . . . so that I could convince myself with my own eyes." Bonifacio Ortega of Jalisco left home for the same reasons, because "we got a desire to come and know this famous country." Greek immigrant Harry Greaves recalled his brother's enticements to move west when Harry worked in New York. "Ah, why you staying here?" his brother asked, "let's go out West and see the country. Why you come to America? Let's go out West!" Such hopes sustained many immigrants through at least parts of their sojourns. One Mexican track worker looked forward especially to the traveling. "I have to go out tonight, I don't know where, but just so I see some more of this country before I settle down."[4] The same high hopes held sway among Italians traveling to western Canada, the last "el Dorado" in North America, according to CPR boosters.

For most immigrants, however, mobility delivered elusive freedoms and benefits.[5] Two aspects of geographic mobility shaped immigrant workers' understanding of the relationship between transience and freedom: movement through space and movement between jobs, the freedom to move and the freedom to quit. Both forms of worker mobility had become sources of tremendous revenue for padrones, with Skliris growing rich by controlling job turnover and Cordasco by

---

[4] Gamio, *The Mexican Immigrant*, 25, 42; Harry Greaves interview by Helen Papanikolas, Salt Lake City, June 1, 1973, Greek Archives; Taylor, *Mexican Labor in the United States*, vol. 2, 260.

[5] On the variety of political meanings that mobility possessed among farm workers in California, see Don Mitchell, *The Lie of the Land: Migrant Workers and the California Landscape* (Minneapolis, 1996), 58–82; Daniel Cletus, *Bitter Harvest: A History of California Farm Workers, 1870–1941* (Ithaca, 1981). On connections between Greek mobility and manhood, see Evthymios Papataxiarchis, "Friends of the Heart: Male Commensal Solidarity, Gender, and Kinship in Aegean Greece," in Loizos and Papataxiarchis, *Contested Identities*, 174.

exploiting movement along one vast set of CPR rails. Both aspects of workers' mobility also became integral to how they defined freedom in North America and resisted padrone power.

Like most wage earners, Italians working for the CPR in British Columbia during the summer could quit whenever they chose. But the costs of such action were indeed high. Quitting not only stranded dependents in Italy without monthly remittances but could also strand oneself in an isolated stretch of the Canadian Rockies. Unlike Ukrainian and Swedish track workers who returned to home-steads and nearby communities in the Canadian plains after quitting, Italians were profoundly isolated, both geographically and culturally. Although "free" to move and to quit, Italians soon discovered that isolation and the necessities of survival transformed such freedoms into misery.

Geographic and cultural isolation were common problems for immigrant sojourners throughout the West. Greek immigrant James Velisaropoulos had high expectations when he joined an extra gang headed for Yellowstone Park, but he discovered far more than he'd bargained for: "We see all kinds of bears and a lot of things right away, and we got scared they are going to eat us up." Terrified, James and his co-workers retreated to a train car, locked themselves in, and waited for the foreman to return. "We got stranded there," he later confessed, a situation that subsequently left him few options in dealing with his foreman who eventually let him out: "I had to do what they tell me to do." Not all isolated workers obeyed their foremen, but quitting or striking involved extraordinary risks in remote regions of the continent. Greek miner Louis Lingos recalled some of the risks he undertook in 1912 when "Leonidas Skliris sent forty of us Greek men to work in Nevada in a deep canyon." The gang decided to quit en masse after a co-worker was injured on the job, but "the company charged us too much for the food" and "would not take us back to Salt Lake." Stranded, they "burned all their luggage and clothes and started back on foot," some of them arriving in Salt Lake City three weeks later, dehydrated and exhausted.[6]

Although Greek workers possessed more work options in Utah than did Italians in British Columbia, Greeks also faced a far greater hurdle in breaking free from Skliris's tribute system. When Louis Lingos arrived back in Salt Lake City in the spring of 1912, he possessed few job options. Having spent his remaining money getting back to town, he was compelled to borrow money from friends to pay Skliris yet another round of job fees to get work. Skliris did not control all potential Greek jobs in Utah, but the main magnets of steady work – the Denver and Rio Grande Railway, the coal mines of Carbon County, the copper smelters in Magna and Garfield, and the open-pit mine at the Utah Copper Company – were under his power by 1912. One had to leave the Intermountain West entirely and all of the friends and kin scattered throughout the region to escape Skliris's tributes.

Quitting one's job was an option many Greeks nonetheless used, often to

---

[6] James Velisaropoulas interview by Louis Cononelos, Salt Lake City, December 11, 1974, American West Center; Louis Lingos interview by Helen Papanikolas, Salt Lake City, April 9, 1970, ibid.

escape the burdens of dangerous work or an abusive foreman. Such actions gave Greek workers a modicum of control over the pace and conditions of work. Mass quittings and spontaneous actions by work gang members were not everyday events, but common enough to dissuade some American labor agents from even hiring Italians, Greeks, or Mexicans over time. One American labor agent in Texas explained in 1927, "I used to ship Greeks, Italians, and Mexicans. When you would fire one, the whole bunch would quit." Another American roadmaster in Chicago recalled that "Italian track workers were always wanting something, ten hours pay for nine hours work, or higher wages, etc. ... And if you discharged one worthless skunk, the others would leave with him." Greeks in Utah used similar patterns of collective action, attacking their American foremen when they fired a member of their work gang or increased their hours. Such collective mobilizations toppled the power of abusive foremen but, until 1912, did not hamper Skliris, who continued collecting job fees from the next foreman.[7]

Mexican workers were individually more successful than Greeks or Italians in making flight an effective means of resisting padrone power. Because Mexican sojourners were closer to home villages than Italians or Greeks, they were more willing to take the risk of quitting a job in a remote region. Moreover, Mexican sojourners were close to Mexican American populations scattered throughout the U.S. Southwest. Although numerous tensions existed between the two groups, as historian David Gutierrez has analyzed, Mexican American communities in Texas, New Mexico, Arizona, and California aided sojourners in numerous ways, providing knowledge about work opportunities, places to recuperate between jobs, and connections to kin in both Mexico and the United States.[8] Mexican sojourners consequently succeeded better than Greeks or Italians in maintaining control over their mobility and in offsetting some of the most coercive aspects of padrone authority and corporate power in the West.

The mobility of Mexican sojourners was indeed remarkable. Labor agent G. A. Hoff of the L. H. Manning Labor Agency in Tucson, Arizona, for example, told sociologist Paul Taylor in 1928 that "forty-six or forty-seven percent of our shipments on the average desert us without paying." On return trips in the fall the percentage of Mexican workers jumping contracts grew even higher. Labor agent Ben Williams of Chicago estimated that "about sixty percent of the Mexicans shipped south leave the job after working a day or so." For labor agent William Clark of the Holmes Supply Company in El Paso, the percentage of desertions reached two-thirds. "Recently we shipped six hundred men for a two hundred man gang around Dawson, Arizona," stated Clark, explaining that "they all leave for cotton. The Mexicans know the locations of the towns."[9]

Mexican mobility between jobs created particular headaches for railroad

[7] Mr. Kennedy interview, S.W.& A. Labor Agency, San Antonio, Texas, doc. no. 26-31, BANC-MSS-74/187c, Paul S. Taylor Papers; Taylor, *Mexican Labor in the United States*, vol. 2, 85.

[8] Gutierrez, *Walls and Mirrors*, 39–68; Sanchez, *Becoming Mexican American*, 87–107.

[9] H. Hoff interview by Paul Taylor, Tucson, 1928, doc. no. 46-556, BANC-MSS-74/187c, Paul S. Taylor Papers; Ben Williams interview by Paul Taylor, Chicago, 1928, ibid.; William Clark interview by Paul Taylor, El Paso, 1928, doc. no. 98-103, ibid.

companies. Gregorio Diaz recalled that in 1908 railroad companies "used to lock the doors on the trains and have a piece of lumber screwed on the outside of the windows" to prevent people from climbing out during stops. But Mexican workers still managed to escape. As Diaz recalled, "The Mexicans used to buy sandwiches and coffee or cigarettes. These were pretexts for jumping the train. Even the illiterates used to know when to jump from the descriptions that had been given to them." Those descriptions not only honed Mexican workers' skills as transients, but also enabled them to get free transportation to jobs of their choice and to communities of kin and fictive kin scattered throughout the U.S. Midwest. Despite railroad company efforts to stop such mobility, it remained the central problem for railroad companies throughout the 1910s and 1920s. According to an American labor agent in Pittsburgh, "We ship in about five hundred Mexicans a month for the Pennsylvania Railroad.... Out of every hundred, twenty stay on the job."[10]

If Mexican mobility foiled corporate attempts to create a "stable" work force, it likewise hindered the padrone's ability to wring a profit from the commerce of migration. Although Mexican job turnover ostensibly increased the volume of business available to labor agents, most Mexicans did not need the padrone's services after they had jumped. Transportation both north and south in North America was not difficult to procure, particularly if one signed a work contract and then quit. Just as no single padrone or labor agent controlled the migration of Mexicans northward in the springtime, there was also no single path of return to Mexico. The train tickets that Mexicans received for signing a padrone's or railroad company's contract were used even if they never showed up for work. According to George Edson, "Mexican workers sell their transportation passes to other men going to Mexico on a visit. They cross the border under an assumed name, and later re-enter under their own name."[11] Padrones like Skliris were hardly the first immigrants in the West to use invented surnames.

Corporations and labor agents attempted to stabilize the turnover of Mexican labor during the 1920s by importing families and women to distant sites of labor demand. According to an employment manager from a steel plant in Kansas in 1928, "the turnover (among Mexicans) was very high at first. Without women and Mexican boardinghouses the men wouldn't stay. So I brought up a Mexican woman to run a boardinghouse and helped her to get started."[12] But such attempts failed to control Mexican workers' mobility. One key reason was the skill Mexican families demonstrated in controlling their freedom to move. Trains did indeed pose a particular challenge for families seeking to jump a contract, especially families with young children. But such disadvantages were offset by the advent of automobiles in the 1920s. According to George Edson, by 1928 "nearly every Mexican family has an automobile, which is regarded as a necessity in this section." The majority of these families traveled to job sites in cotton fields, sugar

---

[10] Gregory Diaz interview by Paul Taylor, Bethlehem, Pa. 1928, doc. no. 113-117, ibid.; Peterson Employment Agency interview by Paul Taylor, Pittsburgh, 1928, ibid.

[11] George L. Edson, "Mexicans in Sugar Beet Work in the Central West: A Summary of Local Reports," April 1927, in "Interviews with Labor Contractors," ibid.

[12] Taylor, *Mexican Labor in the United States*, vol. 2, 67.

beet fields, and factories on their own, with little interference from padrones or corporate commissary systems. The development led sugar beet grower Richard King of south Texas to remark in 1928 that "it is better to get Mexicans in trucks. If they have their own cars they travel every week to see where the cotton is. If they have no other way to move about, it is better."[13] The automobile did not literally emancipate Mexican workers, for as transients they remained underpaid and racially stigmatized. But better than most transient immigrants in the North American West, Mexicans used the automobile to preserve the liberatory potential of mobility between jobs and across arid lands, offsetting corporate domination of their work lives and limiting the exactions of their labor agents.

Suing the Padrone

Mexican workers' skills as transients may have helped them limit padrone power, but these skills also left them poorly positioned to challenge padrone or corporate power using the U.S. legal system. Because of the time, money, and persistence required to file and complete a lawsuit, only a few attempted to use U.S. courts to their advantage. Often it was left to a friend or family member to settle disputes over pay or employment with a company. In 1893, for example, one unnamed Mexican woman walked all the way from Bakersfield, Arizona, to El Paso to get her husband's scrip wages redeemed in hard currency. When officers of the Southern Pacific's Norton-Drake Company refused her request, she promptly told her story to a muckraking journalist for the *El Paso Times*, where the story appeared the next day.[14] The woman could not press charges against the commissary company, however, because the husband was not present: he was still trying to earn some money as a track worker.

When Mexican railroad workers did on occasion sue their American employers, they did so with the help of Mexican American interpreters such as Roman Gonzalez, Robert Zarate, and Isaac Avina. In 1915, Gonzalez represented the family members of Juan Cordero, a deceased Mexican worker, who were seeking damages from the Atchison, Topeka and Santa Fe Railway. Claiming that Cordero had been negligently "run over and killed by an engine," Gonzalez sought ten thousand dollars in damages and lost wages at Cordero's pay rate of nine dollars a week. Although the company denied any liability, it agreed to pay the family $550, a comparatively large settlement in 1913. On rare occasions, Mexican workers sued railroad companies for work-related injuries without the help of interpreters, as when Robert de la Cruz and Leonidez Melendez took the Southern Pacific (SP) to court and won smaller judgments of one hundred dollars each.[15] Such small

---

[13] Richard King interview by Paul Taylor, South Central Texas, 1928, doc. no. 101-691, BANC-MSS-74/187c, Paul S. Taylor Papers.

[14] *El Paso Times*, October 28, 1894, 6.

[15] *R. G. Gonzalez vs. A.T.&S.F. Railway Company*, Case 13168, Records of the 65th District Civil Court, El Paso County Courthouse; *Leonidez Melendez vs. Southern Pacific Railroad Company*, Case 4926, Records of the 34th District Civil Court, ibid.; *Robert de la Cruz vs. Southern Pacific Railroad Company*, Case 13273, Records of the 65th District Civil Court, ibid.

legal victories did not make the U.S. legal system an attractive option for challeng-ing padrone power, particularly when Gonzalez himself represented the worker.

By the 1920s, however, Mexican workers had begun to increase their control over the types of contracts they made with labor agents and employers. According to Patricio Shutter, an American rancher in southern Texas, Mexican cotton pick-ers began preferring written contracts to oral ones because "if the Mexicans are in trouble they can't do anything when the contract is oral." Shutter explained that although "Mexicans ask for written contracts," their landlords typically "say no, their word is good." The result was that "very few contracts, perhaps 10%, are written." Although cotton growers continued to have the upper hand, Mexican workers remained determined to use contracts to their advantage. As Shutter com-mented, "some Mexicans won't work without written contracts."[16]

Part of this change reflected immigrant workers' experience with the United States Employment Service between 1917 and 1919, which guaranteed written contracts for all seasonal Mexican agricultural and railroad workers in the U.S. Southwest. When the federal government suspended its immigration service in 1919, the state of Texas stepped into the void, passing several laws strictly regulating the kinds of contracts and fees that employment agents could charge immigrant workers. Although these laws were passed with mixed motives – Texas labor agency laws in fact sought to restrict worker mobility – immigrant workers correctly perceived in them potential limits to the autocratic power of individual padrones and labor agents.[17]

It would not be long before transient workers in Texas began using the legal system to challenge their labor agents when promises had been broken. In El Paso the first civil action against a labor agent involved Roman Gonzalez during the late summer of 1922, just as his reorganized labor agency was getting off the ground. According to three jointly filed complaints, Gonzalez sent three men to "work as mule skinners" near Kingman, Arizona. But when they arrived they dis-covered that the firm of "Sharp and Fellow" would not hire them. Subsequently, all three ended up in the Kingman jail for ten days on vagrancy charges. When they managed to get out, they were compelled to "board a freight train and hobo it back to El Paso ... suffering hunger and privation" the entire journey across New Mexico's deserts. Each worker claimed that Gonzalez had overcharged him for the job and had not posted the requisite five thousand dollar bond with the city of El Paso, as required by law "for the protection of the general public and the

---

[16] Patricio Shutter interview by Paul Taylor, Robstown, Texas, 1928, doc. no. 147-736, BANC-MSS-74/187c, Paul S. Taylor Papers.

[17] Montejano, *Anglos and Mexicans in the Making of Texas*, 210–213. On the failures of state and federal agencies to reorganize local labor markets during the 1920s, see Licht, *Getting Work*; and Harrison, *Public Employment Agencies*. On the struggles of the United States Employ-ment Service, see Darrell Hevenor Smith, *The United States Employment Service: Its History, Activities, and Organizations* (Baltimore, 1923); and Ruth M. Kellogg, *The United States Employment Service* (Chicago, 1932).

plaintiffs." Because of such legal violations, the workers sought not only a refund of their job fees but "exemplary damages" of two thousand dollars each.[18]

Never before in Gonzalez's career as an enforcer of vagrancy law or in the history of labor agencies in El Paso had transient workers ever sought damages for being made a vagrant. Whether or not Gonzalez appreciated the delicious irony of their claims, he certainly understood their financial implications. The three lawsuits not only threatened him with immediate bankruptcy, but tarnished his refurbished reputation with railroad managers. Although the judge ruled that Gonzalez had only to refund each worker his job fee, his fortunes plummeted thereafter as the railroad companies refused subsequently to do any more business with the now unreliable labor agent. When Gonzalez finally paid the judgments late in 1923, he had lost every contract supplying labor to railroad companies in the Southwest. All remaining business was conducted with sugar beet companies, whose patronage dwindled over the ensuing three years.

Gonzalez would have gone out of business far more quickly had Judge R. R. Price not explicitly instructed the jury to refrain from granting any exemplary damages. Judge Price sought to prevent these cases from becoming a precedent inciting other migrant workers to sue their labor agents. Yet his instructions to the jury were also closely linked to the peculiar nature of racial politics in El Paso. The plaintiffs against Gonzalez – Will Kimble, Will Johnson, and Ernest Young – were not Mexicans or Mexican Americans, but African Americans who had responded to Gonzalez's newspaper advertisement in the *El Paso Times* for "20 colored laborers." Judge Price, along with El Paso's municipal authorities, had little affection for Gonzalez, but did not want to empower "colored" laborers unduly. To the contrary, the legal system in El Paso remained bent on restricting the mobility and rights of African American workers. Yet precisely because Gonzalez was himself not white in the eyes of Judge Price, Kimble was able to squeeze some justice out of the legal proceeding, persuading Price that Gonzalez had "damaged them by false and fraudulent statements."[19] For Gonzalez, the Mexican American who would be a white Spaniard, the verdict must have been excruciating, a not so subtle reminder of his place. Brought down by the same legal system and racial hierarchy that had brought him to power, Gonzalez exemplified how whiteness could be gained as well as lost, even with U.S. citizenship.

Like transient Mexicans, Italian sojourners possessed few if any opportunities to use the Canadian legal system to their advantage between 1901 and the spring of 1904. Not only were they constantly in motion, but Cordasco seemed to be a

---

[18] *Will Kimble vs. R. G. Gonzalez*, Case 22567, Records of the 65th District Civil Court, El Paso County Courthouse; *Will Johnson vs. R. G. Gonzalez*, Case 22568, ibid.; *Ernest Young vs. R. G. Gonzalez*, Case 22569, ibid.

[19] *Kimble vs. Gonzalez*, Case 22567, ibid. As David Montejano has argued, the most successful migrant workers in Texas to sue their employers during the 1920s were "Anglos." See Montejano, *Anglos and Mexicans in the Making of Texas*, 205–206.

master of the Canadian legal system. All Italian workers signed his labor contracts in both Italian and English specifying their daily wage and agreeing to distribute workers' mail "every day, except holydays, from 9:30 to 10 A.M., from 1:30 to 2, and from 4:30 to 5 P.M." Cordasco viewed such details as evidence of his ability to protect Italian workers from the many thieving individuals who would steal from them outright. Interpreters, in particular, were required "to stick to the above rules and give all necessary information to the men."[20] For Italian workers, controlling the mail was another important way Cordasco controlled their mobility and the family relations that sustained it. Cordasco did not, of course, manipulate the content of the information that relatives and kin sent each other, but by functioning as their legal mailman he did control their access to it.

As Italian workers became immobilized in Montreal during the spring of 1904, Cordasco's control over Italian workers' kin connections and consumption habits faded. No longer did workers need Cordasco to be fed, to get their mail, or to send money back to relatives in Italy. Moreover, as Cordasco's social relations with Italian workers soured, the initial premise behind his written contracts – that Italian workers were equal partners in determining the terms of employment – grew ever shakier. Cordasco did himself no favors by evincing contempt for every Italian worker who visited his labor agency. When laborer Giovanni Morillo asked Cordasco why there was no work in June 1904, for example, a frustrated Cordasco bluntly stated "If you do not get out of my office, I will kick you out." And when Vincenzo Sciano, a foreman, demanded his job fees and respect for his "rights," Cordasco replied "you have no rights at all."[21]

Cordasco's autocratic replies only emboldened more Italian workers to demand both their job fees and justice in his office. By June there were several Italian workers willing to testify against him in the Royal Commission's investigation. Scattered through workers' testimonies were assertions of rights, as well as a mixture of betrayal and sadness that Cordasco had not lived up to the terms of his agreements. "He promised to send me out April first or after that date," stated foreman Antonio Giacci. When asked if that date had come, Giacci replied ruefully "not yet." Pietro Bazzani, another foreman, stated "he promised to give me a chance" in the spring of 1904, but moments later grimly remarked "he never gave me a chance."[22] Such comments did not criticize free labor ideology or the notion that a chance at wage labor was fair and free, but rather portrayed Cordasco as a villain because he had eliminated the chance that ostensibly made wage labor "free."

Italian workers' righteous anger grew even hotter after Cordasco reneged on his promise to refund job fees to all unemployed workers in August 1904. According

[20] According to the court testimony of George Burns, "We furnished him with contracts, we sent them to him, I signed them, and he got the contracts signed by the men." See *G. Teolo vs. Antonio Cordasco*, Case 990, Records of the Superior Court, District of Montreal.

[21] Testimony of Giovanni Morillo, *Royal Commission*, 67; Testimony of Vincenzo Sciano, ibid., 32.

[22] Testimony of Pietro Bazzani, ibid., 68.

to Antonio Ganna, Cordasco's former secretary, the list of job fee refunds that Cordasco sent to Judge Ino Winchester in September was "false," containing records of four hundred dollars that had already been refunded before the hearings.[23] Ganna also asserted in a letter to Judge Winchester that Cordasco charged all workers fifty cents for every refund check that he issued and subsequently cashed, a fee that rose as he slid closer to bankruptcy in the fall of 1904.

Cordasco's refusal to refund immigrant workers' job fees fully and expeditiously finally led fifteen Italian workers and foremen to sue him for their unrecovered job fees and lost pay while waiting for promised jobs. Each of the suits claimed the same basic facts: that Cordasco had promised them jobs during the winter of 1903 and failed to deliver the goods or to refund their fees when no jobs became available in 1904. The amounts demanded varied in size from $134.25 by laborer Giuseppe d'Abramo to $350 by foremen Benvenuto Missiti and Alfredo Folco. Together the fifteen suits demanded over $4,000 in lost job fees and wages. Cordasco spent hundreds of dollars defending himself in court over the next four years and lost the most important cases. These legal defeats represented a stunning financial and political blow to the former king, making real his claim in 1905 that he "now was unable to earn a living."[24]

By successfully suing their former boss, foremen such as Pompei Bianco transformed what had been some of Cordasco's chief weapons – contracts and the Canadian legal system – into instruments of their defense and financial gain. Although these cases were not brought as a class-action suit, they were prosecuted in a collective manner, with testimony from one case being cited and used in others. It is not clear where immigrant workers found the collective inspiration – and money – to pursue their court cases. Cordasco believed the lawsuits were entirely the result of the Italian Immigration Aid Society's efforts to discredit him. Ever skilled in the rhetoric of free labor, Cordasco argued in one appeal that the worker Pietro Bazzani "had been forced to institute the said action" by false protectors

---

[23] A. Ganna to the Honorable Judge Winchester, September 25, 1904, ibid. Cordasco reiterated his promise in a letter to Judge Winchester two weeks later, stating that "he would refund the fees paid to me by Italian labourers." Antonio Cordasco to Honorable Judge Winchester, August 2, 1904, Records of the Royal Commission's Investigation, RG 33/99.

[24] See *Giuseppe d'Abramo vs. A. Cordasco*, Case 2787, Records of the Superior Court, District of Montreal; *Pietro Bazzani vs. A. Cordasco*, Case 1359, ibid.; *Beccunliello vs. A. Cordasco*, Case 2136, ibid.; *Pompei Bianco vs. A. Cordasco*, Case 2514, ibid.; *Michelle Cilla vs. A. Cordasco*, Case 2575, ibid.; *Fillip D'Allesandro vs. A. Cordasco*, Case 2357, ibid.; *Alfredo Folco vs. A. Cordasco*, Case 2223, ibid.; *Nicola Fondino vs. A. Cordasco*, Case 3127, ibid.; *Giuseppe Mignella vs. A. Cordasco*, Case 503, ibid.; *Benvenuto Missiti vs. A. Cordasco*, Case 1420, ibid.; *Salvatore Molla vs. A. Cordasco*, Case 2135, ibid.; *Donato Olivastro vs. A. Cordasco*, Case 2198, ibid.; *Domenico Poliseno vs. A. Cordasco*, Case 572, ibid.; *Giuseppe Teolo vs. A. Cordasco*, Case 990, ibid.; *Michelle Tisi vs. A. Cordasco*, Case 2513, ibid. It is unlikely these cases reached the courtroom individually. The judge's ruling on *Bazzani vs. Cordasco*, for example, stated that "evidence taken in Case 990, Giuseppe Teolo as plaintiff, should be common to the present case." See *Pietro Bazzani vs. Cordasco*, March 19, 1906, ibid. See *A. Cordasco vs. the CPR*, Case 2195, ibid. The final judgment in *Giuseppe Teolo vs. A. Cordasco* was not rendered until June 18, 1908.

and that he no longer had "any cause of action or complaint against the defendant."[25] Bazzani never complied with Cordasco's wishful thinking, however, and continued to press for his hard-earned legal judgment. Cordasco preferred not to admit publicly that Bazzani had ever been critical of his authority, suggesting instead that rivals had beguiled his former subjects.

Cordasco was probably correct in suspecting the involvement of his competitors. But recognizing the aid society's role should not obscure the actions of immigrant workers in challenging Cordasco. Indeed, Cordasco was not the only labor agent to be hauled into court by his former "employees" in 1904. In May, Italian track workers Sacco Luigi and Antonio Lamore swore in affidavits that Alberto Dini had "broken his promises" to them, offering them work on a railroad at $1.40 a day in Kirkfield, Ontario. "When we got there," Lamore recalled, "we found not a railway but a canal, very wet, and almost impossible to work."[26] These cases transformed the ways both Dini and Cordasco could do business among their working-class compatriots. For perhaps the first time, padrones were going to be held accountable for the promises they made to immigrant workers. No longer could Italian labor agents dismiss the complaints of their sojourning compatriots or insist they possessed "no rights at all" without reprisals. The contracts that had greased the wheels of Cordasco and Dini's businesses would henceforth be used to challenge, limit, and overturn padrone power.

In contrast to Mexican and Italian sojourners, Greek immigrants in Utah frequently sued one another, even though most were not naturalized citizens and many were unable to speak English or even read and write. Between June 1, 1911, and June 1, 1912, forty Greek plaintiffs originated claims in the town of Bingham out of two hundred total cases, making them just as likely to use the courts as native-born American citizens. The vast majority of these Greeks, most of them workers, sought to collect debts, often by garnisheeing the defendant's wages from their employers. The amounts sought typically ranged between $20 and $50, but some Greek workers went to court over far less. George Melius sued his American landlord John Johnson, a brothel owner, for "the sum of $2.05 for money paid in excess of board without the plaintiff's knowledge or consent." One suspects there was more than a mere day's wage at stake here, perhaps the satisfaction of besting an American pimp and one's landlord. Melius won his case, receiving $2.05 from Johnson plus legal costs, which totaled $5.15.[27]

---

[25] See Cordasco's motion for preemption, May 11, 1906, in *Bazzani vs. Cordasco*, Case 1359, ibid.

[26] All of the fifteen Italians suing Cordasco possessed the same legal counsel, the law firm of Pelissier, Wilson, and Saint Pierre, that also represented Alberto Dini. See *Pompei Bianco vs. Antonio Cordasco*, Case 2514, ibid.; Affidavits by Sacco Luigi and Antonio Lamore, May 2, 1904, and Brugno Serafino and Luigi Turturani, May 26, 1904, Records of the Royal Commission's Investigation, RG 33/99.

[27] *George Melius vs. John Johnson*, September 11, 1912, Town of Bingham Canyon, Register of Actions, Bingham Police Department, Utah State Archives, Salt Lake City, Utah.

Given the facility even newly arrived and illiterate Greek workers had in using the U.S. legal system, one might expect a plethora of court cases against Skliris. Transient workers in Montreal and El Paso, after all, used the courts far less than Greek workers but succeeded in suing Cordasco and Gonzalez. Yet not a single civil or criminal action was ever filed by a Greek worker against Leon Skliris in Utah. One reason was that immigrant middlemen played a critical role in stimulating immigrant workers to use the courts. Greek plaintiffs in Utah typically managed their cases by hiring interpreters, several of whom made their living exclusively by translating grievances into English. One of the most successful in Bingham was George Pappas who advertised in *Ergatis*: "We undertake to translate for those who don't speak English, with guarantees in courts, in hospitals, in companies, and whenever, wherever necessary." His principal competitor was Stavros Skliris, who also claimed in his *Ergatis* advertisements that "we will successfully prosecute in court every kind of political or criminal case. . . . We offer legal advice from an agency with the best lawyers in town."[28] Few Greek workers perceived much hope in taking Leon Skliris to court by hiring his brother, though Stavros had in fact once sued his brother for a larger share of the family business. But Stavros was only one of several interpreters. Why, then, were there no legal actions initiated against Skliris?

We gain potential answers by considering how Greek workers perceived political authority in Utah. Although accustomed to filing lawsuits, Greeks nonetheless perceived Utah to be an autocratic, undemocratic, and capricious state, a regime not unlike the "despotism" they left under the Turks. By seeking help from the governor of Utah, Greek workers hoped political power might be different in "the free country of Amerika." But they also refused to sign their names to the letter for fear of reprisals. "If Skliris learn our names, he'll not let us get a job at any Company he ownes." Skliris was not merely a labor agent to these Greeks, but a man who literally "owned" several companies. By appealing to the governor, the fifty Greeks sought mercy from someone they believed had "appointed Skliris as a labor agent for the Company." Like "despotic" Ottoman rulers in Crete, Skliris seemed to combine political and economic power. Consequently, Greek workers were prepared to testify against Skliris, but only if guaranteed protection: "We are hungry and we don't want to die," concluded the letter. "If you promise us that you will secure us position we are willing to sweare to the God at any court that we paid Skliris."[29] Spry's delayed reply, suggesting they approach Utah Copper managers for a "fair and impartial hearing," confirmed their worst and most conspiratorial fears about the U.S. legal system, even if it remained quite different from Ottoman government in practice.

Greek workers may have erred in seeing Skliris's power as deriving directly

[28] *Ergatis*, September 28, 1907, 4; Stavros Skliris, "Office of Information and Interpretations," ibid., 1.

[29] Fifty Greek and Crete men to the Governor of Utah, February 12, 1911, file "G," box 10, William S. Spry Papers.

from state authority, but they accurately perceived hostility to workers' interests in western statehouses, as the recent trial of Western Federation of Mining leaders William Haywood, Charles Moyer, and George Pettibone made abundantly clear to many western workers. That perception grew stronger when Greek track workers in Pocatello, Idaho, attempted to sue William Caravelis. Unlike Greek workers in Bingham or Big Bill Haywood himself, Greeks in Pocatello had the enthusiastic support of a former Idaho governor, William McConnell. As a "special immigration inspector" for the Department of Justice, McConnell promised Greek workers strict confidentiality in his investigation of Caravelis and succeeded in securing "signatures to a number of affidavits by Greek workers" detailing Caravelis's onerous job fees. But Caravelis survived the threatened legal action by calling in his debts from local officials in Pocatello. Two days after McConnell announced his intention to convict Caravelis of peonage, Bannock county attorney William Terrell announced the case was "premature." Local papers, in turn, praised Caravelis as a fine leader "who stands high among the businessmen, officers, and officials of the railroad."[30] If the "Ali-Pasha of Pocatello" could survive such a legal challenge, with sympathetic governors working against him overtime, what hope did Greek miners in Bingham have?

As their hopes for legal redress dwindled, growing numbers of Greek workers recognized their problems were collective in nature. Indeed, their second letter to Spry was signed by over five hundred Greek workers in Bingham and condemned the lot of the "poor laborer," whose "blood padrones were sucking" throughout the region.[31] As Greek workers searched for more direct means of resisting their czar in the "free country of Amerika," they found the doorstep of the local union hall in Bingham Canyon. To understand the reception they and other new immigrants received, let us consider briefly the historic relationship between organized labor and new immigrants in the West.

American Unions, Immigrant Mobilizations

From its inception on Nevada's Comstock Lode in the 1860s through the rise of the Western Federation of Miners and the Industrial Workers of the World half a century later, the western labor movement featured some of the most radical and militant working-class organizations found anywhere on the continent. It was in the West in 1902 that the Western Federation of Miners (WFM) became one of the first industrial unions in North America officially to endorse socialism. And in 1905 the WFM created the radical Industrial Workers of the World (IWW), committed to emancipating the entire working class, regardless of skill, racial, ethnic, or gender differences. Labor historians in both Canada and the United States have

---

[30] *Pocatello Tribune*, December 3, 1911, 8; ibid., December 8, 1911, 3. On the celebrated trial of Moyer, Haywood, and Pettibone, see J. Anthony Lukas, *Big Trouble: A Murder in a Small Western Town Sets Off a Struggle for the Soul of America* (New York, 1997).

[31] Fifty Greek and Crete men to the Governor of Utah, February 2, 1911, file "G," box 10, William S. Spry Papers.

debated how truly radical and exceptional most western workers were, particularly in comparison to their eastern counterparts. But both sides of this debate have, until recently, equated workers' transience with radicalism, with persistent westerners almost by definition less militant than the truly radical and always transient Wobbly.[32]

Both assumptions about class consciousness in the North American West – its inherently radical expression and its connection to mobility – owe their vitality to the dominant historical and historiographical role of the IWW in the region's labor history. As the telos of much western labor history, the IWW has been portrayed as quintessentially western and radical at the same time, a group of men who provide the best example of an indigenous radicalism in both U.S. and Canadian history. The inspiration for seeing Wobblies as true westerners owes its origins to many Wobblies themselves, who consciously appropriated symbols of the mythic West to forge a countermyth of its capitalist exploitation. While Big Bill Haywood enjoyed discussing his efforts to organize a cowboy's union, less well known Wobblies like Len De Caux recalled his westernness in his autobiography. "The worker riding the western rails," recalled De Caux, "was usually a husky, independent, nervy kind of cuss. From him – and in his words – came much of the fighting message of the IWW." Here indeed were proletarian cowboys that even rugged individualists might recognize and emulate.[33]

[32] On the radical and exceptional character of the western working class in the United States, see Jensen, *Heritage of Conflict*; Schwantes, "The Concept of the Wageworkers' Frontier"; Melvyn Dubofsky, "The Origins of the Western Working Class, 1890–1905," *Labor History* 7 (Spring 1966): 131–154; and Dubofsky, *We Shall Be All*. On the radical working class in Canada, see Stuart Jamieson, *Industrial Relations in Canada* (Ithaca, 1957); David J. Bercuson, *Fools and Wise Men: The Rise and Fall of One Big Union* (Toronto, 1978); Andrew Ross McCormack, *Reformers, Rebels, and Revolutionaries: The Western Canadian Radical Movement, 1899–1919* (Toronto, 1977); and Jeremy Mouat, "The Genesis of Western Exceptionalism: British Columbia's Hard-Rock Miners, 1895–1903," *Canadian Historical Review* 71:3 (September 1990): 317–345. For revisionist treatments of western workers in the United States, see Emmons, *The Butte Irish*; Wyman, *Hard Rock Epic*; Richard H. Peterson, "Conflict and Consensus: Labor Relations in Western Mining," *Journal of the West* 12 (January 1973): 17. For Canada, see Gregory Kealey, "1919: The Canadian Labour Revolt," *Labour/Le Travail* 13 (Spring 1984): 11–44; and James Naylor, *The New Democracy: Challenging the Social Order in Industrial Ontario, 1914–1925* (Toronto, 1991). An important exception to the radical-conservative debate and the tendency to equate transience with radicalism is Elizabeth Jameson, who argues that persistent miners were both reformist and radical. See Jameson, *All That Glitters*, 194–196.

[33] Dubofsky, *We Shall Be All*, 24–26; Philip Taft, "The I.W.W. and the West," *American Quarterly* 12 (Summer 1960): 175–187; Zeese Papanikolas, *Trickster in the Land of Dreams* (Lincoln, 1995), 73–90. William Haywood, *Bill Haywood's Book: The Autobiography of William D. Haywood* (New York, 1929); Len De Caux, *The Living Spirit of the Wobblies* (New York, 1978), 5. Not all histories of the IWW highlight its westernness. See Philip Foner, *History of the Labor Movement in the United States: The Industrial Workers of the World, 1905–1917*, vol. 4 (New York, 1965); Joseph Conlin, *Bread and Roses Too: Studies of the Wobblies* (Westport, Conn., 1970); and Salvatore Salerno, *Red November, Black November: Culture and Community in the Industrial Workers of the World* (Albany, 1989), 45–67; On the gendered nature of Wobbly mobility, see Aileen S. Kraditor, *The Radical Persuasion, 1890–1917:*

Given such a militant and radical labor tradition in the region, one might expect western labor unions in Canada and the United States to have welcomed transient Mexican, Greek, and Italian sojourners with open arms. But such was not the case. Transience in fact possessed a variety of political meanings. Transient workers were not inherently more or less radical than other workers but their conflicts with persistent workers shaped the character of both radicalism and conservatism within the western labor movement. David Emmons, for example, has suggested in his study of Butte, Montana, that the persistent Irish might have voted Socialist but acted like "conservatives" by excluding all transient men from their enclave.[34] Elizabeth Jameson, by contrast, has shown that persistent workers in Cripple Creek, Colorado, were not conservative but were more likely to strike, join the Western Federation of Miners, and assume leadership roles in the union and the Socialist Party. Yet both authors largely ignore transient workers and agree that persistent workers – whether "conservative" or "radical" – excluded their transient cohorts.

Tensions between persistent and transient workers in the western labor movement also assumed racial forms and were as old as the movement itself. The mining frontier's first industrial labor union, located in Gold Hill, Nevada, for example, pledged itself in 1868 to fight the "tyrannical, oppressive power of capital" but simultaneously excluded Chinese workers from underground mining work. The WFM likewise embraced socialism and the class struggle in North America just moments after formally excluding all Asian workers from its ranks. Only the Wobblies organized across lines of race, skill, and gender, though even here, as David Roediger has argued, a powerful streak of "racial paternalism" pervaded much of the Wobblies' organizing literature and campaigns. By no means were all labor radicals in the West racist, but neither were the histories of race and radicalism separate.[35]

While racial boundaries in the western labor movement were dynamic and enduring, many inclusionists nonetheless hoped that "nonwhite" Greek, Italian, and Mexican workers could be assimilated into the region's labor movement.[36]

Aspects of the Intellectual History and the Historiography of Three American Radical Organizations (Baton Rouge, 1981), 187–189.

[34] Emmons, *The Butte Irish*, 222; Jameson, *All That Glitters*, 194–196.

[35] David Roediger, *Towards the Abolition of Whiteness: Essays on Race, Politics, and Working-Class History* (London, 1994), 134. On connections between racialism and radicalism in the western labor movement, see Peck, "Manly Gambles," 706–707; Richard Lingenfelter, *The Hardrock Miners: A History of the Mining Labor Movement in the American West, 1863–1893* (Berkeley, 1974); Saxton, *The Indispensable Enemy*; Jameson, *All That Glitters*, 140–160; Philip Mellinger, "How the IWW Lost Its Western Heartland: Western Labor History Revisited," *Western Historical Quarterly* 28:3 (Autumn 1996): 303–326; and A. Yvette Huginnie, "Strikitos: Race, Class, and Work in the Arizona Copper Industry, 1870–1920" (Ph.D. diss., Yale University, 1992).

[36] On examples of cross-racial alliances among workers outside the North American West, see Eric Arnesen, *Waterfront Workers of New Orleans: Race, Class, and Politics, 1863–1923* (New York, 1991); Leon Fink, *Workingmen's Democracy: The Knights of Labor and American Politics* (Urbana, 1983); Gutman, *Work, Culture, and Society*; Montgomery, *Beyond Equality*, 180; and Montgomery, *Fall of the House of Labor*, 30.

Such hopes were particularly high among members of the Socialist-led United Brotherhood of Railroad Employees (UBRE) in British Columbia during the spring of 1903. In January the UBRE initiated a militant strike involving several nationalities of unskilled railroad workers against the Canadian Pacific Railway. The strike began defensively in reaction to "a kind of secret warfare," in which CPR manager George Burns had been sending men to infiltrate union locals with company spies, firing union leaders, and exploiting ethnic tensions among union members. But anger against the biggest corporation in Canada ran deep and the strike quickly spread beyond its origin in Vancouver throughout the Canadian West, as donations from sympathetic railway workers and fellow Socialists poured in and teamsters from Calgary to Vancouver went out on sympathy strikes. When Italian track workers began to arrive in March, union officials scrambled to find an Italian organizer, while others held their breath and waited. If ever there existed an opportunity for Italian sojourners to find common cause with a host of industrial workers in the West, this seemed to be the moment.[37]

A quick look at the context for Italian migration to British Columbia would have sobered the most sanguine hopes of union officials. Most of the CPR's Italian track workers first came to British Columbia as strikebreakers during the summer of 1901 under Cordasco's new regime, leading one local mine manager to remark that Italian workers were "the strength of the employer and the weakness of the union. How to head off a strike of muckers and laborers for higher wages without the aid of Italian labor ... I do not know."[38] In 1903 this mine manager's assessment of Italian workers once again proved accurate, as George Burns succeeded in using Italian workers to break the strike by May of that year. For members of the UBRE in 1903, the political meaning of Italian transience seemed profoundly conservative rather than radical.

Such conflicts confirmed the worst assumptions many Canadian workers possessed about Italian workers and only heightened tensions between the CPR's "white" employees and its Italian workers. Indeed, even militant and radical union members in western Canada expressed contempt for nonwhite immigrant sojourners after the 1903 strike. One "British Canadian" track worker explained in 1908 to Winnipeg's Socialist newspaper, the *Voice*, why "white men," meaning "English, Scotch, and Irish will not work on the railroads in this country." Part of his explanation focused on the horrifying living conditions on CPR rails, where "anywhere from 20 to 35 men are crowded in an ordinary 35-foot length box car" creating a stench between 11 P.M. and 4 A.M. that could "knock a man down." But his strongest animus was reserved for the nonwhite immigrant sojourner, whose questionable manhood had created the system. After asking "how a married man can exist" on fifteen dollars a week after company deductions, the writer remarked that "of course ... a Canadian will not send his women on the streets to pick up

---

[37] McCormack, *Reformers, Rebels, and Revolutionaries*, 44–46.
[38] Donald Avery, *"Dangerous Foreigners": European Immigrant Workers and Labour Radicalism in Canada, 1896–1932* (Toronto, 1979), 50; Schwantes, *Radical Heritage*, 145–147; Kirby to Blackstock, January 31, 1901, vol. 186, Laurier Papers, Canadian National Archives, Ottawa, cited in McCormack, *Reformers, Rebels, and Revolutionaries*, 9.

wood or steal coal."[39] Immigrant men, by contrast, would throw their families into the lion's den.

Such stereotypes did not make Italian immigrants incapable of organizing themselves and resisting their employers. Had the "British Canadian" track worker looked more carefully at his Italian co-workers, he might have noted how dramatically their rebellion against Cordasco in 1904 had changed their relationship with organized labor. Perhaps the most dramatic consequence of the 1904 rebellion was the transformation of Italian padrone strongholds elsewhere into union locals under the remarkable leadership of a padrone turned labor organizer, Dominic D'Allesandro. As an Italian labor agent in Boston, D'Allesandro carefully watched Cordasco's travails in 1904, but rather than defend himself and other padrones against the mobilizations of Italian workers, he instead set about organizing them into unions. With the help of numerous *prominenti* who wanted to improve the lot and image of Boston's nonwhite Italian workers, D'Allesandro founded the Unione generale dei Lavoratori and quickly affiliated with the American Federation of Labor, renaming it the Laborers and Excavators Union.[40]

In so doing, D'Allesandro not only improved the legitimacy of Italian workers in the eyes of North American workers, but also used the one-thousand-member Boston local as a stepping-stone to greater power by aggressively taking over Italian locals and organizing new ones in padrone-dominated workplaces throughout the East Coast. One of the largest locals D'Allesandro came to control was a union of New York City subway workers, formed in 1902 when thirty thousand Italian subway excavators went on strike demanding the padrone system's immediate abolition. By 1909 D'Allesandro claimed control of ten independent Italian unions in North America, concentrated mainly among urban sewer, subway, and tunnel workers, bootblacks, street cleaners, and street pavers. In each new local that D'Allesandro organized or took over, he replaced the padrone's services with union-run employment offices to regulate the ongoing commerce of migration and to create a closed shop. His efforts against both Italian padrones and Italian labor radicals earned him a reputation that undoubtedly made Cordasco jealous. In March 1908 the Italian monarchy made D'Allesandro a chevalier of the crown of Italy, a royal adornment far more authentic than anything Cordasco or Dini mustered in Montreal. His remarkable career, though exceptional, highlights how padronism could in fact fuel the development of industrial unionism.[41]

[39] *The Voice*, Winnipeg, September 11, 1908, cited in Irving Abella and David Millar, eds., *The Canadian Worker in the Twentieth Century* (Toronto, 1981), 61.

[40] Edwin Fenton, *Immigrants and Unions, a Case Study: Italians and American Labor, 1870–1920* (New York, 1975), 221–226; Montgomery, *Fall of the House of Labor*, 94.

[41] For a brief narrative of the 1902 strike, see John R. Commons, *History of Labor in the United States, 1896–1932*, vols. 3 and 4, ix—xii. According to Fenton, strikes by Italian workers against their padrones were quite common but rarely "peaceful and orderly." See Fenton, *Immigrants and Unions*, 199, 224–234, 237. Many immigration historians have described the mobilization of immigrant workers outside of labor unions as examples of nonradical "ethnic consciousness." See Eric Hobsbawm, *Primitive Rebels: Studies in Archaic Forms of Social*

Although Mexican labor contractors might, in theory, have pushed Mexican workers to join labor unions, most renganchados never acquired sufficient power to compel American-led labor unions to open their doors wide to Mexican members. A few skilled Mexican workers joined craft unions in El Paso and elsewhere between 1900 and 1920, but they possessed little security within them. Mexican iron molder Ignacio Aparacio, for example, joined the International Moulder's Union in Chicago while it was on strike in the early 1920s, a context that pushed the union into a rare moment of racial inclusion. The union won the strike, but the settlement left Aparacio without a job as the company insisted on cutting the size of its work force. As Aparacio recalled, "the union no longer helped me economically and when other workers were asked for they would send the Americans to work and kept leaving me for the last and only gave me work as a helper or at jobs where one earned less than the 'standard' of the union."[42] Throughout this frustrating period, Aparacio was compelled to pay his union dues until he eventually quit the union before returning to El Paso.

Among unskilled Mexicans, the barriers to union membership were even greater. Mexican copper workers made some inroads into the WFM in Arizona and New Mexico after 1903 and especially after 1915, but because they were paid less than their fellow white union members, they frequently found themselves in conflict with them.[43] Before 1915 the American Federation of Labor (AFL) made virtually no efforts to organize Mexicans – skilled or unskilled in El Paso. When Samuel Gompers made a trip to Mexico City in 1916 and concluded that Mexican workers should be brought into his organization, El Paso union officials stubbornly refused to make any such efforts. Some Americans ironically blamed Mexicans for being poorly represented in the labor movement. One official of the UBRE in Chicago, for example, believed that Mexicans "know what good organization is all right," but attributed their poor standing in the union to Mexican culture. "We had a Mexican interpreter go around with me and they would pay me dues, but they would not pay him when he went alone. There had to be a white man along."[44] The official's explanation revealed how race-bound a creation the "brotherhood" was in Chicago and other cities. To these Mexicans, the union was synonymous with white men's rules and regulations. Their failure to pay dues did not reveal any cultural weakness on their part but rather underscored how white the brotherhood was. Put simply, it was not their union.

Like Italian workers, Mexicans could organize themselves without unions on

Protest in the 19th and 20th Centuries (New York, 1959); Mellinger, "'The Men Have Become Organizers': Labor Conflict and Unionization in the Mexican Mining Communities of Arizona, 1900–1915," *Western Historical Quarterly* 23:2 (August 1992): 333; Papanikolas, "Toil and Rage," 121; Zeese Papanikolas, *Buried Unsung: Louis Tikas and the Ludlow Massacre* (Salt Lake City, 1982), 282, 287; and Garcia, *Desert Immigrants*, 108.

[42] Ignacio Aparacio interview by Manuel Gamio, 1927, Z-R-5, Manuel Gamio Papers.

[42] For an account of the slow acceptance of Mexicans by American inclusionists within the WFM, see Philip Mellinger, *Race and Labor in Western Copper: The Fight for Equality, 1896–1918* (Tucson, 1995), 154–173.

[44] Garcia, *Desert Immigrants*, 100–102; Taylor, *Mexican Labor in the United States*, vol. 2, 119.

occasion. Sometimes gang foremen or interpreters helped organize Mexican workers, serving as their bargaining agents. According to C. R. Howard of the Holmes Supply Company in El Paso, interpreters on extra gangs posed special difficulties for his company. "In 1909 or 1910 . . . the interpreters used to collect a dollar a month from the men as well as a special salary. They would put the men up to strike unless they got their demands. At that time most of the track workers were Mexicans." These interpreters were not Mexicans, however, but Spanish-speaking Greeks who succeeded in procuring "running water in each boxcar." The Holmes Supply Company likewise had trouble with its Japanese interpreters. Mr. Mosher, president of the company, recalled that they "were very unsatisfactory. There were a great many strikes; the interpreter did not always interpret."[45] For Mosher, questions of interpretation were only half the problem; the real challenge was controlling the loyalties of his nonwhite foremen, whose sympathies were frequently with sojourning workers rather than the company.

Had there been more Mexican foremen or more powerful Mexican padrones working on the Southern Pacific or Atchison, Topeka, and Santa Fe railroads, conceivably more Mexican track workers might have entered the ranks of organized labor. Such was the case among Japanese miners working in Rock Springs, Wyoming, in 1907. Here, three Japanese labor contractors – Kondo Chikai, Suzuki Rokuhiko, and Ueda Heitaro – signed all seven hundred of "their" Japanese miners into a local chapter of the United Mine Workers of America (UMW) and served as their delegates to a UMW convention in Denver. This anomalous development within a labor union that still officially excluded Asians was a product of local and pragmatic necessity. The seven hundred Japanese miners represented the single largest racial or ethnic group in the work force of Rock Springs and consequently either had to be run out of the community – a solution that had failed twenty years earlier – or accommodated into the union. Chikai, Rokuhiko, and Heitaro also acted out of pragmatic reasons, facing as they were the potential loss of their livelihoods if the UMW excluded all Japanese workers from the coal mining work force as originally planned.[46] Mexican track workers possessed no such powerful padrones who might be redirected, however, precisely because they controlled their freedom to quit and to move far better than Japanese workers and most immigrants in the North American West.

In Bingham, neither Greek workers nor representatives of the local chapter of the WFM were foolish enough to try persuading the "czar of the Greeks" to become a

---

[45] C. R. Howard interview by Paul Taylor, 1928, doc. no. 27-199, BANC-MSS-74/187c, Paul S. Taylor Papers; Mr. Mosher interview by Paul Taylor, Los Angeles, 1928, doc. no. 2-174, ibid.

[46] Yuji Ichioka, "Asian Immigrant Coal Miners and the United Mine Workers of America: Race and Class at Rock Springs, Wyoming, 1907," *Amerasia Journal* 6:2 (1979): 1–23. Chikai, Rokuhiko, and Heitaro sought to protect their power over Japanese laborers by proposing that UMW president John Mitchell make them permanent union representatives, something Mitchell refused to do. For a similar analysis of the WFM's pragmatic inclusion of Mexicans in Arizona, see Mellinger, *Race and Labor in Western Copper*, 168–173.

union representative. If Greeks were ever to become members of the WFM local, it would have to be in opposition to Leon Skliris, a fact that most members of the Bingham local realized as early as 1907. These inclusionists were hopeful that Bingham, with its five thousand resident miners, many of them inhabiting close quarters, could become an ideal arena in which older western "radicals" and new immigrants might find common ground. In May 1905, having just voted to form the Industrial Workers of the World, the WFM local in Bingham also passed a resolution by a resounding majority that "an irrepressible conflict exists between the capitalist class and the working class for supremacy on the industrial field.... There can be no permanent peace between the two."[47] As part of its zealous commitment to waging class struggle, the WFM local redoubled its efforts to organize immigrant workers.

To that end, the Bingham local held special meetings during the summer of 1905 in three languages – English, Finnish, and Serbo-Croatian – and in the fall of 1906 ordered Italian language copies of the WFM's constitution and bylaws to be printed. The effort to organize Italian workers produced some noticeable results. During the first three months of 1907, over 120 Italians joined the Bingham local, swelling its active membership rolls to well above 300. Nearly 50 Italian miners joined the local on February 16, 1907, alone, doubling its Italian membership in just one day. The Bingham local also made efforts to organize Bingham's Greek miners by translating its constitution and bylaws into Greek in 1908 and by offering free English classes in the union library to any immigrants wanting them. A handful of English-speaking Greeks heard the union's call and joined the union in 1907. Union member Thomas Burlison was perhaps the most enthusiastic champion of these inclusionary efforts, giving "lengthy orations about how he would educate the Greeks" and pushing the union to translate its constitution into Greek in 1908.[48] Key to his vision was finding a way to turn Greek workers' ambivalence about their padrones into support for the union.

Unfortunately for Burlison, just 9 percent of Greek workers in Bingham spoke any English as late as 1910. Moreover, not all American union members were enthusiastic about including these unskilled newcomers. Burlison's commitment to inclusion, although idealistic and passionate, was sporadic and fleeting. The union never hired a Greek organizer, even during the strike of 1912, despite the fact that Greeks comprised nearly a third of Bingham's total work force. Although Greeks began to appear on union rolls as early as 1906, only a handful had joined the union by the summer of 1912, in contrast to the Italians and many Serbs who had joined in greater numbers.[49] When the WFM local embraced class struggle in

[47] Bingham Miners' Union no. 67, Minute Books, May 20, 1905, Record Group C-25, Western Federation of Miners and International Union of Mine, Mill, and Smelter Workers Collection, Labor and Management Documentation Center, School of Industrial Relations, Cornell University, Ithaca, N.Y.

[48] Minute Books, July 22, 1905; ibid., October 27, 1906; ibid., February 16, 1907; ibid., August 8, 1908; ibid., November 21, 1908.

[49] The first Greek names to appear in the union's initiation lists were Makis Patmos and Andrew

1905, it made concerted efforts to have interpreters attend membership meetings. But these efforts dissipated over time as interpreters were mostly hired to translate the union's money-raising efforts into various languages. Pledge forms for the construction of a union hall, for example, were printed in three languages, while warnings to delinquent members to pay back dues were posted throughout the camp in several languages. The union declaration of solidarity with the IWW in 1905, by contrast, pledging ceaseless struggle against the "forces of plutocracy," was read and delivered in English only.[50] Equally important, the local's elected leadership remained strictly American between 1904 and 1912, despite a majority foreign-born membership by 1907.

Much of the American union members' ambivalence toward Bingham's new immigrants was rooted in the dramatic economic changes that were transforming Bingham Canyon. Just how closely tied the WFM was to an older order of skilled and persistent white workers was highlighted by the union wage scales it adopted for its members in 1906. Ranging from $3.00 to $4.50 a day, the occupations covered included timbermen, shaftmen, machine men in wet shafts, machine men in dry tunnels, pipemen, tool sharpeners, blacksmiths, and mule drivers. Here was a blueprint for creating a closed shop in Bingham with union pay scales. But these wage rates were all for jobs underground, work that was soon displaced by the Utah Copper Company's open-pit operation in which immigrant muckers made $1.75 a day and shaftmen and timbermen no longer existed. As the Utah Copper Company's open-pit operation gained momentum in 1907, the union began losing many of its best dues-paying members and attendance at monthly meetings dropped steadily from a high of about two hundred in the summer of 1906 to about twenty-five to thirty in the summer of 1908.[51]

Union officials responded to this problem by calling for a halt to the Utah Copper Company's open-pit operations and an immediate end to "the introduction of cheap labor into the mines of Bingham," even as Greeks began to join the union in the fall of 1908. In particular, union leaders praised the muckraking efforts of the local newspaper editor, T. L. Holman, who had "the manliness and courage to expose in his paper the damnable peonage and other outrages perpetrated on the miners of Bingham."[52] Such public outcries against the Greek padrone system were the first to reach the English-speaking press. But they did not stop the rapid and dramatic expansion of the Utah Copper Company, which had not yet made Leon Skliris its sole Greek labor agent. The union's anger was only partially

Bistakis on August 29, 1908. Over the ensuing three months, the following fourteen Greeks joined the Bingham local: Louis Sideris, Zacharios Anagviostakis, George Demos, Makis Andros, Sam Pandajes, Frank Gassas, Anastasios Tsamelo, James Pandajes, Harry Gassas, Andrew Gassas, Pete Tsahamas, George Halaftes, Gust Orman, Nick Comnas. Eleven of these fourteen Greeks recorded Americanized first names, suggesting that most spoke English. See Table 5.2 in Appendix A; Minutes of the Bingham Miner's Union, September 1908–November 1908.

50 Ibid., June 24, 1905; ibid., July 22, 1905; ibid., May 20, 1905.
51 Ibid., June 16, 1906; ibid., June 30, 1906; ibid., December 19, 1908.
52 Ibid., October 3, 1908.

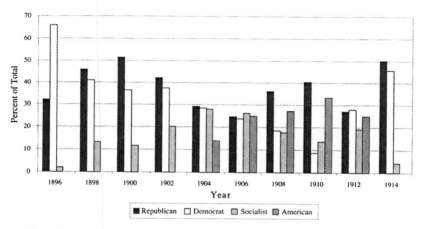

Figure 6.1. Congressional election returns, Bingham, Utah, 1896–1914

directed at the mine operators of Bingham. Many blamed immigrant workers, a reaction reflected in the rapid growth of the nativist American Party in local congressional elections in Bingham (see Figure 6.1). Utah Copper's expansion thus divided Bingham's citizen workers over whom to blame for these dramatic changes: immigrant workers or the Utah Copper Company. For many devoted Socialists in the Bingham Miners' Union, Greeks were not so much an opportunity as a "problem," as the inclusionist Burlison himself put it. To many Socialists and increasing numbers of American Party supporters in the Bingham local, Greeks were as threatening as the Japanese miners, who were their closest cohorts in the open pit.[53]

But inclusionists within the Bingham local continually sought ways to organize Greek workers by turning their growing anger against padrones into union militancy. Sometimes these efforts appeared to do more harm than good for the union. In the spring of 1912, union secretary E. G. Locke wrote a letter to the ambassador of Turkey, protesting the activities of Leon Skliris to his Cretan subjects, with copies sent to Governor William Spry of Utah. Locke overlooked the fact that these same miners possessed considerable loathing for their "official" Turkish protectors. Not surprisingly, his letter earned the union no support from Bingham's Cretan miners, although it did provide Greek banker, Nicholas P. Stathakos, an opportunity to burnish his nationalist credentials by writing his own letter to Spry and Greek workers, excoriating Locke's unpatriotic and meddlesome interference.[54]

Yet Burlison's persistence paid off in the summer of 1912 when total union membership soared from just two hundred fifty in June, to seven hundred in July,

[53] Evidence of a split within the Bingham local over the American Party was revealed in the fall of 1908, when Burlison's desire to donate a modest twenty-five dollars to the local Socialist Party precipitated a discussion "at some length" at the next meeting. Bingham Miners' Union, Minute Books, October 31, 1908, 187.

[54] E. G. Locke to the Ambassador of Turkey, May 12, 1912, box 18, William S. Spry Papers; Nicholas Stathakos to William Spry, August 14, 1912, box 19, ibid.

to twelve hundred in September. Within the space of just six weeks, the Bingham local had become, next to Butte, Montana, the biggest mining local in North America. But Burlison and his fellow inclusionists got more than they bargained for in their new members. In early September, recently initiated Greeks and Italians decided to exercise their newfound rights by pressing American union leaders for a strike. When Charles Moyer, president of the WFM, heard of their plans, he rushed to Bingham by train to dissuade the strike-hungry immigrants. Realizing they would vote for a strike, Moyer nonetheless urged them to "consider the question with great care. It is not certain that you can win this strike if you call one, and therefore, I desire you to use your best judgement." Moyer's reluctance to strike highlighted some of the growing tensions in the WFM between its radical constitution and its increasingly conservative political outlook. With a strike fund nearly bankrupt and the union's legal resources stretched thin, the last thing Moyer desired was a protracted and expensive strike as had recently occurred at the Homestake Mining Company in Lead, South Dakota. Perhaps more important, Moyer was reluctant to relinquish control over the expanding Bingham local to rank-and-file "new" immigrants, whose militancy remained untested and whose numbers and solidarity with Japanese workers challenged the authority of American-born radicals and the racially exclusive organization they had built.[55]

Minutes after Moyer cautioned restraint, the union membership, led by Greek miner John Stanopolis, voted to strike and began celebrating with gunshots and victory toasts. The next morning, over one thousand immigrants laid down their tools and set up pickets around the Utah Copper Company mine and smelter works. Hundreds of nonunion immigrants joined them, including all two hundred Japanese laborers in Bingham. Within twenty-four hours of the strike vote, fully twenty-four different national groups were cooperating in the militant strike effort, digging trenches, breastworks, foxholes, even constructing a makeshift cannon aimed directly at the Utah Copper Company's headquarters. By contrast, a number of skilled American workers, many of them members of the Bingham local, refused to join the strikers and attempted to go to work. When American steam shovel operators began revving up their engines, "a number of strikers, principally Greeks, appeared on the mountainside above the workmen and pelted them with stones and rolled boulders down the mountainside, driving the workers from their places." By noon of the first day, over five thousand workers were idle and "the greatest industrial sight on earth" was completely shut down.[56]

Over the next forty-eight hours, immigrant miners literally took over the town of Bingham, preparing themselves for nothing less than industrial war. In addition to organizing strikers to patrol the breastworks and to build fortifications on the

[55] *Deseret Evening News*, September 16, 1912, 7. For an account of the Homestake Lockout, see Joseph Cash, "Labor in the West: The Homestake Mining Company and Its Workers, 1877–1942" (Ph.D. diss., University of Iowa, 1966).

[56] *Deseret Evening News*, September 16, 1912, 7. *Salt Lake Evening Telegram*, September 18, 1912, 1.

hillside above company headquarters, strike leader John Stanopolis sent a small group of well-armed strikers to the Bingham Mercantile Company to acquire the store's entire remaining supply of guns and ammunition. Strikers kept up a continuous round of gunfire over the small but growing force of deputy sheriffs clustered around the jail in Lower Bingham. Rumors of violence flew as fast as their bullets as sixty-five cases of dynamite were stolen from the Utah Construction Company, allegedly by strikers in order to blow up the railroad should any strikebreakers be imported from Salt Lake City. So powerful was strikers' demonstration of force that company deputies and state police officials refrained from taking any action during the first week of the strike. Wrote the *Salt Lake Evening Telegram*, "The strikers ... from their position could with good marksmanship, good management and disposition of their forces, wreak destruction upon any force that might attempt to take them from the road."[57]

Although these military preparations concentrated immigrant strikers' strength in one place, mobility played a crucial role in the strike movement. The paths of worker mobility between Greek communities that Skliris had formerly exploited were now harnessed by workers in the strike movement. News of the Bingham strike passed like wildfire among friends, cousins, brothers, and uncles, and prompted other Greeks to organize against their padrones. In the week following the Bingham walkout, six hundred Greek miners in Ely, Nevada, joined their WFM local and began agitating to strike against their padrone Louis Cononelos and the Nevada Consolidated Mining Company, a subsidiary of the Utah Copper Company. On October 1, 1912, with the full support of WFM president Charles Moyer, Greek workers in Ely led a walkout that shut down the mine and threw an additional three thousand copper miners out of work.[58] As in Bingham, Greek workers quickly became leaders of a multiethnic strike movement that demanded union recognition, a pay increase, and the abolition of the padrone system. Immobilized for the first time in his career, Skliris spent his days sequestered atop the Hotel Utah, plotting ways to break the regional strike with his subordinates and other Greek padrones who visited him daily.[59]

Although the situation looked bleak for Skliris, he found some hope in the ways that local papers depicted the dramatic strike. According to the *Deseret Evening News*, "The white element has been forced against its will to strike. The Bingham camp is a divided camp today.... On one side is a mob of ... 3,500 aliens.... On the other are 1500 men who refused to strike ... and the merchants and citizens of Bingham itself."[60] By defining Greeks, Italians, Japanese, and Serbs as nonwhite, this reporter reduced all class conflicts in Bingham to a simple racial war of white

[57] *Ogden Evening Standard*, September 19, 1912, 1, 5; *Deseret Evening News*, September 19, 1912, 1,2; *Salt Lake Evening Telegram*, September 19, 1912, 1.
[58] *Ogden Evening Standard*, October 2, 1912, 1; *Salt Lake Tribune*, October 2, 1912, 1.
[59] Nina Cononelos, daughter of the Greek labor agent in Ely, Nevada, recalled a meeting in the Hotel Utah of all Greek padrones in the region a week after the strike began. See Nina Cononelos interview by Louis Cononelos, Salt Lake City, June 27, 1974, American West Center.
[60] *Deseret Evening News*, September 20, 1912, 2.

Americans against nonwhite "aliens." In so doing, he helped create a new opportunity for immigrant leaders such as Skliris, who would seek to reclaim leadership within the Greek community by attempting to whiten his compatriots and gain them admission into the Caucasian race under his leadership.

Although descriptions of the Bingham strike as a race war simplified and distorted events there, tensions between Moyer and strikers confirmed the appearance of a conflict between immigrants and Americans. During the first three days of the strike, Moyer distanced himself publicly from the actions of the militant strikers. To the *Deseret Evening News*, he stated, "I can not be held responsible for the individual conduct of four thousand members." When pressed by the American reporter, Moyer "emphatically asserted that neither he nor the union approved of violent measures." Moyer feared quite accurately that immigrant strikers' use of firearms would weaken any political support for their cause. His concession to Utah's nativist political climate was double-edged, however, for by distancing himself from Greek strikers, he also undercut his authority as a union leader. Wrote the *Ogden Standard*, "Moyer ... seems to be but a nominal leader of the strike,... and it seems that more radical leaders have the ears of the men."[61] This perception was strengthened by the actions of immigrant strikers on the second day of the conflict. When Moyer attempted to talk the strike over with immigrant leaders and began climbing toward strikers' fortifications, he was abruptly driven back by a hail of bullets.

Such militancy thrilled writers for the IWW newspaper, *International Socialist Review*, who chastised Moyer for no longer defending the interests of truly radical industrial workers, having sold out to the conservative trade-union movement by affiliating with the AFL in 1911. And yet the IWW had very little organizational presence in Bingham or any known role in the strike. Only one known Wobbly was in the vicinity of Bingham in 1912, Greek immigrant Louis Theos, and his name never appeared among the strike's Greek leadership roles.[62] Moreover, Wobbly organizers in the Lawrence strike earlier that year responded to the problem of immigrant strikers bearing firearms in precisely the same fashion as Moyer: by distancing themselves from it and trying to build a nonviolent strike movement.

But the Wobbly editorialist highlighted two aspects of the Bingham strike that impressed observers of all political leanings. First, even by the violent and militant standards of the western labor movement, the military preparedness of immigrant strikers was extraordinary. Violence between strikers and company deputies was certainly not new to the region, but normally workers fought their adversaries on defensive terrain. Rarely did strikers establish military superiority over any and

---

[61] Ibid., September 19, 1912, 1; *Ogden Evening Standard*, September 19, 1912, 1.

[62] *International Socialist Review*, October 2, 1912, 1. Dan Georgakas suggests that Theos played an "undercover" role in the Bingham strike, but offers no firm evidence for his claim. See Dan Georgakas, "Greek-American Radicalism: The Twentieth Century," in Dan Georgakas and Paul Buhle, eds., *The Immigrant Left in the United States* (Albany, 1996), 212. On Theos, see also Papanikolas, "Toil and Rage," 122.

all potential adversaries. In Bingham, a bloodbath was avoided not simply because immigrant strikers fired above the heads of deputy sheriffs, but because the company guards and deputy sheriffs wisely realized they would have been crushed had they attempted to dislodge the well-fortified strikers. Although it is tempting to attribute strikers' militancy to a tradition of western outlawry, in fact the Bingham rebellion differed quite dramatically from that tradition.[63] Instead of using stealth and subterfuge, immigrant strikers patrolled the trenches, breastworks, and cannon in plain view of the authorities, as if daring deputy sheriffs, national guardsmen, even the governor of Utah himself, to intervene.[64]

Equally remarkable were the cooperative ties between Bingham's multiethnic strikers. By joining ranks with their Italian, Serbian, and Japanese co-workers, Greek workers accomplished, if only briefly, what few of their predecessors had done in the western mining fields: mobilize Asian and European immigrant workers into one organization. Their alliance was rooted not merely within the shared social spaces of Upper Bingham's boardinghouses, but in their common frustration with the padrone system. Although the names of Japanese padrone Edward Hashimoto and Italian padrone Moses Paggi never made the local papers, Japanese and Italian workers identified with their Greek co-workers' struggle against Skliris. Their shared struggle to break padrone "tyranny" did not make them radical syndicalists as IWW observers hoped, but it did create an organization far more militant and radical in its racial complexion than any local within the western labor movement in 1912.

The Paths to Whiteness

Whether or not the Wobblies and Socialists grasped the full significance of the alliance between Greek and Japanese strikers, they believed that a truly American working class was emerging in Bingham. A reporter for the Socialist daily, the *New York Call*, stated that "out of the practically unorganized mass of workers has sprung up a remarkably strong organization. Bingham now boasts the second

---

[63] For Bingham's strikers, the closest prototype for their military mobilizations was not any tradition of frontier vigilantism or even the region's industrial violence, but more likely the military campaigns of Greek soldiers and citizens against the Ottomans over the previous three decades. See Clogg, *A Concise History of Greece*, 66–98.

[64] Why the Bingham strike received less publicity than the famous Lawrence strike is best explained by the varied outcomes and locations of the strikes. To many labor supporters, the victory of the Wobblies at Lawrence seemed to signal the beginning of a new era in the nation's labor relations. Moreover, the Lawrence strike featured immigrant men, women, and children who garnered considerable support among middle-class reformers. In Bingham, by contrast, not only was the strike lost, but it featured no well-known radicals and only transient men, whose proficiency with guns inspired little sympathy from middle-class onlookers. On the Lawrence strike, see Dubofsky, *We Shall Be All*, 227–252; Salerno, *Red November, Black November*, 98. On the Bingham strike, see Gunther Peck, "Padrones and Protest: 'Old' Radicals and 'New' Immigrants in Bingham, Utah, 1905–1912," *Western Historical Quarterly* 24 (May 1993): 157–178; Papanikolas, "Toil and Rage," 110–125; Mellinger, *Race and Labor in Western Copper*, 106–128.

largest miners' local in the United States. . . . In the face of a common crisis nationalities have been lost and national prejudices have disappeared." If the reporter
for the *Tribune* saw only a racial conflict in Bingham, the *Call* reporter saw ethnicity and nationality, traditional stumbling blocks to class consciousness, being
miraculously set aside, as immigrants finally embraced the WFM's assertion
that "the working class knows but one foreigner and that is the capitalist class."[65]

Yet neither of these competing reportorial narratives – the emergence of race
war or a nationless working class – captured the complex interplay between race,
class, and ethnicity among Bingham's strikers. While the overzealous Socialist
reporter overlooked the vital role of ethnicity and race in shaping the origins and
execution of the Bingham strike, local Americans neglected the complex class
dynamics dividing immigrant workers from their former immigrant leaders. Given
the popularity of both narratives, how did Charles Moyer negotiate these reductive
alternatives and regain his authority as the union's leader? Moyer's strategy, consistent throughout the strike, was to win public support for the union's cause by
"Americanizing" the efforts of its militant immigrant membership. For Moyer,
this meant first enlisting the support of American-born union members in the
Bingham strike and defusing the perception of a race war. By the second week of
the strike, Moyer had succeeded in pressuring the American Brotherhood of Railway Workers and skilled craft unions representing steam shovelmen, machinists,
and teamsters to join the strike and observe immigrant workers' picket lines.
Moyer also managed to persuade American leaders of the WFM local in Ely to
work with their Greek and Italian members. The subsequent walkout in Ely featured close cooperation between American and immigrant strikers as both groups
sought union recognition and the abolition of the padrone system.[66]

Perhaps the most important dimension of Moyer's Americanization campaign
was persuading immigrant strikers to obey local laws regarding firearms. Hoping
to avoid a bloodbath, Moyer called for an open-air meeting between himself,
immigrant strikers, middle-class immigrant leaders, state authorities, and the
governor of Utah, William Spry. Nicholas Stathakos was the first to speak to the
crowd of angry strikers: "For the glory of our nation, you should be law-abiding
here." Stathakos's appeal to Greek patriotism and the American legal system
"deeply agitated" a great number of Greek strikers, whose anger spilled over to the
next speaker, the new Greek Orthodox priest, Vasilios Lambrides. When he made
appeals to Greek patriotism, angry strikers flew into a rage and booed him. As
Lambrides left the podium amid shouts, a number of strikers – principally Greek,
but also Italian, Finnish, and Scottish men – climbed onto the podium and
denounced Skliris as a capitalist parasite and a traitor to his people. All demanded
that company officials abolish the padrone system, with one laborer even asserting

65 *New York Call*, October 3, 1912, 3; *Miner's Magazine*, October 24, 1912, 9.
66 Skilled craft unions in Ely joined the WFM walkout on October 3, 1912. *Salt Lake Tribune*,
     October 4, 1912, 7.

Greeks would return to work if Skliris were fired. The meeting ended with a stern speech by Governor Spry, who warned immigrants to be law-abiding, after which he toured strikers' fortifications with Moyer as his guide.[67]

Moyer's attempt to regain control of the Bingham strike by "Americanizing" the struggle had produced quite a different result. He succeeded in regaining some control over immigrant strikers, as Greeks became the core of a disciplined but now unarmed strike force that patrolled company grounds, inspected all incoming trains for strikebreakers, and manned the picket lines. But by publicly denouncing Skliris and his perceived representatives, immigrant workers of several nationalities redefined the strike's agenda and purpose. This strike was not merely about wages or union recognition, but about the very meaning of free labor for immigrant workers, a message that American newspapers publicized far and near to the disadvantage of both Skliris and the Utah Copper Company.[68]

The mutual accommodation between Moyer and Greek workers marked the beginning of a more cooperative and coordinated relationship between immigrant strikers and the WFM. The efforts of Greek workers, no less militant than at the strike's outset, now earned the praise of WFM leaders. Reflecting the sentiments of E. G. Locke and others, William O'Neill, editor of the *Miner's Magazine* stated, "the Greeks must be given the greatest credit for showing the greatest spirit of solidarity and discipline." The fusion of immigrant and union demands was dramatically evident just one week after the open-air meeting when Skliris announced his resignation from the Utah Copper Company. After celebrating their triumph over Skliris, Greek strikers promptly held a meeting to discuss their options. Although discussion was "animated," they voted unanimously to continue striking for a fifty-cent wage increase and union recognition. Greek workers realized that their success in breaking the padrone system in Bingham had been intimately tied to the efforts of a truly international strike force. And as Stanopolis persuasively pointed out to Greek workers, their accomplishments over Skliris would be quickly undone if they broke ranks with their striking comrades.[69]

Leon Skliris responded to the worst crisis of his career by wrapping himself in the same fraternal rhetoric that was now fueling the militancy of immigrant strikers. In a two-page letter printed on the day of his resignation in the *Deseret Evening News*, Skliris asserted that his Greek brothers "loved him" because he alone was their true defender. He also refused to acknowledge that Greek strikers were committed to industrial unionism and the abolition of padronism. Rather than publicly criticize his countrymen for being radical, and therefore both un-Greek and un-American, Skliris instead embraced the notion that a rival had conspired to take his place as their protector. Skliris concluded his

---

[67] *Salt Lake Tribune*, September 20, 1912, 2; *Deseret Evening News*, September 20, 1912, 3.

[68] For criticisms of the padrone system and the Utah Copper Company, see the *Deseret Evening News*, September 23, 1912, 7.

[69] *Miner's Magazine*, October 10, 1912, 1; *Deseret Evening News*, September 23, 1912, 3; September 24, 1912, 1; September 27, 1912, 1.

letter by denouncing "vicious characters" who were "plotting machinations against my countrymen."[70]

Skliris's resignation produced a crisis within Utah's small middle-class Greek community, which sought to distance itself from Skliris while simultaneously defusing the public perception that Greek strikers were radical. On the day after Greek workers voted to continue striking, George Photopoulos, editor of a new Greek newspaper *To Fos* (The light), stated in the *Salt Lake Evening Telegram* that "the Greeks in Bingham do not understand the significance of a union" and "are ignorant of such American customs." On the same day, Stathakos announced the formation of a new local chapter of the Panhellenic Union, whose purpose in Utah was to "establish schools where Greeks can become familiar with the American language and customs ... and learn to respect the laws of America and in that way become more desirable citizens."[71] Clearly industrial unionism was not one of the "American customs" the Panhellenic Union would teach. Founders of the Panhellenic Union were committed to a respectable and middle-class form of Americanization, one that stood in direct opposition to the American institutions and ideals that Greek workers had embraced in the WFM.

Greek strikers responded to these statements and actions with their own letter to the *Evening Telegram*, which highlighted the class conflicts dividing the Greek community of Utah. Signed by Greek striker George Gatzouros, the letter stated: "We denounce all those self-posed leaders of the Greeks once and for all. . . . It is to their best interests to desist from making themselves prominent and misleading the public regarding the strike situation, or we will be compelled to show them up."[72] Gatzouros's letter captured the combative and boastful quality of Greek strikers' manhood and militancy, while underscoring their abiding commitment to the struggle for union recognition. Despite the efforts of Photopoulos and Stathakos to the contrary, Greeks continued to stand at the forefront of the strike movement.

But if the accommodation of working-class Greeks into the WFM left Skliris and Stathakos bewildered, its implications for other members of Bingham's working class were all too obvious. The Japanese workers who had struck the padrone system with Greek and Italian co-workers were now excluded from the union. The boundaries of working-class organization continued to be racialized in Bingham, boundaries that in fact eased the "Americanization" of working-class Greeks and Italians. Joining the WFM thus represented an ongoing process of both working-class acculturation and racial assimilation for Greek and Italian immigrants. Unlike Mexican sugar beet workers in Oxnard, California, who refused to join the AFL in 1903 unless their Japanese cohorts were included, Bingham's formerly "nonwhite" Greeks sundered ties with their Japanese co-workers as the strike was brought under the direct control of the WFM.[73]

---

[70] *Deseret Evening News*, September 23, 1912, 3.
[71] *Salt Lake Evening Telegram*, September 30, 1912, 12.
[72] Ibid., October 2, 1912, 9.
[73] On the Oxnard strike, see Montgomery, *Fall of the House of Labor*, 87. On the potentially

Not all paths to whiteness proceeded through the doors of the WFM, however. Leon Skliris continued to seek ways to exploit the enduring racial boundaries between Greeks and Americans, even after he had resigned and Greeks had become whitened members of the WFM.[74] Skliris was blessed in this endeavor by the outbreak of the Balkan War in Asia Minor in October 1912, a conflict that joined Greek forces with Bulgarians and Serbians in driving the Ottomans from Europe. Skliris seized the moment by working with Nicholas Stathakos and his former rival William Caravelis to transform the newly formed Panhellenic Union from an instrument of antiradicalism to one of Greek nationalism. Instead of teaching Greek immigrants American customs, the Panhellenic Union made exporting "patriotic" Greeks back home its central mission. Skliris made the most of his rediscovered role as a spokesman of Greek nationalism in the *Salt Lake Tribune*: "To be sure, the empire of the Ottoman is great and its soldiers are fierce and fanatic fighters, but history has yet to show where the Caucasian Race . . . ever went down to defeat in a war so important as this will be. The Turk is doomed."[75] More than a touch of irony shadowed Skliris's manly bravado, given his own recent experience with "fierce and fanatic fighters." Like Moyer, Skliris sought to redeem Greek workers to a nativist public by emphasizing their whiteness. But he did so on terms he defined and could exploit. From Skliris's perspective, truly "white" workers belonged not in the WFM but in their homeland fighting the Turk. Those who stayed in Utah, by implication, were like the Ottomans, "fierce and fanatic fighters," but not Caucasian. Here was Skliris's rejoinder to being described as a "capitalist Turk" by Greek, Finnish, Scottish, and Italian strikers.

To Greek workers, the outbreak of the Balkan War confronted them with an exceptionally difficult dilemma, one made even sharper by the Greek government's executive draft order of October 1, 1912 recalling to active duty all Greek "citizens" between the ages of eighteen and thirty. Should they return to Greece to vanquish their traditional enemy or finish the fight against the Utah Copper Company? The complexities of whiteness and manhood within the Bingham strike movement made the dilemma no simple choice between class war or race war, as Greek workers could fight to be white men in either Bingham or Crete. Initially, most Greek workers stayed in Bingham in solidarity with other strikers in order to finish the fight against the Utah Copper Company. As the strike wore on, however, an increasing number of Greek strikers left town, although it remains unclear whether they returned to Greece. Certainly no Greeks in Bingham used Skliris's "aid" in returning. Their departures nonetheless prompted William O'Neill, editor of the *Miner's Magazine*, to condemn them. "The Greeks who have

---

radical uses of "Americanization" within the working class, see James R. Barrett, "Americanization from the Bottom Up: Immigration and the Remaking of the Working Class in the United States, 1880–1930," *Journal of American History* 79:3 (December 1992): 996–1021; Gerstle, *Working-Class Americanism*, 5–15, 177–87.

[74] These boundaries were quite enduring. Despite the claims of Greek workers, immigrant elites, and union leaders, Greeks remained the focus of nativist hostility in Utah for another thirty years. See Papanikolas, "Toil and Rage," 180.

[75] *Salt Lake Tribune*, October 22, 1912, 3.

gone back belong to the working class," he wrote, "and forget the conditions that drove them to the new world.... But the Greek, like the American, is moved by that sentiment of prejudice, which is commonly known as patriotism."[76] O'Neill condemned patriotic Greeks for fighting the wrong war but, in so doing, obscured the interplay between class, ethnicity, and citizenship rights that fomented and fragmented the strike movement.

If the Balkan War posed a profound dilemma to Greek workers, it provided Daniel Jackling, superintendent of the Utah Copper Company, just the opportunity he needed to begin breaking the strike. Skliris's Greek repatriation effort rehabilitated the padrone system at precisely the moment Jackling most needed its services. As Greek workers pondered which war to fight in early October, Jackling relied upon Skliris's subagent, Gus Paulos, to import one hundred Greek strikebreakers to Bingham, many of them men fleeing the draft.[77] Hundreds of shocked and angry Greek strikers confronted their compatriots at the mine gates and tried to persuade these draft dodgers of their true patriotic duties. But before they could enter the mine a group of well-armed company deputies "swooped down" on the unarmed strikers and forced them to walk to Lower Bingham where one nervous American deputy "accidentally" shot Greek striker Mike Katrakis in the leg. In Ely, Nevada, a similar pattern of coercion and violence was observed. After Greek and Italian strikebreakers were escorted to the mine by company guards, immigrant strikers attempted to enter the mine and throw the scabs out. Deputies promptly opened fire, killing two Greek strikers, Nick Pappas and George Bamosas.[78]

The Utah Copper Company did not break the strike with Greek strikebreakers, however demoralizing that may have been to Greek strikers. Instead, it exploited more enduring and reliable racial boundaries within the western labor movement. First, it offered unionless Japanese workers special wages if they would remain in Bingham. Most Japanese laborers responded to this tragic dilemma with their feet and left Bingham altogether.[79] But the Utah Copper Company maintained good relations with their padrone, Edward Hashimoto, whose connections among "nonwhite" Mexican workers served him well over the ensuing two months. Indeed, these Mexican newcomers played a decisive role in breaking the strike. By the time a defeated WFM leadership formally called the strike off in early December 1912, nearly twice as many Mexicans

[76] Ibid., October 1, 1912, 1; ibid., October 8, 1912, 3, 5; *Miner's Magazine*, November 7, 1912, 4.
[77] Paul Borovilos interview by Helen Papanikolas, Salt Lake City, April 1, 1970, American West Center; Jack Tallas interview by Helen Papanikolas, Salt Lake City, January 18, 1971, Greek Archives; James Korobas interview by Helen Papanikolas, Salt Lake City, October 3, 1974, ibid.; Mrs. Isidore Kastanis interview by Helen Papanikolas, Salt Lake City, March 2, 1973, ibid.; Peter Argentos interview by Helen Papanikolas, Salt Lake City, December 4, 1974, American West Center.
[78] *Salt Lake Tribune*, October 11, 1912, 1, 2. "Martial Law Declared in Ely District," ibid., October 18, 1912, 1.
[79] Ibid., October 2, 1912, 1.

strikebreakers had been imported to Bingham as Greek and Italian strikebreakers combined.[80]

But if the company's strategy of importing Greek and Mexican strikebreakers divided the strikers' solidarity, the tactic also produced mobilizations that challenged, however briefly, the company's apparent control of the situation. On October 25, from the hills above Galena Gulch in Upper Bingham, thirty well-armed Greek strikers opened fire on a startled group of company deputies and Greek strikebreakers as the morning whistle sounded. After firing about five hundred volleys, the Greeks quickly fell back into the cover of the hills. Deputy Sheriff Joseph Sharp immediately organized a posse of over two hundred deputies, but they were unable "to find a trace of the fugitives." Like true western bandits perhaps, Greek strikers were far more familiar with the paths out of town than were American deputies and succeeded with the help of friends, relatives, and compatriots in evading the entire posse. While some hid out with friends in Bingham, others scattered to the coalfields of Colorado, where they encountered Louis Tikas, future martyr of the infamous Ludlow Massacre.[81] The spaces of freedom remained elusive for these men: sometimes fighting in one place seemed the best option, sometimes flight, and on some days, such as October 25, 1912, both seemed reasonable options. For Greek strikebreaker and draft-dodger Harry Spinopoulos, however, questions about the location of freedom soon became irrelevant. Just two weeks after arriving in the "free country of Amerika," Spinopoulos died from injuries sustained in the shooting.

Conclusion

In the spring of 1912, Wobbly songwriter Joe Hill wrote a song commemorating the strike efforts of western railroad workers in British Columbia, many Italians among them. Among other demands, the strikers sought to eliminate the commissary system that continued to exploit transient men on the Canadian Northern Railroad. "For these gunnysack contractors have all been dirty actors, and they're not our benefactors, as every worker knows. So we've got to stick together in fine or dirty weather, and we will show no white feather, where the Fraser River flows" (see Plate 11). The popular song not only punctured the paternalistic veneer of railroad commissary "privileges," but celebrated the power and mobility of transient workers, who like the magnificent Fraser River kept on flowing to their destination, the "one big union." Transience was part and parcel of their radicalism as was the Fraser River itself, which provided an almost mythic backdrop for the heroism of these working-class pioneers. Key to that heroism

---

[80] The impact of these racialized divisions on the Bingham work force were apparent in the subsequent labor history of the community. Bingham would remain without a recognized union until the International Union of Mine, Mill, and Smelter Workers succeeded in winning a union contract in 1946. See Arrington, *The Richest Hole on Earth*, 80–82.

[81] *Ogden Evening Standard*, October 25, 1912, 13; ibid., October 26, 1912, 12; Papanikolas, *Buried Unsung*, 44–46.

was not the western landscape itself but their mobility. Wobbly Len De Caux succinctly captured that connection when explaining what happened to the IWW after 1922. "Among western migratory workers, the IWW retained some strength. But it also dwindled because their numbers dwindled, and their work patterns and manner of life became more stationary."[82] As sedentary men, the living spirit of the Wobblies had gone out of them.

Yet for most transient workers in the North American West, mobility contained far more complex political meanings, however persuasive Joe Hill's and the Wobbly's countermyth of a footloose West may have been. Workers found liberation in mobility not because they lived and worked in an exceptional West, even if it resembled at times a proletarian version of Turner's frontier. Rather, immigrants' passages were transnational and it was that larger context, one that included families in distant Italian, Greek, and Mexican villages, that defined the practice and meaning of mobility and the rights to quit and to move. As most Mexican, Italian, and Greek immigrants quickly realized, those rights were double-edged. Familiarity with the paths out of town greatly benefited many immigrant workers. Italian workers eventually learned to control their mobility to and from North America over time, arranging their own passage to remote industrial islands, to the detriment of labor agents seeking to control Italian migration. Mexican railroad laborers used their knowledge of alternative jobs and geography to limit the power of any Mexican padrone or corporate commissary, knowing when and where to jump the train for better positions in manufacturing plants and sugar beet fields throughout North America. Greek strikers, in turn, exploited their knowledge of pathways in and out of Bingham to pass information to their striking compatriots in Ely, Nevada, and to escape from a local posse after exacting their revenge. In each case, sojourners made mobility subversive to corporate and padrone power by making fight and flight complementary rather than crosscutting strategies of resistance.[83]

But the mobility of immigrant workers also undercut their ability to resist padrone exactions or corporate power. Italian strikers near the mighty Fraser River may have finally joined their "white" co-workers in fighting to improve working and living conditions in 1912, but their mobility as strikebreakers and seasonal workers over the past decade had kept Canadian railroads union-free. During the Bingham strike's waning weeks, many Greek strikers chose flight over fighting, thus hastening the strike's quick conclusion. The mobility of Mexicans workers likewise hampered their ability to resist their labor agents and employers in a collective fashion. As the Mexican consul of Los Angeles stated in 1928, "the difficulty in organizing Mexicans is the continued inflow."[84]

If the freedom to move and to quit remained uncertain paths to freedom, so did

---

[82] De Caux, *The Living Spirit of the Wobblies*, 99, 143. The Canadian Northern strike of 1912 led to a wage increase, although it did not produce union recognition. See McCormack, *Rebels, Reformers, and Revolutionaries*, 107–109.

[83] On the IWW's political uses of mobility, see Don Mitchell's discussion of the Wheatland strike of 1913 in California. Mitchell, *The Lie of the Land*, 36–59.

[84] Consul Pesquiera interview by Paul Taylor, Los Angeles, 1928, BANC-MSS-74/187c, Paul S. Taylor Papers.

the Canadian and U.S. legal systems possess both hazards and opportunities for immigrant sojourners. On the one hand, Cordasco, Skliris, and Gonzalez each used contracts to create their tribute systems. But immigrant workers did not reject contracts or the rights they implied as some Wobblies did. Rather, they used the legal system to contest padrone power whenever possible. Although Greek workers' attempt to sue Greek labor agent Will Caravelis in 1912 failed, Will Kimble of El Paso and Italian foreman Pompei Bianco succeeded in using the language of free labor to damage padrone credibility and nearly put them out of business. By using the law and the courts, immigrant workers did not become uncritical believers in the virtues of U.S. or Canadian citizenship. Their uses of the law and citizenship were selective and occurred in transnational contexts that transformed the meaning of any single national identity. In that regard, Greek workers were only following the lead of Skliris himself, patriotic spokesman for two progressive national identities, when they made the struggle for union rights in the United States a measure of Greek patriotism as well, to the great harm of Harry Spinopoulos.

For all three groups of immigrant workers, the paths to free labor were best realized in collective solidarities with other workers. Yet joining American-led labor unions in the North American West also possessed unforeseen consequences. Greek workers succeeded in driving the czar of the Greeks out of business in Bingham by joining the Western Federation of Miners, transforming the vision and purpose of the Bingham local in the process. But if the accommodation of Greek workers into the WFM made it a more genuinely inclusive and international union, it did not erase the racial boundaries that had helped bring the western labor movement into being half a century earlier. By excluding Japanese strikers from their ranks in the name of working-class radicalism, Greek strikers underscored the crosscutting nature of the emancipation immigrant workers had achieved. These intersections between racialism and radicalism did not make labor history in the region exceptional, but rather distinct, helping explain why so many western workers appeared both exclusive and inclusive, "conservative" and "radical."

The paths to free labor that Greek, Italian, and Mexican workers chose – from mobility to court battles to strikes – did not produce "one big union," much less a unified strategy of resistance. Spaces of freedom for one group of workers remained spaces of oppression for others. But if the strategies that immigrant workers used to resist their padrones undercut one another, each group nonetheless succeeded in undermining its padrone by claiming the legacy of free labor on its own terms. The timing of worker resistance and the collapse of padrone power varied among Mexican, Italian, and Greek immigrants, but the patterns of change were similar. Immigrant workers successfully resisted their padrones by gaining control of the same tools padrones had used to become powerful, transforming coercive practices into liberatory rights. For these immigrants, this struggle was part and parcel of a larger process of working-class formation and acculturation. Their individual and collective protests were not "primitive rebellions," but pragmatic and sophisticated attempts to locate and define the meaning of free labor in North America.

The Vanishing Padrone

During the depth of the Great Depression in 1933, Leonard Slye, later to become Roy Rogers, launched his career by writing a song, "Tumblin' Tumbleweed," that romanticized the famed mobility of the western cowboy. When the song was recorded by Rogers's group, "The Sons of the Pioneers," a year later, it launched a "tidal wave of cowboy romanticism," according to one music historian, as North Americans sang along with the following refrain: "See them tumbling down, pledging their love to the ground, Lonely but free I'll be found, drifting along with the tumblin' tumbleweed." During a moment of acute economic and cultural crisis in which thousands of men and women tramped across the continent in search of work, the song affirmed a romantic vision of the West in which "cares of the past are behind." The cowboy's mistress was the range itself and his roaming bachelorhood a sign of manly individualism and freedom rather than economic coercion or emasculation.[1]

Such sentiments ostensibly reversed the picture of transience familiar to many Americans during the Depression and earlier in the Progressive Era, with one important hitch. Roy Rogers and his famed cowboys were all white, sons of native-born American pioneers, not "bohunks," "dagoes," "wops," or "greasers." Transience among nonwhite men remained deeply troubling to most North Americans and ironically fueled the nostalgia for Roy Rogers's native-born tumbleweeds. While popular musicians looked backward in time to a mythologized and whitened frontier, public and private welfare agencies in the early 1930s looked to the recommendations of Progressive Era urban reformers for creating state-run labor bureaus that would more efficiently connect unemployed workers to jobs in both cities and countryside.

Yet nowhere in 1933 did government bureaucrats discover padrones in their investigations into the causes of transience and unemployment. That omission is striking, given how frequently the celebrated villain had legitimated calls to

---

[1] Ken Griffis, *Hear My Song: The Story of the Celebrated Sons of the Pioneers* (New York, 1990); on the gendered origins of the Western, see Jane Tompkins, *West of Everything: The Inner Life of Westerns* (Oxford, 1992); and Johnson, "'A Memory Sweet to Soldiers.'"

expand the power and authority of both state and federal bureaucracies between 1885 and 1920. But in 1930 on the eve of the New Deal and perhaps the greatest expansion of government power in U.S. history, the padrone appeared nowhere in the New York Industrial Survey Commission's investigation and seemed to have disappeared as an urban or an immigrant problem.[2]

A brief examination of the whereabouts of Gonzalez, Cordasco, and Skliris in 1930 confirms the view that padrones had indeed vanished. Antonio Cordasco survived his legal setbacks between 1904 and 1908 and managed his own steamship agency until 1922, with tickets available for "all classes on all lines to every principal port in the world."[3] But never again did Cordasco demand tributes from his customers or excite much antipathy among either immigrant workers or Canadian reformers. He died in 1924, a reasonably wealthy man surrounded by his wife and children, many of whom had become respectable clerks and shopkeepers in Montreal.

Although Roman Gonzalez outlived his competitors Robert Zarate and Isaac Avina by nearly four decades, he owned little as an older man, inspiring none of the fear or respect that he briefly wielded as El Paso's first Hispanic policeman. After going bankrupt and losing his labor agency for good in 1928, Gonzalez worked as both a day laborer and a night watchman at the El Paso smelter during the depression, before retiring to a modest suburban home in 1946. There, he remained with his wife and daughter until his death in 1963 at the age of ninety-six. As a night watchman during the 1930s, Gonzalez continued to guard boundaries created by corporate America, as did Isaac Avina who became a debt collections officer. But the boundaries that Avina and Gonzalez now guarded were not as varied and profitable as they had been earlier in their careers. Indeed, Gonzalez spent his later years just one step away from the poverty he had long witnessed among his compatriots in Chihuahuita.[4]

If Cordasco and Gonzalez retired to careers of relative obscurity, Leon Skliris quite literally disappeared from the historical record. Initially, Skliris remained in the limelight, surviving the Bingham strike of 1912 and his attempted assassination at the hands of Cretan gunman George Pologeorgi in 1915 to remain in business as a labor agent. On December 5, 1912, he signed a contract with Italian padrone Moses Paggi, agreeing to furnish "unskilled foreign laborers" to the Utah Power and Light Company, a partnership that lasted until 1919. Throughout this period, Skliris and Paggi received a commission of five cents on every dollar earned by Greek and Italian workmen at the Utah construction site. Unlike previous tributes, these commissions were deducted directly from workers' paychecks without any messy problems of enforcement. Skliris also continued to serve as a labor agent for the Denver and Rio Grande Railroad, maintaining offices for the railroad in Chicago, New York, Denver, and San Francisco as late as 1917.

[2] George Trafton, *Employment Agencies Officially Exposed: Sworn Testimony Shows Urgent Need of State Action* (New York, 1930), 2.
[3] See Cordasco's full-page advertisement in *Lowell's Montreal City Directory: 1920–21* (Montreal, 1921), 1256, Canadian National Archives, Montreal.
[4] El Paso, City Directory, 1928–1963, El Paso Public Library.

But by 1920, Skliris and his brothers Evangelos and Stavros had left Utah and the West altogether. Some Greek immigrants claimed in oral histories half a century later that Leon Skliris had fled to Cuba, others that he had become an official in the Mexican government, and still others that he had died penniless and unknown in New York City. The only Skliris to appear in New York City between 1920 and 1950 was a man named George Skliris, who in 1946 briefly operated a travel agency in Brooklyn. Possibly Leon himself, a relative, or an unknown son, "George" disappeared after just one year in the city's directories and tax rolls.[5]

But if padrones had indeed disappeared from public circulation by 1930, labor agents and the workers they moved continued to excite public indignation and government investigations. The central villain of New York State's Industrial Survey Commission in 1930 was not the padrone but a close cousin, the "unscrupulous employment agent." In addition to sending workers to "phoney" jobs and making them pay exorbitant job fees to keep their livelihoods, these "scoundrels" intimidated all laborers who sought to reclaim lost job fees. According to one laborer interviewed in 1930, "I have seen employment men, or clerks, and sometimes the boss himself, not only throw workers downstairs but finish it on the sidewalk.... Nine times out of ten it was some poor foreigner beaten up by the crook upstairs." When asked by the chairman of the New York Industrial Survey Commission, State Senator James Truman, why these workers were beaten up, the witness replied "they was trying to get their money back."[6]

The continuities of these padronelike abuses should not obscure what had, in fact, changed for migrant workers and the men who provided them jobs. Although the "unscrupulous labor agent" exploited workers by sending them to phoney jobs, he rarely exercised the kind of cultural and political power over the lives of immigrant workers that Cordasco and Skliris briefly wielded. Although many labor agents during the depression were immigrants, far fewer specialized in providing jobs only to their compatriots. Perhaps more important, labor agents in the 1930s promised their clients only jobs, rather than help in sending remittances to families overseas, translations for their countrymen in court, or "protection" from American nativists. Many of the tasks previously performed by the padrone had become specialized within immigrant communities or made unnecessary, as immigrants learned English and could send for their relatives themselves. One gleans a

[5] *Moses Paggi vs. Leon Skliris*, March 12, 1919, Case 3216, Records of the Utah Supreme Court. This case was generously brought to my attention by Phil Notarianni of the Utah State Historical Society; see Skliris's advertisement in *The Scenic Lines Employees' Magazine: Official Railroad Journal of the Denver & Rio Grande-Western Pacific* (Denver, 1917), 38; George Lamb interview by Helen Papanikolas, Salt Lake City, September 3, 1972, Greek Archives; Peter John Poulos interview by Helen Papanikolas, Salt Lake City, July 2, 1976, Greek Archives; Nina Cononelos interview by Louis Cononelos, Salt Lake City, June 27, 1974, American West Center; *George Skliris vs. City of New York*, September 1946, Records of Municipal Licenses, Borough of Manhattan, New York Public Library, New York.

[6] George Trafton, *Employment Agencies Officially Exposed*, 2. Walter Licht found that padrones had disappeared among Italians in Philadelphia by the 1930s, but he incorrectly concludes that they never really existed or possessed much influence. See Licht, *Getting Work*, 123.

sense of these changes in Skliris's career after the Bingham strike. By forming a partnership with Italian labor agent Moses Paggi in December 1912, Skliris also began finding work for men of all nationalities. His profits – five cents on every dollar earned – were not so much personal tributes as a bureaucratized tax. Skliris provided his customers employment, but no longer attempted to embody fraternal manhood or mediate the boundaries of ethnic, racial, or national community.

The most important reason padrones lost power, however, was because immigrant workers systematically rejected their authority. The timing of worker resistance varied according to the political and social circumstances of migrant workers and the ways padrones represented their interests. Worker mobilizations against Italian padrones in 1903 and 1904 in cities from New York to Montreal eliminated the padrone system among Italian workers concentrated in urban locations or transformed it into a building block of union power under the leadership of Dominic D'Allesandro. But Italian padrones also survived in diminished fashion in rural pockets such as the Adirondacks and on western railroad lines throughout the 1910s. Similarly, union mobilizations against Skliris crippled the power of all padrones in Utah in 1912, but Skliris and Greek padrones in bootblack shops persisted well into the 1910s. The power of Mexican labor agents had never been as pronounced, but they persisted longer, waxing and waning in strength with the cycles of labor demand on the U.S.-Mexican border throughout the 1920s. Lawsuits against Gonzalez in the early 1920s nonetheless signaled a larger willingness by transient workers in El Paso and elsewhere to use the legal system to their own ends, dramatically weakening the power of Gonzalez and transforming how all labor agencies in El Paso recruited workers. By the late 1920s, resistance by workers against immigrant padrones – whether quitting their jobs en masse, suing padrones, going on strike, joining labor unions, claiming whiteness and citizenship, or asserting the conflicted privileges of manhood – had undermined the ability of most individual padrones to mediate the cultural, geographic, and political spaces separating immigrant workers from North American residents and institutions.

These internal pressures against padronism gave momentum to several external factors that together would sweep padronism from the map by the end of the 1920s. The U.S. government's exclusion of "new" immigrants severely curtailed the number of both Asian and southern European immigrants entering the continent in the early 1920s, eliminating a key source of padrone revenue. Equally important, North American corporations no longer sought the padrone's services. Since the early 1910s, many companies had begun replacing the controversial padrone with a fatherly figure of their own. The corporate personnel manager assumed many of the padrone's former responsibilities, providing "protection" to immigrant workers from abusive foremen, sponsoring citizenship classes, and organizing workers into "respectable" nonunion activities.

Another crucial reason corporations abandoned the padrone system was their decreasing dependence on unskilled labor during the 1930s. Although the depression threatened the economic viability of many corporations, it also represented a period of remarkable growth in worker productivity as mechanization lessened the demand for unskilled workers. As Richard Jensen has demonstrated, companies used the oversupply of labor in all categories to become remarkably selective in their hiring policies during the depression, recruiting only workers who were literate and educated even if they were digging ditches.[7] One gleans a clear sense of this from the changing demands that private employment agents made on the unskilled workers who entered their offices. In 1936 Lorin Andrew Thompson, a "director of research" in the Cincinnati Employment Center, published a book for employment agents outlining the questions prospective workers were now required to answer. In order to get a job as a ditchdigger, for example, one needed to know the names of "four different kinds of pipes in sewers" and that only a "long-handled, round-pointed shovel" could be used to take out "the last dirt."[8]

An important exception to this pattern existed within the nation's agricultural sector and among Mexican immigrants. Although immigration laws encouraged many Mexicans to remain in the United States year-round, solos and families continued to migrate into the United States each work season with the help of Mexican labor contractors, who flourished in specific sectors of agricultural industry. A researcher at Berkeley in 1938, Mary Gorringe Luck, discovered numerous Mexican labor contractors in California agriculture, the most entrepreneurial being a man who collected workers' wages and took his cut from them. These contractors were most concentrated among pea pickers, but were also prominent among "melon, lettuce and other field crops."[9] Mexican labor contractors thrived in the 1930s not only because of the continued northward migration of Mexicans to California, but also because employers nurtured the system in agricultural sectors that remained impervious to labor-saving innovations. The success of Mexican labor contractors in the 1930s – in contrast to their marginal status in previous decades – underscored the continuing importance of corporations as well as the border and its legal enforcement in shaping the growth and development of immigrant labor agents. For perhaps the first time in the history of the U.S-Mexican border, tighter regulation of immigration laws in the 1930s created conditions ripe for the growth of padrone power.

No powerful Mexican padrones emerged in the United States during the 1930s, outside of corporate agriculture, for two reasons. First, padrones throughout the continent experienced increasing competition from philanthropic and public employment agencies in the 1920s and 1930s. Municipal reformers had long sought to curb the padrone's abuses by establishing nonprofit labor agencies and public employment bureaus, both of which provided jobs to clients free of charge. In the first decade of the twentieth century, most philanthropic organizations such as the Italian Emigration Aid Society of Montreal had failed to make significant inroads into the labor-contracting business. Public employment offices such as the

[7] Richard Jensen, "The Causes and Cures of Unemployment in the Great Depression," *Journal of Interdisciplinary History* 19 (Spring 1989): 553–583.

[8] Lorin Andrew Thompson Jr., *Interview Aids and Trade Questions for Employment Offices* (New York, 1936), 60–61.

[9] Emily H. Huntington, *Doors to Jobs: A Study of the Organization of the Labor Market in California* (Berkeley, 1942), 314–315.

Free Employment Bureau of Illinois found jobs for 23,996 individuals in 1901, but this number paled in comparison to the nearly 300,000 unskilled railroad workers mobilized in Chicago's employment district for jobs throughout the Midwest that year. Most of the 24,000 positions were within Chicago's city limits and over 10,000 of these clients were female domestics seeking work in Chicago's middle-class and upper-middle-class homes.[10] By the 1920s, however, charitable and state-run employment offices had become far more adept at sending workers along the paths connecting urban and rural labor markets. Consider the transformation of the National Employment Exchange in New York City, a philanthropic organization that explicitly eschewed making any money from the commerce of migration. In 1910 the exchange initially procured jobs for one hundred manual laborers, most of them as street sweepers for the city. By 1925 the exchange procured jobs for over twelve thousand men, the vast majority of them day laborers on construction projects in the countrysides of upstate New York and New Jersey.[11] Such exchanges took over the same "territory" in which padrones had previously "remained all powerful," according to municipal investigators.

If philanthropic labor agencies usurped the territory of private labor agents, state and federal employment programs during the 1930s and 1940s more dramatically transformed the organization and geography of labor markets in North America. The culmination of federal attempts to organize the unskilled labor market came not with the closing of U.S. borders to European immigration in the 1920s but with the implementation of the Bracero program among Mexican workers during World War II. As in the previous world war, tremendous labor shortages prompted the U.S. government to enter the business of labor recruitment itself. Rather than repeal its exclusive quotas against southern and eastern European immigrants, the government imported thousands of Mexican workers and their families to industrial and agricultural work sites throughout the Southwest and Midwest. The U.S. government took over tasks previously controlled by labor agents and commissary companies by providing all workers with housing, grocery stores, and return transportation to Mexico each work season. Although created by wartime exigencies, the Bracero Program flourished throughout the 1950s and into the 1960s. Il padrone had become Uncle Sam.[12]

But the history of the unscrupulous labor agent in the mid-twentieth century is no simple history of declension in which the forces of modernity – here the corporation and the state in North America – subsumed the padrone's former functions. For such a narrative obscures the reciprocal relationships that continued to

[10] See Abbott, "The Chicago Employment Agency and the Immigrant Worker," 9; State of Illinois, Bureau of Labor Statistics, *Third Annual Report of the Illinois Free Employment Offices, 1901* (Springfield, 1902), 8.

[11] *Annual Report of the National Employment Exchange, First Edition* (New York, 1910); *Annual Report of the National Employment Exchange, Sixteenth Edition* (New York, 1926).

[12] Reisler, *By the Sweat of Their Brow*, 260–261; Linda C. Majka and Theo J. Majka, *Farm Workers, Agribusiness, and the State* (Philadelphia, 1982). On the Bracero program's decline in the early 1960s, see Calavita, *Inside the State*, 141. On the experiences of Bracero workers, see Maria Herrera-Sabek, *The Bracero Experience: Elitelore vs. Folklore* (Los Angeles, 1979).

flourish between border entrepreneurs and the state. The transformation of the U.S. government's role, for example, from preventing the admission of contract laborers in 1885 to organizing the large-scale importation of immigrants under contract in the 1940s, did not eliminate the state's symbiotic relationship with unscrupulous labor agents. During their campaign to create government-run employment offices in the 1930s, for example, the American Association for Labor Legislation used the employment agent as a scapegoat for the immense dislocations of the depression. When wartime lessened the dangers of unemployment, groups as diverse as the Women's Trade Union League and the National Consumers League described the dishonest labor agent as a danger to the nation's self-defense effort, impeding the ability of its workers to produce goods and hindering the growth of their patriotic loyalties. Such vilifications were crucial to legitimating the U.S. government's new Bracero Program in 1942.[13]

If the persistence of these villains reflected the changing political needs of reformers and bureaucrats, it also highlights how padronelike figures remain symbiotically connected to geographic, cultural, and political borders. The boundaries between cities and countrysides, persistent and transient communities, white and nonwhite laborers, fraternal and paternal manhood, citizen and alien have changed since the 1920s. But for today's transnational migrant workers, the forms of oppression encountered by Greek, Italian, and Mexican workers in the early twentieth century are hauntingly familiar. Consider, for example, the recent struggles of Mexican crab pickers imported to the eastern shore of Maryland in the 1990s. In May 1991 Maria Armenta and seven women from Sinaloa, Mexico, set out for Maryland under the supervision of two female labor contractors, Yolanda Felix and Monica Del Croix. The eight Mexican women, all of them mothers ranging from the age of twenty-two to forty-five, had read an advertisement in their local newspaper, *El Debate*, promising wages of one thousand dollars a month above and beyond the costs of room and board in a home filled with amenities and cable television. Instead, Armenta and her cohorts found themselves crowded into small, unfurnished motel rooms, with all costs deducted from their paychecks without their consent. Rather than an eight-hour day, they worked on a piece-rate system for ten and twelve hours with no overtime pay. Unable to speak English and not allowed to drive a car, they were urged "not to speak to strangers" and were entirely dependent on Felix and Del Croix for transportation to and from work and the nearby grocery store.[14]

Although the all-female cast of Maryland's crab pickers and labor agents contrasts sharply with the male-dominated world of the North American West eighty years earlier, Armenta and her cohorts' experience with transnational mobility, geographic and cultural isolation, and constant deductions from their paychecks paralleled the misfortunes of Greek, Italian, and Mexican men.

[13] Calavita, *Inside the State*, 11.

[14] *Maria Lourdes Armenta, et al. vs. David W. Wehrs Seafood, et al.*, November 20, 1991, civil no. L-91-3307, State of Maryland, Records of the U.S. Dist. Civil Court, U.S. District Courthouse, Baltimore. Thanks to Deborah Thompson and John Peter Sarbanes of the Public Justice Center for acquainting me with these cases.

Moreover, their experience with labor agents and employers claiming to protect them recalled the gendered performances of Skliris and Cordasco. In 1996 Mexican crab picker Graciela Guerrero and two female co-workers sued their American employer, Rebecca Rippons, because "they were not allowed to leave their residence after dark" and "could not have men in their place of residence." Rippons's lawyer defended his client, stating, "If she tells them not to go out at night, it's because they don't speak the language and she doesn't want them to wander into trouble. She feels responsible for them." Just as Skliris claimed to be a good brother and Cordasco a model father to immigrant workers, Rippons was, her lawyer suggested, a good mother to her employees. Yet keeping Rippons's "girls" in at night also kept them isolated and, as their complaint stated, "ignorant of their rights in America." As with Skliris and Cordasco, articulating notions of fictive kinship only emboldened immigrant workers to challenge their authority.[15]

If modern padrones and workers continue struggling to define ideas of gender and family obligation to their advantage, so do they fight to control workers' mobility. For Guerrero and other Mexican crab pickers, transience initially empowered both labor contractor and employer. When Guerrero and her cohorts protested their confinement, Rippons fired them and offered them tickets to the U.S.-Mexican border in Laredo, Texas. Though they remained in Maryland, their predicament at that moment was similar to Louis Lingos's in the Nevada desert: they could stay put and be stranded in Maryland or be stranded at the border in Texas, still over one thousand miles from home. In either circumstance, their freedom as wage earners was compromised by geographic and cultural isolation.

The particular variations within whiteness that helped create padrone power in the West have shifted since 1900, but they, too, remain important avenues to power for labor market entrepreneurs. Italian Canadians and Greek Americans no longer comprise a nonwhite racial group, in part because of the economic and poltical success of each group in North America. Few recent Greek and Italian immigrants are unskilled and transient, moreover, unlike their predecessors. Such is not the case with Mexican immigrants, whose transience remains conspicuous and whose numbers in the North and within the regions in which they sojourn continue to grow. Armenta and Guerrero are part of a much larger cohort of migrant Mexicans and central Americans transforming the geography of unskilled work and race throughout North America, from northern Ontario to every nook and cranny of the Old South. What was conspicuous about race relations in the North American West between 1900 and 1920 – a complex and transnational racial hierarchy involving "blacks, Mexicans, Indians, Chinese, Japanese, and other racialized groups" – has become increasingly typical of nearly every region in North America, from the once bipolar U.S. South to the predominantly "white" Canadian East as well. The farm labor market on the east coast today has been

---

[15] *Graciela Palacios Guerrero et al. vs. Rebecca Rippons and Tony's Seafood*, November 21, 1996, Case L-96-3848, State of Maryland, Records of the U.S. District Civil Court, U.S. District Courthouse, Baltimore; *Baltimore Sun*, December 13, 1996, "The Sun in Anne Arundel" section, 2; ibid., April 18, 1998, 1.

"westernized," as Cindy Hahamovitch put it, not so much by migrants born in the West as by immigrants passing through it. The transnational mobility of immigrants that redefined the meaning and shape of free labor at the turn of the twentieth century now transforms the geography of migrant work and free labor throughout North America.[16]

If transnational boundaries of racial and gender difference continue to shape how today's border entrepreneurs gain power, so too does their relationship with border bureaucrats remain symbiotic. Maria Armenta and Graciela Guerrero were both brought to Maryland through Mexico and Texas under a program designed by U.S. lawmakers to facilitate the efficient and ostensibly humane importation of migrant guest workers. Unlike Skliris and other padrones in 1910, Yolanda Felix and Monica Del Croix worked with the formal approval of the U.S. government, which issued them visas for the women they were importing into the nation. Yet labor contractors like Felix and Del Croix have also helped clarify the immigration bureaucracy's often contradictory missions. The sensational discovery of border entrepreneurs like Felix and Del Croix, portrayed in the media as unscrupulous villains rather than as law-abiding citizens, has of late fueled calls to expand further the U.S. Immigration and Naturalization Service's power on U.S. borders.[17] But that bureaucracy's success in discovering border threats may ironically undo its own future as calls mount to find military solutions to what remain cultural and ideological problems. For the bureaucrats who continue to police the human traffic across borders in North America at the end of the Cold War and the twentieth century, free labor will remain an unstable fiction, one whose contours are as contested as they were at the beginning of the century.

The contours of free labor will be rewritten not only by border bureaucrats and labor market entrepreneurs, but by immigrant workers like Maria Armenta and Graciela Guerrero who demand their rights as free laborers in North America. Like Italian, Greek, and Mexican men eighty years earlier, Armenta and Guerrero turned the tables on their alleged protectors and employers using the same devices that brought Felix and Del Croix to power. First, Armenta and Guerrero learned to control their mobility by traveling to Baltimore and finding help at the doorstep of the Public Justice Center, an organization that has helped lead the fight against the exploitation of immigrants throughout Maryland. With their backing, Armenta and Guerrero sued their female employers and labor contractors, not only winning overtime wages and the return of illegal pay deductions totaling forty-nine hundred dollars, but also putting Del Croix, Felix, and Rippons out of business. In winning a measure of justice in the United States, Armenta and Guerrero did not become enthusiastic patriots of the U.S. nation or even its citizens. Like Greek workers in Bingham eighty years earlier, these Mexican women acquired and

---

[16] Foley, *The White Scourge*, 211; Hahamovitch, *Fruits of Their Labor*, 200–201.

[17] See, for example, the sensational coverage and reaction to the discovery of a deaf Mexican importation "ring" in New York City in 1997. Deborah Sontag, "Deaf Mexicans Are Found Enslaved in New York," *New York Times*, July 20, 1997, 1, 19; Sam Dillon, "In Mexico, Tales of Deception Confirm the Fears of the Deaf," ibid., July 21, 1997, 1, 15.

exercised rights in North America selectively. Indeed, when Armenta and Guerreo and their cohorts received their judgments, many had already returned to western Mexico.

If the struggles of Armenta and Guerrero to fight their alleged protectors suggest important commonalities in the experiences of transient workers, they should not obscure the discontinuities as well. Many of the freedoms that Guerrero and Armenta fought for stand in sharp tension with the patriarchal rights that many male sojourners sought to transplant to North America eighty years earlier. Even if Armenta and her cohorts were the principal breadwinners in their families and their husbands performed all of the unpaid labor of domestic childrearing in their absence, these women did not secure a husband's prerogatives over the family's labor and sexuality. Armenta's and Guerrero's stories would just as likely have horrified as inspired Greek strikers in Bingham or workers like Giuseppe Teolo and Will Kimble, whose paternal and fraternal privileges were potentially undone by these women's sojourns. And yet like those immigrant men, Armenta and Guerrero used both flight and fight to their advantage, refashioning the meaning of free labor for their communities in both Mexico and Maryland. Though it was not their intention, Armenta and Guerrero, no less than Greek, Italian, and Mexican men before them, laid the groundwork for the struggles of the next generation of mobile workers in North America, be they male or female, white or nonwhite, "sons of the pioneers" or citizens of the world.

Appendix A: Tables

Table I.I. *Montreal's Growth, 1880–1920*

Year	Total Manufacturing Output	Total Population
1880	$52,510,000	145,580
1890	$67,654,000	220,181
1900	$71,100,000	266,826
1910	$166,297,000	466,197
1920	$593,882,000	863,188

Table I.2. *Land Sales of the Canadian Pacific Railway*

Year	Acres Sold (Thousands)	Price per Acre (Dollars)
1894	49	3.20
1897	199	3.30
1900	268	3.00
1903	2,639	3.60
1906	1,115	5.84
1909	376	13.52
1912	669	15.99

Table I.3. *Utah-Bound Greeks Entering New York City in March*

Year	Salt Lake City	Bingham	Castle Gate	Ogden
1907	50	31	34	4
1910	58	13	9	7
1912	55	73	24	5
1914	22	3	2	10

Table 4.1. *Age Profile of Greek and Italian Immigrants at Peak of Padrone Power (%)*

	17–19	20–22	23–25	26–28	29–31	32–34	35–37	38–40	41–43	44–46	47+
Greeks	1.4	42.1	19.4	12.5	7.4	6.0	7.4	1.9	1.4	0.5	0.0
Italians	11.3	12.4	12.7	13.1	15.9	7.1	8.1	5.3	6.7	2.8	4.6

Table 4.2. *Greek Single Men, Aged 18–23, among the Utah-Bound, 1907–1914*

Year	% Total Migration
1907	40.0
1910	53.5
1912	61.5
1914	24.2

Table 4.3. *Italian Single Men, Aged 18–23, among the Canada-Bound, 1901–1907*

Year	% Total Migration
1901	21.3
1904	23.8
1907	36.1

Table 4.4. *Closest Family Relation in Canada among Canada-Bound Italians, 1901–1907*

Year	%Cousin	%Brother	%Brother-in-Law	%Uncle	%Father	%Husband
1901	16.1	13.2	10.2	5.8	2.0	0
1904	15.9	9.9	7.1	6.4	5.3	4.0
1907	20.8	24.4	13.1	3.6	6.5	8.0

Table 4.5. *Criminal Disturbances by Ethnic Group, Bingham, Utah, June 21–December 17, 1912*

Ethnicity	%Pop	%Total	%DTP	%Pimp	%A&B	%CCW	%Vag	%Oth
Anglo-American	42	66	84	75	56	10	84	83
Greek	23	9	3	0	9	50	0	0
Italian	14	12	0	17	27	10	14	15
Finnish	11	3	6	0	0	0	0	0
Japanese	7	0	0	0	0	0	0	0
Austrian	4	10	6	8	9	30	0	0

Notes: Total = total crimes committed; DTP = disturbing the peace; Pimp = running a baudy house; A&B = assault and battery; CCW = carrying a concealed weapon; Vag = vagrancy; and Oth = other, including "indecent exposure" and "fast riding."
Sources: Records compiled from the Bingham Police Register, 1912, State Archives of Utah. Population figures compiled from the Thirteenth Census of the United States, Population Schedules, Bingham Canyon, Salt Lake County.

Table 5.1. *Ethnic Groups of Bingham, Utah, 1910*

Ethnicity	Freq	%Total	%Unsk	%Semisk	%Sk	%Prof	%Eng	%Cit	%Own
American	113	32	21	31	30	18	100	100	15
British	36	10	19	44	25	11	100	53	14
Swedish	10	3	0	30	40	30	100	80	20
Finnish	29	8	7	83	3	7	86	17	21
Italian	48	14	25	73	0	2	31	4	4
Greek	80	23	73	20	3	5	9	0	1
Japanese	24	7	100	0	0	0	0	8	0
Total	355	100	36	40	15	10	62	44	10

Notes: Freq = number of persons in each ethnic group; %Sk = percent of total having specified level of skill; %Eng = percent of total able to speak English; %Cit = percent of total having U.S. citizenship; and %Own = percent of total owning a residence. Figures represent a one in ten sampling of all occupation holders.

Table 5.2. *Greeks of Bingham and Salt Lake City, 1910*

Occupational Level	Number	%Total	%Eng	Dep	Years in U.S.
Salt Lake City					
Unskilled Laborers	46	78	43	0.04	3.7
Skilled/ Professional	13	22	85	0.69	8.7
Bingham Canyon					
Unskilled Laborers	74	92	5	0.00	3.2
Skilled/ Professional	6	8	50	0.00	7.3

Notes: %Eng = percent of total able to speak English; Dep = average number of dependents (Greeks without an occupation) per individual; and Years in U.S. = average number of years spent in the United States.
Source: Compiled from a one-in-ten sampling of Greeks listed in the Thirteenth Federal Census, Salt Lake County, 1910.

Table 5.3. *Commercial Licenses Purchased by Greek Businessmen in Bingham, Utah, 1908–1913*

License Type	Number	%Total	Years in Operation
Grocer	9	19.1	0.76
Liquor Dealer	8	17.0	0.72
Peddler	8	17.0	0.31
Coffeehouse Owner	7	14.9	0.89
Butcher	5	10.6	0.85
Candy Maker	3	6.4	1.50
Pool Hall Owner	3	6.4	0.33
Milk Dealer	2	1.3	1.75
Baker	2	1.3	0.75
Total	47	100.0	0.79

Source: Town of Bingham Canyon, Ledger, 1908–13, Utah State Archives.

Table 6.1. *Congressional Returns in Bingham, 1896–1914 (% of Total)*

Year	Republican	American	Democrat	Socialist
1896	32.0	0	66.0	2.0
1898	46.0	0	40.8	13.2
1900	51.5	0	36.3	11.7
1902	42.2	0	37.4	20.4
1904	29.3	14.0	28.6	28.1
1906	24.8	25.0	23.8	26.4
1908	36.2	27.3	18.6	17.7
1910	40.5	33.3	8.7	13.9
1912	27.3	25.1	28.2	19.4
1914	50.1	0	45.6	4.3

Source: Compiled from election districts 80–82, 90–92, Salt Lake County, State Archives of Utah.

Appendix B: Tables Used in Preparation of Maps

Map Table 1.1A. *Final Destinations of Canada-Bound Italians, March 1904*

Destination	No. Immigrants	% Immigrants
Montreal	223	79.64
Toronto	19	6.79
Copper Cliff	10	3.57
Alberta	9	3.21
Michel	7	2.50
Ottawa	7	2.50
Revelstoke	3	1.07
Winnipeg	2	0.71

Map Table 1.1B. *Final Destinations of Canada-Bound Italians, March 1907*

Destination	No. Immigrants	% Immigrants
Montreal	36	21.30
Toronto	33	19.53
Michel	30	17.75
Williams Point	20	11.83
Copper Cliff	11	6.51
Sault Ste Marie	8	4.73
Trail	8	4.73
Vancouver	8	4.73
Ottawa	6	3.55
Calgary	3	1.78
Alberta	2	1.18
Winnipeg	2	1.18
Ladysmith	1	0.59
Windsor	1	0.59

Map Table 1.2A. *Final Destinations of Utah-Bound Greeks, March 1912*

Destination	No. Immigrants	% Immigrants
Bingham Canyon	72	33.96
Salt Lake	65	30.66
Price	44	20.75
Sunnyside	12	5.66
Garfield	5	2.36
Scofield	5	2.36
Ogden	4	1.89
Murray	3	1.42
Clear Creek	1	0.47
Logan	1	0.47

Map Table 1.2B. *Final Destinations of Utah-Bound Greeks, March 1914*

Destination	No. Immigrants	% Immigrants
Salt Lake	25	36.76
Ogden	11	16.18
Garfield	10	14.71
Price	10	14.71
Sunnyside	6	8.82
Murray	4	5.88
Bingham Canyon	2	2.94
Clear Creek	0	0.00
Logan	0	0.00
Scofield	0	0.00

Map Table 4.1. *Origins of Greek Emigrants to Utah, 1907–1912*

Place of Origin	No. Emigrants	% Emigrants
Megara	45	17.37
Pireaus	24	9.27
Argos	15	5.79
Apanokhori	14	5.41
Gardiki	13	5.02
Granitsa	12	4.63
Vamos	12	4.63
Haidarli	11	4.25
Korinthos	10	3.86
Glavitsa	9	3.47
Kranidi	9	3.47
Nippos	8	3.09
Pavliani	8	3.09
Crete	7	2.70
Fteri	7	2.70
Pikerni	7	2.70
Stromni	7	2.70
Leonidion	6	2.32
Kalamitsi	5	1.93
Krikouki	5	1.93
Nauplion	5	1.93
Passia	5	1.93
Souri	5	1.93
Spathi	5	1.93
Tripoli	5	1.93

Map Table 4.2. *Origins of Italian Emigrants to Canada, 1901–1904*

Place of Origin	No. Emigrants	% Emigrants
San Elpidio	44	13.21
Bucchianico	28	8.41
Udine	23	6.91
Valvasone	23	6.91
Terracina	15	4.50
Treviso	13	3.90
Francavilla Marittima	11	3.30
Benestare	11	3.30
Caulonia	10	3.00
Arzene	10	3.00
Castropignano	9	2.70
Villareggio	9	2.70
Ardore	8	2.40
Galluccio	8	2.40
Torelo	8	2.40
Bertiolo	8	2.40
Casarsa	8	2.40
Volpago	8	2.40
Chieti	7	2.10
Mignano	7	2.10
San Benedetto	6	1.80
Laurenzana	6	1.80
Lauriano	6	1.80
Narzole	6	1.80
Fergino	6	1.80
Gissi	5	1.50
Vacri	5	1.50
Cellara	5	1.50
Coneas	5	1.50
Mussolente	5	1.50
San Martino	5	1.50
Caerano	5	1.50

Map Table 4.3. *Origins of Mexican Emigrants to the United States, Based on Money Orders Sent Home, July-August, 1926*

State of Origin	No. Immigrants	% Immigrants
Michoacan	4,775	20.0
Guanajuato	4,659	19.6
Jalisco	3,507	14.7
Nuevo León	1,913	8.0
Durango	1,400	5.9
Distrito Federal	1,196	5.0
Zacatecas	1,140	4.8
Chihuahua	1,046	4.4
Coahuila	903	3.8
San Luis Potosi	869	3.7
Tamaulipas	484	2.1
Sinaloa	473	2.0
Aguascalientes	462	1.9
Sonora	294	1.2
Baja California	115	0.5
Puebla	78	0.3
Yucatán	78	0.3
Mexico	66	0.3
Querétaro	58	0.2
Guerrero	57	0.2
Colima	55	0.2
Vera Cruz	54	0.2
Nayarit	51	0.2
Oaxaca	48	0.2
Hidalgo	45	0.2
Tlaxcala	13	0.1
Chiapas	2	0
Tabasco	2	0
Campeche	1	0
Morelos	1	0
Quintana Roo	0	0

Map Table 5.1. *Origins of Naturalized Greeks in Utah, 1902–1912*

Place of Origin	No. Citizens	% Citizens
Megara	44	14.33
Tripoli	37	12.05
Argos	21	6.84
Arahova	18	5.86
Levidhi	17	5.54
Stromni	17	5.54
Pireaus	15	4.89
Crete	14	4.56
Leonidion	13	4.23
Korinthos	12	3.91
Akhladhokambos	8	2.61
Samos	8	2.61
Sparta	8	2.61
Ayios Vasilios	7	2.28
Kalavrita	7	2.28
Hania	6	1.95
Khavari	6	1.95
Patras	6	1.95
Vresthena	6	1.95
Kutsopodi	5	1.63
Lesbos	5	1.63
Limnos	5	1.63
Louka	5	1.63
Nauplion	5	1.63
Krikouki	4	1.30
Apanokhori	2	0.65
Kranidi	2	0.65
Glavitsa	1	0.33
Granitsa	1	0.33
Spathi	1	0.33
Vamos	1	0.33

Bibliography

Primary Documents

Archival and Manuscript Collections

George L. Edson Papers, Bancroft Library, University of California at Berkeley.

Manuel Gamio Papers, Bancroft Library, University of California at Berkeley.

Greek Archives, Marriott Library, University of Utah, Salt Lake City, Utah.

Greek Oral History Collection, American West Center, University of Utah, Salt Lake City, Utah.

Greek Oral History Collection, Marriott Library, University of Utah, Salt Lake City, Utah.

Minutes of the Greek Community of Utah, Holy Trinity Greek Orthodox Church, 1905–1913, Salt Lake City, Utah.

Daniel Jackling Papers, Special Collections, Hoover Library, Stanford University, Palo Alto, Calif.

Panhellenic Grocery Company Papers, Utah State Archives, Salt Lake City, Utah.

Southwest Collection, El Paso City Council Minutes, 1901–1907, El Paso Public Library, El Paso, Texas.

William S. Spry Papers, Personal Correspondence Files, Utah State Archives, Salt Lake City, Utah.

Paul S. Taylor Papers, Bancroft Library, University of California at Berkeley.

Utah Copper Company Papers, Marriott Library, University of Utah, Salt Lake City, Utah.

Western Federation of Miners and International Mine, Mill, and Smelter Workers Union Collection, Executive Board Minutes, 1902–1907, University of Colorado at Boulder

Western Federation of Miners Papers, Local 67, Labor and Management Documentation Center, School of Industrial Relations, Cornell University, Ithaca, N.Y.

Newspapers

Baltimore Sun. Baltimore, Md. 1996, 1998.
Corriere del Canada (Italian). Montreal. 1903, 1904.
Deseret Evening News. Salt Lake City, Utah. 1907–1914.
Eastern Utah Advocate. Price, Utah. 1915.
El Paso Times. El Paso, Texas. 1894, 1900, 1903, 1907.
O Ergatis (Greek). Salt Lake City, Utah. 1907, 1908.
To Fos (Greek). Salt Lake City, Utah. 1911.
International Socialist Review. New York. 1912.
El Latino Americano (Spanish). El Paso, Texas. 1891.
Montreal Star. Montreal. 1904, 1905.
New York Call. New York. 1912.
New York Times. New York. 1900, 1903, 1997.
Ogden Evening Standard. Ogden, Utah. 1912.
Pocatello Tribune. Pocatello, Idaho. 1911–1912.
Salt Lake Evening Telegram. Salt Lake City, Utah. 1907, 1912.
Salt Lake Tribune. Salt Lake City, Utah. 1900–1920.
The Voice. Winnipeg, Manitoba. 1903.

Contemporary Periodicals

Charities Magazine. New York. 1894, 1903, 1904.
Engineering and Mining Journal. Salt Lake City, Utah. 1900–1914.
Engineering Magazine. San Francisco, Calif. 1914.
Federal Reporter. Washington, D.C. 1886, 1891, 1895.
Miner's Magazine. Denver, Colo. 1908–1914.
Pacific Reporter. Seattle, Wash. 1917.
Salt Lake Mining Review. Salt Lake City, Utah. 1904–1912.
Scenic Lines Employees' Magazine: Official Railroad Journal of the Denver and Rio Grande-Western Pacific. Denver, Colo. 1917.
Utah Reports. Salt Lake City, Utah. 1902–1920.

Government Documents: State and Local

Bannock County. Records of the 5th District Civil Court. 1910–1915. Bannock County Courthouse, Pocatello, Idaho.
Bingham Canyon. Public Records Collection. 1901–1923. Utah State Archives, Salt Lake City, Utah.
Borough of Manhattan. Records of Municipal Licenses. 1920–1950. New York Public Library, New York.
District of Montreal. Records of the Superior Court. 1900–1924. Canadian National Archives, Montreal.

El Paso. City Council Minutes. 1901-1907. Southwest Collections, El Paso Public
     Library, El Paso, Texas.
     City Directory. 1893–1963, El Paso Public Library, El Paso, Texas.
El Paso County. Naturalization Files, 1900–1910. El Paso County Courthouse, El
     Paso, Texas.
     Records of the 37th and 65th Districts Civil Court. 1905–1925. El Paso County
     Courthouse, El Paso, Texas.
Montreal. *Lowell's Montreal City Directory.* 1894–1927. Canadian National
     Archives, Montreal.
Salt Lake County. Naturalization Files. 1905–1920. Utah State Archives, Salt
     Lake City, Utah.
     Records of the 3rd District Civil Court. 1900–1920. Utah State Archives, Salt
     Lake City, Utah.
State of Connecticut. *House Journal.* Storrs, Conn. 1865.
State of Idaho. Records of the Bannock County Civil District Court. 1919. Ban-
     nock County Courthouse, Pocatello, Idaho.
State of Illinois. Bureau of Labor Statistics. *Third Annual Report of the Illinois
     Free Employment Offices, 1901.* Springfield, Ill. 1902.
State of Maryland. Records of the U.S. District Civil Court. 1991–1996. U.S. Dis-
     trict Courthouse, Baltimore, Maryland.
State of New York. *Report of the New York State Industrial Survey Commission.*
     New York, 1930.
     *Second Annual Report of the New York State Bureau of Industries and Immi-
     gration.* New York, 1912.
State of Utah. *Eighth Annual Report of the Bureau of Statistics.* Salt Lake City, 1910.
     Records of the Utah Supreme Court. 1908, 1917, 1919. Utah State Archives,
     Salt Lake City, Utah.
State of Washington. Records of the Washington Supreme Court. Washington
     State Archives, Spokane, Wash.
Town of Bingham Canyon. Criminal Dockets, 1908–1915. Utah State Archives,
     Salt Lake City, Utah.
     Ledger, 1908–1913. Utah State Archives, Salt Lake City, Utah.
     Register of Actions, Bingham Police Department, 1911–1912. Utah State
     Archives, Salt Lake City, Utah.

Government Documents: National

Canadian Department of Labour. *Royal Commission Appointed to Inquire into the
     Immigration of Italian Labourers to Montreal and the Alleged Fraudulent
     Practices of Employment Agents.* Ottawa, 1905.
     Records of the Royal Commission's Investigation. RG 33/99, microfiche 3473,
     Canadian National Archives, Ottawa.
Canadian Parliament. *Revised Statutes of Canada.* Ottawa, 1886.
Koren, John. *The Padrone System and Padrone Banks.* Washington, D.C.: U.S.
     Department of Labor Bulletin 9, 1897.

Sheridan, Frank. *Italian, Slav, and Hungarian Unskilled Immigrant Laborers in the United States*. Washington, D.C.: U.S. Department of Labor Bulletin 72, 1907.

U.S. Bureau of Immigration. *The Braun Report*. Immigration Subject Correspondence, file 52320/47. Record Group 85. National Archives, Washington, D.C.

    Contract Labor Violations. Port of Philadelphia, Record Group 85. National Archives, Philadelphia Branch.

    Immigration Subject Correspondence, Commissioner General of Immigration, 1903–1920. Record Group 85. National Archives, Washington, D.C.

    Records of the Office of the Commissioner of Immigration. Port of Philadelphia, Record Group 85. National Archives, Philadelphia Branch.

    Records of the Special Board of Inquiry, 1894–1907. Port of Philadelphia, Record Group 85. Reels 1–16. National Archives, Washington, D.C.

The Stone Report. Immigration Subject Correspondence, files 52546/31A and 52546/31B, box 125. Record Group 85. National Archives, Washington, D.C.

U.S. Bureau of the Census. *Twelfth Census of the United States, 1900. Population Schedules*. Salt Lake County, Utah.

    Thirteenth Census of the United States, 1910. Population Schedules. Salt Lake County, Utah.

U.S. Congress. House. *Congressional Record*. 38th Congress, 1st session, Chapter 246, July 4, 1864.

    House. *Congressional Record*. 43rd Congress, 1st session, June 1, 1874.

    House. *Ford Committee on Contract Labor Violations*. 49th Congress, 1st session, 1888.

    House. *Congressional Record*. 51st Congress, 1st session, 1890. Ex. Doc. 206.

    House. *U.S. Immigration Commission Report on European Immigration*. 52nd Congress, 2nd session, 1893.

    House. *Congressional Record*. 57th Congress, 2nd session, 1903. Chapter 1012.

    House. *Reports of the U.S. Industrial Commission*. 56th Congress, 2nd session, 1901. Vol. 15.

    House. *U.S. Committee on Immigration and Naturalization*. 67th Congress, 1st session, 1921.

    Senate. *Senate Miscellaneous Document*. 38th Congress, 2nd session, 1864. H. Doc. 13.

    Senate. *Report of the Joint Special Committee to Investigate Chinese Immigration*. 44th Congress, 1st session, 1877.

    Senate. *Congressional Record*. 48th Congress, 2nd session, February 26, 1885. Chapter 164.

    Senate. *Congressional Record*. 53rd Congress, 2nd session, June 20, 1894. Ex. Doc. 114.

    Senate. *The Dillingham Commission: Immigrants in Industries*. Vols. 1 and 2. 61st Congress, 2nd session, 1911. Doc.633.

U.S. Department of Justice. Straight Numerical Files. Record Group 60. National
    Archives, Washington, D.C.
U.S. Department of Immigration and Naturalization. Steamship Manifest Lists.
    Port of New York. Record Group 85. National Archives, Washington, D.C.
U.S. Department of State. Central Files. Record Group 60. National Archives,
    Washington, D.C.

Published Books, Autobiographies, and Reminiscences

Adelphotis Arahoviton. *The Adelphotis Arahoviton "Karyae."* New York: Ana-
    tolia Press, 1951.
Alger, Horatio, Jr. *Phil, The Fiddler; or, The Story of a Young Street Musician.*
    Boston: Loring, 1872.
Brandenburg, Broughton. *Imported Americans: The Story of the Experiences of a
    Disguised American and His Wife Studying the Immigration Question.* New
    York: F. A. Stokes, 1904.
Canadian Pacific Railway Company. *The Annual Reports of the Canadian Pacific
    Railway Corporation, 1894–1912.* Montreal: Canadian Pacific Railway,
    1894–1912.
Ciolli, Dominic. "The 'Wop' in the Track Gang," *Immigrants in America Review*
    (July 1916), in Wayne Moquin and Charles Van Doren, eds., *A Documentary
    History of the Italian Americans,* 141–145. New York: Praeger, 1974.
Corresca, Rocco. "The Biography of a Bootblack," *Independent* 5:4 (December 4,
    1902): 2863–2867.
Cozzolino, Thomas. "Tramping and Contracting: An Italian Gang Boss of 1901,"
    in Irving Abella and David Millar, eds., *The Canadian Worker in the Twenti-
    eth Century,* 3–9. Toronto: Oxford University Press, 1981.
Economou, Maria. *Oi Ellines opus tous eida* (The Greeks as I saw them). New
    York: D. C. Divry, 1916.
Gamio, Manuel. *The Mexican Immigrant: His Life Story.* Chicago: University of
    Chicago Press, 1931.
Georgedes, Angelo, *Reminiscences of Life and Moving to America.* Madison:
    State Historical Society of Wisconsin, 1973.
Greek Community of Utah. *By-laws of the Greek Community of Utah.* Salt Lake
    City: Holy Trinity Greek Orthodox Church, 1905.
Industrial Removal Organization. *Annual Reports of the Industrial Removal
    Office.* New York: Industrial Removal Office, 1900–1910.
Italian Immigration Aid Society. *Bollettino della Societa di Patronate Dell' Immi-
    grazione Italiana in Canada Montreal* (Bulletin of the Italian Immigration
    Aid Society). Montreal: Italian Immigration Aid Society, 1903.
    Constitution of the Italian Immigration Society for Canada in Montreal.
    Montreal: Italian Immigration Aid Society, 1902.
    First Annual Report of the Italian Emigration Aid Society for Canada.
    Montreal: Italian Immigration Aid Society, 1904.

Kyranakos, George P. *Biography of George P. Kyranakos from K. Stania Vion, Greece*. Salt Lake City, 1912.

National Consumers League. *Job Brokers Unlimited: The Need for Federal Regulation of Private Employment Agencies Engaged in Interstate Placement*. Washington, D.C.: American Association of Labor Legislation, 1941.

National Employment Exchange. *Annual Reports of the National Employment Exchange, First Edition*. New York, 1910. *Annual Reports of the National Employment Exchange, Sixteenth Edition*. New York, 1926.

Panunzio, Constantine. *The Soul of an Immigrant*. New York: Macmillan, 1921.

Powderly, Terence. *Thirty Years of Labor*. Columbus, Ohio: 1890.

Rizzo, Saverio. "Biography," in Salvatore LaGumina, ed., *The Immigrants Speak: Italian Americans Tell Their Story*, 5–24. New York: Center for Migration Studies, 1979.

Simboli, Cesidio. "When the Boss Went Too Far," *World Outlook* (October 1917), in Wayne Moquin with Charles Van Doren, eds., *A Documentary History of Italian Americans*, 146–149. New York: Praeger, 1974.

Twain, Mark. *The Adventures of Huckleberry Finn*. New York: Oxford University Press, 1996.

Unpublished Autobiographies and Oral Histories

Anton, Theodore. Salt Lake City, January 28, 1971, interview by Theodore Paulos. Greek Archives, University of Utah.

Argentos, Peter. Salt Lake City, December 4, 1974, interview by Louis Cononelos. American West Center, University of Utah.

Armijo, Charles. El Paso, Texas, 1971, interview by Leon Metz, David Salazar, and Christina Garcia. Institute of Oral History, University of Texas at El Paso.

Avrantinis, Harry. Salt Lake City, November 10, 1971, interview by Theodore Paulos. Greek Archives, University of Utah.

Bapis, Michael. Salt Lake City, January 25, 1973, interview by Georgiana Angelos. Greek Archives, University of Utah.

Biakakis, Mrs. Mae Pappas. Salt Lake City, November 26, 1977, interview by Helen Papanikolas. Greek Archives, University of Utah.

Borovilos, Paul. Salt Lake City, April 1, 1970, interview by Helen Papanikolas. American West Center, University of Utah.

Calleros, Cleofas. El Paso, September 14, 1972, interview by Oscar Martinez. Insitutute of Oral History, University of Texas at El Paso.

Cayias, George. Salt Lake City, July 16, 1972, interview by Helen Papanikolas. Greek Archives, University of Utah.

Chipianos, Anastacio. Salt Lake City, July 1, 1974, interview by Louis Cononelos. American West Center, University of Utah.

Cononelos, Nina. Salt Lake City, June 27, 1974, interview by Louis Cononelos. American West Center, University of Utah.

Demeris, John. Salt Lake City, May 4, 1974, interview by Louis Cononelos. Greek
    Archives, University of Utah.

Demiris, Peter. Salt Lake City, June 30, 1972, interview by Helen Papanikolas.
    Greek Archives, University of Utah.

Galanis, James. Salt Lake City, March 1974, interview by Louis Cononelos, Greek
    Archives, University of Utah.

Gigounakis, George. Salt Lake City, July 25, 1974, interview by Louis Cononelos.
    Greek Archives, University of Utah.

Greaves, Harry. Salt Lake City, June 1, 1973, interview by Helen Papanikolas.
    American West Center, University of Utah.

Jerefos, Nick and Katherine. Salt Lake City, September 8, 1973, interview by
    Helen Papanikolas and Georgia Angelos. American West Center, University
    of Utah.

Kalaides, Steve. Salt Lake City, March 22, 1973, interview by Helen Papanikolas.
    Greek Archives, University of Utah.

Kambouris, Haralambos. "Pages of My Life and Various Poems: My Leaving for
    Greece and My Sojourn in America." September 1912 – January 1915. Greek
    Archives, University of Utah.

Kastanis, Mrs. Isidore. Salt Lake City, March 2, 1973, interview by Helen
    Papanikolas. American West Center, University of Utah.

Korobas, James. Salt Lake City, October 3, 1974, interview by Louis Cononelos.
    Greek Archives, University of Utah.

Kotsovos, John. Salt Lake City, September 19, 1974, interview by Louis Conone-
    los. American West Center, University of Utah.

Kouris, Gus. Salt Lake City, April 27, 1973, interview by Helen Papanikolas.
    American West Center, University of Utah.

Lamb, George. Salt Lake City, September 3, 1972, interview by Helen Papaniko-
    las. Greek Archives, University of Utah.

Leonudakis, George. Salt Lake City, June 28, 1974, interview by Louis Conone-
    los. American West Center, University of Utah.

Lingos, Louis. Salt Lake City, April 9, 1970, interview by Helen Papanikolas.
    American West Center, University of Utah.

Mantos, John Harry. Salt Lake City, December 9, 1974, interview by Louis
    Cononelos. American West Center, University of Utah.

Marganis, Theodore. Salt Lake City, May 4, 1974, interview by Louis Cononelos.
    Greek Archives, University of Utah.

Maverakis, Immanuel. Salt Lake City, January 4, 1973, interview by Georgia
    Angelos. American West Center, University of Utah.

Miles, Harry. Salt Lake City, August 10, 1970, interview by Helen Papanikolas.
    Greek Archives, University of Utah.

Pallios, Mrs. Stellios. Salt Lake City, March 2, 1973, interview by Helen
    Papanikolas. American West Center, University of Utah.

Papadikas, Gus. Salt Lake City, August 29, 1973, interview by Zeese Papanikolas.
    American West Center, University of Utah.

Papanikolas, George, Salt Lake City, December 2, 1974, interview by Louis
    Cononelos. American West Center, University of Utah.
Papoulis, John, Salt Lake City, April 10, 1972, interview by Helen Papanikolas.
    American West Center, University of Utah.
Poulos, Peter John. Salt Lake City, July 2, 1976, interview by Louis Cononelos.
    Greek Archives, University of Utah.
Rondoyiannis, Samuel. Salt Lake City, September 30, 1974, interview by Louis
    Cononelos. Greek Archives, University of Utah.
Tallas, Jack. Salt Lake City, January 18, 1971, interview by Theodore Paulos.
    Greek Archives, University of Utah.
Velisaropoulos, James. Salt Lake City, December 11, 1974, interview by Louis
    Cononelos. American West Center, University of Utah.
Zekas, John. Salt Lake City, June 17, 1973, interview by Helen Papanikolas.
    American West Center, University of Utah.

Secondary Sources

Books and Articles

Abbott, Edith, ed. *Immigration: Select Documents and Case Records*. Chicago:
    University of Chicago Press, 1924.
Abbott, Grace. "The Chicago Employment Agency and the Immigrant Worker,"
    American Journal of Sociology 14:3 (November 1908): 296–305.
    "Railroad Gangs," in *Report of the Mayor's Commission on Unemployment*.
    Chicago: 1914.
Abella, Irving, and David Millar, eds. *The Canadian Worker in the Twentieth Cen-
    tury*. Toronto: Oxford University Press, 1981.
Alexiou, Margaret. "Sons, Wives, and Mothers: Reality and Fantasy in Some
    Modern Greek Ballads," *Journal of Greek Studies* 1:1 (1983): 73–111.
Allen, James B. *The Company Town in the American West*. Norman: University of
    Oklahoma Press, 1966.
Allen, Theodore. *The Invention of the White Race*. Vol. 1. London: Verso, 1994.
Almaguer, Tomas. *Racial Fault Lines: The Historical Origins of White Supremacy
    in California*. Berkeley: University of California Press, 1994.
Anderson, Benedict. *Imagined Communities: Reflections on the Origin and
    Spread of Nationalism*. London: Verso, 1983.
Anderson, Henry P. *The Bracero Program in California*. New York: Arno Press,
    1976.
Anderson, Nels. *The Hobo: The Sociology of the Homeless Man*. Chicago: Uni-
    versity of Chicago Press, 1923.
    Men on the Move. Chicago: University of Chicago Press, 1940.
Archdeacon, Thomas. *Becoming American: An Ethnic History*. New York: Free
    Press, 1983.
Arnesen, Eric. "'Like Banquo's Ghost, It Will Not Down': The Race Question and

the American Railroad Brotherhoods," *American Historical Review* 99 (December 1994): 1601–1634.

Waterfront Workers of New Orleans: Race, Class, and Politics, 1863–1923. New York: Oxford, 1991.

Arrington, Leonard. *The Richest Hole on Earth: A History of the Bingham Copper Mine.* Logan: Utah State University Press, 1963.

Avery, Donald. *"Dangerous Foreigners": European Immigrant Workers and Labour Radicalism in Canada, 1896–1932.* Toronto: McClelland and Stewart, 1979.

Reluctant Host: Canada's Response to Immigrant Workers, 1896–1914. Toronto: McGill & Stewart, 1995.

Baily, Samuel, and Frank Ramella. *One Family, Two Worlds: An Italian Family's Correspondence across the Atlantic, 1901–1922.* New Brunswick: Rutgers University Press, 1988.

Bakhtin, Mikhail. *The Dialogic Imagination: Four Essays.* Austin: University of Texas Press, 1981.

Banfield, Edward C. *The Moral Basis of a Backward Society.* Glencoe, Ill., 1958.

Barbagli, Mazio, and David Kertzer. "An Introduction to the History of Italian Family Life," *Journal of Family History* 15:4 (1990): 369–383.

Baron, Ava. "Gender and Labor History," in Ava Baron, ed. *Work Engendered: Toward a New History of American Labor*, 1–47. Ithaca: Cornell University Press, 1991.

Barrera, Mario. *Race and Class in the Southwest: A Theory of Racial Inequality.* Notre Dame: University of Notre Dame Press, 1979.

Barrett, James R. "Americanization from the Bottom Up: Immigration and the Remaking of the Working Class in the United States, 1880–1930," *Journal of American History* 79:3 (December 1992): 996–1021.

Work and Community in the Jungle: Chicago's Packinghouse Workers, 1894–1922. Urbana: University of Illinois Press, 1987.

Barton, Josef F. *Peasants and Strangers: Italians, Rumanians, and Slovaks in an American City, 1890–1950.* Cambridge, Mass.: Harvard University Press, 1975.

Basler, Roy F., et al. eds., *The Collected Works of Abraham Lincoln.* New Brunswick: Rutgers University Press, 1953.

Bauer, Arnold. "Rural Workers in Spanish America: Problems of Peonage and Oppression," *American Historical Review* 59:1 (1979): 34–63.

Baxevanis, John. "Population, Internal Migration, and Urbanization in Greece," *Balkan Studies* 6 (1965): 83–98.

Bederman, Gail. *Manliness and Civilization: A Cultural History of Gender and Race in the United States, 1880–1917.* Chicago: University of Chicago Press, 1995.

Beese, Susan K. *Restructuring Patriarchy: The Modernization of Gender Inequality in Brazil, 1914–1940.* Chapel Hill: University of North Carolina Press, 1996.

Bell, Rudolph. *Fate and Honor, Family and Village: Demographic and Cultural Change in Rural Italy since 1800.* Chicago: University of Chicago Press, 1979.

Bennett, John W., and Seena B. Kohl. *Settling the Canadian-American West, 1890–1915: Pioneer Adaptation and Community Building, an Anthropological History.* Lincoln: University of Nebraska Press, 1995.

Bercuson, David J. *Fools and Wise Men: The Rise and Fall of One Big Union.* Toronto: University of Toronto Press, 1978.

Bernstein, Iver. *The New York City Draft Riots: Their Significance for American Society and Politics in the Age of the Civil War.* New York: Oxford University Press, 1990.

Bilbao, Jon, and William A. Douglass. *Amerikanuak: Basques in the New World.* Reno: University of Nevada Press, 1975.

Blewett, Mary H. *Men, Women, and Work: Class, Gender, and Protest in the New England Shoe Industry.* Urbana: University of Illinois Press, 1988.

Blok, Anton. *The Mafia of a Sicilian Village, 1860–1960: A Study of Violent Peasant Entrepreneurs.* New York: Harper and Rowe, 1974.

Bobeck, Hans. "The Main Stages in Socio-Economic Evolution from a Geographical Point of View," in Philip Wagner and Marvin Mikesell, eds., *Readings in Cultural Geography*, 218–247. Chicago: University of Chicago Press, 1962.

Bodnar, John. *The Transplanted: A History of Immigrants in Urban America.* Bloomington: Indiana University Press, 1985.

Bodnar, John, Roger Simon, and Michael Weber. *Lives of Their Own: Blacks, Italians, and Poles in Pittsburgh, 1900–1960.* Urbana: University of Illinois Press, 1982.

Bonacich, Edna. "A Theory of Ethnic Antagonism: The Split Labor Market," *American Sociological Review* 37 (1972): 574–579.

"A Theory of Middlemen Minorities," *American Sociological Review* 38 (1973): 583–594.

Bonacich, Edna, and Ivan Light. *Immigrant Entrepreneurs: Koreans in Los Angeles, 1965–1982.* Berkeley: University of California Press, 1988.

Boris, Eileen, and Cynthia Daniels. *Homework: Historical and Contemporary Perspectives on Paid Labor at Home.* Urbana: University of Illinois Press, 1989.

Bowman, Shearer Davis. *Masters and Lords: Mid-19th-Century U.S. Planters and Prussian Junkers.* New York: Oxford University Press, 1993.

Boydston, Jeanne. *Home and Work: Housework, Wages, and the Ideology of Labor in the Early Republic.* New York: Oxford University Press, 1990.

"To Earn Her Daily Bread: Housework and Antebellum Working-Class Subsistence," *Radical History Review* 35 (April 1986): 7–25.

Boyer, Paul. *Urban Masses and Moral Order in America, 1820–1920.* Cambridge, Mass.: Harvard University Press, 1978.

Brading, David A. *Haciendas and Ranchoes in the Mexican Bajio: 1700–1860.* Cambridge: Cambridge University Press, 1978.

Braverman, Harry. *Labor and Monopoly Capital: The Degradation of Work in the Twentieth Century*. New York: Monthly Review Press, 1974.

Briggs, John. *An Italian Passage: Immigrants to Three American Cities, 1890–1930*. New Haven: Yale University Press, 1979.

Bristow, Edward J. *Prostitution and Prejudice: The Jewish Fight against White Slavery, 1870–1939*. Oxford: Clarendon Press, 1982.

Buder, Stanley. *Pullman: An Experiment in Industrial Order and Community Planning, 1880–1930*. New York: Oxford University Press, 1967.

Butler, Ann. *Daughters of Joy, Sisters of Mercy: Prostitution in the American West, 1865–1900*. Urbana: University of Illinois Press, 1985.

Butler, Judith. *Gender Trouble: Feminism and the Subversion of Identity*. New York: Routledge, 1990.

Cafantzoglou, Roxanne. "The Household Formation Pattern of a Vlach Mountain Community of Greece: Syrako, 1898–1929," *Journal of Family History* 19:1 (1994): 79–98.

Calavita, Kitty. *Inside the State: The Bracero Program, Immigration, and the I.N.S.* New York: Routledge, 1992.

U.S. Immigration Law and the Control of Labor, 1820–1924. London: Academic Press, 1984.

Camarillo, Albert. *Chicanos in a Changing Society: From Mexican Pueblos to American Barrios in Santa Barbara and Southern California, 1848–1930*. Cambridge, Mass.: Harvard University Press, 1979.

Campbell, John. *Honour, Family, and Patronage: A Study of Institutions and Moral Values in a Greek Mountain Community*. New York: Oxford University Press, 1964.

Cardoso, Lawrence. *Mexican Emigration to the United States, 1897–1931: Socio-Economic Patterns*. Tucson: University of Arizona Press, 1987.

Careless, J. M. S. *Frontier and Metropolis: Regions, Cities, and Identities in Canada before 1914*. Toronto: University of Toronto Press, 1989.

Carnes, Mark C. *Secret Ritual and Manhood in Victorian America*. New Haven: Yale University Press, 1989.

Cassavetti, Demetrius John. *Hellas and the Balkan Wars*. New York: Dodd, Mead, 1914.

Castillo, Richard Griswold del. *La Familia: Chicano Families in the Urban Southwest, 1848–Present*. South Bend: University of Notre Dame Press, 1984.

Chambers, Iain. *Migrancy, Culture, Identity*. London: Routledge, 1994.

Chan, Suchen. *Asian Americans: An Interpretive History*. Boston: Twayne, 1991.

Chandler, Alfred. *The Visible Hand: The Managerial Revolution in American Business*. Cambridge, Mass.: Belknap Press, 1977.

Chauncey, George. *Gay New York: Gender, Urban Culture, and the Making of the Gay Male World, 1890–1940*. New York: Basic Books, 1994.

Cheng, Lucie, and Edna Bonacich, eds. *Labor Immigration under Capitalism: Asian Workers in the U.S. before World War II*. Berkeley: University of California Press, 1984.

Chevalier, François. *Land and Society in Colonial Mexico: The Great Hacienda*. Berkeley: University of California Press, 1963.

Cinel, Dino. *From Italy to San Francisco: The Immigrant Experience*. Stanford: Stanford University Press, 1982.

　The National Integration of Italian Return Migration, 1870–1929. Cambridge: Cambridge University Press, 1991.

　"The Seasonal Emigration of Italians in the Nineteenth Century: From Internal to International Destinations," *Journal of Ethnic Studies* 19 (1982): 43–69.

Clawson, Mary Ann. *Constructing Brotherhood: Class, Gender and Fraternalism*. Princeton: Princeton University Press, 1989.

Cletus, Daniel. *Bitter Harvest: A History of California Farmworkers, 1870–1941*. Ithaca: Cornell University Press, 1981.

Clogg, Richard. *A Concise History of Greece*. Cambridge: Cambridge University Press, 1992.

Coatsworth, John. "Obstacles to Economic Growth in Nineteenth-Century Mexico," *American Historical Review* 83 (1978): 80–100.

Cobble, Dorothy Sue. *Dishing It Out: Waitresses and Their Unions in the Twentieth Century*. Urbana: University of Illinois Press, 1991.

Coffin, Judith. *The Politics of Women's Work: The Paris Garment Trades, 1750–1915*. Princeton: Princeton University Press, 1996.

Cohen, Lizabeth. *Making a New Deal: Industrial Workers in Chicago, 1919–1939*. Cambridge: Cambridge University Press, 1990.

Cohen, Lucy M. *Chinese in the Post-Civil War South: A People without a History*. Baton Rouge: Louisiana State University Press, 1984.

Collomp, Catherine. "Unions, Civics, and National Identity: Organized Labor's Reaction to Immigration, 1881–1897," in Marianne Debouzy, ed., *In the Shadow of the Statue of Liberty: Immigrants, Workers, and Citizens in the American Republic, 1880–1920*, 229–256. Urbana: University of Illinois Press, 1992.

Commons, John R. *A History of Labor in the United States*. Vols. 3 and 4. New York: Macmillan, 1935.

Con, Harry. *From China to Canada: A History of the Chinese Communities in Canada*. Toronto: McClelland and Stewart, 1982.

Conlin, Joseph. *Bread and Roses Too: Studies of the Wobblies*. Westport, Conn.: Greenwood Publishers, 1969.

Consulo, Ronald S. *Italian Nationalism: From Its Origins to World War II*. Malabar, Fla.: R. E. Krieger, 1990.

Coolidge, Mary. *Chinese Immigration*. New York: Holt & Rinehart, 1909.

Cooper, Patricia. *Once a Cigar Maker: Men, Women, and Work Culture in American Cigar Factories, 1900–1919*. Urbana: University of Illinois Press, 1987.

　"'Travelling Fraternity': Union Cigar Makers and Geographic Mobility, 1900–1919," in Eric Monkkonen, ed., *Walking to Work: Tramps in America, 1790–1935*, 118–138. Lincoln: University of Nebraska Press, 1984.

Courtwright, David T. *Violent Land: Single Men and Social Disorder from the*

Frontier to the Inner City. Cambridge, Mass.: Harvard University Press, 1996.

Cowie, Jefferson R. *Capital Moves: RCA's Seventy-Year Quest for Cheap Labor*. Ithaca: Cornell University Press, 1999.

Crew, David. *Town in the Ruhr: A Social History of Bochum, 1860–1914*. New York: Columbia University Press, 1979.

Cronon, William. "Kennecott Journey: The Paths out of Town," in William Cronon, George Miles, and Jay Gitlin, eds., *Under An Open Sky: Rethinking America's Western Past*, 28–51. New York: Norton, 1992.

Nature's Metropolis: Chicago and the Great West. New York: Norton, 1991.

"Revisiting the Vanishing Frontier: The Legacy of Frederick Jackson Turner," *Western Historical Quarterly* 18:2 (April 1987): 157–176.

Daniels, Pete. *The Shadow of Slavery: Peonage in the South, 1901–1969*. Urbana: University of Illinois Press, 1972.

Davis, John A. *Land and Family in Pisticci*. London: Athlone Press, 1973.

Merchants, Monopolists, and Contractors: A Study of Economic Activity and Society in Bourbon Naples, 1815–1860. New York: Arno, 1981.

People of the Mediterranean. London: Routledge, 1977.

Davis, Mike. *City of Quartz: Excavating the Future in Los Angeles*. London: Verso, 1990.

De Caux, Len. *The Living Spirit of the Wobblies*. New York: International Publishers, 1978.

Deutsch, Sarah. *No Separate Refuge: Culture, Class, and Gender on an Anglo-Hispanic Frontier in the American Southwest, 1880–1940*. New York: Oxford, 1987.

Docker, Edward Wybergh. *The Blackbirders: The Recruiting of South Seas Labor for Queensland, 1883–1907*. Sydney: Angus & Robertson, 1970.

Douglass, William A. *Emigration in a South Italian Town: An Anthropological History*. New Brunswick: Rutgers University Press, 1984.

Dubisch, Jill. "Gender, Kinship, and Religion: Reconstructing the Anthropology of Greece," in Peter Loizos and Evthymios Papataxiarchis, eds., *Contested Identities: Gender and Kinship in Modern Greece*, 29–46. Princeton: Princeton University Press, 1991.

Dubofsky, Melvyn. "The Origins of the Western Working Class, 1890-1905," *Labor History* 7 (Spring 1966): 131–154.

The State and Labor in Modern America. Chapel Hill: University of North Carolina Press, 1994.

We Shall Be All: A History of the Industrial Workers of the World. Chicago: Quadrangle Books, 1969.

Du Boulay, Juliet. "The Meaning of Dowry: Changing Values in Rural Greece," *Journal of Modern Greek Studies* 1:1 (1984): 243–270.

Portrait of a Greek Mountain Village. Oxford: Oxford University Press, 1974.

Dumenil, Lynn. *Freemasonry and American Culture, 1880–1939*. Princeton: Princeton University Press, 1984.

Dykstra, Robert. *The Cattle Towns*. New York: Knopf, 1968.

"Field: Overdosing on Dodge City," *Western Historical Quarterly* 27 (Winter 1996): 505–514.

Eagle, John A. *The Canadian Pacific Railway and the Development of Western Canada*. Montreal: McGill-Queens' University Press 1989.

Edelman, Murray. *Constructing the Political Spectacle*. Chicago: University of Chicago Press, 1988.

The Symbolic Uses of Politics. Urbana: University of Illinois Press, 1964.

Edwards, Richard, David Gordon, and Michael Reich. *Segmented Work, Divided Workers: The Historical Transformation of Labor in the United States*. Cambridge: Cambridge University Press, 1982.

Emmons, David. *The Butte Irish: Class and Ethnicity in an American Mining Town, 1875–1925*. Urbana: University of Illinois Press, 1989.

Erikson, Charlotte. *American Industry and the European Immigrant, 1860–1885*. Cambridge, Mass.: Harvard University Press, 1957.

Ernst, Morris L. *Public Employment Exchanges: Report of the Committee Appointed by the Trustees of the City Club of New York on December 17, 1913 "to inquire into the need of public employment exchanges in New York"*. New York: City Club of New York, 1914.

Fabian, Ann. *Card Sharps, Dream Books, and Bucket Shops: Gambling in Nineteenth-Century America*. Ithaca: Cornell University Press, 1990.

Faragher, John Mack. "Americans, Mexicans, Metis: A Community Approach to the Comparative Study of North American Frontiers," in William Cronon, George Miles, and Jay Gitlin, eds., *Under An Open Sky: Rethinking America's Western Past*, 90–109. New York: Norton, 1992.

Feiss, Richard A. "Personal Relationship as a Basis for Scientific Management," *Bulletin of the Society to Promote the Science of Management* 1 (1914): 6.

Fenton, Edwin. *Immigrants and Unions, a Case Study: Italians and American Labor, 1870–1920*. New York: Arno, 1975.

Fermor, Patrick Leigh. *Mani: Travels in the Southern Peloponnese*. New York: Harper, 1958.

Ferraro, Thomas J. "Blood in the Marketplace: The Business of Family in the Godfather Narratives," in Werner Sollors, ed., *The Invention of Ethnicity*, 176–207. Oxford: Oxford University Press, 1990.

Fink, Leon. "The New Labor History and the Powers of Historical Pessimism: Consensus, Hegemony, and the Case of the Knights of Labor," *Journal of American History* 75 (June 1989): 115–136.

Workingmen's Democracy: The Knights of Labor and American Politics. Urbana: University of Illinois Press, 1983.

Flamming, Douglas. *Creating the Modern South: Millhands and Managers in Dalton, Georgia, 1884–1984*. Chapel Hill: University of North Carolina Press, 1992.

Flower, Juliet. *The Regime of the Brother: After the Patriarchy*. London: Routledge, 1991.

Foerster, Robin. *The Italian Emigration of Our Times*. Cambridge, Mass.: Harvard University Press, 1919.

Foley, Neil. *The White Scourge: Mexicans, Blacks, and Poor Whites in Texas Cotton Culture*. Berkeley: University of California Press, 1997.

Foner, Eric. *Free Soil, Free Labor, Free Men: The Ideology of the Republican Party before the Civil War*. New York: Oxford University Press, 1970.

Nothing but Freedom: Emancipation and Its Legacy. Baton Rouge: Louisiana State University, 1983.

The Story of American Freedom. New York: Norton, 1998.

"Why Is There No Socialism in the United States?" *History Workshop* 17 (Spring 1984): 57–80.

Foner, Philip. *History of the Labor Movement in the United States: The Industrial Workers of the World, 1905–1917*. Vol. 4. New York: International Publishers, 1965.

Forbath, William. "The Ambiguities of Free Labor: Labor and the Law in the Gilded Age," *Wisconsin Law Review* (1985): 787–809.

Law and the Shaping of the American Labor Movement. Cambridge, Mass.: Harvard University Press, 1991.

Foster, George. "The Dyadic Contact: A Model for the Social Structure of a Mexican Peasant Village," *American Anthropologist* 63:66 (December 1961): 1173–1192.

Friedman, Gerald. "The Decline of Paternalism and the Making of the Employer Class: France, 1870–1914," in Sanford Jacoby, ed., *Masters to Managers: Historical and Comparative Perspectives on American Employers*, 153–172. New York: Columbia University Press, 1991.

Friedman, Lawrence. *Contract Law in America: A Social and Economic Case Study*. Madison: University of Wisconsin Press, 1965.

A History of American Law. New York: Simon & Schuster, 1978.

Gabaccia, Donna Rae. *From Sicily to Elizabeth Street: Housing and Social Change among Italian Immigrants, 1880–1930*. Albany: State University of New York Press, 1984.

Militants and Migrants: Rural Sicilians Become American Workers. New Brunswick: Rutgers University Press, 1987."

"Neither Padrone Slaves, Nor Primitive Rebels," in Dirk Hoerder, ed., *"Struggle a Hard Battle": Essays on Working-Class Immigrants*, 95–117 Dekalb: Northern Illinois University, 1986.

"Worker Internationalism and Italian Labor Migration," *International Labor and Working-Class History* 45 (Spring 1994): 63–79.

Gamio, Manuel. *The Mexican Immigrant, His Life Story: Autobiographic Documents*. Chicago: University of Chicago Press, 1931.

Mexican Immigration to the United States: A Study of Human Migration and Adjustment. Chicago: University of Chicago Press, 1930.

Gans, Herbert. *The Urban Villagers: Group and Class in the Life of Italian Americans*. New York: Free Press, 1962.

Garcia, Mario. *Desert Immigrants: The Mexicans of El Paso, 1880–1920*. New Haven: Yale University Press, 1981.

Genovese, Eugene. *Roll Jordan Roll: The World the Slaves Made*. New York: Pantheon Press, 1974.

Georgakas, Dan. "Greek-American Radicalism: The Twentieth Century," in Dan Georgakas and Paul Buhle, eds., *The Immigrant Left in the United States*. Albany: State University of New York Press, 1996.

ed. *New Directions in Greek American Studies*. New York: Pella Press, 1991.

Gerstle, Gary. *Working-Class Americanism: The Politics of Labor in a Textile City, 1914–1960*. Cambridge: Cambridge University Press, 1989.

Gilfoyle, Timothy J. *City of Eros: New York City, Prostitution, and the Commercialization of Sex, 1820–1920*. New York: Norton, 1992.

Gilmore, David G. "Introduction: The Shame of Dishonor," in David Gilmore, ed., *Honor and Shame and the Unity of the Mediterranean*, 2–21. Washington, D.C.: American Anthropological Association, 1987.

Manhood in the Making: Cultural Concepts of Masculinity. New Haven: Yale University Press, 1990.

Glenn, Susan. *Daughters of the Shtetl: Life and Labor in the Immigrant Generation*. Ithaca: Cornell University Press, 1990.

Glickman, Lawrence. *A Living Wage: American Workers and the Making of Consumer Society*. Ithaca: Cornell University Press, 1997.

Glickstein, Jonathan. *Concepts of Free Labor in Antebellum America*. New Haven: Yale University Press, 1991.

Goldin, Claudia, and Stanley Engerman. *Seasonality in Nineteenth Century Labor Markets*. Cambridge, Mass.: National Bureau of Economic Research, 1990.

Goldman, Marion S. *Gold Diggers and Silver Miners: Prostitution and Social Life on the Comstock Lode*. Ann Arbor: University of Michigan Press, 1981.

Gomez-Izquierdo, José Jorge. *El movimiento antichino en Mexico, 1871–1934: Problemas del racismo y del nacionalismo durante la revolucion Mexicana*. Mexico City: Instituto Nacional de Anthropologia e Historia, 1991.

Gordon, Linda, and Allen Hunter. "Not All Male Dominance is Patriarchal," *Radical History Review* 71 (1998): 71–74.

Gorn, Eliot. *The Manly Art: Bare-Knuckle Prize Fighting in America*. Ithaca: Cornell University Press, 1986.

Graziano, Luigi. "Patron-Client Relationships in Southern Italy," *European Journal of Political Research* 1 (1973): 1–16.

Greene, Victor R. *American Immigrant Leaders, 1800–1910: Marginality and Identity*. Baltimore: Johns Hopkins University Press, 1987.

For God and Country: The Rise of Polish and Lithuanian Ethnic Consciousness in America, 1860–1910. Madison: University of Wisconsin Press, 1975.

Gregory, Derek. *Geographical Imaginations*. Cambridge: Blackwell, 1994.

Griffen, Clyde, and Mark Carnes, eds. *Meanings for Manhood: Constructions of Masculinity in Victorian America*. Chicago: University of Chicago Press, 1990.

Griffis, Ken. *Hear My Song: The Story of the Celebrated Sons of the Pioneers*. Camarillo, Calif.: Norken, 1994.

Grittner, Frederick K. *White Slavery: Myth, Ideology, and American Law*. New York: Garland, 1990.

Guerin-Gonzalez, Camille. *Mexican Workers and American Dreams: Immigration, Repatriation, and California Farm Labor, 1900–1939*. New Brunswick: Rutgers University Press, 1994.

Gutierrez, David. *Walls and Mirrors: Mexican Americans, Mexican Immigrants, and the Politics of Identity*. Berkeley: University of California Press, 1995.

Gutierrez, Ramon. *When Jesus Came, the Corn Mothers Went Away: Marriage, Sexuality, and Power in New Mexico, 1500–1846*. Stanford: Stanford University Press, 1991.

Gutman, Herbert. *Work, Culture, and Society in Industrializing America: Essays in American Working-Class and Social History*. New York: Knopf, 1976.

Haag, Pamela. "'The Ill-Use of a Wife': Working-Class Violence in Domestic and Public New York City, 1860–1880," *Journal of Social History* 25:3 (Spring 1992): 447–478.

Hahamovitch, Cindy. *The Fruits of Their Labor: Atlantic Coast Farmworkers and the Making of Migrant Poverty, 1870–1945*. Chapel Hill: University of North Carolina Press, 1997.

Hall, Jacquelyn, James Leloudis, Robert Korstad, Mary Murphy, Lu Ann Jones, and Christopher B. Daly. *Like a Family: The Making of a Southern Cotton Mill World*. Chapel Hill: University of North Carolina Press, 1987.

Hardwick, Julie. *The Practice of Patriarchy: Gender and the Politics of Household Authority in Early Modern France*. University Station: Pennsylvania State University Press, 1998.

Hareven, Tamara, and Randolph Langenbach. *Amoskeag: Life and Work in an American Factory-City*. New York: Pantheon Books, 1978.

Harney, Robert. "The Commerce of Migration," *Canadian and Ethnic Studies* 9:1 (1977): 42–53.

"Montreal's King of Italian Labour: A Case Study of Padronism," *Labour/Le Travailleur* 4(1979): 57–84.

"The Padrone and the Immigrant," *Canadian Review of American Studies* 5(1974): 100–118.

Harrison, Shelby M. *Public Employment Offices: Their Purpose, Structure, and Methods*. New York: Russell Sage Foundation, 1924.

Hart, John M. *Revolutionary Mexico: The Coming and Process of the Mexican Revolution*. Berkeley: University of California Press, 1987.

Harvey, David. *The Condition of Postmodernity: An Enquiry into the Origins of Cultural Change*. Oxford: Blackwell, 1989.

The Urbanization of Capital: Studies in the History and Theory of Capitalist Urbanization. Baltimore: Johns Hopkins University Press, 1985.

Hattam, Victoria. *Labor Visions and State Power: The Origins of Business Unionism in the United States*. Princeton: Princeton University Press, 1993.

Haywood, William. *Bill Haywood's Book: The Autobiography of William D. Haywood*. New York: International Publishers, 1929.

Hedges, James B. *Building the Canadian West: The Land and Colonization Policies of the Canadian Pacific Railway*. New York: Macmillan, 1939.

Herrera-Sabek, Maria. *The Bracero Experience: Elitelore vs. Folklore*. Los Angeles: UCLA Latin American Center Publications, 1979.

Herzfeld, Michael. "'As in Your Own House': Hospitality, Ethnography, and the Stereotype of Mediterranean Society," in David Gilmore, ed., *Honor and Shame and the Unity of the Mediterranean*, 75–89. Washington, D.C.: American Anthropological Association, 1987.

   The Poetics of Manhood: Contest and Identity in a Cretan Mountain Village. Princeton: Princeton University Press, 1985.

   "Social Tensions and Inheritance by Lot in Three Greek Villages," *Anthropological Quarterly* 53:2 (1980): 91-100.

Higgins, Benjamin. *The Rise and Fall? of Montreal: A Case Study of Urban Growth, Regional Expansion, and National Development*. Montreal: Canadian Institute for Research on Regional Development, 1986.

Higgins, William C. "Tearing Down Mountains at Bingham," *Salt Lake Mining Review* 10:8 (30 July 1908): 1.

Higham, John, ed. *Ethnic Leadership in America*. Baltimore: Johns Hopkins University Press, 1978.

   Strangers in the Land: Patterns of American Nativism, 1860–1925. New York: Atheneum, 1963.

Hionidou, Violetta. "Nuptiality Patterns and Household Structure on the Greek Island of Mykonos, 1849–1959," *Journal of Family History* 20:1 (1995): 67–102.

Hobsbawm, Eric J. *Nations and Nationalism since 1780: Programme, Myth, Reality*. Cambridge: Cambridge University Press, 1990.

   Primitive Rebels: Studies in Archaic Forms of Social Movement in the 19th and 20th Centuries. New York: Praeger, 1959.

Hofsommer, Donald. *The Southern Pacific, 1901–1985*. College Station: Texas A&M Press, 1986.

Hu-DeHart, Evelyn. "Racism and Anti-Chinese persecution in Sonora, Mexico, 1876–1932," *Amerasia* 9:2 (1982): 1–27.

Huntington, Emily H. *Doors to Jobs: A Study of the Organization of the Labor Market in California*. Berkeley: University of California Press, 1942.

Huston, Reeve. "Land and Freedom: The New York Anti-Rent Wars and the Construction of Free Labor in the Antebellum North," in Eric Arnesen, Julie Greene, and Bruce Laurie, eds., *Labor Histories: Class, Politics, and the Working Class Experience*, 19–44. Urbana: University of Illinois Press, 1998.

Ichioka, Yuji. "Asian Immigrant Coal Miners and the United Mine Workers of America: Race and Class at Rock Springs, Wyoming, 1907," *Amerasia Journal* 6:2 (1979): 1–23.

   The Issei: The World of the First Generation Japanese Immigrants, 1885–1924. New York: Free Press, 1988.

Ignatiev, Noel. *How the Irish Became White*. London: Routledge, 1995.

Ingham, John N. "A Strike in the Progressive Era: McKees Rocks, 1909," *Pennsylvania Magazine of History and Biography* 90 (July 1906): 353–377.

Jacobson, Matthew. *Special Sorrows: The Diasporic Imagination of Irish, Polish, and Jewish Immigrants in the United States*. Cambridge, Mass.: Harvard University Press, 1995.

    Whiteness of a Different Color: European Immigrants and the Alchemy of Race. Cambridge, Mass.: Harvard University Press, 1998.

Jacoby, Sanford. *Employing Bureaucracy: Managers, Unions, and the Transformation of Work in American Industry, 1900–1945*. New York: Columbia University Press, 1985.

    Modern Manors: Welfare Capitalism since the New Deal. Princeton: Princeton University Press, 1997.

    ed. *Masters to Managers: Historical and Comparative Perspectives on American Employers*. New York: Columbia University Press, 1991

Jacques, Leo M. "The Anti-Chinese Legislative and Press Campaign in Sonora, Mexico, 1916–1921," *Immigrants and Minorities* 5:2 (July 1986): 167–180.

Jameson, Elizabeth. *All that Glitters: Class, Conflict, and Community in Cripple Creek*. Urbana: University of Illinois Press, 1998.

    "Women as Workers, Women as Civilizers: True Womanhood in the American West," in Susan Armitage and Elizabeth Jameson, eds., *The Women's West*, 145–164. Norman: University of Oklahoma Press, 1987.

Jamieson, Stuart. *Industrial Relations in Canada*. Ithaca: Cornell University Press, 1957.

Janiewski, Dolores. "Southern Honor, Southern Dishonor: Managerial Ideology and the Construction of Gender, Race, and Class in Southern Industry," in Ava Baron, ed., *Work Engendered: Toward a New History of American Labor*, 70–91. Ithaca: Cornell University Press, 1991.

Jensen, Richard. "The Causes and Cures of Unemployment in the Great Depression," *Journal of Interdisciplinary History* 19 (Spring 1989): 553–583.

Jensen, Vernon. *Heritage of Conflict: Labor Relations in the Nonferrous Metals Industry up to 1930*. Ithaca: Cornell University Press, 1950.

Johnson, Susan. "'A Memory Sweet to Soldiers': The Significance of Gender in the History of the American West," *Western Historical Quarterly* 24:4 (November 1993): 495–517.

Jones, Jacqueline. *The Dispossessed: America's Underclasses from the Civil War to the Present*. New York: Basic Books, 1992.

Joseph, Gilbert M., and Daniel Nugent, eds. *Everyday Forms of State Formation: Revolution and the Negotiation of Rule in Modern Mexico*. Durham: Duke University Press, 1994.

Karsten, Peter. "'Bottomed on Justice': A Reappraisal of Critical Legal Studies Scholarship Concerning Breaches of Labor Contracts by Quitting and Firing in Britain and the U.S., 1630–1880," *Journal of American Legal History* 34:3 (July 1990): 213–261.

Katz, Friedrich. "Labor Conditions on Haciendas in Porfirian Mexico: Some Trends and Tendencies," *Hispanic American Historical Review* 54:1 (February 1974): 1–47.

    The Secret War in Mexico: Europe, the United States, and the Mexican Revolution. Chicago: University of Chicago Press, 1981.

    ed. *Riot, Rebellion, and Revolution: Rural Social Conflict in Mexico.* Princeton: Princeton University Press, 1988.

Katz, Michael B., ed. *The "Underclass" Debate: Views from History.* Princeton: Princeton University Press, 1993.

Kealey, Gregory. "1919: The Canadian Labour Revolt," *Labour/Le Travail* 13 (Spring 1984): 11–44.

Kellogg, Ruth M. *The United States Employment Service.* Chicago: University of Chicago Press, 1932.

Kenny, Kevin. *Making Sense of the Molly Maguires.* New York: Oxford University Press, 1998.

Kertzer, David I. *Family Life in Central Italy, 1880–1910: Sharecropping, Wage Labor, and Coresidence.* New Brunswick: Rutgers University Press, 1984.

Kertzer, David I., and Dennis P. Hogan. *Family, Political Economy, and Demographic Change: The Transformation of Life in Casalecchio, Italy, 1861–1921.* Madison: University of Wisconsin Press, 1989.

Kimmel, Michael. *Manhood in America: A Cultural History.* New York: Free Press, 1996.

Knight, Alan. *The Mexican Revolution.* Vols. 1–2. Cambridge: Cambridge University Press, 1986.

Koliopoulos, John. *Brigands with a Cause: Brigandage and Irredentism in Modern Greece, 1821–1912.* New York: Oxford, 1987.

Korver, Tom. *The Fictitious Commodity: A Study of the U.S. Labor Market, 1880–1940.* New York: Greenwood, 1990.

Kraditor, Aileen S. *The Radical Persuasion, 1890–1917: Aspects of the Intellectual History and the Historiography of Three American Radical Organizations.* Baton Rouge: Louisiana State University Press, 1981.

Kroeber, Clifton B., and Walker D. Wyman. *The Frontier in Perspective.* Madison: University of Wisconsin Press, 1957.

Kwong, Peter. *Forbidden Workers: Illegal Chinese Immigrants and American Labor.* New York: New Press, 1997.

LaGumina, Salvatore J., ed. *The Immigrants Speak: Italian Americans Tell Their Story.* New York: Center for Migration Studies, 1979.

Lamar, Howard. "From Bondage to Contract: Ethnic Labor in the American West, 1600–1890," in Steven Hahn and Jonathan Prude, eds., *The Countryside in the Age of Capitalist Transformation: Essays in the Social History of Rural America*, 293–324. Chapel Hill: University of North Carolina, 1985.

Lamar, Howard, and Leonard Thompson, eds. *The Frontier in History: North America and Southern Africa Compared.* New Haven: Yale University Press, 1981.

Lamb, William Kaye. *History of the Canadian Pacific Railway.* New York: Macmillan, 1977.

Lane, A. T. *Solidarity or Survival?: American Labor and European Immigrants, 1830–1924*. New York: Greenwood, 1987.

Larson, Lawrence H., and Barbara J. Cottrell. *The Gate City: A History of Omaha.* Boulder: Pruett, 1982.

Laslett, Peter. "Family and Household as Work Group and Kin Group: Areas of Traditional Europe Compared," in Richard Wall, Jean Robin, and Peter Laslett, eds., *Family Forms in Historic Europe*, 513–563. Cambridge: Cambridge University Press, 1983.

Leiserson, William. *Adjusting Immigrant and Industry*. New York: Harper, 1924.

Lerner, Gerda. *The Creation of Patriarchy*. New York: Oxford University Press, 1986.

Lescohier, Donald D. *The Labor Market*. New York: Macmillan, 1919

Licht, Walter. *Getting Work: Philadelphia, 1840–1950*. Cambridge, Mass.: Harvard University Press, 1992.

Limerick, Patricia. *The Legacy of Conquest: The Unbroken Past of the American West*. New York: Norton, 1987.

Lingenfelter, Richard. *The Hardrock Miners: A History of the Mining Labor Movement in the American West, 1863–1893*. Berkeley: University of California Press, 1974.

Loizos, Peter, and Evthymios Papataxiarchis. "Introduction." In Peter Loizos and Evthymios Papataxiarchis, eds., *Contested Identities: Gender and Kinship in Modern Greece*, 3–9. Princeton: Princeton University Press, 1991.

Lomnitz, Larissa, and Marisol Perez-Lizaur. "Dynastic Growth and Survival Strategies: The Solidarity of Mexican Grand-Families," in Elizabeth Jelin, ed., *Family, Household and Gender Relations in Latin America*. London: Kegan Paul International, 1991.

A Mexican Elite Family, 1820–1980. Princeton: Princeton University Press, 1987.

London, Jack. *The Road*. London: Macmillan, 1907.

Lukas, Anthony J. *Big Trouble: A Murder in a Small Western Town Sets Off a Struggle for the Soul of America*. New York: Simon and Schuster, 1997.

Madison, Grant. *The Passing of a Great Race: Or, the Racial Basis of European History*. New York: Charles Scribner's Sons, 1916.

Majka, Linda C., and Theo J. Majka. *Farm Workers, Agribusiness, and the State*. Philadelphia: Temple University Press, 1982.

Maraspini, A. L. *The Study of an Italian Village*. Paris: Mouton, 1968.

Martinez, Oscar. *Border Boom Town: Ciudad Juarez since 1848*. Austin: University of Texas Press, 1978.

Mavrogordatos, Iannis. *Stillborn Republic: Social Coalitions and Party Strategies in Greece, 1922–1936*. Berkeley: University of California Press, 1983.

McBride, George McCutchen. *The Land Systems of Mexico*. New York: American Geographical Society, 1923.

McCormack, Andrew Ross. *Reformers, Rebels, and Revolutionaries: The Western Canadian Radical Movement, 1899–1919*. Toronto: University of Toronto Press, 1977.

"Wobblies and Blanketstiffs: The Constituency of the IWW in Western

Canada," in W. J. C. Cherwinski and Gregory S. Kealey, eds., *Lectures in Canadian Labour and Working-Class History*, 101–112. St. John's, New-foundland: Committee on Canadian Labour History and New Hogtown Press, 1985.

McGrath, Roger D. *Gunfighters, Highwaymen, and Vigilantes: Violence on the Frontier*. Berkeley: University of California, 1984.

McGrew, William. *Land and Revolution in Modern Greece, 1800–1881: The Transition in the Tenure and Exploitation of Land from Ottoman Rule to Independence*. Kent, Ohio: Kent State University Press, 1985.

Meade, Teresa, and Pamela Haag. "Persistent Patriarchy?: Ghost or Reality?" *Radical History Review* 71 (1998): 91–93.

Mellinger, Phillip. "How the IWW Lost Its Western Heartland: Western Labor History Revisited," *Western Historical Quarterly* 28:3 (Autumn 1996): 303–326.

———. "'The Men have Become Organizers': Labor Conflict and Unionization in the Mexican Mining Communities of Arizona, 1900–1915," *Western Historical Quarterly* 23:2 (August 1992): 333.

———. *Race and Labor in Western Copper: The Fight for Equality, 1896–1918*. Tucson: University of Arizona Press, 1995.

Miller, Kerby. "Class, Culture, and Immigrant Group Identity in the United States: The Case of Irish-American Identity," in Virginia Yans-Mclaughlin, ed., *Immigration Reconsidered: History, Sociology, and Politics*, 96–129. New York: Oxford University Press, 1990.

Mink, Gwendolyn. *Old Labor and New Immigrants in American Political Development: Union, Party, and State, 1875–1920*. Ithaca: Cornell University Press, 1986.

Mitchell, Don. *The Lie of the Land: Migrant Workers and the California Landscape*. Minneapolis: University of Minnesota Press, 1996.

Montejano, David. *Anglos and Mexicans in the Making of Texas, 1836–1986*. Austin: University of Texas, 1987.

Montgomery, David. *Beyond Equality: Labor and the Radical Republicans, 1862–1872*. New York: Knopf, 1967.

———. *Citizen Worker: The Experience of Workers in the United States with Democracy and the Free Market during the Nineteenth Century*. Cambridge: Cambridge University Press, 1993.

———. *The Fall of the House of Labor: The Workplace, the State, and American Labor Activism, 1865–1925*. Cambridge: Cambridge University Press, 1987.

———. "Nationalism, American Patriotism, and Class Consciousness among Immigrant Workers in the United States in the Epoch of World War One," in Dirk Hoerder, ed., *"Struggle a Hard Battle": Essays on Working-Class Immigrants*, 327–351. Dekalb: Northern Illinois University Press, 1986.

———. *Worker's Control in America: Studies in the History of Work, Technology, and Labor Struggles*. Cambridge: Cambridge University Press, 1979.

Moon, Michael. "'The Gentle Boy from the Dangerous Classes': Pederasty, Domesticity, and Capitalism in Horatio Alger," *Representations* 19 (Summer 1987): 87–110.

Moriyama, Alan Takeo. *Imingaisha: Japanese Emigration Companies and Hawaii, 1894–1908*. Honolulu: University of Hawaii Press, 1985.

Morrison, C. J. "Short-Sighted Methods in Dealing with Labor," *Engineering Magazine* 46 (January 1914): 563–574.

Moskos, Charles C. "Georgakas on Greek Americans: A Response," *Journal of Hellenic Diaspora* 14:1–2 (Spring 1987): 5–77.

Mouat, Jeremy. "The Genesis of Western Exceptionalism: British Columbia's Hard-Rock Miners, 1895–1903," *Canadian Historical Review* 71:3 (September 1990): 317–345.

Murray, Mary. *The Law of the Father?: Patriarchy in the Transition from Feudalism to Capitalism*. London: Routledge, 1995.

Naylor, James. *The New Democracy: Challenging the Social Order in Industrial Toronto, 1914–1925*. Toronto: University of Toronto Press, 1991.

Nelli, Humbert. *From Italy to San Francisco: The Immigrant Experience*. Palo Alto: Stanford University Press, 1982.

"The Italian Padrone System in the United States," *Labor History* 5 (Spring 1964): 153–167.

Italians in Chicago, 1880–1930: A Study in Ethnic Mobility. New York: Oxford University Press, 1970.

Nelson, Daniel. *Managers and Workers: Origins of the New Factory System in the United States, 1880–1920*. Madison: University of Wisconsin Press, 1975.

Noiriel, Gerard. "Du 'patronage' au 'paternalisme': La restructuration des formes de domination de la main-d'oeuvrière dans l'industrie metalurgique français," *Le Mouvement Social* 144 (1988): 17–36.

Northrup, David. *Indentured Labor in the Age of Imperialism, 1834–1922*. Cambridge: Cambridge University Press, 1995.

Nye, David. *Narratives and Spaces: Technology and the Construction of American Culture*. New York: Columbia University Press, 1997.

O'Connor, Harvey. *The Guggenheims: The Making of an American Dynasty*. New York: Covici Friede, 1937.

Oestreicher, Richard. *Solidarity and Fragmentation: Working People and Class Consciousness in Detroit, 1875–1900*. Urbana: University of Illinois Press, 1986.

Okihiro, Gary. *Margins and Mainstreams: Asians in American History and Culture*. Seattle: University of Washington Press, 1994.

Orren, Karen. *Belated Feudalism: Labor, the Law, and Liberal Development in the United States*. Cambridge: Cambridge University Press, 1991.

Papanikolas, Helen, ed. *The Peoples of Utah*. Salt Lake City: Utah Historical Society, 1976.

"Toil and Rage in a New Land: The Greek Immigrants of Utah," *Utah Historical Quarterly* 38:2 (Spring 1970): 100–204.

Papanikolas, Zeese. *Buried Unsung: Louis Tikas and the Ludlow Massacre*. Salt Lake City: University of Utah Press, 1982.

Trickster in the Land of Dreams. Lincoln: University of Nebraska Press, 1995.

Papataxiarchis, Evthymios. "Friends of the Heart: Male Commensal Solidarity, Gender, and Kinship in Aegean Greece," in Peter Loizos and Evthymios Papataxiarchis, eds., *Contested Identities: Gender and Kinship in Modern Greece*, 156–179. Princeton: Princeton University Press, 1991.

Parker, Carleton. *The Casual Laborer, and Other Essays*. New York: Harcourt, Brace, and Howe, 1920.

Pascoe, Peggy. *Relations of Rescue: The Search for Female Moral Authority in the American West, 1874–1939*. New York: Oxford University Press, 1990.

Pateman, Carole. *The Sexual Contract*. Stanford: Stanford University Press, 1988.

Peck, Gunther. "Crisis in the Family: Padrones and Radicals in Utah, 1908–1912," in Dan Georgakas and Charles C. Moskos, eds., *New Directions in Greek American Studies*, 73–94. New York: Pella Press, 1991.

"Divided Loyalties: Immigrant Padrones and the Evolution of Industrial Paternalism in North America," *International Labor and Working-Class History* 53 (Spring 1998): 49–68.

"Manly Gambles: The Politics of Risk on the Comstock Lode, 1860–1880," *Journal of Social History* 26:4 (Summer 1993): 701–723.

"Mobilizing Community: Migrant Workers and the Politics of Labor Mobility in the North American West, 1900–1920," in Eric Arnesen, Julie Greene, and Bruce Laurie, eds., *Labor Histories: Class, Politics, and the Working Class Experience*, 175–200. Urbana: University of Illinois Press, 1998.

"Padrones and Protest: 'Old' Radicals and 'New' Immigrants in Bingham, Utah, 1905–1912," *Western Historical Quarterly* 24 (May 1993): 157–178.

"Reinventing Free Labor: Immigrant Padrones and Contract Laborers in North America, 1885–1925," *Journal of American History* 83 (Winter 1996): 848–871.

Peristiany, J. G. *Honour and Shame: The Values of Mediterranean Society*. Chicago: University of Chicago Press, 1966.

Mediterranean Family Structures. Cambridge: Cambridge University Press, 1976.

Peterson, Richard H. "Conflict and Consensus: Labor Relations in Western Mining," *Journal of the West* 12 (January 1973): 17.

Petrik, Paula. *No Step Backward: Women and Family on the Rocky Mountain Frontier: Helena, Montana, 1865–1900*. Helena: Montana Historical Society, 1987.

Phiphard, Charles. "The Philanthropist Padrone: What Is Being Done to Raise the Standard through Competition and Example," *Charities Magazine* 12 (1904): 470–472.

Ping, Chiu. *Chinese Labor in California, 1850–1880: An Economic Study*. Madison: State Historical Society of Wisconsin, 1967.

Piore, Michael. *Birds of Passage: Migrant Labor and Industrial Societies*. Cambridge: Cambridge University Press, 1979.

Pitt-Rivers, Julian. *The People of the Sierra*. Chicago: University of Chicago Press, 1961.

Poovey, Mary. *Uneven Developments: The Ideological Work of Gender in Mid-Victorian England*. Chicago: University of Illinois Press, 1988.

Portes, Alejandro, and Robert L. Bach. *Latin Journey: Cuban and Mexican Immigrants in the United States*. Berkeley: University of California Press, 1985.

Puzo, Mario. *The Godfather*. New York: G. P. Putnam's Sons, 1969.

Ramirez, Bruno. "Brief Encounters: Italian Immigrant Workers and the CPR, 1900–1930," *Labour/Le Travail* 17 (Spring 1986): 9–27.

"The Italians of Montreal: From Sojourning to Settlement, 1900–1921," in Robert Harney and Vincenza Scarpaci, eds., *Little Italies in North America*. Toronto: Multicultural History Society of Ontario, 1981.

On the Move: French-Canadian and Italian Migrants in the North Atlantic Economy, 1860–1914. Toronto: McClelland and Stewart, 1991.

Les premiers Italiens de Montreal: L'origine de la petite Italie du Quebec. Montreal: Boreal Express, 1984.

Reisler, Mark. *By the Sweat of Their Brow: Mexican Immigrant Labor in the United States, 1900–1940*. Westport, Conn.: Greenwood, 1976.

Rhoads, Edward J. M. "Asian Pioneers in the Eastern United States: Chinese Cutlery Workers in Beaver Falls, Pennsylvania, in the 1870s," *Journal of Asian American Studies*, forthcoming.

Roediger, David. *Towards the Abolition of Whiteness: Essays on Race, Politics, and Working-Class History*. London: Verso, 1994.

The Wages of Whiteness: Race and the Making of the American Working Class. London: Verso, 1991.

Romo, Ricardo. *East Los Angeles: History of a Barrio*. Austin: University of Texas, 1983.

Roper, Michael, and John Tosh, eds. *Manful Assertions:Masculinities in Britain since 1800*. London: Routledge, 1992.

Ross, Edward Alsworth. *The Old World in the New: The Significance of Past and Present Immigration to the American People*. New York, 1914.

Rotundo, Anthony. *American Manhood: Transformations in Masculinity from the Revolution to the Modern Era*. New York: Basic Books, 1993.

Roy, Patricia E. *A White Man's Province: British Columbia Politicians and Chinese and Japanese Immigrants, 1858–1914*. Vancouver: University of British Columbia Press, 1989.

Ruiz, Vicki L. *Cannery Women, Cannery Lives: Mexican Women, Unionization, and the California Food Processing Industry, 1930–1950*. Albuquerque: University of New Mexico Press, 1987.

Salerno, Salvatore. *Red November, Black November: Culture and Community in the Industrial Workers of the World*. Albany: State University of New York Press, 1989.

Saloutos, Theodore. *The Greeks in the United States*. Cambridge, Mass.: Harvard University Press, 1964.

Sanchez, George. *Becoming Mexican American: Ethnicity, Culture, and Identity in Chicano Los Angeles, 1900–1945*. New York: Oxford University Press, 1993.

Sant Cassia, Paul, with Constantine Bada. *The Making of the Modern Greek Family: Marriage and Exchange in Nineteenth Century Athens*. Cambridge: Cambridge University Press, 1992.

Saraceno, Chiara. "Women, Family and the Law, 1750–1942," *Journal of Family History* 15:4 (1990): 427–442.

Saunders, Kay. *Workers in Bondage: The Origins and Bases of Unfree Labour in Queensland, 1824–1916*. St. Lucia: University of Queensland Press, 1982.

Saville, Julie. *The Work of Reconstruction: From Slave to Wage Laborer in South Carolina, 1860–1870*. Cambridge: Cambridge University Press, 1994.

Sawyer, Roger. *Slavery in the Twentieth Century*. London: Routledge, 1986.

Saxton, Alexander. *The Indispensable Enemy: Labor and the Anti-Chinese Movement in California*. Berkeley: University of California Press, 1971.

The Rise and Fall of the White Republic: Class Politics and Mass Culture in Nineteenth-Century America. London: Verso, 1990.

Sayler, Lucy. *Laws Harsh as Tigers: Chinese Immigrants and the Shaping of Modern Immigration Law*. Chapel Hill: University of North Carolina Press, 1995.

Schlicter, Sumner. *The Turnover of Factory Labor*. New York: D. Appleton, 1919.

Schwantes, Carlos. "The Concept of the Wageworkers' Frontier: A Framework for Future Research," *Western Historical Quarterly* 18 (January 1987): 39–55.

Radical Heritage: Labor, Socialism, and Reform in Washington and British Columbia, 1885–1917. Seattle: University of Washington Press, 1979.

Scott, James C. *Domination and the Arts of Resistance: Hidden Transcripts*. New Haven: Yale University Press, 1990.

Seed, Patricia. *To Love, Honor, and Obey in Colonial Mexico: Conflicts over Marriage Choice, 1574–1821*. Stanford: Stanford University Press, 1988.

Silverman, Sydel F. "Agricultural Organization, Social Structure, and Values in Italy: Amoral Familism Reconsidered," *American Anthropologist* 70:1 (February 1968): 1–20.

"Patronage and Community-Nation Relationships in Central Italy," *Ethnology* 4:2 (April, 1965): 172–189.

Slotkin, Richard. *The Fatal Environment: The Myth of the Frontier in the Age of Industrialization, 1800–1890*. New York: Atheneum, 1985.

Smith, Darrell Hevenor. *The United States Employment Service: Its History, Activities, and Organizations*. Baltimore: Johns Hopkins University Press, 1923.

Smith, Henry Nash. *Virgin Land: The American West as Symbol and Myth*. Cambridge, Mass.: Harvard University Press, 1950.

Smith, Timothy. "New Approaches to the History of Immigration in Twentieth-Century America," *American Historical Review* 71 (July 1966): 1265–1279.

Smith, William George. *A Study in Canadian Immigration*. Toronto: Ryerson Press, 1920.

Soja, Edward W. *Postmodern Geographies: The Reassertion of Space in Critical Social Theory*. London: Verso, 1989.

Solenberger, Alice. *One Thousand Homeless Men: A Study of Original Records*. New York: Charities Publication Committee, 1911.

Stanley, Amy Dru. "'Beggars Can't Be Choosers': Compulsion and Contract in Postbellum America," *Journal of American History* 78:4 (March 1992): 1265–1293.

"Conjugal Bonds and Wage Labor: Rights of Contract in the Age of Emancipation," *Journal of American History* 75:2 (September 1988): 471–500.

From Bondage to Contract: Wage Labor, Marriage, and the Market in the Age of Slave Emancipation. Cambridge: Cambridge University Press, 1998.

Steinfeld, Robert. *The Invention of Free Labor: The Employment Relation in English and American Law and Culture, 1350–1870.* Chapel Hill: University of North Carolina Press, 1991.

"Law in the Construction of Wage Labor and Peonage: A Critical Legal History," paper delivered at the 15th annual North American Labor History Conference, Wayne State University, October 1993.

Stern, Steven J. *The Secret History of Gender: Men, Women, and Power in Late Colonial Mexico.* Chapel Hill: University of North Carolina Press, 1995.

Stromquist, Shelton. *A Generation of Boomers: The Pattern of Railroad Labor Conflict in Nineteenth-Century America.* Urbana: University of Illinois Press, 1987.

Sturino, Franc. *Forging the Chain: A Case Study of Italian Migration to North America, 1880–1930.* Toronto: Multicultural History Society of Ontario, 1990.

Sutherland, Edwin Hardin. *Unemployed and Public Employment Agencies.* Chicago: Cameron, Amberg, 1914.

Sutton, Susan Buck. "What Is a Village in a Nation of Migrants?" *Journal of Modern Greek Studies* 6 (1988): 187–215.

Taft, Phillip. "The I.W.W. and the West," *American Quarterly* 12 (Summer 1960): 175–187.

Takaki, Ronald. *Iron Cages: Race and Culture in Nineteenth-Century America.* New York: Knopf, 1979.

Tatsios, Theodore G. *The Megali Idea and the Greek-Turkish War of 1897: The Impact of the Cretan Problem on Greek Irredentism, 1866–1897.* New York: Columbia University Press, 1984.

Taylor, Paul S. *Mexican Labor in the United States.* Vol. 1. Berkeley: University of California Press, 1928.

Mexican Labor in the United States: Chicago and the Calumet Region. Vol. 2. Berkeley: University of California Press, 1928.

Tenorio-Trillo, Mauricio. *Mexico at the World's Fairs: Crafting a Modern Nation.* Berkeley: University of California Press, 1996.

Thistlewaite, Frank. "Migration from Europe Overseas in the Nineteenth and Twentieth Centuries," in *XIe Congres International des Sciences Historiques. Rapports. V. Historie Contemporaine*, 32–60. Goteborg, Stockholm and Uppsala: Almquist & Wiksell, 1960.

Thompson, Lorin Andrew, Jr. *Interview Aids and Trade Questions for Employment Offices.* New York: Harper, 1936.

Tomlins, Christopher L. *Law, Labor, and Ideology in the Early American Repub-lic*. Cambridge: Cambridge University Press, 1993.

The State and Unions: Labor Relations, Law, and the Organized Labor Movement in America, 1880–1960. Cambridge: Cambridge University Press, 1985.

Tomlins, Christopher, and Andrew J. King, "Labor, Law, and History," in Christo-pher Tomlins and Andrew King, eds., *Labor Law in America: Historical and Critical Essays*. Baltimore: Johns Hopkins University Press, 1992.

Tompkins, Jane. *West of Everything: The Inner Life of Westerns*. New York: Oxford University Press, 1992.

Tone, Andrea. *The Business of Benevolence: Industrial Paternalism in Progres-sive America*. Ithaca: Cornell University Press, 1997.

Trafton, George. *Employment Agencies Officially Exposed: Sworn Testimony Shows Urgent Need of State Action*. New York: American Association for Labor Legislation, 1930.

Tsoucalas, Constantine. "On the Problem of Political Clientelism in Greece in the Nineteenth Century," *Journal of Hellenic Diaspora* 5:1 (1978): 5–15.

Tuck, Joseph. "The United Brotherhood of Railway Employees in Western Canada, 1898–1905," *Labour/Le Travail* 11 (Spring 1983): 55–73.

Tullidge, Edward W. *The History of Salt Lake City and Its Founders*. Salt Lake City: F. W. Tullidge, 1896.

Turbin, Carole. "Reconceptualizing Family, Work, and Labor Organizing: Work-ing Women in Troy, 1860–1890," *Review of Radical Political Economics* 16 (Spring 1984): 1–16.

Turner, Frederick Jackson. *The Frontier in American History*. New York: Henry Holt, 1920.

Turner, Mary, ed. *From Chattel Slaves to Wage Slaves: The Dynamics of Labour Bargaining in the Americas*. Bloomington: Indiana University Press, 1995.

Tutino, John. "Agrarian Social Change and Peasant Rebellion in Nineteenth-Century Mexico: The Example of Chalco," in Friedrich Katz, ed., *Riot, Rebellion, and Revolution: Rural Social Conflict in Mexico*, 95–146. Prince-ton: Princeton University Press, 1988.

Valdes, Dennis Nodin. "Betabeleros: The Formation of an Agricultural Proletariat in the Midwest, 1897–1930," *Labor History* 30:4 (Fall 1989): 536–562.

Al Norte: Agricultural Workers in the Great Lakes Region, 1917–1970. Austin: University of Texas Press, 1991.

Vargas, Zaragosa. *Proletarians of the North: A History of Mexican Industrial Workers in Detroit and the Midwest, 1917–1933*. Berkeley: University of California Press, 1993.

Vecoli, Rudolph. "'Free Country': The American Republic Viewed by the Italian Left, 1880–1920," in Marianne Debouzy, ed., *In the Shadow of the Statue of Liberty: Immigrants, Workers, and Citizens in the American Republic, 1880—1920*, 23–44. Chicago: University of Illinois Press, 1992.

"Italian American Workers, 1880–1920: Padrone Slaves or Primitive Rebels?" in Silvano M. Tomasi, ed., *Perspectives in Italian Immigration and Ethnicity.* Staten Island: Center for Migration Studies, 1977.

Verdicchio, Pasquale. *Bound by Distance: Rethinking Nationalism through the Italian Diaspora.* Madison: Fairleigh Dickinson University Press, 1997.

Viazzo, Pier Paolo, and Dionigi Albera. "The Peasant Family in Northern Italy, 1750–1930: A Reassessment," *Journal of Family History* 15:4 (1990), 461–482.

Villari, Luigi. *Italian Life in Town and Country.* New York: G. P. Putnam's Sons, 1903.

Waldrep, Christopher. "Substituting Law for the Lash: Emancipation and Legal Formalism in a Mississippi County Court," *Journal of American History* 82 (March 1996): 1425–1451.

Walkowitz, Daniel. *Worker City, Company Town: Iron and Cotton-Worker Protest in Troy and Cohoes, New York, 1855–1884.* Urbana: University of Illinois Press, 1978.

Wallerstein, Immanuel. *The Modern World-System: Capitalist Agriculture and the Origins of the European World- Economy in the Sixteenth Century.* New York: Academic Press, 1976.

Wang, Sing-Wu. *The Organization of Chinese Emigration, 1848–1888: With Special Reference to Chinese Emigration to Australia.* San Francisco: Chinese Materials Center, 1978.

Ward, Peter. *White Canada Forever: Popular Attitudes and Public Policy towards Orientals in British Columbia.* Montreal: McGill-Queens University Press, 1990.

Warren, Louis. *The Hunter's Game: Poachers and Conservationists in Twentieth-Century America.* New Haven: Yale University Press, 1997.

Watson, Tony J. *The Personnel Managers: A Study in the Sociology of Work and Employment.* Boston: Routledge, 1977.

Watt, Stewart. *Chinese Bondage in Peru: A History of the Chinese Coolie in Peru, 1849–1874.* Durham: Duke University Press, 1951.

Way, Peter. *Common Labour: Workers and the Digging of North American Canals, 1780–1860.* Cambridge: Cambridge University Press, 1993.

"Evil Humors and Ardent Spirits: The Rough Culture of Canal Construction Laborers," *Journal of American History* 79:4 (March 1993): 1397–1428.

Webb, Walter Prescott. *The Great Plains.* Boston: Ginn, 1931.

Weber, David J., ed. *New Spain's Far Northern Frontier: Essays on Spain in the American West, 1540–1821.* Albuquerque: University of New Mexico Press, 1979.

West, Cornell. *Race Matters.* Boston: Beacon Press, 1993.

Weston, Kath. *Families We Choose: Lesbians, Gays, Kinship.* New York: Columbia University Press, 1991.

White, Richard. "Outlaw Gangs of the Middle Border: American Social Bandits," *Western Historical Quarterly* 12 (October, 1981): 387–408.

Wiebe, Robert. *The Search for Order, 1877–1920.* New York: Hill and Wang, 1967.

Wilentz, Sean. "Against Exceptionalism: Class Consciousness and the American Labor Movement, 1790–1920," *International Labor and Working Class History* 26 (Fall 1984): 1–24.

Chants Democratic: New York City and the Rise of the American Working Class, 1788–1850. New York: Oxford University Press, 1984.

Williams, Phyllis H. *South Italian Folkways in Europe and America: A Handbook for Social Workers, Visiting Nurses, School Teachers, and Physicians.* New Haven: Yale University Press, 1938.

Williams, Rosalind. *Notes on the Underground: An Essay on Technology, Society, and the Imagination.* Cambridge, Mass.: MIT Press, 1990.

Wilson, Neill Compton, and Frank J. Taylor. *Southern Pacific: The Roaring Story of a Fighting Railroad.* New York: McGraw Hill, 1952.

Wingert, Mary. "Rethinking Paternalism: Power and Parochialism in a Southern Mill Village," *Journal of American History* 83 (1996): 872.

Wright, Gavin. "Labor History and Labor Economics," in Gavin Wright, ed., *The Future of Economic History*, 313–341. Boston: Kluwer-Nijhoff, 1987.

Wyman, Mark. *Hard Rock Epic: Western Miners and the Industrial Revolution, 1860–1910.* Berkeley: University of California Press, 1979.

Yans-McLaughlin, Virginia. *Family and Community: Italian Immigrants in Buffalo, 1880–1930.* Ithaca: Cornell University Press, 1977.

ed. *Immigration Reconsidered: History, Sociology, and Politics.* New York: Oxford University Press, 1990.

Zahavi, Gerald. *Workers, Managers, and Welfare Capitalism: The Shoeworkers and Tanners of Endicott Johnson, 1890–1950.* Urbana: University of Illinois Press, 1988.

Zamora, Emilio. *The World of the Mexican Worker in Texas.* College Station: Texas A&M University Press, 1993.

Zunz, Olivier. *Making America Corporate, 1870–1920.* Chicago: University of Chicago Press, 1990.

Unpublished Master's Theses and Dissertations

Bean, Philip A. "Fatherland and Adopted Land: Irish-, German-, and Italian-American Nationalism, 1865–1950." Ph.D. diss., University of Rochester, 1994.

Cash, Joseph. "Labor in the West: The Homestake Mining Company and Its Workers, 1877–1942." Ph.D. diss., University of Iowa, 1966.

Cononelos, Louis. "Greek Immigrant Labor in the Intermountain West, 1900–1920." M.A. thesis, University of Utah, 1979.

DePastino, Todd Allen. "From Hobohemia to Skid Row: Homelessness and American Culture, 1870–1950." Ph.D. diss., Yale University, 1996.

Garcilazo, Jeffrey Marcos. "'Traqueros': Mexican Railroad Workers in the United States, 1870–1930." Ph.D. diss., University of California at Santa Barbara, 1995.

Gomilla, Michele. "Los Refugiados y los Comerciantes: Mexican Refugees and Businessmen in Downtown El Paso, 1910–1920." M.A. thesis, University of Texas at El Paso, 1990.

Huginnie, Yvette. "Strikitos: Race, Class, and Work in the Arizona Copper Industry, 1870–1920." Ph.D. diss., Yale University, 1991.

Johnson, Susan. "Of Fiddles and Fandangos." IN "'The Gold She Gathered': Difference, Domination, and California's Southern Mines, 1848–1853." Ph.D. diss., Yale University, 1993.

Morrone, Marco. "The Making of an American Mafia: Italians in New Orleans, 1890–1910." M.A. thesis, University of Texas at Austin, 1998.

Tuck, Joseph. "Canadian Railways and the International Brotherhoods: Labour Organization in the Railway Running Trades in Canada, 1865–1914." Ph.D. diss., Western Ontario University, 1975.

Wong, Aliza A. "Green, White, Red – and Yellow: The Imaging of China in the Construction of the Italian Nation." M.A. thesis, University of Colorado, 1997.

Wood, Patrica. "Nationalism from the Margins: The Development of National and Ethnic Identities among Italian Immigrants in Alberta and British Columbia, 1880–1980." Ph.D. diss., Duke University, 1995.

Zo, Kil Young. "Chinese Emigration into the United States, 1850–1880." Ph.D. diss., Columbia University, 1971.

Index